Crime, Law and Society in Nigeria

Afrika-Studiecentrum Series

VOLUME 37

The titles published in this series are listed at *brill.com/asc*

Crime, Law and Society in Nigeria

Essays in Honour of Stephen Ellis

Edited by

Rufus Akinyele
Ton Dietz

BRILL

LEIDEN | BOSTON

Cover illustration: Roundtable event "History of Organised Crime in Nigeria", Lagos University, 28 October 2016. Photograph by Akinyinka Akinyoade.

Library of Congress Cataloging-in-Publication Data

Names: Akinyele, R. T., editor. | Dietz, Ton, editor. | Ellis, Stephen, 1953-2015, honouree.
Title: Crime, law and society in Nigeria : essays in honour of Stephen Ellis / edited by Rufus Akinyele, Ton Dietz.
Description: Leiden ; Boston : Brill, 2019. | Series: Afrika-Studiecentrum series ; v. 37 | Includes bibliographical references and index.
Identifiers: LCCN 2019010105 (print) | LCCN 2019016418 (ebook) | ISBN 9789004396289 (ebook) | ISBN 9789004396241 (pbk. : alk. paper)
Subjects: LCSH: Crime--Nigeria--History. | Criminal justice, Administration of--Nigeria.
Classification: LCC HV7165.5 (ebook) | LCC HV7165.5 .C755 2019 (print) | DDC 364.9669--dc23
LC record available at https://lccn.loc.gov/2019010105

Typeface for the Latin, Greek, and Cyrillic scripts: "Brill". See and download: brill.com/brill-typeface.

ISSN 1570-9310
ISBN 978-90-04-39624-1 (paperback)
ISBN 978-90-04-39628-9 (e-book)

This book is printed on acid-free paper and produced in a sustainable manner.

Contents

Book Review

Acknowledgements

We owe a debt of gratitude to several people and institutions in the course of publishing this book. Firstly, we wish to thank the widow of Stephen Ellis, Prof. Gerrie ter Haar, for agreeing to write the introductory chapter on the life and work of Stephen Ellis. Her enthusiasm and moral support went a long way in encouraging us to forge ahead.

We also want to thank Prof. ter Haar, as well as Prof. Chibuike Uche and Dr. Akinyinka Akinyoade for accompanying Prof. Ton Dietz, the Director of the African Studies Centre, Leiden to the University of Lagos, Nigeria, on 28 October 2016 for the public presentation of Stephen Ellis' book, *This Present Darkness: A History of Organised Crime in Nigeria.*

At the University of Lagos, we hereby express our gratitude to the former Vice-Chancellor, Prof. Rahamon A. Bello, for the warm reception of the Africa Studies Centre Leiden (ASCL) team and fruitful deliberations on the areas of collaboration between the university and ASCL. We are grateful to the Dean of Faculty of Arts, Prof. Muyiwa Falaiye, and those who played prominent roles in organising the roundtable for the book presentation. In this regard, we would like to single out Prof. Ayodeji Olukoju and Dr. David Aworawo of the Department of History and Strategic Studies. We gratefully acknowledge the editorial assistance received from Dr. Tunde Oduwobi of the same department. Finally, we thank the African Studies Centre Leiden, its publications team (Dr. Harry Wels and Machteld Oosterkamp) and Brill Publishers for agreeing to publish this book as a way of keeping the memory of Stephen Ellis alive. We sincerely hope that the publication of this book will help to cement the relationship between the University of Lagos and ASCL, which has been forged through the recently created Institute of African and Diaspora Studies at the University of Lagos.

Notes on Contributors

A.E. Akintayo
is a Lecturer in the Department of Public Law, University of Lagos. He has published extensively on criminal justice administration.

Rufus Akinyele
is a Professor of African History and Chair of the Department of History and Strategic Studies, University of Lagos. His articles have appeared in high impact journals including *African Affairs, Asian and African Studies, African Studies Review* and *Africa Development*. Akinyele is on the Editorial Advisory Board of *African Affairs* (2008–2017).

Jackson A. Aluede
is Ph.D student in the Department of History and Strategic Studies, University of Lagos. He is about to conclude his thesis titled, "Nigeria's Foreign Policy and Trans-Border Crime: A Historical Analysis of the Nigeria-Benin Border, 1960–2013".

Franca Attoh
is a Senior Lecturer in the Department of Sociology, University of Lagos. She is an alumnus of the CODESRIA Gender Institute and a Fellow of the Institute of Security in Nigeria. She is also on the Council for the Development of Social Science in Africa.

Ayodele Atsenuwa
is the Dean, Faculty of Law, University of Lagos. Her research and teaching interests are Human Rights, Criminal Justice, Gender Studies, and Health Law.

Edmund Chilaka
obtained his PhD in History from the Department of History and Strategic Studies, University of Lagos, specializing in Maritime History. He lectures at the School of Transport, Lagos State University, Ojoo. He is the publisher of a dredging and maritime magazine, *Dredge, Drill and Hall*, which can be accessed online.

Ton Dietz
is Professor Emeritus of the Study of African Development at the University of Leiden. He is currently engaged as a Senior Researcher at the African Studies

Centre, Leiden where he was the Director between May 2010 and September 2017.

Samson Folarin
is a graduate of the Department of Mass Communication, University of Lagos. He is a reporter with the Punch Newspaper in Lagos.

Gerrrie ter Haar
is Professor Emerita of Religion and Development at the International Institute of Social Studies, Erasmus University, Rotterdam. She is a founding member of the African Association for the study of Religions [AASR]. Her research interests cover the areas of Human Rights, Conflict and Peace, Religion and Migration.

Ayodeji Olukoju
is a Professor of Maritime History, Department of History and Strategic Studies, University of Lagos. Olukoju has held several fellowships including the Japan Foundation Academy, Chapman, Leventis and IDE (Japan) Fellowships. He has also served on the editorial boards of *Journal of African History*, *African Economic History*, and *History in Africa*. He is a former Vice-Chancellor of Caleb University, Imota, Nigeria.

Abiodun Oluwadare
is a Lecturer at the Department of Political Science and Defense Studies, Nigerian Defence Academy, Nigeria. His area of specialisation is Defence and Strategic Studies.

Paul Osifodunrin
is a Senior Lecturer in the Department of History and Strategic Studies, University of Lagos. He is an urban historian and has published extensively on crime in Lagos. Osifodunrin is a member of the Lagos Studies Association.

Leo Enahoro Otoide
is a Professor of History and International Diplomacy and current Dean of Arts, University of Benin, Nigeria. He was editor of the Journal of Historical Society of Nigeria [JHSN]. He has published widely in the areas of International Relations, Cultural History and Historiography. He is a Fellow of the Historical Society of Nigeria.

Introduction

Rufus Akinyele and Ton Dietz

This volume in honour of Stephen Ellis is a follow-up to the public presentation of his book on the history of organised crime in Nigeria at the University of Lagos, Nigeria on 28 October 2016. At the roundtable organised for the event, four papers were presented on various aspects of crime in Nigeria in addition to the book review. These were: "Theft in Early Colonial Lagos, 1861–1906", "Currency Counterfeiting and 'Substantial Justice' in Colonial Nigeria", "Crime at the University of Lagos: Insight from the Akoka Campus", and "Reporting Crime in Lagos".

The interest the papers generated compelled us to bring the issues raised to the attention of a wider audience; hence the decision to invite more papers on crime in Nigeria to complement the four papers. The result is what is contained in this book. Some of the papers amplify the points raised by Stephen Ellis, while others highlight new areas. On the whole, the papers provide a fresh insight into the nature of crime, law, and society in Nigeria.

Stephen Ellis' book *This Present Darkness. A History of Nigerian Organised Crime* was his last. It was published in April 2016 by Hurst, who published several of Stephen's books. Stephen died in July 2015, and he was working on this book as a senior researcher at the African Studies Centre in Leiden almost to his last moments.

Stephen has always had an interest in the hidden sides of African society. Before he came to Leiden he was the editor of *Africa Confidential*, the journal that uncovers Africa's secrets. Later, he studied the war in Liberia, where the state had become a criminal state, and its leaders thrived because of their involvement in warfare, smuggling, and everything else that could be regarded as "illegal".

Stephen Ellis was born in Nottingham, the United Kingdom on 13 June 1953. He studied modern history at the University of Oxford where he did his doctoral exam in 1981. He studied a revolt in Madagascar in the late 1890s, which was published as *The Rising of the Red Shawls* (by Cambridge University Press in 1985). He would later publish another book about Madagascar in French *Un Complot à Madagascar* (1990, Karthala). In 1979–1980 he worked as a lecturer at the University of Madagascar, but that was not his first time in Africa. When he was eighteen years old he worked as a teacher in Douala, Cameroon. Between 1982 and 1986 he was head of the African sub-region at the International Secretariat of Amnesty International in London, followed by a position as Editor for the *Africa Confidential* newsletter. In 1991–1994, Stephen became the General

 | DOI:10.1163/9789004396289_002

Secretary and later Director of the African Studies Centre in Leiden, followed by an assignment for the Netherlands Ministry of Foreign Affairs for the Global Coalition for Africa. This resulted in his book *Africa Now*, published in 1996. After 1994, Stephen became a senior researcher at the African Studies Centre in Leiden until his death. He was also appointed Desmond Tutu Professor at the Vrije Universiteit in Amsterdam in 2008.

Stephen Ellis was the ASCL's most prominent scholar, and one of the key researchers in African Studies in the world. The ASCL library holds 82 of his publications, many of which deal with recent or historical political developments in Africa or, often together with his partner Gerrie ter Haar, about religion in Africa. He wrote most extensively about South Africa, Madagascar, Liberia and Nigeria, but also about Togo, Zambia, and Sierra Leone. Stephen Ellis' personal page on Google Scholar shows that more than 5000 colleagues have cited his many publications to date. His most popular book is *The Criminalization of the State in Africa*, which he wrote together with Jean-François Bayart and Béatrice Hibou, and which was published in 1999 (subsequent to a French version that was published two years earlier). Other renowned books include *The Mask of Anarchy: The destruction of Liberia and the religious dimension of an African civil war* (2001), *Worlds of Power: Religious thought and political practice in Africa* (together with Gerrie ter Haar, 2004) and *Comrades against Apartheid: The ANC & the South African Communist Party in exile* (together with Tsepo Sechaba, 1992). Among his recent publications are: *External Mission: The ANC in exile, 1960–1990* (2013), *Season of Rains: Africa in the world* (2012; there is also Dutch version called *Het Regenseizoen*), and *West Africa's International Drug Trade* (2009).

Christopher Clapham, scholar at the University of Cambridge, shows that many of Stephen's interests come together in his last book, about the history of organised crime in Nigeria:

> This is quite simply a dynamite book, striking first of all for the sheer depth of research that has gone into it. It is remarkable, too, in the way that it is able to fit this material into a bigger picture, created not only by a thorough familiarity with Nigerian history and politics, but also by an awareness especially of the spiritual dimensions of Nigerian life, and the ways in which these feed through into crime as well as virtually every other aspect of Nigerian affairs (text on the book cover).

This follow-up book contains ten chapters, mostly written by Nigerian scholars. The book ends with a review of *This Present Darkness*, which was presented at the roundtable at the University of Lagos, in November 2016, followed by a curriculum vitae of Prof. Stephen Ellis.

In Chapter 1, Gerrie ter Haar provides a window into the life and work of Stephen Ellis, beginning with his birth as a British citizen of mixed English-Irish stock in 1953. She devotes attention to the aspects of his life concerning Voluntary Service Overseas, particularly his involvement in human rights missions and liberation struggles in Africa. She highlights the new direction he gave to research and scholarship as Director of the Africa Studies Centre Leiden, especially in pushing for the study of Africa "within" and fostering research collaboration with scholars on the Africa continent. The impressive review of the publications of the Oxford-trained historian shows that he was not only aware of the power of history to explain the present, but that he also recognised the important intersection between Africa's religious history and African politics. This incisively written chapter supports the observation that the life and work of Stephen Ellis are "bound together in a profoundly holistic manner", and that he was, to say the least, "a philosopher, a generous human being and a meticulous scholar". The second chapter, contributed by Paul Osifodunrin, examines the problem of theft in early colonial Lagos. The central question of the paper is: What was responsible for the upsurge of theft during this period? His analysis reveals that unlike in the first half of the nineteenth century, when theft was induced mainly by public disorder, the situation in the later period is best explained in the context of new opportunities in the social, economic, and political arenas of the growing urban centre. The author skilfully synthesizes information from existing literature with new data from oral tradition, newspaper, and colonial records.

In Chapter 3, Jackson Aluede situates smuggling across the Nigeria-Benin border in a global context. He traces the nature and dimensions of the problem from the colonial period, highlights the roles played by the factors of different economic policies on the two sides of the border, population disparity, the Structural Adjustment Policy, as well as the influence of globalisation. The analysis shows how the surreptitious support of the government of the Republic of Benin for smuggling across the border has frustrated attempts by Nigeria to curb the ruinous effect of smuggling across the troublesome border.

In the next chapter, Edmund Chilaka examines the nature and trend of criminal activities in the Nigerian ports environments. As the Nigerian economy is the destination of nearly 70 per cent of West Africa's sea trade, it is, therefore, understandable why crimes within the port environments in Nigeria are of striking significance. The chapter reveals that there has been a sharp decline in criminal activities in and around the ports since the strict enforcement of the International Ships and Port Facility Security Code (ISPS) in 2004.

In Chapter 5, Leo Otoide complements the work of Stephen Ellis on human trafficking by focusing on the societal and institutional responses to the problem of prostitution in Edo State, which is believed to be the source of most of the girls that are trafficked abroad. One of his recommendations to curb the menace is that the bank accounts of convicted traffickers should be frozen and the assets confiscated by the state in order to generate money for the rehabilitation of the victims.

The focus of Chapter 6, contributed by Abiodun Oluwadare was on the Niger Delta. As is well known, the crisis that began as a popular struggle for environmental justice and accelerated development in the Niger Delta has been hijacked by the political elite and oil theft syndicates who now manipulate the ethnic militias to perpetrate crime in the Niger Delta. The chapter demonstrates how the militancy degenerated into criminality and provides an insight into the complex nature of the phenomenon.

In the next chapter, Franca Attoh illuminates the nature and dimension of crime in a Nigerian University, using the Akoka Campus of the University of Lagos as a case study. The analysis is done in the context of the architectural design of the built environment on the campus, the proximity of the institution to the sprawling ghettoes of llaje and Iwaya, and the inadequate provision of modern security gadgets to monitor and control crime on campus.

Chapter 8 relates the lived experience of a crime reporter. Even in advanced countries, crime is generally underreported, partly due to fear of reprisal attacks by the perpetrators. In this chapter, Samson Folarin provides an insight into the nature and dimensions of crime in metropolitan Lagos, where about 67 per cent of the population live in constant fear of becoming a crime victim, and the nature of the danger an investigative journalist constantly faces. The specific risks he identifies include threats to life, problems of sourcing information from victims and eyewitnesses, and being sued for libel, especially by the rich and powerful. Summing up his own experience as an investigative journalist with a major newspaper in Lagos, he writes, "the investigative reporter is in no lesser danger than the police or the undercover detectives, especially when it comes to reporting crime in a city like Lagos".

The last two chapters of this book shift attention to the criminal justice systems in the colonial and post-colonial periods. In Chapter 9, Ayodeji Olukoju notes that in colonial Nigeria, the criminal justice system treated offences against property and the state, alongside homicide, with great severity. In particular, the government was against currency counterfeiting because it was a big threat to the integrity of the colonial monetary, fiscal, and commercial systems. Olukoju used the Tijani Ali case, which is the focus of the chapter, to illustrate the miscarriage of justice that characterised the colonial justices system. The main argument is that Tijani was dealt a serious injustice in the absence of evidence by a flawed administration of "substantial justice" in colonial Nigeria.

In Chapter 10, A.E. Akintayo offers a new interpretation of the mind-boggling problem of corruption in the Nigeria judiciary. His argument is that the bribery and corruption for which many of the judges have been indicted is not, as is popularly believed, a symptom of the craving for material possessions by a new breed of judges, but rather a legal deficiency that has its roots in the inherited British legal system and tradition that privileged the rich over the poor. The analysis reveals the symbiotic relationship between the class-based criminal law regime, the interests of the political class and the judiciary, and how this has made it difficult to win the war on corruption in Nigeria.

The final part of this book contains the book review presented by Ayodele Atsenuwa during the public launch of *This Present Darkness* at the University of Lagos in October 2016. The incisive review, which underscores the interconnectedness of disciplines in the Humanities, was done with the probing mind of a legal luminary and presented in an elegant style.

CHAPTER 1

Stephen Ellis: His Life and Work

Gerrie ter Haar

I have been asked to open this volume with a chapter introducing the life and work of Stephen Ellis. Although I am happy to do so, as his closest partner in both senses of the term, I also find it a challenging task, primarily for personal reasons. I find myself reluctant to share details of his personal life with others who have not been part of it. Fortunately, writing about Stephen's life inevitably also means writing about his work, an area that I am more comfortable sharing with a broader audience. Stephen's life and work have been closely interconnected, and his works actually provide an excellent lens for reflecting on relevant aspects of his life.[1]

In the following sections, I will provide an overview of Stephen's life that will place his works in context. I will allow other voices to speak about the way he performed his academic tasks and responsibilities, before offering my personal reflections on how his life and works are bound together in a profoundly holistic manner.

1 The English Period: Life and Work in Britain

When Stephen died on 29 July 2015 he had just turned 62. He was born a British citizen in Nottingham, on 13 June 1953, the youngest of three children from an average middle-class family of mixed English and Irish stock. The latter also explains his Roman Catholic upbringing by his mother, even though his father's side of the family stood firmly in the Protestant tradition. Until he went to university, he attended a Catholic boys school in Nottingham for his primary and secondary education. As elsewhere in the world, Catholic schools in Britain were known for the quality of their education. Stephen was a good pupil and his old school friends remember him as a "very bright" and "extremely smart"

1 An extensive overview can be found in Jos Damen, *Stephen Ellis Bibliography*. The original version was published online in November 2016: https://openaccess.leidenuniv.nl/handle/1887/44389. A revised edition has recently been published in book form: Jos Damen, *Stephen Ellis Bibliography*, 2nd revised and enlarged edition, African Studies Centre, Leiden University, 2018 (ASCL Occasional Publication 35). Also available online.

 | DOI:10.1163/9789004396289_003

boy, who would later become a "learned man who never assumed that you didn't know as much as he did".[2] Stephen took his A-levels in History, French, and Latin with excellent results. This gave him an entry ticket to Oxford University, which, in those days, was still pretty much the exclusive reserve of the traditional British upper class.

Before joining university, Stephen decided to take a year out to do voluntary work through the Voluntary Service Overseas (VSO). He was sent to Cameroon to teach English at Collège Libermann, a Catholic missionary school for boys in Douala, founded in the 1950s by the Holy Spirit Congregation but soon taken over by the Jesuits. One of the Jesuits was Eric de Rosny, who attained fame from his explorations of the spirit world as experienced by many Cameroonians.[3] De Rosny was in charge of the college at the time that Stephen arrived, at just 18, young and inexperienced. He looked after Stephen not only as his formal boss, but in other ways too. Later in life, Stephen remembered with fondness how De Rosny took him to the townships of Douala where his mentor used to spend hours talking to people about the past.[4] The memory of these experiences also resonated with him when we became a couple in the 1980s, complementing each other with our different knowledge of Africa: Stephen as a historian and me as a scholar of religion, both focusing in our work on sub-Saharan Africa. Our first trip to Africa together was to Zambia, in 1986, where I was conducting research into the spiritual healing activities of the former Catholic Archbishop of Lusaka, Emmanuel Milingo, which had led to a serious clash with the Vatican and had culminated in a crisis of many sorts in Zambia.[5] The subject matter immediately triggered Stephen's interest, as it had done in Cameroon years earlier; it led to our first-ever joint publication in his favourite journal *African Affairs*, whose editor he would later become.[6]

After finishing his year of service for VSO, Stephen went to Oxford to take up his undergraduate studies in history at St Catherine's College, one of the university's newer colleges. This was at a time when the traditional gender segregation at Oxford colleges was becoming outdated. St Catherine's was among the first to abolish this practice; when Stephen arrived the college had already

2 Personal messages from childhood friends.

3 Eric de Rosny, *Healers in the Night*. Maryknoll: Orbis Books, 1985. Originally published in French in 1981 as *Les yeux de ma chèvre*.

4 In the Acknowledgements to his last book, *This Present Darkness: A History of Nigerian Organised Crime*. London: Hurst & Co./New York: Oxford University Press, 2016.

5 Gerrie ter Haar, *Spirit of Africa: The Healing Ministry of Archbishop Milingo of Zambia*. London: Hurst & Co., 1992. Also published in French and Italian.

6 Gerrie ter Haar and Stephen Ellis, "Spirit possession and healing in modern Zambia: An analysis of letters to Archbishop Milingo", *African Affairs*, 87: 347 (1988), pp. 185–206.

admitted women students. One of these women was Benazir Bhutto,[7] born, like Stephen, in June 1953, and probably the college's most famous alumna. Incidentally, St. Catherine's was also the college of Matthew Schoffeleers, like De Rosny a reputable (Dutch) Catholic missionary priest and anthropologist, who drew me – and by association also Stephen – into the so-called Milingo affair, which was still to unfold at the time that Stephen moved to live at St Catherine's in 1972. Stephen spent three happy years there, forging lasting bonds with fellow students, one of the pleasurable consequences of Oxford college life. Stephen and I liked to compare the type of bonding among college friends, with its elements of mutual obligation, reciprocal relations, and solidarity within the group, to the social bonds forged in African societies, such as initiation societies in West Africa or the Broederbond in South Africa. Regular reunions, known as gaudies, are organised by the Oxford colleges to bring together alumni of the same year groups about once every decade. These gatherings, accompanied by a formal dinner at the college, serve to keep the bonds alive. The last gaudy that Stephen and I attended was in June 2014, where Stephen announced to his peers, with typical stoicism, that he was dying. In 1975, Stephen graduated with a BA in Modern History, with first-class honours. He left St Catherine's to pursue a PhD at St Antony's college, a leading centre for the study of modern history and known for area studies, including Africa.

When Stephen left St Catherine's he wanted to specialize in African history, a subject that had first caught his interest during his stay in Cameroon. He followed a course on African history at St Antony's that was taught by Anthony Kirk-Greene, known for his studies on Nigeria. It was he who introduced Stephen to the idea of studying Madagascar, which, at that time, was largely the preserve of French academics. Since Stephen was proficient in French, there would be no formal language barrier, nor any obstacles to consulting French colonial records. As part of his doctoral research, Stephen spent considerable time in the national archives of France, particularly in Paris and Aix-en-Provence, where the overseas colonial archives are held. He perfected his French in the process, as he loved the language and French culture generally, and would continue to visit France for the rest of his life for work, but also for pleasure. We spent many holidays there, exploring various parts of the country, mostly by bicycle.

The decision taken, Stephen left to conduct research on a revolt in Madagascar in the late nineteenth century, which was later published by Cambridge

7 Prime Minister of Pakistan between 1988 and 1990 and again between 1993 and 1996. She was assassinated in 2007.

University Press.[8] He became affiliated with the University of Antananarivo, where he taught English once again, this time to earn an income. He learned enough Malagasy to be able to read the language, as needed for research purposes, and had a basic grasp of the spoken language, which was less important since the official language is French. Day-to-day life in Madagascar was quite different from the formal lifestyle in Britain, both institutionally and in terms of personal relationships, and suited him down to the ground. Indeed, it fit with Stephen's personality in every way, and for years to come he would dish out stories and anecdotes, provoking lots of laughter. Blessed with a sharp and disciplined mind, he completed his studies quickly and easily. He even started a writing project on the side, about economic aspects of the history of Madagascar, in collaboration with his friend Robert Archer, which due to circumstances was never completed.[9] In 1980, Stephen submitted his dissertation, followed by the official graduation ceremony in Oxford on 7 March 1981.

By that time, he had already started to publish in academic journals. Typically, Stephen had his first-ever academic article published in the historical journal of Madagascar,[10] before considering international journals. *The Journal of African History* was the first to publish on the specific subject of his PhD – the nineteenth-century revolt – and thereafter brought out several of his articles on Madagascar, as well as many of his book reviews.[11] Although his academic life took him in many other directions, Stephen earned a reputation as one of the best academic experts on the history and politics of Madagascar. In 1987, we visited the country together, and Stephen went there several times again subsequently, the last time in 2012 for a study of labour unions in Madagascar that had been commissioned by one of the main Dutch trade unions.[12] Doing research and writing about it, as we will see, would remain his passion throughout his life.

---

8 *The Rising of the Red Shawls: A Revolt in Madagascar 1895–1899*. Cambridge University Press, 1985. A French edition was published in 1998 with Karthala.

9 Personal archives. In January 1987, Stephen presented a paper at SOAS based on this secondary project, entitled "Madagascar's place in the international slave trade in the 19th century".

10 "Un texte du XVIIième siècle sur Madagascar", *Omaly sy Anio*, 9: 1 (1979), pp. 151–166.

11 "The political elite of Imerina and the revolt of the menalamba: The creation of a colonial myth in Madagascar, 1895–1898". *The Journal of African History*, 21: 2 (1980), pp. 219–234. The *Stephen Ellis Bibliography* compiled by Jos Damen, provides about 25 entries on articles and book reviews by Stephen.

12 The study was carried out for the CNV, a federation of Christian trade unions in the Netherlands, together with Solofo Randrianja.

Having returned to Britain, it proved difficult to find a job, especially since the UK was experiencing a recession at that time. To make ends meet, Stephen took up various short-term jobs, including a brief stint in the civil service, till in 1982 when he was offered a contract by Amnesty International to work as a researcher for West Africa at its London headquarters. This is how Stephen and I got to know each other, since in those days I was one of the many volunteers in the Dutch section of Amnesty International, working as a country coordinator for West Africa, the region that Stephen became responsible for. As one of the largest and most active sections of the international human rights organisation, contacts between London and Amsterdam tended to be as frequent as they were inevitable: the Dutch could simply not be ignored. Although this sometimes irritated other researchers in the head office, Stephen immediately displayed some of the personal characteristics that would also become manifest later in his academic work: he approached resistance with disarming charm and humour, and with a healthy sense of compromise. As part of his job he would regularly travel to West Africa on human rights missions, either to visit prisoners of conscience imprisoned without trial or to meet heads of state to discuss the human rights situation in their country. Such high-level missions could at times also produce situations that would later evoke much laughter, such as when Stephen, accompanied by one of Amnesty's international human rights lawyers and a medical doctor, went on a mission to Togo, where he was held at the airport in Lomé, by order of the president, Gnassingbé Eyadéma. He spent a few hilarious days in the President's VIP room before being deported, as nobody really knew what to do with the Amnesty delegates.[13]

His capacity to approach life with humour never prevented Stephen from revealing unpleasant truths. As an Amnesty researcher, he wrote several reports about the human rights situation in various countries in the region and the appalling conditions in which detainees were usually held and otherwise treated. Later in life, having left Amnesty, he did exactly the same when it concerned African liberation movements, such as SWAPO and the ANC, revealing serious human rights abuses by these political organisations, especially against dissidents. Such revelations would provoke the same indignant responses from those in power as they had during his time with Amnesty. Stephen's ability as a historian, used to working in archives, proved an asset, even after his death. When, in 2016, former Chadian president Hissène Habré, who had come to office in 1982, was eventually convicted in Senegal by an African tribunal for

13 [...] "I can tell anyone who will believe me that I have spent New Year's Eve locked in the President of Togo's bedroom with a doctor, a lawyer, and two bottles of champagne". Quotation taken from a personal note to a Dutch Amnesty colleague, dated 16 May 1986.

gross human rights abuses during his rule, this was also facilitated by evidence produced from the meticulously detailed information that Stephen had left in the Amnesty archives during his tenure as West Africa researcher in the early 1980s. Although at the time of the trial Stephen's illness prevented him from testifying in person, he was gratified to know that one of his former colleagues was able to make use of his work.[14] These are just a few examples of how Stephen displayed in his work what philosophers have described as epistemic virtues, as reflected in his intellectual honesty and humility, and in his courage to pursue the truth irrespective of the consequences.

These same virtues marked the following step in his career. In 1986, Stephen left Amnesty to become the editor of *Africa Confidential*, a small London-based newsletter that has been reporting on current affairs in Africa since 1960.[15] The change from Amnesty to Africa Confidential gave him full freedom to write freely about the dark sides of African politics and allowed him to take on the rich and powerful in ways that he had not been able to do before. One of the main policy rules in Amnesty at the time was that its researchers were not allowed to publish on issues regarding the countries under their professional responsibility, other than anonymous output in the form of official Amnesty reports and other documents. Although Stephen faithfully obliged, he increasingly felt the constraints of not being able to talk or write freely about the things that mattered to him. When the opportunity presented itself, he left Amnesty to become an investigative researcher and journalist. During this period he developed a long-standing friendship with Richard Dowden, former director of the Royal African Society in London and also a leading journalist on Africa. In Stephen's obituary, he recalls their first meeting: "We first met when he [Stephen] waited to be interviewed for the editorship of the journal, Africa Confidential. I was disappointed not to get the job but when I realised who I had been up against I realised why. We became good friends and colleagues and worked on several stories together".[16] He relates how "Stephen always wanted to dig deeper than journalism. He was an excellent interviewer, posing simple,

14 Personal communication with Mike Dottridge, former Amnesty International researcher for the Central Africa region.

15 *Africa Confidential* remains a leading journal on Africa's politics: see https://www.africa-cionfidential.com.

16 Richard Dowden, "Stephen Ellis – Obituary – A cool observer of Africa who took on big themes", 30 July 2015. Published on the RAS website: http://www.royalafricansociety.org/blog/stephen-ellis-obituary-cool-observer-africa-who-took-big-themes#sthash.uot2h-PwL.dpuf. Also available on the ASC website where some 25 obituaries can be found. See http://www.ascleiden.nl/news/memoriam-stephen-ellis-1953-2015/. The joint articles are included in the *Stephen Ellis Bibliography* under the heading "Press articles".

almost casual, questions to find the threads that led to the truth. He meticulously unravelled them and pondered on their meaning and implications".[17]

Stephen's revelations often did not amuse those in power, whether in Africa or in Europe. He would regularly come under great pressure not to publish, for example, about the secret involvement in dubious affairs of European royalty or members of the British aristocracy,[18] African presidents or wealthy businessmen, and others with social positions that enabled them to wield undue political influence. Among them were ANC leaders, living in exile in London, who tried to smear his reputation by denouncing him as an agent working for MI6, Britain's secret intelligence service. The notorious English libel laws would be another instrument to try to silence him,[19] as was frequently the case during his academic career. The most contentious of these was the libel charge initiated by Charles Taylor, then President of Liberia, whose anger had been incurred by Stephen's ground-breaking book about the civil war in Liberia, *The Mask of Anarchy*.[20] In it, Stephen revealed some of the gruesome practices for which Taylor was responsible, which an article in the British *Times* described as "cannibalism".[21] Eventually, Taylor had to drop the case. Throughout his career, Stephen was threatened, but he was never to be deterred.

Stephen took up the editorship of *Africa Confidential* at a time when the political dynamics in Africa were changing fast, especially in southern Africa. In South Africa, the apartheid regime was running out of steam and, as one of his colleagues at the paper recalled, "a rearguard action was well under way in the apartheid government and its feared National Intelligence Service [...] was very active in London, a centre of opposition to the SA regime".[22] Here lay the beginnings of Stephen's particular interest in South Africa. In her obituary of Stephen, the same colleague stated how he would later devote "his considerable investigative powers" to an impressive series of scholarly books

17 Dowden, "Obituary".

18 For example, their engagement in covert operations relating to the World Wide Fund for Nature (WWF) with the code name Operation Lock. In the early 1990s, Stephen published several articles in the British and Dutch press, among which: "Prince paid thousands into wildlife sting", *The Independent*, 18 January 1991. A draft book manuscript: "Operation Lock: How South African death squads use nature conservation" is in the personal archives that are kept at the African Studies Centre's library in Leiden.

19 Stephen Ellis, "Face to face with England's libel laws", *Socio*, 3 (2014), pp. 49–61.

20 *The Mask of Anarchy: The Destruction of Liberia and the Religious Dimension of an African Civil War*. London: C. Hurst & New York: New York University Press, 1999. A second, revised and updated version with a new preface was published in 2007.

21 Michael Dynes, "Liberia's gruesome top 20 killers", *The Times*, 2 November 1999.

22 Gillian Lusk, "In remembrance of Stephen Ellis", *Africa Confidential*, 56: 16, 6 August 2015. Available on the ASCL website.

based on the original research done during his time at *Africa Confidential*.[23] Stephen worked for the newsletter, recognisable by its format and distinctive blue colour for five years, during which time he built a formidable network of contacts that he had already started to develop while working for Amnesty. According to Jean-François Bayart,

> [Stephen] probably had one of the best address books a specialist in African affairs could boast of: in it, leading lights of the international scholarly community rubbed shoulders with civil servants of all nations, activists, journalists, bankers, brokers, ex-mercenaries, business figures sometimes with a background in armed struggle, priests and pastors, environmentalists, diamond merchants, and a host of anonymous people he had met in the course of his travels, especially in Africa, to whom he evinced a respect which did not cloud his clear-sightedness.[24]

This multi-dimensional approach to his work would be perpetuated in the academic career that became the next step in Stephen's working life.

2 The Dutch Period: Life and Work in the Netherlands

In 1991, while still living in London, Stephen was approached to become the director of the African Studies Centre (ASC) in Leiden. He had obtained a reputation as an expert on Africa, was highly qualified for the job as an academic, and likely to be interested in living in the Netherlands due to his Dutch partner. For several years Stephen and I had been commuting between London and Amsterdam, and in 1990 we had settled in London for the time being. It looked like an attractive option. In the early 1990s, the centre was a mere hint of what it later became; at the time, it was pretty much a playground for individuals with a professional interest in Africa, who could use its seemingly unlimited resources (including finances) unfettered. Stephen was excited about the possibility of steering the ASC onto a new, dynamic course as he could see its potential to become a leading institution in the world of African studies, especially with all the resources at its disposal. He embarked on his new responsibilities with enthusiasm, formulating ambitious goals and starting the

23 *Ibid.*

24 Jean-François Bayart, "Stephen Ellis 1953–2015: A tribute from Jean-François Bayart to Stephen Ellis", 5 August 2015. Obituary originally published in French on the website of Karthala. Both versions are available on the ASCL website.

necessary changes.[25] But he was soon to discover that there was no common vision at the centre, or the desire to develop one under the direction of an outsider aiming to bring about change. He became disillusioned with what he considered a lack of intellectual ambition that promoted self-interest and nepotism, including at the top. Inevitably, the situation led to conflict with competing interests at stake, and Stephen decided not to waste his energy on a battle that he realised he was not going to win. Nor was he prepared to compromise his personal and academic integrity, which meant more to him than any other aspect of his life and work.

Since his heart was in stimulating and promoting research on Africa, in 1994 he accepted an invitation from Jan Pronk, then minister for Development Cooperation, to take a year off to write a study for the Global Coalition for Africa (GCA) analysing the changes taking place on the African continent and their implications for development. What would the future of Africa look like in the coming decades, politically and economically, but also socially and culturally? Making use of his vast network of African scholars and other intellectuals, Stephen produced a shrewd analysis of Africa's future offered to the 1995 GCA plenary meeting on "Africa's Future and the World" that was hosted by the Dutch government.[26] Fifteen years later, Stephen would write a second book about Africa's place in the world, again at the request of the Ministry of Foreign Affairs, which became compulsory reading for all civil servants in the Netherlands, including diplomats, aspiring to engage with Africa.[27]

Stephen believed that the African Studies Centre should be finding out how Africa "works" at every level in close collaboration with African academics. He strived for a broader approach to and wider focus in African studies, taking African realities as a point of departure rather than the latest theoretical fashions in Europe or America. He stimulated the growth of the ASC fellowship programme, which allowed African researchers to spend time at the centre with free access to its resources, and he was instrumental in setting up a European network of African study centres that subsequently developed into AEGIS, the Africa-Europe Group for Interdisciplinary Studies.[28] He considered supporting scholars from Africa to be one of his most important tasks as ASC director. Sharing some personal memories of Stephen, one of his colleagues at the

25 See Ton Dietz, "Introductory speech on the occasion of the handing over of the position of director of the African Studies Centre", 12 April 2010.

26 Stephen Ellis (ed.), *Africa Now: People, Policies and Institutions*. London: James Currey, 1996. French and Dutch editions were published in 1995.

27 Stephen Ellis, *Season of Rains: Africa in the World*. London, Hurst & Co/Johannesburg: Jacana, 2011; University of Chicago Press, 2012. A Dutch edition was published in 2011.

28 aegis-eu.org.

centre has described him as "an invaluable colleague and an inspiring mentor", who generously shared information, views, and contacts, and brought to the ASC "a whole range of visitors, seminar speakers, and visiting fellows, opening up a rather sedate centre to the exciting world of ground-breaking research".[29]

Stephen also emphasised the need for the ASC to get out of the ivory tower and show its relevance also to outside institutions, which was not a widely accepted idea in the early 1990s. In an early interview, shortly after his appointment at the ASC, he explained what he meant. Relevant research in African studies, meant to him "research related to issues which are either of obvious or overwhelming importance". "And", he added, "if there is an argument, we should say: what Africans themselves identify as such",[30] highlighting thus once more the need for research collaboration with African colleagues. Being relevant also implied the need for publishing research results in different ways, for different publics and in different languages; notably for the ASC this also included publishing in Dutch to inform and enlighten the Dutch public.

In 1995, Stephen returned to the centre as senior researcher, content to leave the directorship to a Dutch colleague.[31] In retrospect, it is clear that the seeds for change were sown under his directorship, providing the foundation on which the academic future of the centre could be built further. For the next twenty years, until his death in 2015, Stephen enjoyed working at the ASC, sharing with and advising others if and whenever they wanted, making maximum use of the great research opportunities offered by the centre. The ASC library in particular became his favourite place. "He absorbed books, journal articles and newspapers about Africa", writes ASC's chief librarian Jos Damen in the *Stephen Ellis Bibliography* he published after Stephen's death.[32] Stephen became widely known for his erudition; the bibliography is testimony to the width and depth of his knowledge on Africa and Africa's place in the world, both past and present. An impressive list of books he reviewed are included in the bibliography, as are the non-academic contributions he made to the debate on Africa. He also gave numerous interviews to media all over the world seeking his views on what was happening in Africa. Stephen took his role and responsibility as a public intellectual very seriously. In a blog about the future of Africa, written in 2011, he observed how people in Europe continue to underestimate the importance of Africa. "Africa", he wrote, "is now more important than at any time

29 Ineke van Kessel, "In memoriam of Stephen Ellis", *NVAS* [Dutch Society of African Studies] *Newsletter*, 2 August 2015. Available on the ASCL website.

30 Interview in *IMWOO Bulletin*, 19: 3, 1991, pp. 3–5.

31 Dr. Gerti Hesseling, who would be ASC director between 1996 and 2004. She died in 2009.

32 Damen, *Stephen Ellis Bibliography* (2018), p. 7.

in the last fifty years. You would never think so, to judge from the small-minded attitude of European publics and the shallow generation of politicians they have voted into office".[33] He warned that European governments should be careful not to lose what little they have. "Otherwise they will find themselves squandering the influence that they have acquired, at great cost in blood and treasure, both their own and that of others, over generations".[34]

We can hear in these comments an echo of the inaugural address Stephen gave following his appointment in 2008 as Desmond Tutu Professor in the Faculty of Social Sciences at VU University Amsterdam, a position he combined with his research post at the ASC. In his speech, he emphasised the need to "decolonize" our minds, not only in Africa, but also in Europe.[35] It was the main reason why he thought writing and publishing about Africa was so important. The Global Initiative against Transnational Organized Crime, one of the many networks that Stephen was associated with, commented in its obituary that "[h]is research is unparalleled, both for its depth and breadth", and that Stephen was "one of the rare and gifted individuals who effectively bridged the gap between research and policy".[36] Ton Dietz, outgoing ASC director at the time of writing, states: "Stephen was a welcome guest at the Ministry of Foreign Affairs and many diplomats have asked his advice. He gave that with dedication, based on his deep insights in many African countries, and with complete sincerity and integrity".[37]

Integrity is the word that characterises Stephen best, personally and professionally. In the many obituaries and tributes following his death, the word "integrity" frequently recurs to describe his life and work, as "a standard of moral courage and intellectual independence".[38] According to these various commentators, Stephen was one of the most authoritative Africanists of our time, "one of the greatest Africanists of his generation".[39] If he ever thought

33 Blog *African Arguments*, "What future for Africa?", 20 June 2011. http://africanarguments.org/2011/06/20/what-future-for-africa-by-stephen-ellis/.

34 *Ibid.*

35 *South Africa and the Decolonization of the Mind* (2009). Online version: http://hdl.handle.net/1871/15351.

36 "In Memoriam: Stephen Ellis, 1953–2015", 29 July 2015. http://globalinitiative.net/in-memoriam-stephen-ellis-1953-2015/.

37 Ton Dietz in his speech at the inauguration of the Stephen Ellis Chair on 4 April 2017. http://www.ascleiden.nl/sites/default/files/speech-ton-dietz-launch-stephen-ellis-chair-04042017.pdf.

38 Paul Trewhela, "Stephen Ellis: A standard of moral courage", *South African Historical Journal*, 67: 3, 2015, pp. 381–384.

39 Dowden, "Obituary".

so himself – which he didn't – Stephen would certainly never have said it or even suggested so. The reason is very simple, because, as one of his colleagues stated at his funeral, unlike many other academics with a reputation in their field, Stephen was not a "conceited jerk".[40] Stephen was always excited about his work, but he never boasted about it. In my own speech at the funeral, I gave a short summary of how others had described him in their numerous messages to me as an academic:

> [A] wonderful man and a superb scholar; somebody without match in sheer range and depth; by far the most accomplished, productive and dedicated scholar of Africa of his generation, whose contribution will remain the gold standard with respect to modern scholarship on Africa; somebody with a brilliant brain, an extraordinarily talented person with a terrific memory; a gem truly lost. The idiom of the fallen tree, one person wrote, is overused, but if ever there was a giant baobab it was Stephen Ellis.[41]

The African Studies Centre in Leiden, too, through its director Ton Dietz, has hailed Stephen at many occasions as its most prominent and most influential researcher.[42] Stephen's qualities as a researcher, however, must be considered in reference to his personality. Thus, colleagues who wrote to me after his death referred to him not only as a great scholar, but as:

> [A] lovely man; a warm and witty person with a sharp mind; a person with no airs and graces; with a basic humility and humanity, who lacked arrogance and treated everybody as his peer, without a trace of condescension or suggestion of hierarchy; somebody to be trusted and respected absolutely, who not only brought intellectual excitement but also much love and laughter in the lives of others.[43]

40 Ton Salman, head of the Department of Social and Cultural Anthropology of VU University, in his funeral speech. http://www.ascleiden.nl/sites/default/files/speech_ton_salman_vu_0.pdf/.

41 Funeral speech available on the ASCL website: http://www.ascleiden.nl/sites/default/files/speech_gerrie_ter_haar.pdf/.

42 For example, at the launch of *This Present Darkness* at the ASC in Leiden. http://www.ascleiden.nl/news/tribute-stephen-ellis-and-book-launch-present-darkness/. The book was published posthumously.

43 Personal messages quoted in funeral speech: http://www.ascleiden.nl/sites/default/files/speech_gerrie_ter_haar.pdf/.

Stephen was always driven by curiosity, and his intellectual curiosity also included areas of knowledge practiced outside the academy. It brought him into contact with an amazing range of people, with whom he interacted in a totally unbiased manner. His disarming way of talking to people allowed him to interview persons from different backgrounds and all walks of life and to collaborate with them effectively. In the course of his academic career, he worked, for example, with the Truth and Reconciliation Committee in South Africa (1997–1998), as director of the Africa Programme at the International Crisis Group (2003–2004), and as scientific advisor to the West Africa Committee on Drugs (2012–2014) chaired by former Nigerian President Olusegun Obasanjo. At the same time, he served as an editorial board member of various journals, and for many years (1998–2006) he was editor of *African Affairs*, the journal of the Royal African Society in London, which remembers him as "a greatly respected editor [...], who played an important role in making the journal the success that it is today". In his honour, the journal introduced the Stephen Ellis Prize for the most innovative article "to highlight and promote the kind of thought-provoking, politically engaged and path breaking analysis that Stephen Ellis pioneered throughout his hugely influential career".[44]

The sections above illuminate the interwovenness of Stephen's life and work. Without understanding his personal character one cannot fully understand the nature of his work.

3 Stephen Ellis and His Works: The Role of History

It is important to remember that Stephen was a *historian*, first and last; a historian of Africa, the continent that had been his passion ever since his early student days. The historical perspective provides the foundation for all of his writings, from his first book on a nineteenth-century revolt in Madagascar[45] to his last one on Nigerian organised crime in today's world.[46] His last book is actually a perfect example of the way he understood his task as a historian; at the same time, it is proof of the way in which his thinking on how to write about history has developed over the years. For him, history was not something concerning the past; it meant much more than that. In an essay he wrote for *The Journal of African History*, he argued that historians need to engage with the history of contemporary Africa, both as a way of throwing new light on

44 https://academic.oup.com/afraf/pages/the_stephen_ellis_prize/.

45 *The Rising of the Red Shawls.*

46 *This Present Darkness.*

Africa's more remote past and as a way of understanding the present.[47] Past and present, in his view, are inextricably linked, and the two should be studied not separately, but in relation to one another. In other words, the present does not explain itself. Rather, we have to understand where it comes from. In his last book, too, an analysis of Nigerian organised crime, Stephen asks the essential question: how did Nigeria get there? The short answer, summarized in the final pages of the book is: it comes from its particular history.[48]

Bringing the past to bear on the present required Stephen to identify themes that would help him to carry out what he considered the real task of a historian: to pursue the truth. This is what led him to investigate and write about crime in Africa.[49] Typically, Stephen knew that for a proper understanding of the phenomenon one needs to understand not only the African context – which he did very well through his numerous research activities in different parts of the continent – but also the global context; hence his books about the place of Africa in the world.[50] His ground-breaking studies of specific countries such as Liberia, Nigeria, and South Africa are all informed by such a contextual perspective.[51] His way of working also required an interdisciplinary approach, which became one of the distinctive attributes of Stephen's scholarly work. He collaborated with scholars and experts from other disciplines, including some less obvious ones – at least at first sight – such as scholars of religion like myself. His book about the criminalisation of the state in Africa, co-authored with political scientists Jean-François Bayart and Béatrice Hibou, is one of the best-known examples.[52] Another is the book on religion and politics in Africa, jointly written by Stephen and I.[53] Both books have become highly influential in the academic debate, as they broke with conventional patterns of analysis.

47 "Writing histories of contemporary Africa", *The Journal of African History*, 43: 1, 2002, pp. 1–27.

48 *This Present Darkness*, pp. 215–230.

49 See his last article, written jointly with Mark Shaw, which was published posthumously: "Does organised crime exist in Africa?", *African Affairs*, 114: 457, 2015, pp. 508–528. Reprinted in Nic Cheeseman, Lindsay Whitfield, and Carl Death (eds.), *The African Affairs Reader: Key Texts in Politics, Development, and International Relations*, Oxford: Oxford University Press, 2017, pp. 88–111.

50 *Africa Now* (1996) and *Season of Rains* (2012).

51 *The Mask of Anarchy* [about Liberia], *This Present Darkness* [about Nigeria], and *External Mission: The ANC in Exile, 1960/1990*. Johannesburg: Jonathan Ball/London: Hurst & Co, 2012 & New York, Oxford University Press, 2013 [about South Africa].

52 Originally published in French: *La criminalisation de l'Etat en Afrique*. Bruxelles: Éditions Complexe, 1997. English edition published in 1999: *The Criminalization of the State in Africa*. Oxford: James Currey/ Bloomington: Indiana University Press.

53 *Worlds of Power: Religious Thought and Political Practice in Africa*. London: Hurst/New York: Oxford University Press, 2004.

Stephen was never a slave to passing academic fashions; his erudition did simply not allow for that. He had a totally unapologetic view of Africa, its history and contemporary realities, and he researched these with intellectual rigour. In his obituary of Stephen, Jean-François Bayart remarked on Stephen's scrupulous attention to sources and the diversity of sources on which he drew.[54] It is no surprise, then, that Stephen became widely known for the breadth of his academic appeal.

His view on the task of a historian necessitated him to write about contemporary African realities, such as war, crime, and corruption, but always to do so from a historical perspective. The historical context he provided on these topics in his studies were crucial to a good understanding and an antidote to conventional essentialising analyses. Initiating research and engaging in debates on such issues required moral courage, since they implied taking on the rich and powerful in Africa and holding them accountable for their deeds. It did not make him popular in certain circles. Stephen's testimony to the Special Court for Sierra Leone in The Hague was vital in having Charles Taylor sentenced to – in effect – life imprisonment.[55] His revelations about the ANC in exile[56] caused much controversy, particularly provoking the anger of the ANC leadership in South Africa, although all the unpleasant truths he published, starting already during his time at *Africa Confidential*, were subsequently proven to be true.[57] In a lecture in memory of Stephen, South African Professor Jonathan Jansen, then vice chancellor of the University of the Free State, stated: "I know of no other historical work that better explains the state we are in by taking 1994 as a marker of not only change but continuity with the fractured past of the liberation movements, principally the ANC".[58] As Lansana Gberie has suggested, the real reason for the ANC leadership's anger lay in the fact that Stephen confronted "the depredations and betrayed promises of the post-colonial state and liberation movements in Africa".[59] Insults and threats, however, did not prevent Stephen from pursuing the truth, a vital responsibility of a historian in his

54 Bayart, "A tribute".

55 "Charles Taylor and the war in Sierra Leone: Report for the Special Court for Sierra Leone" (2006). Personal archives. In January 2008, Stephen testified for two days as an expert witness at the special court in The Hague.

56 *External Mission*.

57 Trewhela, "Stephen Ellis: A standard of moral courage".

58 Jonathan Jansen, "A quiet contemplation on the new anger: The state of transformation in South African universities", Stephen Ellis Memorial Lecture, 9 October 2015, Pretoria. Available on the ASCL website.

59 Lansana Gberie in his obituary in *Africa Confidential* on 6 August 2015. Available on the ASCL website.

view. At the same time, as a friend once put it, Stephen never thought in terms of good guys and bad guys, but instead tried to understand the human frailties that had have helped situations to develop the way they have.

Stephen's specific understanding of his tasks and responsibilities as a historian enabled him to write about many aspects of Africa's history: from politics and war to crime and corruption, from governance and states to religion and economy, from wildlife to witchcraft, from drugs and oil to human trafficking, from secret societies to secret services, to mention only some.[60] His work covered West Africa as well as southern Africa, particularly, though not exclusively (see his expert work on Madagascar), and addressed local as well as global issues. It is telling that since his death in 2015, the (five) articles and (one) book that have been published posthumously deal with very diverse subjects, geographically and theoretically. Diverse as these subjects may seem, they are tied together by the main features of Stephen's encompassing approach to Africa's history, which I choose to qualify as "holistic", in conformity with the way in which many African scholars have written about how Africans tend to view the world.

The term "holistic" is often used rather loosely in academia, but I want to apply it here in a precise manner to describe the way Stephen carried out his task as a historian, namely by developing an encompassing approach to Africa's history based on a thorough knowledge of its nature, the functions and properties of its components, the interactions between these and their relationship to the whole.[61] Stephen adopted a holistic approach in his research at every level: in his choice of methods and disciplines, in his use of sources, in the way he addressed local and global contexts in his analyses, and, most significantly, by consistently taking into account the indivisibility of the different spheres of life – visible and invisible, material and spiritual – thus acknowledging the *reality* (note: not the truth) of African worldviews that distinguish but do not separate the material from the spiritual realm of life. The latter, in particular, has become a defining feature of his work.[62]

4 Histories of Invisible Africa: The Role of Religion

In the course of his academic career, Stephen developed an increasing interest in the role of religion in African politics. Or, rather, of a religious *worldview* in

60 As reflected in the more than 160 academic articles that Stephen published: see Damen, *Stephen Ellis Bibliography*.
61 Working definition based on a definition provided at BusinessDictionary.com/.
62 See notably *The Mask of Anarchy*, *Worlds of Power*, and *This Present Darkness*.

Africa's history and its profound influence on African politics, a subject he subsequently pursued with his usual academic rigour and the open-mindedness that characterised his personality in every field of life. Although his first book *The Rising of the Red Shawls* shows that he was aware of the importance of what was then labelled "ancestral religion", it is only later that he became fully conscious of the significance of religion in the life of most Africans. His scholarly view of history and the way in which politics evolved in Africa also led him to delve into Africa's spiritual history. This is an aspect of his work that makes it rather unusual compared to that of many observers of Africa, scholarly and other, who often refuse to take African spirit beliefs seriously, discarding them as either backward or outdated.

In the course of his numerous travels to Africa and through his engagement with Africans of all walks of life, Stephen came to realise that, as a historian, he also had to understand Africans' relationship to and interaction with the invisible world that many of them consider to be the cradle of all power, including political power.[63] In many of his works, including his last book *This Present Darkness*, Stephen demonstrates that, in Africa, power has historically been conceived partly in spiritual terms and that the spiritual domain is one in which power is actively contested. He shows that there is a huge gap between the legal universe that formally exists and the lived reality of governance; a gap, he argues, that is also a moral and even a spiritual one.[64] It is this awareness that brought him increasingly to investigate Africa's spiritual history in relation to African politics.

Stephen developed a growing interest in Africa's spiritual history not for its own sake, but because of the significance ascribed to religion by most Africans and the way in which it continued to affect their lives. This became most clear in his book about the war in Liberia.[65] In it, he showed how much political conflict was entangled with religion, a concept not to be understood primarily in institutional terms, but in terms of a religious consciousness that connects the visible, material world with the invisible spiritual world that, in this case, Liberians believed to exist.[66] In virtually all of his subsequent writings, Stephen continued to draw attention to this vital aspect of African societies in order to

63 As explained at length in *Worlds of Power*.

64 *This Present Darkness*, p. 207.

65 *The Mask of Anarchy*.

66 As pointed out in our joint work, in the context of Africa, "religion" can best be understood as "a belief in the existence of an invisible world, distinct but not separate from the visible one, that is home to spiritual beings with effective powers over the material world". See *Worlds of Power*, p. 14. Note that this is a working or operational definition and, like all such definitions, used as an analytical tool.

clarify the nature of especially African politics.[67] The crucial point he made in this respect is that the very existence of a widespread belief in the spirit world turns the spirit world itself into a political instrument.

Albeit via different paths, Stephen and I had both arrived at the insight that understanding the African spirit world was crucial to understanding life in Africa. Through my own work as a scholar of religion with a research focus on Africa, I had first come to this conclusion in the mid-1980s, inspired by my study of the "Milingo affair".[68] In the 30 years that Stephen and I lived together, we inevitably ended up influencing each other with ideas and insights emerging from our different academic backgrounds: history and politics, on the one hand, and the study of religion, on the other. During all those years, our "partnership of head and heart"[69] led to mutually beneficially forms of academic cooperation that resulted in a number of joint publications, the best known of which is our book *Worlds of Power: Religious Thought and Political Practice in Africa*, but also includes a number of important journal articles.[70] This partnership allowed us, as Paul Trewhela wrote with specific reference to South Africa, to bring "a broad, humane and spiritual vision to some of [South] Africa's harsh and most knotty issues".[71] This can only be done by taking African epistemologies seriously,[72] and trying to understand Africa on its own terms.

Belief in a spirit world is part of Africa's religious history. I consider Stephen's emphasis on the significance of a religious worldview in Africa's history and its profound influence on African politics to be one of his most important contributions to our understanding of African history and politics. By drawing attention to the significance of the realm of the invisible in Africa, Stephen showed how people in Africa, including African politicians, make use of religious repertoires that are, in fact, established, i.e. *historical* repertoires of action. In *This Present Darkness*, he shows that this is no different in matters of governance and crime, which are also marked by such repertoires. Here, Stephen demonstrates the pervasiveness of people's belief in a spirit world in many areas of life and among all sectors of society, irrespective of people's rank and education, underscoring the importance that many Africans assign to the spirit world.

---

67 See notably our joint articles in the *Journal of Modern African Studies*: "Religion and politics in sub-Saharan Africa" (36: 2, 1998, pp. 175–201), and "Religion and politics: Taking African epistemologies seriously" (45: 3, 2007, pp. 385–401).

68 Ter Haar, *Spirit of Africa*.

69 Trewhela, "Stephen Ellis: A standard of moral courage".

70 See further Damen, *Stephen Ellis Bibliography*.

71 Trewhela, "Stephen Ellis: A standard of moral courage", p. 383.

72 Ellis and Ter Haar, "Religion and politics: Taking African epistemologies seriously".

This particular aspect of Stephen's work makes it rather unusual compared to that of many other commentators on African politics, and it challenges several of the academic disciplines in which the study of contemporary Africa is most often conceived (we may think particularly of anthropology and political science, but also development studies), since the social sciences have been developed over generations on the assumption of a separation between the realms of the secular and the religious. However, Africa's contemporary realities point to the fact that most Africans understand and interpret the world partly through the prism of religion (in the defined sense). It is therefore important to adapt our analytical tools accordingly and incorporate the spiritual dimension into political theories concerning Africa. African politicians have long been known for their efforts to access the power they believe to reside in the realm of the invisible, as demonstrated by Stephen's works. These highlight the importance that many Africans assign to spiritual power, i.e. power believed to reside in the spirit world; a type of power to which human beings can get access through various means of communication, such as divination, dreams, and visions, or through spirit possession and forms of trance, or through the use of oracles, as in Nigeria, for example. All of these are historically formed expressions of "spiritual technology" that highlight the "open frontier"[73] nature of African worldviews, in which interaction between the material and the spiritual world is considered both common and normal.

Hence, the world as most Africans view and experience it – i.e. including the realms of the visible and the invisible – became an important point of analysis in Stephen's work. By successfully bringing the concepts of political power and spiritual power together in one analytical frame, Stephen provided great insights into the relation between religion and politics that are of broad relevance and of comparative interest. The concept of spiritual power also explains why, in Africa's history, spiritual movements have so often led to the political mobilization of local populations, and why colonial as well as post-colonial governments have always tried to control and repress these. Religion, Stephen has shown, is of great political importance in Africa as a historically tested instrument of governance. In our joint work, we have also demonstrated how many Africans use a "spirit idiom" – that is, how they employ the language of religion – to express dissatisfaction with poor governance.

As a historian, Stephen was not afraid to engage with another aspect of religion in Africa that many Western social scientists tend to eschew: theology.

73 The term "open frontier" is taken from Andrew F. Walls, "Christian scholarship and the demographic transformation of the Church", in Rodney L. Petersen (ed.), with Nancy M. Rourke, *Theological Literacy for the Twenty-First Century*. Grand Rapids, MI: Eerdmans, 2002, pp. 166–183.

Stephen understood that, in Africa, theology constitutes an important intellectual trend that represents a coherent set of ideas, even if these do not follow our own logic, and, as such, it also constitutes an important historical source. It became clear to him that religious knowledge, whether in the form of traditional spiritual knowledge or "world religion" theologies, contains not simply dogmatic knowledge, but *historical* knowledge that is indispensable for understanding Africa's past and present. Stephen recognised that, in African traditions of learning, spiritual knowledge is an important part of understanding the world and that it was therefore important to incorporate an understanding of religion in its different facets into his work. This is what makes his work as insightful as it is exceptional. His last book is a final testament to the crucial insight that life in Africa – in past and present – cannot be understood without paying due attention to its religious and spiritual history.

Stephen's understanding of the interconnectedness of the visible and the invisible in Africa also impacted his personal life. Being brought up in the Catholic tradition, he came to appreciate its mystical aspects. At the time of his death, he had not returned so much to the Catholic faith (which had never left him anyway) – as some have suggested – but rather to his spiritual roots. Stephen eschewed dogmatic beliefs and ideologies, whether religious or secular, but he had learned from Africa the value of mysticism, as "the spiritual apprehension of knowledge inaccessible to the intellect, that may be attained through contemplation and self-surrender".[74] Catholicism offered him a familiar framework to focus on its mystical dimensions, allowing him also to reflect on his passing life and approaching death. Stephen loved his life but also believed, to quote the American poet Christian Wiman, "that there is some way of dying *into* life rather than simply away from it".[75] When I had to announce his actual death on 29 July 2015, I could therefore state with confidence that Stephen had been "happy in life, happy in death".[76]

5 In Conclusion

The numerous tributes that followed Stephen's death in 2015 bear witness to his lasting impact in the world of African studies. For many years he had been setting the tone of academic debates on Africa, notably on the nature of politics in Africa. In doing so, he showed both courage and intellectual honesty,

74 Cf. online "definition mysticism".

75 Christian Wiman, *My Bright Abyss: Meditation of a Modern Believer*, New York: Farrar, Straus and Giroux, 2013, p. 35.

76 Motto used on the funeral card.

two important virtues that challenge not only those in power in the political world, but also in academia. Being a responsible academic, Stephen has shown, is not a futile job. As a historian he considered it his task to pursue the truth, and if and where necessary to uncover what others might have preferred to remain hidden. That he did so "without fear or favour"[77] gained him respect in many circles. "Stephen Ellis died as he had lived", wrote Jean-François Bayart, "as a philosopher, a man of faith, a perfect gentleman", praising his social skills, his warmth, and sense of humour.[78] Jonathan Jansen, in his memorial lecture, stated how:

> From the time of our first meeting Stephen Ellis struck me as a fine English gentleman, a generous human being and a meticulous scholar. I was not surprised that he would be invited to share the honour of Desmond Tutu Professor, an association he always carried with great pride. It was only later, however, that I would come to appreciate the stature of this Oxford-trained historian in the academic world not only as Editor of two prestigious publications, Africa Confidential and African Affairs, but also as author or co-author of a collection of truly outstanding books on the African condition alongside his towering presence in leading world journals concerned with African Studies.[79]

Apart from being "[o]ne of the most prominent Africanists of our time", as his colleague Ineke van Kessel wrote, "Stephen also left his mark as a talent scout, mentoring numerous young talented researchers in Africa and beyond [...] [H]e helped to open up the bastion of academic journals for more contributions from Africa, notably from young researchers".[80] Stephen was very interested in the work of young scholars, particularly from Africa, and was always prepared to read and comment on and to help them publish their work. As editor of *African Affairs*, he would make it his business to hunt for promising students and young researchers from Africa at international conferences, and he generously shared his ideas with them. There are many reasons for which he will be remembered as a great scholar, not only in African Studies, but also among the many broader publics that got to know him in his role as public intellectual and for which he received due recognition.

77 Ineke van Kessel, "Researching and reporting Africa without fear or favour: Stephen Ellis (13 June 1953/29 July 2015)", *Modern Africa*, 3: 2, pp. 13–16. Available on the ASCL website.
78 Bayart, "A tribute".
79 Jonathan Jansen in the introductory part of his memorial lecture.
80 Van Kessel, "Researching and reporting Africa without fear or favour". Quotes on p. 15.

In 2017, Leiden University honoured Stephen by establishing a chair in his name at the African Studies Centre, the Stephen Ellis Chair for the Governance of Finance and Integrity in Africa.[81] The new chair is currently occupied by the Nigerian scholar Chibuike Uche, thereby becoming the first official ASC professor at Leiden University. This was made possible by the recent integration of the African Studies Centre into the university of Leiden. For ASC director Ton Dietz, the appointment of an African member of staff to this position was "a dream come true".[82] Had Stephen still lived, he would have agreed, as he enjoyed the fact that in his last years some of his own dreams about the course of the centre had eventually materialised. At the celebratory launch of the chair, Ton Dietz recognised Stephen's important role as the ASC's most distinguished scholar and one of the best-known Africanists in the world.[83] At the same occasion, the Dutch Minister of Foreign Affairs, Bert Koenders, who had supported the initiative financially in recognition of Stephen's work for the Ministry, spoke warmly in a video message about Stephen and his importance for policy thinking at Foreign Affairs. "In pursuing our policies on Africa and in redressing our relationship with Africa, I hope we are able to act in the same spirit as Stephen Ellis", he concluded.[84]

My final conclusion, however, goes one step further. Stephen's way of working not only tells us something about his academic qualities, which were indeed formidable, but it also says something about Stephen as the bearer of these qualities: an academic who combined the necessary passion with the thoughtful attention and balanced weighing of arguments that, in Greek mythology, were associated with the god Kairos, the alert god of time, who, unlike his grandfather Chronos, was able to create and seize the right moment in the continuous stream of time in order to bring about necessary change.[85] In the struggle against apartheid in the history of South Africa, *kairos* has become a well-known concept, especially in religious circles, to express that very idea. As an academic with an in-depth knowledge of Africa, Stephen embodied the ability to create "kairotic" moments that have profoundly influenced the way we think about the continent (and which, I assume, is the reason why his death

81 http://www.ascleiden.nl/news/stephen-ellis-chair-governance-finance-and-integrity-festively-launched/.

82 Farewell interview with Ton Dietz. On http://www.ascleiden.nl/content/farewell-interview-ton-dietz-director-african-studies-centre-leiden.

83 http://www.ascleiden.nl/sites/default/files/speech-ton-dietz-launch-stephen-ellis-chair-04042017.pdf.

84 https://www.youtube.com/watch?v=3nPV_-qXKQE&t=3s/. Available on the ASCL website.

85 Joke J. Hermsen, *Kairos: Een nieuwe bevlogenheid*. Amsterdam: Arbeiderpers, 2014. My philosophical reflections are inspired by this book.

has provoked such a global response). Michel Foucault, the French philosopher oft-quoted in African studies, has connected the concept of kairos with another Greek philosophical concept, *parrhesia*, which stands for speaking the truth in a free and open manner, and, above all, in an honest manner. According to Foucault, parrhesia implies taking risks in speaking the truth, even if it means risking your own social position.[86] During his academic life, Stephen consistently chose to tell the truth against established opinion, out of a profound sense of intellectual honesty and moral duty. In doing so, he has introduced kairotic moments into the study of Africa. It is part of the unique legacy that he has left us with.

Bibliography

Bayart, Jean-François, "Stephen Ellis 1953–2015: A Tribute from Jean-François Bayart to Stephen Ellis", 5 August 2015. Available at www.ascleiden.nl.

Bayart, Jean-François, Stephen Ellis, and Béatrice Hibou, *The Criminalization of the State in Africa*. Oxford: James Currey/Bloomington, IN: Indiana University Press, 1999 (First published in French in 1997).

Damen, Jos, *Stephen Ellis Bibliography*. Leiden: African Studies Centre, Leiden University. 2nd, enlarged and revised edition, November 2018, ASCL Occasional Publication 35. (Originally published November 2016).

De Rosny, Eric, *Healers in the Night*. Maryknoll, NY: Orbis Books, 1985. (Originally published in French, 1981).

Dowden, Richard, "Stephen Ellis – Obituary: A Cool Observer of Africa Who Took on Big Themes", 30 July 2015. Available at http://www.royalafricansociety.org/blog/stephen-ellis-obituary-cool-observer-africa-who-took-big-themes#sthash.uot2hPwL.dpuf.

Dynes, Michael, "Liberia's Gruesome Top 20 killers", *The Times*, 2 November 1999.

Ellis, Stephen, "'Un texte du XVIIième siècle sur Madagascar", *Omaly sy Anio*, 9:1 (1979), pp. 151–166.

Ellis, Stephen, "The Political Elite of Imerina and the Revolt of the Menalamba: The Creation of a Colonial Myth in Madagascar, 1895–1898", *The Journal of African History*, 21: 2 (1980), pp. 219–234.

Ellis, Stephen, *The Rising of the Red Shawls: A Revolt in Madagascar 1895–1899*. Cambridge: Cambridge University Press, 1985. (French edition Karthala, 1998).

86 Michel Foucault: "Discourse and Truth: The Problematization of Parrhesia". (Lecture 1 in a series of 6 lectures given at the University of California, Berkeley, Oct.–Nov. 1983). Available online at: http://foucault.info/documents/parrhesia/.

Ellis, Stephen, "Madagascar's Place in the International Slave Trade in the 19th century". Paper presented at SOAS, London, January 1987.

Ellis, Stephen, "Prince Paid Thousands into Wildlife Sting", *The Independent*, 18 January 1991.

Ellis, Stephen, "Operation Lock: How South African Death Squads Use Nature Conservation", c. 1991. (Personal archives African Studies Centre, Leiden University).

Ellis, Stephen (ed.), *Africa Now: People, Policies and Institutions*. London: James Currey, 1996. (French and Dutch editions published in 1995).

Ellis, Stephen, "Writing Histories of Contemporary Africa", *The Journal of African History*, 43: 1 (2002), pp. 1–27.

Ellis, Stephen, "Charles Taylor and the War in Sierra Leone: Report for the Special Court for Sierra Leone" (2006). (Personal archives ASCL).

Ellis, Stephen, *The Mask of Anarchy: The Destruction of Liberia and the Religious Dimension of an African Civil War*. London: C. Hurst/ New York: New York University Press, 1999. Second edition, revised and updated with new preface, 2007.

Ellis, Stephen, *South Africa and the Decolonization of the Mind*. Faculty of Social Sciences, VU University Amsterdam, 2009.

Ellis, Stephen, *Season of Rains: Africa in the World*. London, Hurst & Co/ Johannesburg: Jacana, 2011; University of Chicago Press, 2012. (Dutch edition 2011).

Ellis, Stephen, "What Future for Africa?", 20 June 2011. Blog *African Arguments*. Available at: http://africanarguments.org/2011/06/20/what-future-for-africa-by-stephen-ellis/.

Ellis, Stephen, *External Mission: The ANC in Exile, 1960–1990*. Johannesburg: Jonathan Ball/London: Hurst & Co, 2012 & New York, Oxford University Press, 2013.

Ellis, Stephen, "Face to Face with England's Libel Laws", *Socio*, 3 (2014), pp. 49–61.

Ellis, Stephen, *This Present Darkness: A History of Nigerian Organised Crime*. London: Hurst & Co./New York: Oxford University Press, 2016.

Ellis, Stephen, and Gerrie ter Haar, "Religion and Politics in Sub-Saharan Africa", *Journal of Modern African Studies*, 36: 2 (1998), pp. 175–201.

Ellis, Stephen, and Gerrie ter Haar, *Worlds of Power: Religious Thought and Political Practice in Africa*. London: Hurst/New York: Oxford University Press, 2004. (Spanish edition published in 2005).

Ellis, Stephen, and Gerrie ter Haar, "Religion and Politics: Taking African Epistemologies Seriously", *Journal of Modern African Studies*, 45: 3 (2007), pp. 385–401.

Ellis, Stephen, and Mark Shaw, "Does Organised Crime Exist in Africa?", *African Affairs*, 114: 457 (2015), pp. 508–528. Also published in Nic Cheeseman, Lindsay Whitfield, and Carl Death (eds.), *The African Affairs Reader: Key Texts in Politics, Development, and International Relations*, Oxford: Oxford University Press, 2017, pp. 88–111.

Foucault, Michel, "Discourse and Truth: The Problematization of *Parrhesia*", Lecture 1 in a series of 6 lectures given at the University of California, Berkeley, Oct.–Nov. 1983. Available at: http://foucault.info/documents/parrhesia/.

Gberie, Lansana, "Stephen Ellis, 1953–2015: An obituary", *Africa Confidential*, 56: 16, 6 August 2015. Available online at: https://www.africa-confidential.com/article/id/11190/Stephen_Ellis%2c_1953-2015.

Hermsen, Joke J., *Kairos: Een Nieuwe Bevlogenheid*, Amsterdam: Arbeiderpers, 2014.

Jansen, Jonathan, "A Quiet Contemplation on the New Anger: The State of Transformation in South African Universities", Stephen Ellis Memorial Lecture, 9 October 2015, Pretoria. Available at: www.ascleiden.nl.

Lusk, Gillian, "In Remembrance of Stephen Ellis", *Africa Confidential*, 56: 16, 6 August 2015.

Ter Haar, Gerrie, *Spirit of Africa: The Healing Ministry of Archbishop Milingo of Zambia*. London: Hurst & Co., 1992. (Also published in French and Italian).

Ter Haar, Gerrie, and Stephen Ellis, "Spirit Possession and Healing in Modern Zambia: An analysis of Letters to Archbishop Milingo", *African Affairs*, 87: 347 (1988), pp. 185–206.

The Global Initiative, "In Memoriam: Stephen Ellis, 1953–2015", 29 July 2015. Available at: http://globalinitiative.net/in-memoriam-stephen-ellis-1953-2015/.

Trewhela, Paul, "Stephen Ellis: A Standard of Moral Courage", *South African Historical Journal*, 67: 3 (2015), pp. 381–384.

Van Kessel, Ineke, "In Memoriam of Stephen Ellis", *NVAS Newsletter*, 2 August 2015. Available at: www.ascleiden.nl.

Van Kessel, Ineke, "Researching and Reporting Africa Without Fear or Favour: Stephen Ellis (13 June 1953–29 July 2015)", *Modern Africa*, 3: 2, pp. 13–16.

Veldhuis, M. "Interview met Stephen Ellis, directeur Afrika Studiecentrum", *IMWOO Bulletin*, 19: 3 (1991), pp. 3–5.

Walls, Andrew F., "Christian Scholarship and the Demographic Transformation of the Church", in Rodney L. Petersen (ed.), with Nancy M. Rourke, *Theological Literacy for the Twenty-First Century*, Grand Rapids, MI: Eerdmans, 2002, pp. 166–183.

Wiman, Christian, *My Bright Abyss: Meditation of a Modern Believer*. New York: Farrar, Straus and Giroux, 2013.

CHAPTER 2

Theft in Early Colonial Lagos, 1861–1906

Paul Osifodunrin

1 Introduction

Colonial rule effectively started in Lagos in 1863 and within two years of its commencement, theft became the most reported crime in this incipient colonial enclave, and it remained so till 1906 when the Lagos colony was merged with the Southern Nigeria protectorate to form the Colony and Protectorate of Southern Nigeria. Theft was also one of the offences for which three convicts were publicly hanged by the new colonial administration in Lagos in 1863.[1] In two separate studies on aspects of life in nineteenth-century Lagos, Spencer Brown and Michael Echeruo have drawn attention to the frequency of theft of property in the city.[2] Spencer Brown in particular noted the prevalence of stealing, which he described as the most publicised crime in Lagos from 1861 to 1886.[3] Indeed, the issue of theft was well reported in all the newspapers in circulation during the first four decades of colonial rule. The *Anglo-African*, the first newspaper to be published in Lagos, starting in 1863, reported in 1865 that there was scarcely a dwelling occupied by civilised, that is, rich or educated people in Lagos which had not been entered into and robbed between May and October of that year. Poor people were also targeted by thieves. According to Brown, it was not uncommon for such poor people to be removed, naked, from their bed, either bound and gagged or rendered unconscious by a narcotic and then left in the street while the thieves stole whatever valuables they had.[4] Annual official crime statistics returned in the *Lagos Blue Books* from 1863 to 1871 also confirm the prevalence of theft over other offences recorded in Lagos. The figures returned for the same offence between 1872 and 1906 fluctuated considerably (see Tables 2.1 and 2.2). Public opinion was unequivocal in condemning the police for inefficiency in tackling and preventing the menace of theft, while also fingering some policemen as known thieves. Some Sierra

1 S.H. Brown, "A History of the People of Lagos, 1852–1886" (PhD thesis Northwestern University, 1964), pp. 381–382.

2 *Ibid.* See also, Michael Echeruo, *Victorian Lagos: Aspects of Nineteenth Century Lagos Life* (London: Macmillan, 1977), pp. 21–22.

3 Brown, "History", p. 382.

4 *Ibid.* pp. 381–382.

 | DOI:10.1163/9789004396289_004

Leonean returnees resident in Lagos during this period actually blamed the British colonial administration for the emergence and prevalence of theft in the town.[5]

My task in this chapter is to offer explanations on how theft became prevalent in Lagos during the period under review, in view of the claims by elderly indigenous Lagosians and some Sierra-Leonean returnees that theft was not a very common offence in pre-colonial Lagos. Even though written evidence on the occurrence of theft in Lagos before the nineteenth century is virtually non-existent, oral evidence suggests that the compact and communal life of the community and the principle of collective responsibility for offences committed by a family member made it difficult for anyone to steal. Besides, since theft was both a social and religious offence, the belief was that offenders could not escape punishment either by the gods, or the traditional authority, as recorded in one of the verses of *Ifa*, the Yoruba deity of divination.[6] The argument, therefore, is that cultural and social restrictions, which cosmopolitanism and colonialism later undermined, had prevented people from engaging in theft without scruples in pre-nineteenth-century Lagos, since almost everyone knew that the punishment for stealing was severe, whether meted out by the earthly king (trial by ordeal) or the gods.[7] If theft, as claimed by tradition, was unattractive to Lagosians in the pre-nineteenth century era, how, then, can we explain the upsurge of the offence from the mid- to the late nineteenth century? My argument here is that the transformations that began in Lagos in the late eighteenth century, and which intensified in the political, social, and economic arenas in the nineteenth century, induced a host of activities that encouraged the offence of theft.[8] The study examines these transformations and argues that the prevalence of theft in Lagos in the second half of the nineteenth century fits the general pattern of crime in pre-modern cities transforming into modern cities.[9] In Lagos, during our period, higher levels of theft and a lower level of violence were recorded as the city transformed into a

5 *Times*, 10 October 1883.

6 The Ifa Verse goes thus: *If the earthly king does not see you, the heavenly king is looking at you. Thus declares the oracle to the one who steals under the cover of darkness, who says that the earthly king does not see him. God sees the thief and will surely punish him.* See S.A. Adewale, "Crime and African Traditional Religion" Orita XXVI/1–2 (1994), pp. 54–66.

7 Robin Law, "Trade and Politics behind the Slave Coast: The Lagoon Traffic and the Rise of Lagos, 1500–1800", *Journal of African History*, 24: 3, (1983), pp. 321–348.

8 For more detailed reasons for the annexation of Lagos in 1861, see A.I. Asiwaju, "The Western Province under Colonial Rule", in *Groundwork of Nigerian History ,Obaro Ikime (ed)* (Ibadan: Heinemann, 1980), pp. 429–445.

9 For example, V.A.C. Gatrell, "The Decline of Theft and Violence in Victorian and Edwardian England", in V.A.C. Gatrell, Bruce Lenman, and Geoffrey Parker (eds) *Crime and the Law: The Social History of Crime in Western Europe since 1500* (London: Europa Publications, 1980),

cosmopolitan centre. Whereas political violence was the main problem of city life in Lagos during the first half of the nineteenth century, by the second half, this had been replaced by theft. The starting date for this research marks the beginning of British direct rule over Lagos and a suitable point of departure for assessing colonial records and newspaper reports on theft that were generated beginning from that period. The historical context for the study, however, precedes the emergence of colonial rule. An attempt to understand the nature of theft in Lagos before 1861 increases our understanding of the state of theft before and after colonial rule was established. 1906 is a convenient date to end the study because it marked the end of the production of separate official crime statistics for Lagos. Generally, the study synthesises the few existing knowledge of theft in Lagos during our period in extant literature while infusing new information derived from oral tradition, newspapers, and colonial records.

2 Changing Socio-Economic and Political Landscape in Lagos before 1861

The pre-colonial history of Lagos between 1800 and 1861 can be framed around three main themes that allow an understanding of how events during this period shaped the future of the city between 1861 and 1906. The first is the involvement of Lagos in the Atlantic slave trade. By getting Lagos directly involved in slave trading, Oba Akinsemoyin is generally regarded as the architect of modern Lagos, an era that began around 1760.[10] Before his reign, Lagos played a less prominent role in the Atlantic slave trade along the Bight of Benin, even though its economy was still above subsistence level as traders from neighbouring towns and the hinterland converged on Lagos markets to buy and sell mainly agricultural produce and textile materials. The direct involvement of Lagos in the Atlantic slave trade however, transformed the town into the most important slaving port along the Slave Coast, stretching from the Volta River to the Lagos Lagoon from the late eighteenth till the mid-nineteenth century, thus supplanting and relegating older slave ports such as Badagry to the background. Lagos traditional elites, particularly members of the royal house,

passim. For an interesting discussion of the historiography of crime in Europe, see Clive Emsley and Louis A. Knafla (eds) *Crime History and Histories of Crime: Studies in the Historiography of Crime and Criminal Justice in Modern History* (Westport, CT: Greenwood Publishers, 1996), *passim*.

10 Ade Adefuye, "Oba Akinsemoyin", in Ade Adefuye, Babatunde Agiri, and Jide Osuntokun (eds) *History of the Peoples of Lagos State* (Ikeja: Literamed, 1987), pp. 33–46. See also, Law, "Trade", pp. 344–348.

prospered immensely from the trade even as slave markets and depots were established at different locations in the town. Domestic slavery also became entrenched in the process as many chiefs began to acquire slaves as a measure of wealth and opulence, thus inadvertently changing the demographics of the emerging city. Although oral evidence is silent on how much theft was committed by the large of number of slaves domesticated in Lagos, we know that it was slaves and strangers, not indigenes, who were often the perpetrators of this crime, as was the case in Elmina in the nineteenth century.[11] Meanwhile, the violence (succession disputes) that characterised Lagos politics in the first half of the nineteenth century has been linked to the struggle for the control of the revenues that accrued from the slave trade by Lagos princes.[12] Though Robert Smith disagrees with this view, and rather blames the irregularity or lack of clarity in the succession process to the Lagos throne as the main cause of the series of succession disputes in Lagos, it is probable that the violence that attended the dynastic dispute was escalated by the participation of Lagos princes in the slave trade.[13] Kristin Mann agrees this much when she notes that "the growth of slave trade in Lagos increased the stakes in succession disputes and made winning or losing more consequential".[14] The differing positions held by different scholars on this issue are indeed enriching, as each of the perspectives offer deep insights that promote an understanding of the violence that erupted in Lagos in the mid-nineteenth century.

Although relative peace was enjoyed in Lagos in the first two decades of the nineteenth century, by the third decade, civil wars broke out between successive kings and rival claimants to the throne. The most important of these wars were fought between King Oluwole and the sons of King Eshilokun in 1835; and by King Akintoye and King Kosoko between 1845 and 1851. If these wars created a disorderly environment, the fear and rumours of war that permeated Lagos thereafter continually unsettled the city with dire socio-economic consequences. As might be expected, economic activities in Lagos were seriously hampered as trading and fishing were often disrupted.[15] Both economic

11 See Larry W. Yarak, "Murder and Theft in Early Nineteenth-Century Elmina", in Donald Crummey (ed.) *Banditry, Rebellion and Social Protest in Africa* (London: James Currey, 1986), pp. 33–47.

12 For more details on these disputes, see Patrick Cole, *Modern and Traditional Political Elites in the Politics of Lagos* (London: Cambridge University Press, 1975), pp. 21–22.

13 Robert Smith, *The Lagos Consulate, 1851–1861* (Berkeley, CA: University of California Press, 1979), pp. 11–15.

14 See Kristin Mann, *Slavery and the Birth of an African City: Lagos, 1760–1900* (Bloomington, IN: Indiana University Press, 2007), p. 83.

15 See Cole, *Modern*, 21.

activities became dangerous vocations as the waterways, trading routes, and market places became unsafe as rival factions tried to outwit one another on land and water. The resultant impact and responses of Lagosians to the crises were varied. First, there was general hunger as people lost almost everything, became unemployed, and exhausted stockpiled foodstuffs as supply routes became insecure. Apart from starvation occasioned by blockades and the burning of houses during such conflicts, even fresh water was often scarce forcing people to drink from the brackish water of the Lagos lagoon, as experienced during the *Olomiro* war in 1835. The Yoruba hinterland experienced similar situations during the nineteenth-century wars as interruptions of trade and the inability to farm resulted in unemployment, hunger, and even death in extreme cases.[16] Hunger-driven theft thus emerged in Lagos as a survival strategy during our period, and the offence was largely excused by the feeble and unstable traditional authority since notions of justice were in flux.[17] Second, as loyalists of rival factions (combatants/warriors) burnt and looted houses, their ranks were swelled by non-aligned civilians freeloading for survival. Lagos historians are yet to investigate the full impact of the nineteenth-century Lagos civil wars on the civilian population. We note here, however, that apart from petty theft and looting occasioned by the wars, many became poor as means of livelihood were lost. Refugees emerged as homes were lost, forcing many to emigrate to the mainland and to the north, west, and east of Lagos. These forced Lagos migrants are remembered today as the founders of such riverine communities as Ijede, Baiyeku, Offin, Oreta-Ile, Ibese, and Ebute-Iga, all lying close to the market town of Ikorodu.[18]

---

16 John Iliffe, *African Poor: A History,* (Cambridge: Cambridge University Press, 1987), p. 87.

17 Since the nineteenth century was generally a period of war in Yorubaland, many towns and cities experienced a disintegration of the political and economic framework of society. The collapse of Oyo in the 1830s and the resultant political vacuum and wars that followed it led to a period of political experimentation. These experiments underpinned new political economies with their concomitant moral economies. Expectedly, notions of justice were in flux. Refugees became a significant problem, as well as the proliferation of martial skills. Several communities excused individual petty crime driven by hunger, just as plunder and pillage by war lords became a political instrument for accumulation. In the end, as new political experiments such as Abeokuta and Ibadan became successful native states, attempts were made to confront the growing tide of crime. Gang criminality, which along with its attendant violence and loss of lives, had become problematic, was met with summary executions, especially as these crimes were committed by ordinary people.

18 B.A. Agiri, "Lagos-Ikorodu Relations, 1894–1950"; in Adefuye et al., (eds), *History of the Peoples of Lagos* p. 197. See also Cole, *Modern*, pp. 20–22.

The second theme around which we can frame the history of Lagos before 1861 was the shift from slave trade to legitimate trade. Details of this transformation have been well-documented by scholars.[19] What is important to note here is that the abolition of the slave trade in 1807 and its enforcement in the Lagos area challenged an existing political economy that had been entrenched for almost a century. Diversifying the economy and orientating it towards dependence on the sale of mainly agricultural produce was not readily acceptable, particularly to the traditional elite, who were the key players and the main beneficiaries of the defunct trade. As the British naval squadron intensified efforts to capture and seize slave ships along the Slave Coast, so the revenue of Lagos chiefs dwindled, since their involvement in legitimate commerce was not as profitable.[20] The fierceness with which such pro-slave trade chiefs fought against anti-slave trade forces between 1830 and 1861 should be considered as a fight for both personal and group survival. The loss of revenue was indeed shocking for most Lagos chiefs as the erosion of their economic base threatened their lifestyle, largely built around the ownership and sustenance of a large slave holding in view of the halting profits of the new commerce. The chiefs losses were twofold: they lost profits from the disrupted trade, but there was also a gradual disintegration of their slave holdings. The consequence was a weakening and redefined social relationship between the chiefs and their slaves as the latter struggled to take advantage of the new dispensation by trading in palm oil and other articles including textiles. Unlike before, when the traditional elites had a monopoly on the slave trade, legitimate commerce welcomed everybody. Indeed, legitimate commerce was initially more beneficial to commoners and slaves than to the traditional elites.[21] Some slaves saw their participation in the new commerce as an opportunity to purchase their freedom and cater for themselves, much to the chagrin of their masters. Although the traditional elites – pro- or anti-slave trade, resisted the attempt by the British to intervene in issues involving domestic slavery, and actually condemned the consul Benjamin Campbell (1853–1859) for issuing emancipation documents to runaway slaves, the emerging political economy and Christianity were indeed two of the new forces that were expected to weaken the institution of slavery as more slaves either escaped, or traded to buy their freedom. Yet, even more slaves seemed to have remained in slavery, rather than escape or buy their freedom, either due to a lack of the necessary

---

19 See Robin Law, "Introduction", Robin Law (ed.) *From Slave Trade to "Legitimate" Commerce: The Commercial Transition in Nineteenth-Century West Africa* (Cambridge: Cambridge University Press, 1995), pp. 1–31.

20 See Antony G. Hopkins, "Property Rights and Empire Building: British Annexation of Lagos, 1861", *The Journal of Economic History*, 40: 4 (Dec. 1980), pp. 782–784.

21 Hopkins, "Property", p. 785.

credit to engage in trade, or because it was too risky to return to the interior, where they could be caught and resold into slavery.[22] Lack of credit was also a major hindrance for the Lagos poor becoming fully involved in the new commerce in order to escape poverty.

Meanwhile, caught in the trap of revenue loss and the risk of becoming socially irrelevant, since the measure of wealth in the city was changing, some of the chiefs attempted to resist the new order while others simply reinvented themselves. There are suggestions that some chiefs simply resorted to augmenting their revenue base by encouraging their slaves to steal. In extant literature, two Lagos kings, King Oluwole and King Kosoko, and their followers have actually been accused of theft and criminality. The allegation against King Oluwole (1834–1841) was that he encouraged his servants to rob both indigenous Lagosians and strangers. A case in point was the robbing of about 265 Sierra Leonean immigrants, who landed at the port of Lagos on their way to Abeokuta during his reign. The warmth and excessive hospitality shown towards these immigrants provided the perfect atmosphere for stealing their property and money. From all indications, this technique of welcoming strangers by stealing from them worked effectively, as all the immigrants arrived in Abeokuta empty-handed.[23] In trying to make sense of the allegation above, J.B. Losi suggests that the king's servants and not the king himself were the culprits, having acted independently in the name of the king, given the unstable nature of law and order during this period. Describing them as generally wicked, J.B. Losi contends that the pastime of these kingly servants was to "lay hold on foodstuffs and any other things they came across on their way",[24] while accompanying the king on his numerous outings as necessary. This explanation is interesting as the insight offered resonates also in Ganda and Nyoro societies of East Africa in the nineteenth century, where Ganda officials, also acting in the name of the Kabaka (official title of the King of Buganda), raided and virtually robbed their own people.[25] Two extremely interesting glimpses into this situation are furnished by two first-hand accounts written by Grant and Speke, both nineteenth-century travellers to Buganda. The first described how state officials systematically plundered the dwellings of Ganda inhabitants, stealing food and property, while the latter looked on helplessly. The second account described how the escort attached to the Wanyambo, as the king's guest, stole what they liked while he tried and failed to stop the practice.

22 Mann, *Slavery*, Ch. 6.

23 See S.O. Biobaku, *Egba and their Neighbours* (Ibadan: University Press, 1991), p. 28.

24 J.B. Losi, *History of Lagos* (Lagos: African Education Press, 1967), pp. 27–28.

25 Jan Kuhanen, "Poverty and Wealth in Traditional African Societies; Considerations Regarding Wealth, Well-Being, and Nutrition in the Ganda and Nyoro Societies, c. 1800 to 1875", *Nordic Journal of African Studies* 9:1, (2000), pp. 70–97.

Jan Kuhanen's interpretation of the two accounts is interesting and instructive for our purpose here. First, he considers the issues of stealing and plundering as an aspect of an entrenched system of elite organised coercion. More importantly, he interprets the coercion as the *realpolitik* of entertainment and extraction practised by the Ganda during that period. The politics of entertainment revolves around the commitment of the Kabaka and his court to welcome foreigners (royal guests) and treat them well at the expense of their own people, even if that meant plundering and stealing from the latter. The extraction of firearms, ammunitions, and possibly the manufacture of cannons by the guest was the ultimate objective of this often excessive hospitality, which was meant to guarantee the position of Buganda as the dominant power in the East African region.

While not disputing J.B. Losi's insight, one must be quick to draw attention to a theft-induced curse story also involving King Oluwole. Although historians of Africa are yet to interrogate curse as an agency of historical change, numerous traditions seem to suggest serious intersections between curses and causes in African history. In this case, it was alleged that King Oluwole stole expensive jewellery belonging to one of his wives. The story was told of how, having failed to find the missing jewellery, the woman placed a curse on the thief, unaware that the king (her husband) was the culprit. Coincidentally, tradition recalls that in the room where the curse was issued was a powerful deity that gave potency to her wishes, which were: (a) a shameful death for the culprit, and (b) an inglorious life for his/her descendants. Although the king's death has been described as mysterious, evidence from traditional sources suggests that he died in an explosion of gun powder in his palace, his body mangled beyond recognition save for the royal beads on his body by which he was identified.[26] Indeed, there are those who interpret the unsavoury reputation associated with some of his descendants, and the notoriety of Oluwole Market (a haven for fraudsters demolished by the Lagos State Government in 2007) in contemporary Lagos as manifestations of the timelessness of the curse on the king's descendants and anything, including even a public space, named after him.

King Kosoko and his servants were also accused of theft and criminality by Sierra Leonean immigrants, the British, and the Egba. Kosoko himself was said to have wondered how he could have been labelled a criminal by those who collaborated to dislodge him from Lagos. Unlike Oluwole, Kosoko's thieveries were dictated by political and economic exigencies occasioned by his competition with Lagos rather than outright criminality. Before his deposition, Kosoko hated immigrants, particularly those from Sierra Leone, and sought every means possible to punish them. Not only did he not allow them to settle

26 Smith, *Consulate*, p. 16.

in large numbers in the city between 1845 and 1851, but he also ensured that many of them were dispossessed of their property, even though Lagos was a transit point rather than a destination for many of them. In the aftermath of his deposition and consequent expulsion from Lagos, Kosoko unleashed a reign of terror on the city-state through coordinated piracy that almost ruined its economy. Traders were attacked on waterways, their goods and canoes were confiscated, while the traders (mostly women) were captured and sold into slavery. Lagos itself was attacked on several occasions or under the threat of attack by Kosoko from 1852 until his return to Lagos in 1862.[27] Lagosians called him a thief, but his followers revered him greatly because of his charisma and great leadership qualities.

The third theme around which we can frame Lagos history before colonisation was the influx of people into the city and the creation of new dwelling and commercial spaces as new and alternative centres of power and social and economic influence by the new settlers. Although Lagos had attracted a lot of people during the slave trade era, its abolition and the shift to legitimate trade brought even more people, particularly after 1851. Generally, we can categorise the kinds of people that were attracted to Lagos during this period. They included African returnees – Sierra Leoneans and Brazilians, who settled in the Olowogbowo and Popo-Aguda areas located to the west and east of Lagos Island, respectively. Many of these new settlers were traders, artisans, and educated. As noted by Robert Smith, many of them, particularly the Sierra Leoneans, had superior skills and later acquired a dominant position in trade.[28] Needless to say, they benefitted far more from the new commerce than the local peoples. Their settlements were actually better planned and they introduced new architecture that, by the standards of that period, was better than most of the designs in downtown Lagos. Their lifestyle and demeanour were Western and many of them saw themselves as superior to the indigenous population. Moderation was not their watchword, and their hubristic pride and arrogance invited envy from the indigenous population. The natural sequel to such a strained relationship was tension and rivalry, and a lot of these were generated in Lagos between the two groups before 1861. The feeling of insecurity generated by such a strained relationship was probably one of the reasons why young Sierra Leoneans – as the moving spirits behind the tensions – had to carry knives in the streets of Lagos, ostensibly for self-defence.[29] Other important settlers were European merchants who lived and

27 See Toyin Falola, "Brigandage and Piracy in Nineteenth-Century Yorubaland", *Journal of the Historical Society off Nigeria*, XII: 1 & 2, (1995), pp. 94–95.

28 Smith, *Consulate*, 80.

29 *Ibid.*

established their commercial houses along the Marina (formerly Ehin Igbeti). Although Dutch travellers to the West African coast had mentioned Lagos in many of their reports before the eighteenth century, and the Portuguese had arrived in Lagos in the eighteenth century as slavers and close business associates of the royal house, it was the British that intervened most in the local politics of Lagos. Beyond enforcing the abolition law and policing the West African coast, the British were actively involved in two major developments that were to shape the history of Lagos before its eventual annexation in 1861. First, was the establishment of the Lagos Consulate in 1851, and second was the bombardment of Lagos in the last month of the same year. While the latter action had the immediate impact of destroying almost half of the town, sending more people into the abyss of penury, deposing Kosoko, and reinstating Akitoye to the throne of Lagos, the impact of the former action was of a *longue durée* culminating in the eventual annexation of Lagos in 1861. Under consul Benjamin Campbell (1853–1859), the role of the consulate fluctuated greatly, albeit within its mandate of ensuring the eradication of the slave trade and promoting legitimate commerce. Although British influence in Lagos politics was entrenched during this period, opposition to the activities of the consulate emanated from the different sections of the society – merchants (Europeans and Africans), traditional elites, and even the missionaries. It is not my intention to go into the details of the opposition here, but it is sufficient to note that the consulate performed a Herculean task managing various interests in Lagos. It was seen by a section of the traditional elites as a stumbling block, whose leadership must be assassinated.[30] At times, it was the stabilising force that helped to uphold the authority of the native government, as illustrated by the expulsion of Madam Tinubu from Lagos by King Dosunmu in 1856. At other times, its situation became precarious as it was perceived to be supporting or opposing Kosoko via different interest groups in Lagos society, even as it tried to resolve the problem of the disruption of Lagos trade occasioned by the terroristic and piratical activities of Kosoko and the continued interest of the Ijebu and Ibadan in the slave trade. Overall, the consulate years reduced open violence in Lagos, although trust among the different segments of the Lagos population was lacking. Rumours of war continued to haunt Lagosians, but public order was never really compromised enough to create an atmosphere for unbridled looting. There is a suggestion by Campbell's successor – William McCoskry (locally called Apongbon) – that King Dosunmu could not control his people, and that Africans accused of theft, robbery, or other

30 Smith, *Consulate*, pp. 73–74.

offences sought the protection of Lagos chiefs.[31] But his antecedents render such insinuations unreliable. Although he had served as vice-consul of Badagry under Campbell, he disliked his boss for forcing him to obey the authority of a native government, which he would rather have ignored. On one occasion in 1856, to his dismay, Campbell had actually forced him to pay a fine imposed by Oba Dosunmu for secretly visiting Kosoko, in violation of the interdiction of trade between Lagos and Epe.[32] Thus, it is not surprising that, as acting consul, he had little respect for King Dosunmu's authority. The alacrity with which he implemented the annexation policy of the British in Lagos also suggests that these allegations were probably exaggerated, though not wholly false.

Finally, there were also European and African missionaries who migrated to Lagos between 1852 and 1861. The missionary factor in Lagos history has been well outlined by scholars such as J.F. Ade Ajayi. Here, it is sufficient to note that agents of the Church Missionary Society (CMS), such as Charles Andrew Gollmer (German) and Catechist James White (African returnee), were very influential in Lagos politics and converted a number of Lagos chiefs to Christianity, stopped human sacrifice, and sometimes gave protection to people who could have been sold into slavery. On arrival in Lagos, the missionaries initially resided among indigenous Lagosians in downtown Lagos, before spreading out to the east and west of the Island. As these overseas migrants were settling down, immigrants from the Yoruba interior, mostly poor people, were also arriving. They included, among others, ex-war boys, runaway slaves, and other refugees in search of a new life and opportunities. Hausa migrants – traders, clerics, ex-slaves, and herders – were also represented in Lagos. Added to these layers of migrants were people from Liberia and the Gold Coast, particularly Kru men who thronged to Lagos as canoe boys. These latter settlers established themselves not only in downtown Lagos among the indigenous peoples, but also on the mainland. Thus, on the eve of colonial rule, Lagos was already sprawling and populated in such a way that defined new centres of power, influence, and authority, even as individualism began to supplant communal life. It is therefore clear that, before 1861, Lagos was a city in transition in political, economic, and spatial terms. Trust was a scarce commodity and class, based on the level of participation in the new economy, was definitely an issue. Although Robert Smith suggests that the king still exercised a lot of authority, even as late as the consular era, there is no doubt that his authority was greatly weakened by divided loyalties to the throne. As noted earlier, it

31 Tekena Tamuno, The *Police in Modern Nigeria, 1861–1965: Origins, Development and Role* (Ibadan: University Press, 1970), p. 13.

32 Smith, *Consulate*, pp. 75–77.

became increasingly difficult for the throne in Lagos to enforce its rules without the support of the consulate.

3 Colonisation and Theft in Lagos, 1861–1906

By 1861, Lagos was already cosmopolitan, but it was still a compact society in terms of space occupied. As the natural entrepôt of a massive hinterland, Lagos was the centre of the legitimate trade in palm oil. Compared to other neighbouring towns, such as Badagry, Lagos was also more prosperous and the main destination for traders and migrants from the interior. The creation of a British colony in Lagos in 1861 also made it the first foothold of colonialism in Nigeria. Lagos residents reacted differently to the imposition of colonial rule. While the traditional elites resented the idea and wrote several petitions to London, European merchants, African returnees, and the missionaries seemed to have welcomed the development for three main reasons – commerce, Christianity, and civilisation.[33] The subordination of the native government and its territory to British rule was painful to the traditional elites, just as the loss of the profits from the slave trade. King Dosunmu, for instance, lost the customary revenue of about 2000 bags of cowries of export duty, fines, and summons as well as import duty on tobacco and cowries at the landing places, including extensive presents from the merchants.[34] War chiefs were more miserable, while the misfortune of land-owning chiefs (Idejos) in Lagos were no less small as they feared the loss of their land, which, after annexation, was becoming commercialised and a new source of revenue and security for loans in the cities expanding credit system.[35] Until Governor Henry Freeman assured them that the annexation would not deprive them of their power and rights over their land, they remained in opposition to the cession.[36]

At a wider society level, sources are silent on the immediate reaction of people in general to the annexation, but, as might be expected, the annexation of Lagos had certain implications for the administration of the new colony. First, it permitted the gradual extension of the territorial extent of Lagos so that, by 1894, the colony area included the villages lying to the north of Lagos, Badagry, Ikorodu, and Epe. Second, the annexation necessitated the introduction and wider application of British laws and their enforcement. This brought

33 P.M. Mbaeyi, "Lagos and the British, 1871–1874", *Ikenga*, 1: 1 (1972), pp. 28–29.

34 Mbaeyi, "Lagos", p. 29.

35 Mann, "Women, Landed Property and the Accumulation of Wealth in Early Colonial Lagos", *Signs* 16: 4 (1991), pp. 682–706.

36 Mbaeyi, "Lagos", p. 29.

about certain changes hitherto unknown in this West African city: a gaol was built, and a small force was set up in October 1861 by Acting Governor, William McCoskry, to tackle the problem of insecurity, although the number was inadequate as there were only 25 police constables for a population of about 30,000. In 1862, Governor Henry Stanhope Freeman increased the strength of the police department to 100 constables under the supervision of one superintendent, four sergeants, and eight corporals. A Police Court, Criminal and Slave Court, and Commercial Tribunal were also established. By 1863, two police branches – one civil, the other semi-military or Armed Hausa Police – had emerged to enforce the supremacy of European law.[37]

With the new bureaucracy and legal system in place, no one was left in doubt as to the readiness of the new administration to exercise the power of life and death over Lagosians and to ensure stability in the new territory. Yet, a lot of theft, among other crimes such as murder, kidnapping, and so on, were reported in Lagos between 1863 and 1906, indicating that it was easier to acquire rather than to administer the new colonial enclave. Three possibilities are suggested for this turn of events. The first is that the occurrence of theft was promptly tackled by the new administration. The second is that colonialism created a new system and with it came new opportunities and crimes. The third is that the British lacked understanding of the culture of the terrain that they acquired, and hence introduced laws or policies that either criminalised or forced people into crime. Each of these scenarios represents a phase in the cumulative occurrence of theft in Lagos, as would soon be demonstrated.

The criminal statistics available for Lagos between 1863 and 1905 suggest that the new colonial administration identified and tackled the offence of theft head on. As shown in the criminal statistics presented in Table 2.1 below, theft ranked highest among the three offences recorded separately, and was only lower to the rate of offences jointly recorded as "other offences" in 1863. Theft was more common than the indictable offences against persons, and shows a steady increase compared to other offences from 1865–1871. Considered alone, the table depicts a fluctuating rate of reported cases of theft, rather than a steady increase. The number of reported thefts since 1865, however, grew steadily until 1869, when a lower figure was recorded only for a higher figure to be reported in 1870 and a lower figure in 1871. The table also produces an interesting revelation about the age of offenders, thus suggesting the early involvement and predominance of youths in criminality during this period in Lagos. As indicated in the "number in confinement" column and those who were committed for trial, the latter were obviously more numerous than the former. Although the figures seem unbelievably high, the table shows

37 Tamuno, *Police*, pp. 15–17.

a steady increase from 1863 to 1871, with the exception of 1864 and 1867 (figures for which are not available), and of 1866, for which a ridiculously low figure of 10 was returned, and 1869 which recorded a lower figure than the previous year. Generally, however, the figures show a steady increase in the number of arrests made and those committed for trial, suggesting that the machinery of justice during this period was efficient.

The number in confinement also indicates the level of importance that the colonial government attached to incarceration as a mode of punishment during this period, in spite of the fact that the phenomenon was new in Lagos and, indeed, relatively rare in sub-Saharan African societies before the advent of colonial rule. A "more common form of detention was to restrain prisoners by attaching them to a log or tree".[38] David Killingray has noted that punishment of offenders, and not their rehabilitation, prevailed in early colonial Lagos until after 1922 when the 1893 proposal of the Gladstone Committee,

TABLE 2.1 Theft and other Offences, and Number Confined in Lagos Prison, 1863–1871

	Felony	Theft	Assault	Other offences	No. In confinement	No. Com. under 18	No. Com. that cannot read
1863	0	165	51	196	324	413	5
1864	0	0	0	0	0	0	0
1865	46	127	69	185	107	428	0
1866	16	224	98	197	106	10	0
1867	0	0	0	0	0	0	0
1868	19	350	89	253	136	710	0
1869	11	272	97	210	149	632	0
1870	17	286	283	160	162	868	0
1871	19	281	99	244	180	693	0

SOURCE: COMPILED FROM PUBLIC RECORDS OFFICE (NOW NATIONAL ARCHIVES), UNITED KINGDOM, CO 151/2, *COLONY OF LAGOS*, 1863 AND CO 151/3-9, *LAGOS BLUE BOOKS OF STATISTICS*, 1865-1871.[a]

NB. Com. = Committed

a Statistics for 1861 and 1862 are not available. A plausible reason for this is that the colonial administration was yet to settle down to the business of administering the Lagos colony. *The* statistical data for 1864 is missing. Meanwhile, available records indicate that the publication of the *Lagos Blue Book* commenced in 1865. Thus, as shown above, statistics relating to the Colony in 1863 were published in a book simply titled *Colony of Lagos*.

38 David Killingray, "Punishment to Fit the Crime? Penal Policy and Practice in British Colonial Africa", in Bernault, Florence (dir.), *Enfermement, prison et châtiments en Afrique du 19 è siècle à nos jours* (Paris: Karthala, 1999), p. 181.

which favoured reform rather than punishment, was eventually implemented.[39] Until that time, penal labour, such as working on paths, roads, and buildings, was the rule and prisoners earned nothing at the Lagos Prison located at Faji.[40] Initially, each cell at the Lagos prison was capable of accommodating six inmates at a time. And when more than one prisoner slept in one cell, it could accommodate twenty prisoners in 1863. The Gaol, as it was called, was built of mud and floored with boards. The hours of labour within the common gaol were between 8am and 5pm. Prison facilities were improved when a 300-capacity building patterned after the British model was opened for prisoners on Broad Street in 1872.[41]

Although the above table gives the impression that the police and the court were efficient in the first decade of colonial rule in Lagos, an alternative source suggests otherwise. As early as 1863, for instance, the *Anglo-African* had reported that the police, rather than concentrate on tackling "real nuisances which would only give them trouble without recompense, found abundant occupation of the kind for which there was extra remuneration".[42] Some Sierra Leoneans who lived in Lagos at this time also hint of a stricter system of enforcement exercised by native governments in the interior of Yorubaland compared to the lenient British judicial system in Lagos.[43] Leniency in this context can be explained in two ways. First, it arose from the British principle of individual rather than group liability for offences committed. Second, it relates to a respect for the rights and liabilities of a criminal offender as distinct from that of his family. Third, it also refers to the British idea of the presumption of innocence, i.e. considering all offenders innocent until they are proven guilty. Before long, criminals were exploiting this inbuilt leniency and other loopholes in the new judicial system.

The popular dictum – "Lagos accommodates the thief and the indolent" (*Eko gb'ole o gb'ole'*) helps to explain one of the possible reasons for the rising rate of theft in Lagos after annexation. Theft, as indicated earlier, occurred in pre-colonial Lagos in the period of political instability, and was committed mainly by people associated with traditional authority. In the first decade of colonial rule, however, the offence seems to have been committed by two groups of people – individual poor townsmen of varying background, and by gangs with bases on the outskirts of Lagos. Emerging evidence suggests that theft was a common occurrence in coastal towns with a fairly mixed population in

39 Killingray, "Punishment", p. 188.
40 National Archives, UK, CO 151/2, *Colony of Lagos, 1863*.
41 Killingray, "Punishment", p. 188.
42 Brown, "History", pp. 381–382.
43 *Times*, October 1883.

nineteenth-century West Africa.[44] Poor townsmen were mostly strangers and ex-slaves who had flocked to Lagos shortly before and after colonialism. Many were unemployed and responded individually to their situation by stealing for survival.[45] Even those who were employed occasionally as canoe men still found it convenient to steal. Clearly, the early colonial status of Lagos made it a haven not just for the indolent and the unemployed, but also for fleeing criminals escaping harsher treatment by native governments in the interior. Many such dislodged criminals found villages on the Lagos mainland and its environs a more conducive, riper, and less dangerous field of operation. In 1865, the *Anglo-African* reported the activities of several of these gangs terrorising Lagos from their bases on the mainland.[46] In 1868, the police in Lagos was on high alert following the dispersal of a band of one hundred thieves in Ilorin after their leader was executed; many of the scattered thieves were expected to make their way to Lagos. In the same vein, as a sequel to the clampdown on burglars by the Egba Government in 1886 and 1887, many thieves also escaped to Lagos.[47] This was why S.H. Brown noted, rightly, that

> every clean-up of an interior caused more professional thieves to make their way to the coast and once there, they either formed or joined a gang and usually lived at Ebute-Metta, Apapa, Igamu (Iganmu) or some other places within easy canoe distance of Lagos. Gangs with their residence at Badagry and even as far as Porto-Novo would also come to steal by night and then slip away with their loot by canoe before dawn.[48]

Table 2.2 below shows the criminal statistics for 1872 to 1905. Specifically, it indicates a steady reduction in the total number of offences reported to the police from 1872–1876, although it represents a higher figure relative to those returned from 1868–1871. By 1877, the figure rose slightly, only to continue the downward trend in succeeding years. The fluctuating figures from 1886 were especially low, raising questions about their reliability and the possible existence of a "dark figure",[49] that is, unknown criminality.

---

44 See for instance, Emmanuel Akyeampong, *Between the Sea and the Lagoon: An Eco-Social History of the Anlo of Southeastern Ghana, c. 1850 to Recent Times* (Athens, OH: Ohio University Press, 2001), p. 88.

45 Iliffe, *African Poor*, pp. 175, 165.

46 See *Anglo-African*, 22 July 1865. Also *Anglo-African*, 28 October 1865.

47 Brown, "History", pp. 381–382.

48 *Ibid.*

49 The "dark figure" or unknown criminality refers to those crimes neither discovered by the police, nor reported by citizens. It also includes crimes that are reported but not recorded. For more details, see Anna Alvazzi Del Frate, *Victims of Crime in the Developing World*, (Rome: United Nations Interregional Crime and Justice Research Institute Publication

TABLE 2.2 Number of offences reported to the police or the magistrate in Lagos, 1872–1905

	Total no. of Off. rep.	Off. Agst. person	Cattle stealing and arson	Off. Agst. Pro. than cattle stealing	Other off.
1872	2357	1219	65	520	553
1873	1525	439	38	477	571
1874	1328	154	61	720	393
1875	1099	251	30	601	217
1876	971				
1877	1060	349	15	410	256
1878	949	289	34	306	270
1879	995	269	46	400	280
1880	709				
1881	414	168	23	134	89
1882	804	295	18	235	256
1883	576	279	69	76	152
1884	794	457	65	69	203
1885	648	315	16	169	118
1886	12	21	0	0	8
1887	28	4	1	23	0
1888	25	3	0	22	0
1889	22	0	0	22	0
1890	51	0	0	51	1
1891	29	1	0	28	0
1892	35	5	0	28	2
1893	36	2	0	31	0
1894	133	0	0	0	0
1895	5	20	20	18	0
1896	36	2	0	34	0
1897	27	1	0	25	0
1898	41	2	0	39	0
1899	32	2	0	30	0
1900	30	1	0	29	0
1901	320	120	5	69	126
1902	25	1	0	24	0
1903	29	3	0	25	1
1904	27	0	1	26	0
1905	32	2	3	27	0

SOURCE: COMPILED FROM PUBLIC RECORDS OFFICE (NOW NATIONAL ARCHIVES, UNITED KINGDOM), CO 151/10-43, *LAGOS BLUE BOOKS*, 1872–1905

Moreover, in 1874, there were complaints that organised crime had increased and that no man's house was safe, as thieves thought nothing of digging through walls of houses built of mud or sun-dried brick, or door burning if no easier access route was available. This was in addition to carrying weapons, which they did not hesitate to use to injure or in extreme cases kill anyone who endangered their personal safety or professional success.[50] Again, the dampened morale of the law enforcement groups in the post-Glover years was definitely not an inducement for their efficiency.[51] The public itself demonstrated a loss of confidence in the police, typified in a petition addressed to Lord Derby, the Secretary of State for the Colonies in 1884 and an observation at a General Meeting held in Lagos the same year. The petition alleged that "the policemen most of whom were known thieves and Kru men of bad character had failed to protect the citizens at a time when cases of murder, arson and burglaries were rife".[52] The meeting observed that "instances have been known when a robbery is committed, those to whom is entrusted the protection of life and property have been found to form allies (sic) with the thieves".[53] The meeting subsequently denounced the Lagos Police in no uncertain terms: "the Police Force supposed to be for protection is useless for that purpose; it has among its members men known to be thieves".[54] *The Mirror* put it quite simply in a comment of 18 February 1888 that "the rampant stupidity and ignorance of the police [was] proverbial"[55] and therefore not new. Given the above, it should not be surprising that Brown concluded that the purported drop in the number of crimes and convictions during this period of great anxiety was questionable.[56] It was possible that fewer crimes were reported as the Lagos public became discontented with the police. It might also be the case that as more crimes were reported less crime was recorded, due perhaps to a less efficient police force. The crime rate in Lagos almost certainly continued to rise as the population increased and migrant criminal gangs fed, parasitically on the colony.

Yet, the table above gives fresh insight into the nature and trend of criminality in Lagos from 1872 to 1905. First, contrary to what obtained in the first decade of colonial rule when offences against property – theft, burglary, and

No. 57, 1998), pp. 6–11. Walker calls it the unrecorded percentage of the events that one is trying to study. See also Nigel Walker, *Crimes, Courts and Figures: An Introduction to Criminal Statistics* (Harmondsworth: Penguin Books, 1971), pp. 15–21.

50 Brown, "History", pp. 381–382.

51 Tamuno, *Police*, pp. 23–26.

52 *Ibid.*

53 Echeruo, *Victorian Lagos*, p. 22.

54 *Ibid.*

55 *Ibid.*

56 Brown, "History", p. 384.

robbery – were highest, in the early years of the following decade, a shift seems to have taken place as the criminal statistics show an initial tilt towards the commission of offences against persons in 1872 and 1873. If, however, we add the figures in the first two rows of the fourth and fifth columns, both of which constitute offences against property, the total for the first row would still trail behind the figures quoted for offences against property in the same years in 1872, the exception being a slightly higher figure for offences against persons for 1873. By 1874, the offences against property once again bounced back to prominence and thereafter competed against offences against persons till 1905. Second, the table above also reveals that cattle stealing and arson were particularly widespread during this period. Indeed, arson was sometimes an adjunct of housebreaking, burglary, or robbery in nineteenth-century Lagos.[57] Brown put it thus: "To set fire to houses accidentally while attempting to burn the door or deliberately in order to force the occupants to flee hurriedly, was an approved technique among burglars especially during the eighties".[58]

The point must be made that all categories of people, not excluding those who were considered poor by the standards of that period, were at the receiving end of these criminal activities, although the degree of losses differed. Understandably, the Europeans, immigrants, and some local merchants who were rich, or were considered so, were most affected by the gangs of thieves that came from the neighbouring towns and those who operated from within. Patrick Cole, in his study of elites in Lagos, wrote that many of them made their life as pleasant and comfortable as possible, even as early as the 1850s. They "built huge houses and furnished them with floors nearly all of inlaid marble and pictures of the best modern Italian masters, most of them surrounded by pretty gardens, tastefully laid out".[59] Residential houses were not the only places targeted by thieves for stealing people's property like money, cloth, and other personal effects. As would later become clear, warehouses for storing agricultural produce and imported materials were also targeted.

The impact on crime of the wealth of Lagos relative to that of its hinterland must be emphasised. The legitimate commerce that emerged before 1861 intensified in the post-annexation era bringing many more people into the city. Lagos was the preferred destination for many traders from the interior supplying agricultural produce. As an entrepôt, it was also the location for the supply of imported materials before their distribution into the interior.

57 For details, see C. Onyeka Nwanunobi, "Incendiarism and Other Fires in Nineteenth-Century Lagos, 1863–1888", *Africa*, 60:1 (1990), pp. 111–120.

58 Brown, "History", pp. 381–382.

59 See Cole, *Modern*, pp. 9–10.

Although the benefits derived from the trade were lopsided, it was clear that Lagos was reaping a lot of financial benefits from the trade. Antony Hopkins noted while studying the economic history of Lagos during this period that the fundamental changes taking place in the economy of Lagos in the early colonial period were advantageous, at least to some people, despite the initial disruptive tendencies.[60] Colonial policies in the first four decades of colonial rule were therefore geared towards ensuring the free flow of trade between Lagos and the interior. As revenues from trade were ploughed into infrastructure development, even more people were attracted to the city. Ayodeji Olukoju's study on infrastructure development and urban facilities in Lagos has shown how Lagos benefitted from the various schemes that were put in place to transform the city.[61] Here, it is sufficient to note that these developments – urbanisation, introduction of modern transport facilities, monetisation of the economy, establishment of a modern banking system, introduction of wage labour – and, at the social level, the new status that education, wealth, and affluence conferred on people, in addition to the fine structures that people erected, went a long way in making Lagos not only the preferred destination of all migrants seeking employment or trading opportunities, but invariably a breeding ground for unemployment and, consequently, crime. That Lagos itself was at times a generative city that induced economic growth in neighbouring towns is incontestable. However, as the experience of Badagry indicates, at least until 1887,[62] Lagos proved to be a parasitic city, as it drained the prosperity of Badagry in the aftermath of the abolition of the slave trade. One of the implications of this development was that more criminals from Badagry became active in Lagos during this period.[63] It must be noted, however, that trade was not always profitable and it would appear that the downturn in the economy from 1880 to 1905 negatively affected not just the merchants, traders, and producers who had to adjust to the more demanding conditions of trade that resulted from this slump, but also the common men who had to rediscover their role within the emerging colonial context. The story of Bello Jaguda, associated locally with this period of economic downturn, demonstrates clearly that there was a connection between British laws and the occurrence of theft in Lagos during our period.

---

60 Antony Hopkins, "An Economic History of Lagos, 1880–1914", PhD Thesis (University of London, 1964), p. 377.

61 Ayodeji Olukoju, *Infrastructure Development and Urban Facilities in Lagos, 1861–2000*, (Ibadan: IFRA, 2003), *passim*.

62 *Ibid.*, pp. 79–81.

63 *Ibid.*

4 Bello Jaguda, Noise Ordinance and Theft in Colonial Lagos

Bello Jaguda, a native of Akokoland in eastern Yorubaland, went to Lagos sometime in the late nineteenth century. Little is known about his early life or his village or town in Akoko, but he was one of the numerous nineteenth-century migrants from the interior of Yorubaland that thronged into Lagos in search of opportunities in the first four decades of colonial rule. Tradition remembers him as a talented and well-patronised drummer. Since entertainment was an integral part of the life of indigenous Lagosians, who particularly enjoyed dancing and praise singing, it was not difficult for Bello Jaguda to assemble a band of drummers with whom he roamed the lanes and streets of Lagos, entertaining different categories of people and making money in the process. Life was good and Bello Jaguda became popular because of his dexterity at playing all kinds of drums and singing to the satisfaction of his clients.[64] It is not clear whether Bello Jaguda had a family, but he was certainly able to assemble a group of boys on the streets that followed and sang with him. It would appear that he also had his way with women and enjoyed life. His livelihood, however, was threatened when the British colonial administration introduced the ordinance to control what they regarded as noise-making in the town.[65] Singing and drumming, which hitherto went on throughout the day, were restricted to specific hours. The ordinance soon became a point of contention between the British, who loved serenity, and Lagosians, who enjoyed entertainment and frowned on British insensitivity to their culture. Several Lagos chiefs condemned the ordinance on noise-making, noting the plight of drummers and singers like Bello Jaguda, who were most affected by the law, and the lull in the town, which they complained impacted negatively on the general well-being of the entire community. But British officials insisted on compliance and continued to enforce the restriction on the hours when drums could be sounded in the town.

The ordinance formed part of the urban planning and social control strategy of the colonial administration. It was one of the ways that the colonial administration exercised its power and authority over the colonised people

64 Dr (now) Prof. Yomi Akinyeye first drew my attention to this story in 2007. Later, I met Prince Dimeji Ajikobi of the Department of Linguistics African and Asian Studies, who corroborated and provided more information about Bello Jaguda. I am also grateful to the octogenarian, Pa J.K. Osinowo, who explained the meaning of *Jaguda-Pali-baba-Bilisi* to me in a way that I never really imagined. I certainly hope to probe this theme further. I am also grateful to Pa Hakeem Oduga, the Olootu of Aige Family in Ikorodu, for his numerous interventions and explanations of the Jaguda phenomenon.

65 For details on the drumming question, see Echeruo, *Victorian*, pp. 67–79.

in Lagos. But while the traditional elite grumbled and protested, but eventually acquiesced to the ordinance, it would appear that Bello Jaguda and his boys felt otherwise, since they were directly on the receiving end. As a result, a reinvention occurred. Rather than continue to drum and sing, Bello Jaguda redirected his energy into stealing as an alternative to drumming and singing. Recruiting boys to steal was not a problem as he was popular and already had many followers from the interior, including runaways and children.[66] Redirecting their energy towards stealing on the streets, in homes, and in market places was not a problem, as many of the boys were already exposed to street life and even petty theft. Indeed, the Jaguda boys operated with such dexterity in Lagos that the name Jaguda entered into the Yoruba lexicon as synonymous with a petty thief or pickpocket. Equally entrenched in the social thought of the people is the description of the aggressive, swift, risky, and dishonourable manoeuvres of the group, as encapsulated in the phrase: *Jaguda-Pali-Baba-Bilisi*. This can be interpreted as meaning a most determined and devilish thief, who would stop at nothing to achieve his goal, notwithstanding the risks. The Bello Jaguda story surely requires further research to clarify some grey areas. As illuminating and insightful as it sounds, it is surprising that the exploits of Bello Jaguda were neither recorded in the newspapers, nor captured in the colonial records of that period. Although tradition is silent on whom the victims of Jaguda and his boys were, it seems that their targets were mostly the returnees, particularly the Agudas. In fact, we think that his real name was not Jaguda, which explains why the newspapers of that period and colonial records never mentioned him. Since they robbed and stole mainly from this set of people, the indigenous people of Lagos might have simply committed their exploits and victims to memory using a description such as, *Ja-Aguda-lole*, meaning one who steals from the returnees, later corrupted to Jaguda, while *ole-jija* or *ja-le* is the general descriptive phrase or compound word for describing the action of a thief among the Yoruba. If we recall the constant rivalry between the returnees and indigenous Lagosians, it is also not unlikely that Bello Jaguda was protected by indigenous Lagosians, which would explain why he was neither caught, nor brought to justice.

Not surprisingly, Jaguda (the action) not Bello (the person) became the stereotype for a thief among the Yoruba, and the word has endured till today. In Lagos in the 1920s, 1930s, and 1940s, the word was used extensively to describe

66 Between 1877 and 1887, 2695 children were registered as having been brought into Lagos from the interior of Yorubaland and elsewhere. A few were fostered by relatives needing child labour. Many were probably just brought to Lagos and abandoned. See Iliffe, *African Poor*, p. 165.

several gangs of juvenile delinquents not only in Lagos, but also in Ibadan, as shown in the study by Simon Heap.[67] The story of Anikura, a notorious robber in Lagos of the 1950s underscores the timelessness of the Jaguda phenomenon. One of the poems in his honour is "*Awon jaguda kekeke l'olopa Ekoo mu, Anikura mbe nile won o lee mu u. Anikura baba omokomo. Anikura olori ole tii da boro. Agba ole a basuwon gbooro*" (meaning Nigeria Police in those days only harassed petty thieves; not Anikura whom they are unable to touch; Anikura, the father of rascals. Anikura the head of robbers, with an extra-long purse).[68] Overall, the Bello Jaguda story is very instructive, in that it links the occurrence of theft in Lagos during our period to the issue of law and social control. While it would be hasty to interpret the Jaguda story as representing a form of organised resistance to colonial rule, it seems logical to say that in an attempt to solve one problem, the colonial government inadvertently created another one.

Meanwhile, beyond the issue of the Noise Ordinance as the major motivation for the Jaguda affair, it would appear that several other factors, including depression or boom in Lagos trade, impacted theft in Lagos during this period. Trade was not always profitable and it would appear that the downturn in the economy from 1880 to 1905 negatively affected not just the merchants, traders, and producers, who had to adjust to the more demanding conditions of trade that this slump brought about, but also the common men who had to rediscover their role within the emerging colonial context. The point should be made at the outset that prosperity and poverty can both influence the rate of criminality in a given environment, as lack and unequal distribution of wealth can breed criminality in both conditions. The 1880s no doubt represented a period of slump in Lagos trade. In his study of the economic history of Lagos from 1880–1914, Hopkins concludes that trade in the 25 years before 1906 suffered a depression, and that these were years of fluctuating fortunes, while the subsequent years, from 1906–1914, heralded prosperity.[69] Yet, as already noted, the criminal statistics returned in the period of depression (1880–1906) suggest a downward trend in crime that seems illogical. In any case, newspaper reports on crime during this period show that crimes were on the increase and that gangs were being more efficiently organised and supported by key figures resident in Lagos. A Muslim priest called Sunmanu and a Yoruba Priest, Bada

67 Simon Heap has an article on "'Jaguda boys': Pickpocketing in Ibadan, 1930–60 (with emphasis on the district of Ekotedo)", *Urban History*, 24: 3 (1997) pp. 324–342. However, no reference whatsoever was made to the existence of Bello Jaguda.

68 *Guardian*, 23 February 2006.

69 Hopkins, "Economic", p. 377.

Foresythe, were accused of making money from gangs of thieves through the sale of charms that protected them from apprehension in 1883 and 1884, respectively.[70] Some members of the police force were also accused of co-operating with the thieves.[71] It was also alleged in 1882 that many thieves had formerly served in the police force just to learn the law and how to circumvent it.[72] Press reports also noted that the government strategy of recruiting non-Yoruba into the force to reduce the degree of co-operation between some of the Yoruba policemen and the Yoruba thieves achieved little as the men, mostly of Kru origin, made little difference.[73]

In the same vein, on 10 October 1883, the *Times* complained that thefts and robberies were becoming increasingly rampant. It noted that some of the gangs were under the patronage of certain persons considered to be respectable in the society who employ them to steal and rob for them and whom they pay with a portion of the property stolen. The same newspaper wrote that the robberies in Lagos were probably a creation of the new Christian cosmopolitan civilisation in Lagos, noting that "much larger countries of Abeokuta and Ibadan, independent Yoruba states, had a much lower amount of flagrant crimes than Lagos",[74] suggesting that the "summary executions [which those states dealt out for] murders, incendiarism, thefts and robberies, and the exposure of the bodies of the executed to public dishonour had a very deterrent effect".[75] While it is true that colonialism altered the mode of crime in Lagos, inducing new forms of property crimes and white-collar crimes such as fraud and embezzlement, it would be unjust to say that it created theft or robbery. That said, the newspaper's allusion to a Christian-cosmopolitan-civilisation-induced criminality in Lagos has the potential to illuminate our understanding of property crime in the city during this period. First, it drew attention, however implied, to the difficulties that efficient crime control in adjacent jurisdictions posed to Lagos during this period. Second, the assertion of the paper that robbery was a colonial creation provides a glimpse of the opinion of a section of the Lagos public – Africans – on criminality during this period. Indeed, a Yoruba dictum on criminality, which probably had its roots in the colonial period retorts: *Oyinbo o ko ole, afara lo ko*.[76] This can be interpreted as meaning that stealing is permissible to the European, provided the thief is smart.

70 Brown, "History", p. 384.

71 *Ibid.*

72 Brown, "History", p. 388.

73 *Ibid.*

74 Echeruo, *Victorian*, pp. 21–22. See also, *The Lagos Times*, 1882–1883.

75 *Ibid.*

76 Oral Information, Dimeji Ajikobi, Lecturer, Department of Linguistics, African and Asian Studies, University of Lagos. It is important to note that *afowora* in Yoruba Language means petty theft, hence *ole-afowora*.

Meanwhile, the story of a celebrated murder case in Lagos in 1884, involving one Adeoshun, a refugee from Dahomey, has been told by both Spencer Brown and TekenaTamuno.[77] However, it is necessary to recount it here because it shows that killing was sometimes an adjunct of robbery in nineteenth-century Lagos. Relying on the two accounts, the story revolved around the recurring disappearance of women in Lagos under mysterious circumstances for about eight or nine years before nemesis caught up with the offender in 1884 when his last victims, Mrs Selina Cole and her servant, disappeared. Their skeletons, together with those of two others, were later discovered in a bush near Ikoyi. Police investigations directed by Superintendent A.C. Willoughby, acting on a clue, discovered Mrs Cole's property at the residence of the culprit who "in the assumed role of a 'doctor, alchemist and conjurer' had succeeded in enticing superstitious women to his home or other convenient spot where he robbed and subsequently murdered them".[78] His trial and conviction for the murder of the two victims and another named Catherine Clegg resulted in his being hung.

On 8 August 1885, the editor of the *Eagle* again drew the attention of the public to the fact that burglars in Lagos were becoming daring, armed with spears, cutlasses, knives, and other weapons absolutely necessary for aggressive procedures.[79] Four years later, the *Record* also described the numerous and daring burglaries in December 1891, which it claimed had made Lagos unsafe, thus requiring better and increased measures of protection.[80] By 1895, the Civil Police was still being accused of inefficiency and complicity with criminals. In fact, it was said that the low wages payable to police officers attracted people of low status and shady character into the force.

Another newspaper report gives insight into the modus operandi of some of the criminals. Earlier, we noted the digging of holes through walls. In the 1880s, the use of fire and burning of houses became rampant. Although fires often occurred in residential areas in Lagos during civil wars, criminals began to use it more effectively during the colonial period.[81] Understandably, the Marina, the emerging commercial centre of Lagos, suffered most. The commercial stores of Jacob E. Williams, Messrs William Brothers & Co, and several other Lagos merchants were looted after the entrance to the stores were burnt to facilitate entry. Such criminal activities usually led to the theft of large quantities of goods. In the case of the William Brothers, the store was set on fire after the burglars

77 Brown, "History", p. 384 and Tamuno, *Police*, p. 26.

78 *Ibid.*

79 Echeruo, *Victorian*, p. 21.

80 *Ibid.*

81 Nwanunobi, Incendiarism, pp. 114–116.

had removed a large quantity of rum and gin.[82] It was also recorded in the mid-1880s that Lagos thieves found it convenient to rob during the rainy season. The advantages were many. First, policemen and night watchmen usually took cover during the rains. Second, walls were easier to tunnel through. Third, the nights were darker and escape was easier, and the chances of grounding on a sand bar and having to jettison part of the loot were less. This seasonal pattern was still evident in 1900.[83]

5 Official Responses to Theft

The colonial authority tried to fight crime in several ways. Governor Glover in particular did much to fight crime in Lagos and its environs. He continued the policy of appointing one or two local men to staff their usually one-man police posts as a part of their rural policing team, generally comprising headmen, and those described as "Natives Chiefs Sergeants".[84] Ewu, Isasi, Isolo, Idimu, Janike (Ijanikin) Igamu (Iganmu) Agbara, Ojo, Oto, Igando, Werakun, and Onibeju, communities hitherto in the outlying districts of Lagos but now absorbed into the Greater Lagos idea, were all affected by this policy. By 1872, these outfits numbered about 63 in the Eastern District of Lagos, suggesting its popularity. Meanwhile, in 1873, a sum of £800 was reserved for them in the annual Estimate.[85] In the heart of Lagos, efforts were made to increase police presence in the neighbourhood through the proliferation of police stations. There was only one civil police station located at Olowogbowo where the returnees lived in 1871. In the same year, effort was made to site one at Tinubu Square, one in Tapa's quarter near Dosunmu and yet another in Olowogbowo.[86]

Following his departure, however, Glover's efforts could not be sustained for various reasons. First, the change in leadership meant the introduction of a new approach to administration. Second, as the administration of Lagos was still intertwined with that of Sierra Leone and later that of the Gold Coast, from 1874–1886, J.P. Hennessy, Administrator-in-Chief could not immediately appreciate the police needs of Lagos. Third, the Isaac Willoughby affair,[87] which needs no elaboration here, significantly beclouded what should

82 *Ibid.*, 116.

83 Brown, "History", p. 384.

84 Tamuno, *Police*, pp. 20–21.

85 *Ibid.*

86 Brown, "History", p. 388.

87 He was the first African Superintendent of Police in Lagos from 1862–1873. The affair borders on theft of government money by a brother of the superintendent, and the latter's

otherwise have been the commendable efforts of Glover at encouraging rural policing and invariably enhancing internal security in Lagos. These reasons, coupled with the fact that the Civil Police was bedevilled with problems of inefficiency, recruitment of illiterates from "the very lowest off-scourings of people",[88] mostly from the interior-ex-slaves and porters, made Lagos residents – especially the merchant class, irrespective of race – to seek the help of the Colonial Government in providing more and better police supervision as well as the introduction of police detectives to fight crime.

In the aftermath of the separation of Lagos administration from that of the Gold Coast in 1886, new efforts were made to tackle criminality in Lagos. One major response was to improve the efficiency of the police. Governor Alfred Moloney planned and subsequently received approval from the Colonial Office to re-organise the Lagos Constabulary by increasing their "strength, improve the beat system, entrust them with the duties of a fire brigade and make them responsible for street lighting which took off effectively in 1898".[89] The improvement in the beat system yielded some positive results, but the effect soon wore off as "the thieves soon learned the schedule of the patrols".[90] Granted, Alfred Moloney, at different times Governor of the colony in acting, deputising and substantive capacities in, respectively, 1878–1880, 1883, and 1886–1887, and 1890,[91] had obliged the merchants' request for more police presence by increasing the strength of the Civil Police with fourteen constables and the introduction of six detectives,[92] it is doubtful whether the force could have performed as creditably as the statistics seem to suggest.

The government also initiated the process of enhancing street lighting in Lagos. By 1898, it had succeeded in replacing the kerosene and gas lanterns that had once illuminated the streets of Lagos with electric lighting. In fact, press reports suggest that the lack of street lighting was the cause of frequent burglaries in Lagos.[93] This might be true of those criminals who worked, perhaps effortlessly, under the cover of darkness, but the introduction of street lighting did not stop burglaries in the city. Besides, police business requires a balance

unwillingness to prosecute him, and perceived high-handedness of the ASP by the public. For details, see Tamuno, *Police*, pp. 21–23.

88 *Ibid.*, 25.

89 Tamuno, *Police*, p. 26.

90 Brown, "History", p. 389.

91 L.C. Gwam, "An Inventory of the Administrative Records Assembled from the Colony Province, Ibadan: National Archives Headquarters, 1961", p. 77.

92 Tamuno, *Police*, p. 24.

93 Echeruo, *Victorian*, p. 21.

of illumination and darkness to thrive.[94] At another level, the government also tried to improve the calibre of men who sought enrolment in the force. In 1887, for the first time it solicited the recruitment of "intelligent men who could speak English and Yoruba to become lance corporals in the civil police force".[95] This laudable idea, however, proved unworkable as "the pay of thirteen pence a day was no inducement for capable men".[96] The low income only attracted men of little honour to the force. Spencer Brown notes that the Civil Police remained a neglected force and still wore the short, baggy trousers that some Sierra Leoneans thought a disgrace. By 1887, in spite of the armed Hausa and Civil Police patrols, a general insecurity about life and property had returned.[97]

Another dimension of the official response to criminality was evident in the co-operation the government sought with an adjacent power through treaty-making and boundary demarcation. The enactment of treaties by the British has been interpreted as a frantic "search for [...] some appearance of legal certainty and claims over territories that were illegally acquired by imperial force".[98] But beyond the issue of legally protecting territorial claims, treaty-making was also a means by which the British tried to control criminality in Lagos. In doing this, it had to co-operate with a rival colonial power – France – to ensure that criminals or suspects emanating from the colony did not take advantage of situation in adjacent jurisdictions to undermine colonial security. For instance, in 1876, the British signed a treaty with the French Colonial Government in Dahomey to achieve the extradition of criminals fleeing prosecution into French territory.

The bilateral treaty included a proviso that normal diplomatic procedure would be bent for a less rigorous one to hasten the process of inter-colonial extradition. The treaty was signed at a time when the grip of the two colonial powers on their colonial territories was still wobbly.[99] Furthermore, the Agreement of 1889 between the British and the French, demarcated the frontier between Lagos and Porto-Novo from "the north of the Ajarra Creek northwards

94 See NAI, Comcol 1 FN 1532, "Street Lighting in the Municipality of Lagos", pp. 22–24.

95 Brown, "History", p. 389.

96 *Ibid.*

97 *Ibid.*

98 O.A. Adewoye, *The Judicial System in Southern Nigeria, 1854–1954: Law and Justice in a Dependency* (London: Longman, 1977), p. 17.

99 Reference to the existence of the treaty can be found in Porto-Novo, Republic of Benin in, Des Archives Nationales, Quando (D.A.N.Q.), 1F 58/ 365 , Police, Extradition d'indigènes entre le Nigeria et le Dahomey, 1909 and D.A.N.Q., 1F 57/ 360, Police, Extradition: Convention Franco- anglaise, 1911. The original treaty may have been lost, although it is not impossible that it may be somewhere in the Archives of the Minister for Foreign Affairs in France (Le Ministère des Affaires Etrangères).

to the north parallel".[100] Subsequently, the British established protectorates over border communities such as Igbessa, Ipokia, Addo, and Ajilete up to Ilaro. While political reasons had been generally adduced for this demarcation, it is not unlikely that the action also inevitably became about curbing criminals, who often came from the neighbouring communities on the Dahomean side to rob, and, when under pressure, retreated to their communities, thus exploiting the closeness of these villages. For instance, Egbado appears to have been a source region from many of the criminals who terrorised the outlying districts of Lagos during the colonial period. The effect of the demarcation on trans-border crime was, however, limited.

Notwithstanding all these efforts, criminals continued to operate in Lagos until 1906, when the Colony and Protectorate of Lagos was amalgamated with the Protectorate of Southern Nigeria (formerly the Niger Coast Protectorate) to constitute the Colony and Protectorate of Southern Nigeria. In 1900, there were reports of thieves entering the premises of one Mr. S.J. Sawyer on Joseph Street and stealing a watch. A considerable quantity of stolen property could have been carted away but for the fact that the victim woke up in the process, forcing the thieves to escape hurriedly.[101] In the same year, the *Record* reported a robbery at Government House, suggesting that there was nowhere that could not be robbed in Lagos.[102] Indeed, as early as 1867, a similar incident occurred when burglars, apparently untroubled by the safeguards put in place, broke open the buildings of the Supreme Court at Tinubu Square and made away with public money.

6 Conclusion

This chapter has offered explanations on the prevalence of theft in early colonial Lagos. Unlike in the first half of the nineteenth century, when theft was induced mainly by public disorder, in the colonial era, theft seems predominantly to be a consequence of the influx of criminals from neighbouring towns and villages into Lagos. While it is true that Lagos might have had homegrown thieves organised by disgruntled chiefs for survival, it seems that most of the crimes in Lagos had external roots, even as the idea of Lagos began to expand.

100 Hopkins, "Economic", p. 111. For more on boundary matters, see A.I. Asiwaju, "Law in African Borderlands: The Lived Experience of the Yoruba Astride the Nigeria-Dahomey Border", in Kristin Mann and Richard Roberts (eds.), *Law in Colonial Africa* (Portsmouth: Heinemann, 1991), pp. 224–238.

101 Echeruo, *Victorian*, p. 22.

102 *Ibid.*

Of course, as cosmopolitanism grew and the growth of individualism as opposed to communalism increased, more disadvantaged indigenous Lagosians might have committed more theft than is usually ascribed to them. Studies of criminality in nineteenth-century European and American cities suggest that low levels of property crime and a high level of violence were characteristic of pre-modern villages and rural areas in Europe and America. But, as industrialisation increased and as modernisation set in, these rural areas tended to transform into metropolitan areas with low levels of violence and a higher level of theft. To a certain extent, Lagos seems to fit this model, as colonialism, not industrialisation, made life less communal. As issues of survival became more personal, many found crime a profitable venture especially in Lagos, which had a lenient judicial system compared to what obtained in the interior of Yorubaland. The British annexation of Lagos in 1861, which made it the earliest British colony in West Africa outside of Sierra Leone, also had serious implications for property crime in the city. This novel political experiment increased the number of expatriates, expanded commerce, and brought about the physical transformation of Lagos, with areas exhibiting a concentration of wealth, including the Marina, where the large businesses were concentrated thus becoming easy targets for criminals. Also, colonial justice with its rule of law and due process in Lagos seemed lenient, with criminals compared to the summary justice of the interior Yoruba states, hence turning the former into a haven for criminals.

Bibliography

Brown, Spencer H., "A History of the Peoples of Lagos, 1852–1886", PhD Thesis, North Western University, 1964.

Echeruo, Michael J.C., *Victorian Lagos: Aspects of Nineteenth Century Lagos Life*, (London and Basingstoke: Macmillan, 1977).

Fourchard, Laurent, "Urban Poverty, Urban Crime and Crime Control: The Lagos and Ibadan Cases, 1929–1945", in S. Salm and T. Falola (eds.), *African Urban Spaces in Historical Perspective*, Rochester, NY: Rochester University Press, 2003, pp. 291–319.

Iliffe, John, *African Poor: A History*, Cambridge: Cambridge University Press, 1987.

Law, Robin, "Trade and Politics behind the Slave Coast: The Lagoon Traffic and the Rise of Lagos, 1500–1800" *Journal of African History*, 24: 3, 1983, pp. 321–348.

Nwanunobi, C. Onyeka, "Incendiarism and Other Fires in Nineteenth-Century Lagos, 1863–1888", *Africa, Journal of the International African Institute* (*Revue de l'Institut Africain International*), 60: 1 (1990), pp. 111–120.

Osifodunrin, Paul, "Violent Crimes in Lagos, 1861–2000: Nature, Responses and Impact", PhD Thesis, University of Lagos, 2008.

Tamuno, Tekena, *The Police in Modern Nigeria, 1861–1965: Origins, Development and Role*, Ibadan: University Press, 1970.

CHAPTER 3

Smuggling across the Nigeria: Benin Border and Its Impact on Nigeria's Economic Development

Jackson A. Aluede

> Smuggling is a serious menace to the economy and that all hands must be on deck to flush it out. As you know, when goods are illegally brought into the country through smuggling, it is not just the revenue that is lost, local industries are affected and jobs are lost.[1]

1 Smuggling in Global Perspective

Smuggling in its various forms, namely human trafficking, smuggling of contrabands such as petroleum products, hard drugs, arms and ammunition, among others, constitutes a key component of the illicit enterprise popularly known as transnational organised crime. The nature of the threat smuggling and other transborder crimes pose to human and national security, in all parts of the world, has compelled world leaders to seek ways to combat the menace. The first attempt to address the problem globally was in 1994, in Naples, Italy, when a meeting was convened under the auspices of the World Ministerial Conference on Organised Transnational Crime. The conference ended with a communiqué titled "Political Declaration and Global Action Plan against Organised Transnational Crime", in which Ministers initiated principles, specific guidelines, and plans to be followed by member states at the national and international levels to combat the menace of transborder crime.[2] Furthermore, in December 2000, the United Nations Convention against Transnational Organized Crime was held in Palermo, Italy.[3] The Convention demonstrated the

1 Rotimi Akinwumi and Ahmed Musa "Smuggling Import N7trn worth of Goods annually, say Senate" *Daily Independent* July 18, 2017, p. 2.

2 Sabrina Adamoli et al., *Organised Crime around the World* (Helsinki: European Institute for Crime Prevention and Control, 1998), p. 1.

3 *United Nations Security Council*, Report of the Secretary–General on Illicit Cross-Border Trafficking Movement. 19 October 2012, p. 2.

 | DOI:10.1163/9789004396289_005

political will of the international community to provide a global response to a global challenge. The resolve of the world body was aptly captured in the slogan that, "if crime crosses borders, so must law enforcement".[4] The convention defined what transnational organised crime is, its nature, and patterns as well as what the global response should be. A unique feature of smuggling the world over is that it takes place within states and across international borders, particularly in borderlands.[5]

Smuggling is the oldest illicit enterprise embedded in the concepts of cross-border crime, transborder, and transnational organised crime. Sometimes, these concepts are used interchangeably.[6] The interchangeable use of these terms, however, demands clarification. It is interesting to note that they all connote the same meaning, which is the perpetrating of criminal activities across the border of two or more countries. For instance, cross-border crime refers to illicit conduct that jeopardises the legally protected interests in more than one national jurisdiction and which is criminalised in at least one of the states/jurisdictions concerned.[7] Transnational organised crime, according to the United Nations Convention against Transnational Organised Crime signed in Palermo in 2000 refers to a crime committed in more than one state in which a substantial part of its preparation, planning, direction, or control takes place in another state, involving an organised criminal group.[8] Transborder crime has, in turn, been defined as the illegal activities carried out by individuals and groups across national and international boundaries, either for financial gain, or for socio-political and religious considerations.[9] Succinctly put, criminal acts whose perpetrators and repercussions go beyond territorial borders. The use of each of these terms depends on the discretion of individuals analysing or studying the illicit cross-border phenomenon.

Transborder and transnational organised crimes are recent terms, used to explain the phenomenon of cross-border criminal activities since the last

4 UNODC, "United Nations Convention against Transnational Organized Crime and the Protocols Thereto" (Vienna: United Nations Publications, 2004), p. iii.

5 Thomas M. Wilson and Hastings Donnan, "Border and Border Studies" in Thomas M. Wilson and Hastings Donnan (eds.), *A Companion to Border Studies* (Oxford: Blackwell Publishing Ltd, 2012), p. 1.

6 Petrus C. van Duyne, "Organized Crime Markets in a Turbulent Europe" *European Journal on Criminal Policy and Research*, 1: (1993): pp. 10–29.

7 Nikos Passas "Cross-border Crime and the Interface between Legal and Illegal Actors", in Petrus C. van Duyne, Klaus von Lampe, Nikos Passas (eds.), *Upperworld and Underworld in Cross-Border Crime* (Nijmegen: Wolf Legal Publishers, 2002), p. 13.

8 UNODC, "United Nations Convention against Transnational Organized Crime and the Protocols Thereto", p. 6.

9 Simon Odey Ering, "Trans-border Crime and Its Socio-economic Impact on Developing Economies" *Journal Sociology and Anthropology*, 2: 2 (2011): pp. 73–80.

decades of the twentieth century. This is due largely to the influence of globalisation on the cross-border flow of goods and services as well as the opening of borders to promote trade and regional integration in the West, especially in Europe. The impact of globalisation, through the interconnectedness of global economics and innovations in information technology, was exploited by criminal gangs operating across borders to make their trade more organised in scope and reach. The term cross-border crime predates transborder and transnational organised crime in usage. There are those, however, who share the view that not all cross-border crimes are equally serious, sophisticated, or organised.[10] Notwithstanding this, all the concepts under review involve criminal activities prohibited by law, whether locally or internationally. As already indicated, the focus of this study is smuggling, a component of transborder crime.

Smuggling, in the words of Isaac Olawale Albert, is an age-old worldwide business in which smugglers seek to maximise profit or gains by illegally smuggling and trafficking items prohibited by law into and outside their countries, in collaboration with their partners or fellow smugglers in other countries.[11] Smuggling has been in existence for centuries in different parts of the world. It is difficult to date precisely when smuggling started. However, some scholars have traced the origin of the illicit enterprise to the formation of the state system in Europe. For others, smuggling predates the post-Westphalia era. Interestingly, however, in some cases, some countries had sponsored smuggling as a state policy in the past. In an article titled "Gangster's Paradise: The Untold History of the United States and International Crime", Peter Andreas reveals the United States' involvement in the illicit enterprise in the early years of her independence. In his words:

> Far from being a passive victim, the United States has fostered as rich a tradition of illicit trade as any other country in the world. Since its founding, the United States has had an intimate relationship with clandestine commerce, and contraband capitalism was integral to the rise of the U.S. economy.[12]

10 Nikos Passas "Cross-border Crime and the Interface between Legal and Illegal Actors", p. 13.

11 Isaac Olawale Albert, "Smuggling Second-hand Cars through the Benin-Nigeria Borders", in A.I. Asiwaju et al. (eds.), *Cross Border Crimes and Community Policing: Prospects and Challenges in Nigeria-Benin Cross-Border Areas of Ogun State* (Imeko: African University Institute, 2006), p. 65.

12 Peter Andreas, "Gangster's Paradise: The Untold History of the United States and International Crime", *Foreign Affairs* (March/April 2013), pp. 23–24.

Apart from the United States, the British government in the eighteenth and nineteenth centuries embarked on state-sponsored smuggling against her rivals in North America and Asia. For instance, illegal trade between Britain and Spanish colonies was a deliberate British policy in the first half of the eighteenth century and helped to bring about the collapse of Spain's commercial empire.[13] In East Asia, and particularly in China, the British sponsored smuggling of opium led to the mid-nineteenth-century Opium Wars with China.[14]

In Africa, smuggling assumed a worrisome dimension following the establishment of colonialism by the respective colonial masters, namely the British, French, German, Portuguese, and Spanish. In West Africa, smuggling was more intense in rival European colonies sharing colonial boundaries, such as British and French colonial West Africa. On the Nigeria–Benin border, rival colonial economic policies with respect to trade, taxes charged on goods, and the prohibition of the movement of certain items from one colonial territory to another made smuggling a lucrative business in the border communities, particularly in the southern part of the Nigeria–Dahomey colonial border.[15] For instance, the low tariff on the price of goods in Porto-Novo in French West Africa, capital of present-day Benin, encouraged traders to smuggle goods into British West Africa from Lagos and Badagry. L.C. Dioka explained how the tariff war between British and French colonial authorities fuelled smuggling across the Nigeria–Benin border during the colonial period. According to him:

> The Anglo-French agreement of 10th August 1889 transformed the colonial boundaries into the international boundary. But rather than curtail the excessive degree of smuggling, the boundary exacerbated it; hence with it (the boundary), smuggling became a stable feature of the region. British and French nationals were confined to their own side of the boundary while waging tariff wars. While the French, in order to encourage investment and settlement of their nationals in keeping with their policy of assimilation imposed low tariffs, the British on the other hand, imposed high tariffs on their colonies to cover administrative cost.[16]

13 David Felsen, & Akis Kalaitzidis, "A Historical Overview of Transnational Crime", in Philip Reichel (ed.), *Handbook of Transnational Crime & Justice* (London: Sage Publications, 2005), p. 10.

14 *Ibid.*

15 Ogunsola John Igué, "Évolution du commerce clandestin entre le Dahomey et le Nigeria depuis la guerre du Biafra", *Canadian Journal of African Studies / Revue Canadienne des ÉtudesAfricaines*, 10: 2 (1976): pp. 235–257.

16 L.C. Dioka, *Lagos and Its Environs* (Lagos: First Academic Publishers, 2001), pp. 201–202.

The illicit enterprise survived through the colonial into the post-colonial era. Moreover, it expanded in scope and dimension. It has gone beyond the smuggling of agricultural produce and imported contrabands from abroad, to include the smuggling of people, hard drugs, petroleum products, and arms and ammunitions. Igue and Soule observe that the "entrepôt states" in West Africa, notably Benin, Togo, and The Gambia, base their economic development strategies on enhancing their attractiveness as trading hubs to serve as conduits for both legal transit to landlocked countries in West Africa (Mali, Niger, and Burkina Faso), and illegal trade to more protectionist neighbours such as Senegal and Nigeria.[17] They have achieved this by deliberately maintaining low import barriers and relatively well-functioning ports to lower import and transshipping costs.

Concerning North, South, and Central America, especially with reference to the United States and Mexico, so much has been written on the smuggling of drugs from Mexico into the United States through the US/Mexico borders.[18] The proximity of Europe to Central Asian countries, especially Turkey and Afghanistan, and the removal of barriers with Eastern European countries has encouraged the smuggling of heroin and other items from Central Asia into Western Europe.[19] The same trend is noticeable in East and Southern Africa. Kenya and South Africa have had similar experiences. Both countries have not only seen smugglers from the neighbouring countries of Tanzania, Uganda, Somalia, Zimbabwe, Zambia, Mozambique, Angola, and Swaziland, but have become transit countries for the trafficking and smuggling of persons, arms, heroin, and cocaine to Europe, the United States, China, Turkey, Pakistan, and India.[20]

Another salient feature of the nature and pattern of smuggling is that the illicit enterprise bridges the gap between demand and supply, restricted by law and trade regulations between states. It is paradoxical that smuggled items in one country are in in demand across the border in another country. For instance, smugglers and traffickers smuggle cocaine and heroin from South America and

17 J.O. Igue′ & B.G. Soulé, *L'Etat Entrepôt au Benin: Commerce Informelou Reponse ala Crise?* (Karthala: Paris, 1992), cited in Stephen S. Golub, "Entrepôt Trade and Smuggling in West Africa: Benin, Togo and Nigeria", *The World Economy* (2012), p. 1.

18 Eric L. Olson *et al.*, "Introduction", in Eric L. Olson, David A. Shirk & Andrew Selee (eds.), *Shared Responsibility: US-Mexico Policy Options for Confronting Organized Crime* (Washington, DC: Mexico Institute, Woodrow Wilson International Center for Scholars, 2010), pp. 1–3.

19 Petrus C. van Duyne, "Organized Crime Markets in a Turbulent Europe", p. 13.

20 Peter Gastrow, "African Actors in International Organized Crime" in John T. Picarelli (ed.), *International Organized Crime: The African Experience* (Courmayeur Mont Blanc: International Scientific and Professional Advisory Council of the United Nations Crime Prevention and Criminal Justice Programme ISPAC, 2010), pp. 31–41.

Asia, where they have a surplus of hard drugs, to Africa, the United States, and Europe, where they are in demand. The same applied to other forms of smuggling, such as human trafficking, whereby young women from Africa, Asia, and Latin America are transported to Europe and the United States to engage in prostitution. In recent times, globalisation, advances in technology, and the emergence of smuggling cartels, among others, have influenced and encouraged smugglers in different parts of the world to profit from such enterprises.

In the context of the threat posed by smuggling to the corporate existence of a state, this paper examines the impact of smuggling in the Nigeria–Benin border area on Nigeria's economic development. The paper is in three parts. The first part focuses on the nature and dimension of smuggling at the border during the colonial era, the second examines the factors that have encouraged the illicit trade in recent times, while the third section analyses the economic implications of smuggling on Nigeria as well as the efforts made by the governments of Nigeria and the Republic of Benin to address the problem.

2 Colonial Origin of the Nigeria-Benin Border and the Bifurcation of the Ecosystem

One common feature of borders worldwide is that they are artificial creations, aimed at separating peoples for socio-cultural, economic, and political reasons. According to Zartman, borders are sharp, clear, deep lines where political lines are reinforced by "natural" distinctions in terms of physical and human geography; that is, where populations are clearly different on either side of the line and where they are thinned out by clearly marked, less inhabitable distinctions, such as natural walls and moats, mountains ridges, or water bodies.[21] Most borderlands are an amalgam of ethnic nationalities, separated by the boundaries of two states, such as the US/Mexico, Ghana/Togo, and the Nigeria/Benin (formerly Dahomey) borders. Niles Hansen describes borderlands as "sub-national areas whose economic and social life is directly and significantly affected by proximity to an international boundary".[22] Borderlands are both melting pots and hotspots.[23]

21 I. Williams Zartman, "Identity, Movement and Response", in I. William Zartman (ed.), *Understanding Life in the Borderlands: Boundaries in Depth and in Motion* (Athens, GA: The University of Georgia Press, 2010), p. 5.

22 Niles Hansen, *The Border Economy: Regional Development in the Southwest* (Austin, TX: University of Texas Press, 1981).

23 Constanze Blum, *Cross-Border Flows Between Nigeria and Benin: What Are the Challenges for (Human) Security?* (Abuja: Friedrich-Ebert-Stiftung, 2014).

The Nigeria–Benin epitomises the aforementioned characteristics. Nigeria and Benin share a land boundary of approximately 770 kilometres in length (see map 3.1), made up of three distinct sections: the Atlantic coast to Okpara River (203 kilometres); Okpara River to Thalwag (161 kilometres); and Okpara to the Niger River.[24] The Nigeria–Benin border was created by the British and the French, through a series of boundary agreements following claims and counter-claims over their respective "spheres of influence" and the "right to effective occupation", having secured parts of the territories by signing treaties of protection with the traditional rulers. The 1889 Anglo-French Convention, and the 1906 and 1914 Anglo-French Boundary Agreements, define the boundary between Nigeria and Benin as it exists today.[25]

Fundamentally, colonial boundaries have had an enormous impact on post-independent African states, particularly concerning border-related challenges between and among neighbouring states on the continent. The works of Williams Zartman, Alan J. Day, Saadia Touval, A.I. Asiwaju, and Judith Vorrath shed light on some of the negative effects such as irredentism, clashes over mineral resources, genocide, ethnic clashes, and transborder crimes, which the inherited colonial boundaries have bequeathed to post-independent Africa.[26] Before the eruption of border-related problems between African states, some African leaders at the 1964 Organisation African Unity (OAU) meeting had called for the redrawing of the continent's political map in order to undo the negative effects of colonial boundaries on post-independence Africa. However, the majority of the leaders opposed the proposition, instead agreeing a resolution

24 Alec C. McEwen, "The Establishment of the Nigeria/Benin Boundary, 1889–1989", *The Geographical Journal*, 157, 1 (1991): 62.

25 See J.C. Anene, *The International Boundaries of Nigeria 1885–1960: The Framework of an Emergent African Nation* (London: Longman Group Limited, 1970); J.D. Hargreaves, "The Making of the Boundaries: Focus on West Africa", in A.I. Asiwaju (ed.), *Partitioned Africans: Ethnic Relations across Africa's International Boundaries 1884–1984* (London: C. Hurst & Company 1985), p. 20; Alec C. McEwen, "The Establishment of the Nigeria/Benin Boundary, 1889–1989".

26 I. Williams Zartman, "Identity, Movement and Response", in *Understanding Life in the Borderlands: Boundaries in Depth and in Motion, Athens, GA: The University of Georgia Press, 2010.*;Alan J. Day (ed.), *Border and Territorial Disputes* (London, Longman Group Limited, 1982), pp. 111–116; Saadia Touval, "Partitioned Groups and Inter-State Relations", in A.I. Asiwaju (ed.) *Partitioned Africans: Ethnic Relations across Africa's International Boundaries* 1884–1984 (London: C. Hurst & Company, 1985); Judith Vorrath, "On the Margin of Statehood? State-Society Relations in African Borderlands", in I. William Zartman (ed.), *Understanding Life in the Borderlands: Boundaries in Depth and in Motion* (Athens, GA: The University of Georgia Press, 2010), pp. 87–91; A.I. Asiwaju, *Boundaries and African Integration: Essay In Comparative History and Policy Analysis* (Lagos: Panaf Publishing, Inc, 2003), pp. 3–543.

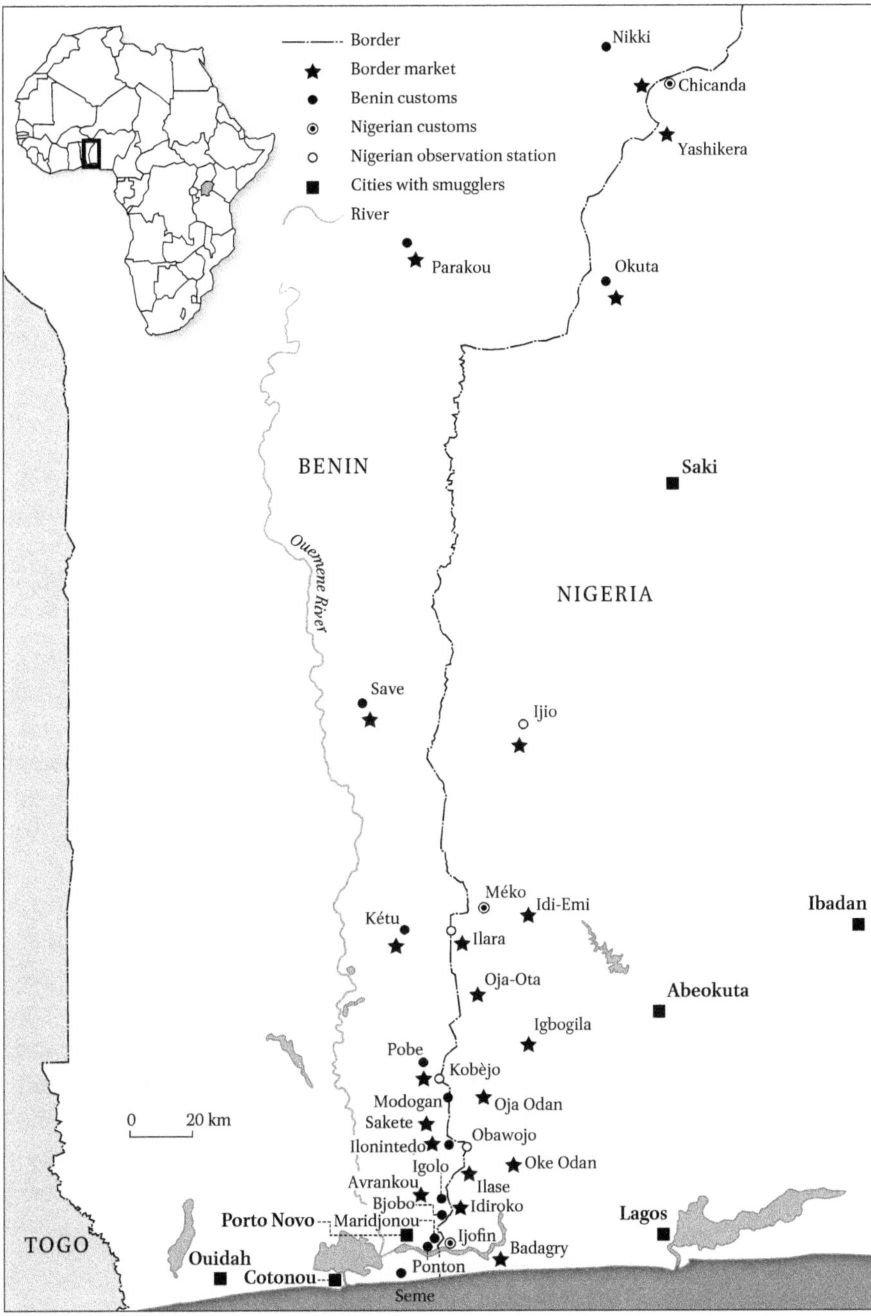

MAP 3.1 Border Nigeria – Benin
Nel de Vink (DeVink Mapdesign), based on Wikimedia.
SOURCE: HTTPS://COMMONS.WIKIMEDIA.ORG/WIKI/FILE:DAHOMEY-NIGERIA_BOUNDARY_LOC_76696106JPG (ACCESSED 15 OCTOBER 2018).

that "all member-states pledge themselves to respect the borders existing on their achievement of national independence".[27] Thus, the concept of Uti Possidetis, a principle of international law that provides that newly formed sovereign states retain the borders they had before independence, entered into the African political equation. However, as events across the continent have shown, the colonial boundaries have continued to pose challenges to relations between neighbouring states, threatening peace and economic, political, and socio-cultural relations.

3 Smuggling across the Nigeria-Benin Border since the Colonial Period

Several factors have influenced smuggling across the Nigeria–Benin border since the colonial era. The first was the economic policies of the British and the French colonial masters. These policies were influenced by a desire to protect the home industries from other competitive European states. This was evident in the different tariffs imposed on alcohol, firearms, and other goods by both the British and French colonial authorities.[28] For instance, a British Colonial Office Committee Report in the latter part of the eighteenth century on the effect of the spirit trade on Southern Nigeria contended that the trade in alcohol could be checked by a sharp tariff increase, but held that such a step could not be taken unilaterally because the lower duties in force in Dahomey (now the Benin Republic) would encourage the entry of smuggled spirits into Yorubaland.[29] Generally, the tariff on imported and exported goods was cheaper on the French side of the Nigeria–Benin border, compared to that on the British territory. The same can be said of duties levied on goods. This development encouraged smuggling as traders and businessmen in Lagos and Badagry flocked into Porto Novo bringing smuggled goods with them.[30] Moreover, the strict control of goods across the border and the high import duties charged on goods crossing from the British to French colonial territories in West Africa, equally affected the free movement of agricultural produce at the Nigeria–Benin border. The development contributed to the smuggling of cash crops particularly in the border regions across West Africa; a development that was encouraged

27 Alan J. Day (ed.), *Border and Territorial Disputes*, p. 95.

28 James J. Cooke, "Anglo-French Diplomacy and the Contraband Arms Trade in Colonial Africa, 1894–1897", *African Studies Review*, 17: 1 (1974), pp. 34–35; A. Olorunfemi, "The Liquor Traffic Dilemma in British West Africa: The Southern Nigerian Example, 1895–1918", *The International Journal of African Historical Studies*, 17: 2 (1984): pp. 240–241.

29 *Ibid.*

30 L.C. Dioka, *Lagos and Its Environs*, p. 201.

by price differentiation in the respective colonies. For instance, at the Nigeria–Niger border, groundnut farmers in Niger under French colonial rule smuggled their produce into neighbouring Hausa land in Nigeria to get a higher price, especially during the Second World War and the immediate post-war period. According to John Davison Collins, over 90% of Niger's commercial groundnut crop is purchased in the four neighbouring districts of Maradi, Tessaoua, Metameye, and Magaria, each of which has a southern border with Nigeria.[31]

At the Nigeria–Benin border, cocoa, kola nuts, palm kernel, and palm oil were the main cash crops smuggled from the Nigerian side of the border into the Republic of Benin. Cocoa later dominated other cash crops before it was replaced by fuel in the second half of the twentieth century. Cocoa farmers and middlemen involved in the sale of the agricultural produce from the western part of Nigeria transported large quantities of their cocoa produce to the border between Nigeria and Benin, where they were sold at a favourable price, and later smuggled into the Benin Republic.[32] There was a high demand for cocoa in the French colonies, where it was re-exported to France. Likewise, local industries, including beverage companies, operating in Benin wanted cocoa too. Since cocoa was not cultivated in Benin, the beverage companies relied on external supply, which came mainly from the neighbouring British colony of Nigeria through smuggling.[33] On the other hand, several imported items were smuggled from the Benin Republic into Nigeria, such as fabric, spirit, liquor, cigarettes/tobacco, smoked fish, enamel, and used clothes, among others.[34]

The French and the British colonial authorities failed to do anything remarkable to stop the smuggling of goods across their respective borders during the colonial period. This is because it favoured their economic interest, especially that of the French colonial authorities. Throughout the colonial period, French firms imported several goods into their respective colonies in West Africa, which were then smuggled into British and other European territories in the West Africa sub-region. Since the independence of the two countries, this smuggling has gained a new dimension and is partly aided by the geographical features of the border region and the lucrative nature of the trade. Although smuggling progressed from the colonial into the post-colonial era, at the Nigeria–Benin border it has been observed that many of those involved on the

31 John. Davidson Collins, "The Clandestine Movement of Groundnuts across the Niger–Nigeria Boundary", *Canadian Journal of African Studies* 10: 2 (1976), pp. 262–267.

32 Chief Omolade Popola Olabokunde (The Balogun Olorunda Ifonyin Itedo, Owode/Yewa South Local Government Area of Ogun State, Nigeria) in discussion with Jackson Aluede, 24 December 2015.

33 *Ibid.*

34 Ogunsola John Igué, "Clandestine trade developments between Dahomey and Nigeria since the Biafra war".

Nigerian side were not indigenes of the border communities, but Nigerians from other parts of the country with a history of long-distance trade. They are the Ijesha, Ikire, Ogbomosho, and the Osun people.[35] These Yoruba-speaking people settled on both sides of the Nigeria–Benin border among the indigenes who were mainly farmers. They also served as guards to the alternative border route. Nevertheless, the Nigeria civil war changed their perception of the illicit trade. After the war, the border communities became major actors in the smuggling of different goods across the borders between the two countries.

At independence, little or nothing was done by the governments of Nigeria and the Benin Republic to address the threat that smuggling posed to their economy, development, and security. However, the explanation for this lies in the dependent structure of the economy of both countries. They were still tied to the apron strings of their former colonial masters.[36] According to Olukoshi and Obi, as in the colonial period, both economies were vertically linked to the metropoles' advanced market economy, to which they supply the primary products of agricultural production and mineral resources.[37] As a result, most of the newly independent Africa leaders or governments paid little attention to interstate trade between neighbouring countries. This is particularly true of the informal sector of those individuals and groups in the borderlands where smuggling of contraband became a major business. Thus, while the Nigerian post-colonial economy served the interests of the British, those of its immediate Francophone neighbours, namely, Benin (then Dahomey), Niger, Chad, and Cameroon, were fashioned to serve the needs of France. In the process, formal trade between Nigeria and her immediate neighbours decreased significantly due to the concentration of her trade and other economic relations on the capitalist and advanced economies of the West. However, informal trade and the smuggling of contraband among indigenes or nationals of both countries flourished. On this development, Olukoshi and Obi wrote that:

> Within this scenario, trade relations between Nigeria and its neighbours accounted for a very small proportion of their total foreign trade. It has

35 Chief OmoladePopola Olabokunde (The BalogunOlorundaIfonyinItedo, Owode/Yewa South Local Government Area of Ogun State, Nigeria).

36 Nkem Onyekpe, "The Nature and Problems of Nigeria's Dependent Economic Status", in Yomi Akinyeye (ed.), *Nigeria and the Wider World in the 20th Century: Essay in Honour of Professor Akinjide Osuntokun* (Ibadan: Davidson Press, 2003), pp. 40–41.

37 A.O. Olukoshi and C.I. Obi, "The State of Nigeria's Trade Relations with its Neighbours: Issues and Problems", in G.A. Obiozor, A.O. Olukoshi, C.I. Obi (eds.), *West African Regional Economic Integration: Nigerian Policy Perspectives for the 1990s* (Uppsala: NordiskaAfrika Institute, 1996), p. 12.

> been pointed out that a lot of unrecorded or informal trade continues to take place across the "artificial borders of Nigeria and its immediate neighbours," almost overshadowing the low level of formal trade between and among them, taken together, these informal flows still constitute a small proportion of the total trade of the sub-region.[38]

Similarly, the different post-independence economic policies of the newly independent states of Nigeria and the Benin Republic were influenced by their colonial experiences, and to a large extent accounted for the ongoing smuggling in their borderlands. In Nigeria, different administrations encouraged the protection of local or infant industries with high tariffs on imported goods and an embargo on certain goods entering the country. On the other side of the border, from the moment of independence the Beninese economy was open to the importation of all kinds of goods, which were then smuggled into neighbouring countries, including Nigeria. An important factor in the Benineois government opening her port to all kinds of overseas goods (with the exception of toxic waste, arms, and ammunition), is the fact that a major source of her internally generated revenue comes from import duties charged on imported goods. In the process, Benin's government has maintained favourable custom duties to ensure quick clearing of imported goods.[39]

In the same vein, the population difference between the two countries has encouraged smugglers to continue the illicit trade. At independence, Nigeria had a population of 60 million, while the Benin Republic had 10 million inhabitants. This difference, according to Ogunsola John Igué, means Nigeria is a very large market that attracts more goods of different kinds.[40] The development has sustained the illicit enterprise into the post-independence era.

Smuggling across the Nigeria–Benin border, before and after independence, happens in circuits; that is, via tracks well known to smugglers linking both sides of the border, waterways, and official routes connecting the borders of both countries. The following tracks are used, among others, to smuggle goods between Nigeria and Benin: the Ilara-Ketu track via Iselu; the Igolo-Idiroko track; the Saki-Parakou track via Okuta; the Porto-Novo-Ponton track via Malahoui; the Seme border track; the Save (Saki) track via Ayegun-Imeko; and the

38 *Ibid.*

39 Emeka Nwokedi, "Nigeria-Benin Relations: The Joys and Anguish of Bilateralism", in Bassey E. Ate & Bola Akinterinwa (eds.), *Nigeria and Its Immediate Neighbours: Constraints and Prospects of Sub-Regional Security in the 1990s* (Lagos: Nigerian Institute of International Affairs (NIIA), 1992), pp. 129–131.

40 Ogunsola John Igué, "Évolution du commerce clandestin entre le Dahomey et le Nigeria depuis la guerre du Biafra", *Canadian Journal of African Studies*, pp. 235–257.

Saki-Parakou track via Okuta.[41] The official land routes are roads that pass through the borders of both countries and where security personnel, especially customs and immigration officers, carry checks on vehicles and commuters for contraband. Interestingly, commercial bus drivers and traders smuggle goods across the Nigeria–Benin border mainly by giving the drivers huge sums of money to bribe customs and security personnel along the roads.

Apart from the land routes, waterways are also used by smugglers operating across the border. These include the Ouemene River, which passes through the villages of Hetin, Kessounou, and the city of Porto-Novo, and the River Agougu in Badagry, which is used to smuggle goods within Badagry and its environs. These waterways serve as channels to some tracks, such as the Ijofin-Maridjonou route. The majority of the waterways used for smuggling are located in the southern part of the border between Nigeria and the Benin Republic.[42] Waterways in particular are used to smuggle luxury goods, especially jewellery, tobacco, and alcohol.

Mastery of the geographical environment has enabled the smugglers operating across the Nigeria–Benin border to carry out their illicit trade effectively. For instance, the absence of natural or physical obstacles such as mountains and dangerous gorges makes it easy for smugglers to navigate the forest tracks and bush paths to smuggle contraband across the border. The exception is the Okpara River that separates the Sabe (Shabe) Yoruba-speaking people on both sides of the border. In the rainy season, this river usually overflows its banks, thus inhibiting communication between the two parts as well as the movement of contraband.[43]

Smuggling was more widespread in the southern parts of the Nigeria–Benin border region compared to the northern and central parts, which are not as densely populated. The central and northern parts are savannah, open grassland that is not favourable for smuggling. Moreover, the Islamic injunction that admonishes Muslims to refrain from criminal activities such as smuggling and the consumption of alcohol is also believed to have contributed to the low rate of smuggling in the area.[44]

Prior to 1967, the central and northern parts of the Nigeria–Benin border were under the administration of the Northern Region, headed by the Sarduna

41 *Ibid.*, p. 239.

42 *Ibid.*

43 Flynn K. Donna, "'We Are the Border': Identity, Exchange, and the State along the Bénin Nigeria Border", *American Ethnologist*, 24: 2, (1997), p. 328.

44 T.G.O. Gbadamosi & M.O. Junaid, "Islamic Culture and Nigerian Society", in Akinjide Osuntokun & Ayodeji Olukoju (eds.), *Nigerian Peoples and Cultures* (Ibadan: Davidson Press, 1997), p. 123.

of Sokoto, Sir Ahmandu Bello. The southern part was under the control of the government of the Western Region. Lagos, the centre of power, was under the Federal Government of Nigeria. Unlike the northern and central parts, the southern part is densely populated with several towns and villages closely linked to each other, despite the boundary separating them. Among them are Meridjonou, Adjara, Ifonyin Itedo, Avrankou, Saki, Sabe, Kobejo, Pobb, Ketu, Ilara, Save, and Chikanda.[45] It is very easy for smugglers residing in these border towns to network. Equally, the interlocking pattern of some of these border towns makes it easy for smugglers to operate. For instance, in Ilara, some of the houses have their frontage in Nigeria and their backyard in the Benin Republic.[46] It is therefore very complicated and difficult to apprehend smugglers operating in Ilara town. Contraband, such as agricultural produce, consumables, and luxury items are smuggled easily across the border through Ilara.

Ifonyintedo is another border town within the Idiroko border region where smugglers freely operate across the Nigeria–Benin border. In the 1960s and after the civil war, the entire area was agrarian. Agricultural produce was smuggled from Nigeria into Benin Republic from Ifonyintedo. Significantly, the southern part of the border is linked to major cities on the Nigeria side, notably Lagos, Abeokuta, Ibadan Ilaro, Sango Ota, Ijebu-Ode, and Sagamu.[47] Traders from these major towns and cities come to the border towns between Nigeria and Benin to purchase contraband.

Prior to the outbreak of the Nigerian Civil War (1967–1970), the main items smuggled across the borders from Nigeria include agricultural produce, namely: cocoa; groundnuts; palm kernels; enamel; bicycles; motorcycles and their accessories. On the Beninois side, alcohol, tobacco, cigarette, consumables and luxurious items were smuggled into Nigeria. However, the decision of the Beninois government to allow its airbase to be used by the International Committee of the Red Cross to provide relief material for Biafra resulted in strained relations that led to the closure of Nigeria's border with Benin Republic in 1969.[48] Shortly after war, the border was re-opened following the restoration of diplomatic relations between the two countries.

45 Ogunsola John Igué, "Évolution du commerce clandestin entre le Dahomey et le Nigeria depuis la guerre du Biafra", *Canadian Journal of African Studies*, pp. 235–257.

46 Mr. Michael Amosun (a retired teacher, politician and businessman, Owode/Yewa South Local Government Area of Ogun State, Nigeria) in discussion with Jackson Aluede, 30 December 2015.

47 Ogunsola John Igué, "Évolution du commerce clandestin entre le Dahomey et le Nigeria depuis la guerre du Biafra", *Canadian Journal of African Studies*, p. 249.

48 Emeka Nwokedi, "Nigeria-Benin Relations: The Joys and Anguish of Bilateralism", in *Nigeria and Its Immediate Neighbours: Constraints and Prospects of Sub-Regional Security in the 1990s*, p. 128.

During and immediately after the Nigerian Civil War, the production capacity of the local industries in Nigeria fell significantly. The development influenced the importation of various items into the country as well as the various goods that were smuggled into the country, especially through the Benin Republic whose seaport was opened to all kinds of goods from the economically advanced countries of Europe, North America, and Asia. After the war, several new items were smuggled across the borders of both countries. From Benin, came Western-made goods, such as fabric (textile materials), used clothes, liquor, consumables, and cigarettes, among others. On the Nigeria side, the items included, among others, used vehicles, motorcycles and their accessories, agricultural products, which were later replaced by petroleum products such as fuel and kerosene, and currencies. Interestingly, there is a paucity of statistical records or data to shed light on the volume of informal trade and smuggled goods across the borders of both countries. Nevertheless, the records of import and export trade, especially of goods that passed through the land borders between Nigeria and Benin Republic from 1966 to 1974, provide an insight into the main items smuggled across their borders during the period (see Tables 3.1 & 3.2, below).

It is interesting to note that the majority of the exporters are expatriates: Europeans, North Americans, Japanese, Indians, and Lebanese. Other prominent actors include a few Benineois and some Igbo who fled Nigeria to Benin during the Nigerian Civil War.

TABLE 3.1 Imports from Nigeria to the Benin Republic 1966–1973 (import units: 1000000)

Goods	1966	1967	1968	1969	1970	1971	1972	1973
Enamels	47	180	117					
Cycles & acc.	11	3					41	
Biscuits	35	31						
Fabrics	35							
Wood saws	32							
Cocoa	328	900	1385	1728	1371.8			
Palm oil				59		48.1		
Miscellaneous	130	300	420	600	200	150	200	435
TOTAL	188	553	600	928	1100	1594	1928	1869.9

SOURCE: IGUÉ, 1976.[a]

a Ogunsola John Igué, "Évolution du commerce clandestin entre le Dahomey et le Nigeria depuis la guerre du Biafra", *Canadian Journal of African Studies*, p. 248.

TABLE 3.2 Exports from the Benin Republic to Nigeria 1966–1973
(Export units: 1000000)

Products	1966	1967	1968	1969	1970	1971	1972	1973
Smoked fish	20	30						
Food products	53	176	216					
Tobacco/ cigarettes	66	137	207	560.40	873.20	680	1680.40	1173.90
Textiles / thrift shop		134	123	1525.00	2696.00	4270	2970.002.	569.60
Liquor	34	87	18	24645	600	265.00	640.00	572.00
Beer			28					
Pets			41					
Preserves			160.00	207.40	446.80	5005	57.40	
Miscellaneous	5	167	192	145.00	325.00	164	200.60	308.60
TOTAL	158	721	855	236.85	4366.60	6214	5297.80	5241.50

SOURCE: IGUÉ, 1976.[a]
a *Ibid.*, p. 249.

These foreigners import goods into the Benin Republic, from where they are re-exported to Nigeria and other West African countries through the formal and informal sectors. Among the foreign companies involved in the movement of goods across the border are CFAO, AOCS, John Holt, John Walden, Sodaic, Cica, Critel Fabre, Unicomer, and Hollando. Between 1971 and 1972, illegal exports from Benin to neighbouring countries were valued at a record 10.2 billion francs. This value was calculated from the surveys conducted by the Central Bank of the States West Africa (BCEAO) in department stores, Benin Republic retailers, and foreign businessmen in Cotonou. Of these 10 billion, 200 million CFA francs were exchanged with Nigeria, representing 93% of the total.[49]

Three types of goods dominated the re-export trade and smuggling across the Nigeria–Benin border during and immediately after the Nigerian Civil War: fabric/used clothing (English wax, Dutch wax, Japanese fabric, Vichy basin, terga, head scarves, handkerchiefs, and Indian and Japanese poplin); tobacco from Britain, the United States, and other European countries (cigarette brands including, among others Benson and Rothmans); alcohol/liquor (Dubonnet,

49 *Ibid.*, p. 250.

whisky, cognac, gin, rum, champagne, schnapps).[50] After the war, the demand for cloth in Nigeria increased significantly. This influenced the re-export and smuggling of fabric of various kinds, including second-hand clothes, known as *okrika*, into Nigeria. Alcohol and tobacco consumption in the country during and after the Nigerian Civil War was influenced largely by the demands of the military.

Smuggled items from the Benin Republic into Nigeria across the Nigeria–Benin border expanded from the 1980s onwards to include (frozen) poultry, meat, beer, wine, milk products, tomato preserves, wheat dough, spaghetti, noodles, fruit juice in retail packs, used cars, used tyres, and pharmaceuticals, to mention but a few.[51]

After the Nigerian Civil War, fuel soon became the main item smuggled across the Nigeria–Benin border from Nigeria. It replaced agricultural products such as cocoa, groundnuts, palm kernels, palm oil, lantern glass, and motorcycles. The smuggling of fuel from Nigeria goes beyond Benin Republic, as far as Togo and other West Africa countries in need of the commodities. One of the main factors fuelling the smuggling of petroleum products such as fuel, kerosene and gas across the Nigeria–Benin border since the 1970s is the subsidized price of such products in Nigeria, compared to neighbouring countries where the prices are higher. As a result, Nigerians involved in the illicit enterprise in collaboration with their partners in other parts of West Africa, assisted by security personnel at the borders as well as indigenes of the border communities, all connive to smuggle petroleum products to other markets in the sub-region where the price is higher.

This phenomenon started immediately after the Nigerian Civil War. Following the exportation of crude oil abroad, the Gowon-led military government decided to subsidise petroleum meant for local consumption in an attempt to satisfy certain social demands and contribute to strengthening the peace.[52] Smuggling of petroleum products across Nigeria's borders into the Benin Republic, Chad, Niger, and Togo has been encouraged by the awareness of the price differentials in Nigeria and neighbouring countries. This has encouraged the growth of the black market since the 1970s in which the border communities have become a major player. It is interesting to note that several towns and villages on the Benineois side of the border do not have filling stations to sell petroleum products to people. For instance, there is no supply centre in

50 *Ibid.*, p. 252.

51 Stephen S. Golub, "Entrepot Trade and Smuggling in West Africa: Benin, Togo and Nigeria", *The World Economy* volume 35, issue 9, (2012), pp. 6–7.

52 Nigeria Infos: L'actualitenigeriane en francais, (The Nigerian news in French) "Fuel Smuggling in Nigeria, Benin and Togo: an intractable trade", nigeriainfosblog.com.ng (accessed 28 January 2015).

Igolo, Meridjonou, Ifoyintedo, Gbawojo, Ita-Jebou, or Ipinle.[53] Even the supply towns, such as Sakete, Pobe, and Ketu do not have big storage facilities to stock petroleum products such as kerosene to meet the demands of the people, who sell in tanks and bottles of various sizes. Sakete and its environment has about 100,000 inhabitants, but there is only one filling station serving the area. Likewise, the Pobe district with 70,000 inhabitants and two industrial complexes, namely the Research Institute for Oils and Oilseeds (IRHO) and the Agonvi Agro-Industrial Complex, has only one filling station.[54] The inadequate supply of petroleum in these towns has encouraged smuggling of the product as the only way to meet demand.

The smuggling of cars (second-hand vehicles called *tokunbo* cars) into Nigeria via Benin is just one of a thriving list of criminal enterprises conducted by the men of the underworld. Several factors have encouraged this development, including: Benin's liberal economy policy, which has allowed the importation of all kinds of items into the country;[55] the low tariffs and custom duties compared to the charges and duties in Nigeria; efficient port administration; and the absence of restrictions on the age of imported vehicles, unlike Nigeria. Importers and buyers take advantage of these liberal conditions in order to evade paying customs duties and to smuggle or "fly" very old vehicles that are not allowed into Nigeria.[56] The smuggling of second-hand cars into the country usually takes place in the middle of the night via illegal routes following the bribing of customs personnel.

4 Factors Influencing Smuggling in the Nigeria-Benin Border

This section will highlight a number of factors that have encouraged smuggling in the Nigeria–Benin border area since the 1990s.

4.1 *Lack of Employment Opportunities and Increasing Poverty*

Smugglers operating in the southern area of the Nigeria–Benin border often blame their involvement in illicit enterprises on their inability to secure

53 Ogunsola John Igué, "Évolution du commerce clandestin entre le Dahomey et le Nigeria depuis la guerre du Biafra", *Canadian Journal of African Studies*, p. 255.

54 *Ibid.*, p. 256.

55 Isaac Olawale Albert, "Smuggling Second-hand Cars through the Benin-Nigeria Borders", in A.I. Asiiwaju, G. Ogun and E.C. Ojukwu,(eds.), *Cross Border Crimes and Community Policing: Prospects and Challenges in Nigeria-Benin Cross-Border Areas of Ogun State, Imeko, African University Institute, 2016,* pp. 65–67.

56 Mr. L.S. Sule, (Deputy Officer II, Customs Enforcement Unit, Statistics, Nigerian Customs Headquarters, Abuja, Nigeria) in discussion with Jackson Aluede, 21 August 2015.

employment and escape poverty.[57] Smuggling across the Nigeria–Benin border has become a lucrative venture that has improved the lives of the people residing in the Idiroko, Ilara, and Seme border towns. According to Michael Amosun, "to live comfortably in the Nigeria–Benin border area and its environs, such a person must be engaging in illicit enterprise".[58] The inability of the Nigerian government to engage the country's youth in productive ventures has continued to serve as an excuse for those in the border area to engage in smuggling as a way out of poverty.

4.2 *Failed Structural Adjustment Programme* (SAP)

The Structural Adjustment Programme (SAP) embarked upon by several African governments in the 1980s, under the influence of the International Monetary Fund (IMF) and the World Bank, failed to produce the required result. SAP was embraced by countries in Africa, Asia, and Latin America as a panacea for their economic misfortunes. It was meant to address debt repayments to commercial banks, governments, and the World Bank.[59] In the course of the implementation of SAP, many African governments, including Nigeria and the Benin Republic, were forced to adopt stringent economic policies that were unfavourable to their citizens. Some governments were even forced to introduce a moratorium on job recruitment, while others devalued their currencies. Contrary to the expectations of many African leaders, SAP brought untold hardship to their citizens.

In Nigeria, SAP was introduced in 1986 by the government of General Ibrahim Babangida. Prior to this, the country's economy was already showing signs of recession, which started during the civilian administration of Alhaji Shehu Shagari. The austerity measures put in place by the civilian government failed to address the economic situation. The failures of the austerity measures worsened the already ailing economy. The official inflation rate of the country in 1983 was 23.2%. It rose to 39.6% in 1984.[60] Several private companies laid off employees, while the federal government lacked the capacity to recruit the increasing number of unemployed Nigerians into the federal ministries

57 Chief Omolade Popola Olabokunde (The BalogunOlorundaIfonyinItedo, Owode/Yewa South Local Government Area of Ogun State, Nigeria).

58 Mr. Michael Amosun (a retired teacher, politician, and businessman, Owode/Yewa South Local Government Area of Ogun State, Nigeria).

59 Anup Shah, *Structural Adjustment – A Major Cause of Poverty,* www.globalissues.org (accessed 20 December 2015).

60 "Structural Adjustment Programme", Washington DC: The World Bank Group (2003).

and agencies. Smuggling consequently received a boost during this period, as residents of border communities engaged in illicit enterprises to sustain their livelihoods.[61]

One of the reasons the Babangida-led military regime approached the IMF and World Bank was to achieve a bailout for Nigeria, which was in the grip of economic recession. Along with the loan received from the global financial institutions came the policies of SAP. Nigerians protested against the IMF loan, knowing full well it would be accompanied by unfavourable stringent measures.[62] The implementation of the harsh economic policies of SAP led several Nigerians to seek greener pastures in foreign lands for themselves and their families. Smuggling in the Nigeria–Benin border region blossomed during this period.

In Benin Republic, the experience was similar. Following the near collapse of the country's economy in the late 1980s, President Mathieu Kerekou went to the IMF and World Bank to negotiate a loan to bailout his country. In return, the Kerekou government accepted the policies of SAP in 1989.[63] Like Nigeria, many jobless Beninois turned to smuggling across the Nigeria–Benin border to fend for themselves.

4.3 *Contrasting Economic Policies between the Neighbouring Countries*

Another factor that has encouraged smuggling along the Nigeria–Benin border is, as previously mentioned, the different economic policies of both countries. Unlike Nigeria, the economic policy of the Benin Republic is import-driven, i.e. it depends on the importation of consumables and other items. Nigeria's economy, on the other hand, although also import-driven, prohibits entry of certain goods into the country in order to protect the local industries.[64] This disparity in policy is a strong incentive for smuggling.

61 See Isaac Olawale Albert, "Smuggling Second-hand Cars through the Benin-Nigeria Borders", Flynn K. Donna, "We Are the Border": Identity, Exchange, and the State along the Bénin Nigeria Border, American Ethnologist, 24:2, 1997, p. 328.

62 Adebayo Olukoshi, "The March of Adjustment in Nigerian Economy" in Adebayo Olukoshi (ed.), *Crisis and Adjustment in the Nigerian Economy* (Lagos: JAD, 1991), p. 29, cited in Okechukwu Ibeanu and Abubakar Momoh (2008), *State Responsiveness to Public Security Needs: The Politics of Security Decision-Making, Nigerian Country Study* (London: Conflict, Security and Development Group Kings College).

63 Structural Adjustment Programme The Whirled Bank Group (2003).

64 Mr. Ambrose Obeji, (Director of Economic Manufacturing Association of Nigeria (MAN), 77 Awolowo Way, Ikeja, Lagos) in discussion with Jackson Aluede, 12 May 2015.

4.4 *Lucrative Nature of the Smuggling*

Another factor responsible for smuggling along the Nigeria–Benin border, and, indeed, other borderlands around the world, is the lucrative nature of the business. Of course, it is very difficult to estimate the annual profits of smugglers in different parts of the world, especially in the Nigeria–Benin borderland. The reasons are obvious. Smuggling is carried out in secrecy. There is no documentation of transactions by the parties involved. The illicit enterprise is carried out as an informal trading activity, devoid of official inspection and supervision. This enables smugglers to reduce risk and maximize profits. Consequently, some indigenes of the border communities have abandoned farming and other traditional occupations for the more lucrative business of smuggling, popularly called "*fayawo*", which literally translates as the business of crawling on the belly.[65]

Many people have also channelled the proceeds of smuggling into other enterprises. Some have opened filling stations, hotels, shopping centres, or embarked on transport businesses, etc.[66] The lucrative nature of the enterprise, and the ability of smugglers to outmanoeuvre security personnel at the border posts and exploit alternative routes, have encouraged many people within and outside the border communities to persist in illegal trade.

5 Impact of Smuggling on Nigeria's Economic Development

Smuggling is a major impediment to the economic development of many countries around the world. Comparatively, however, the effect of smuggling is greater in developing economies than in developed ones. Smuggling hinders the growth of the manufacturing sector of developing economies and deprives governments of much-needed revenues. Jorge I. Dominguez highlights the effects of smuggling on developing economies, which are particularly relevant to Nigeria:

> Smuggling destabilises relations with allies. It is a source of frustration in areas ranging from industrial protection to population growth. It dulls the effectiveness of foreign policy instruments, such as trade and immigration acts. And it can affect the internal structure of a society by creating new actors, power bases, and patterns of consumption. Smuggling

65 Mr. Michael Amosun (a retired teacher, politician and businessman, Owode/Yewa South Local Government Area of Ogun State, Nigeria).

66 *Ibid.*

> maybe the extreme instance of loss of state control. A part of frenzy in less developed countries to regulate the activities of multinational enterprises stems from the concern that not all of their activities are legal. ... smuggling is a more complex problem than illegal trade because it often requires the establishment of alternative market systems in the target country.[67]

The economic sabotage being committed by smugglers operating in the Nigeria–Benin border area led the governments of General Mohammadu Buhari and President Olusegun Obasanjo to close Nigeria's border with the Republic of Benin in 1984 and 2003, respectively. An Editorial in the Nigerian newspaper *The Tribune* attempts to justify the 2003 border closure with the following words:

> Earlier this month, Nigeria abruptly closed its border with The Republic of Benin. A military tank was conspicuously positioned to underscore Nigeria's seriousness about the closure. [...] Before the border closure, many Nigerians quaked in their expensive cars. These cars were the very easy targets of many cross-border robbers. The bandits terrorised major Nigerian cities in search of these cars. Everyday was a field day for smugglers. Custom officials were usually no match for them- either for their firepower or their bribes, which often disarmed the officers faster than the bullets from sophisticated guns.[68]

Nigeria has being a victim of Benin's deliberate tactics to exploit the Nigerian protective trade policy to its own advantage. Although the high tariffs are meant to protect local industries and encourage the growth of the non-oil sector, the objective has been frustrated by smuggling, particularly along the Nigeria–Benin border.[69] For instance, a 2007 report by the World Trade Organization (WTO) shows import bans and trade restrictions have been on the rise in Nigeria since 2001. Critics of the country's trade policy argue that:

> Supply, however, has failed to respond to the restrictive trade policy and tariff differentials with neighbouring countries. Instead, these measures

67 Jorge I. Domínguez, "Smuggling" *Foreign Policy*, 20 (1975), p. 87.

68 "The Benin Border Closure", *The Tribune*, 25 August 2003, p. 10.

69 Gaël Raballand and Edmond Mjekiqi, "Nigeria's Trade PolicyFacilitates Unofficial Trade but Not Manufacturing in Putting Nigeria to Work", in Volker Treichel (ed.), *A Strategy for Employment and Growth* (Washington, DC: The International Bank for Reconstruction and Development / The World Bank, 2010), p. 206.

> have created strong incentives for traders and importers to smuggle goods from neighbouring countries, such as Bénin to meet demand, inducing a non-compliant and non-transparent culture among traders, which is aggravated by corrupt behaviour on the part of many customs officials.[70]

However, the Nigerian government has continued to maintain that its economic and trade policies are aimed at protecting and promoting local industries, particularly the manufacturing sector of the economy. This explains the continuous upward review of its trade tariffs, which are now some of the highest in the world. Although bringing Nigeria's trade policies in line with those of Benin would remove the incentives that encourage smuggling along the Nigeria–Benin border, this is not a solution as it would open up Nigeria to an invasion of foreign products at the expense of local production. The option available to Nigeria, therefore, is to remain protective and increase local production to meet demand in terms of quality and quantity and to strengthen border policing and surveillance to curb smuggling.

6 Collapse of Local Industries

The activity of smugglers operating in the Nigeria–Bénin border region has contributed to the near collapse of some of the local industries in Nigeria, particularly the textile industry. Indeed, the Nigerian textile industry today is a shadow of its former self. The once flourishing industry of the 1980s and early 1990s, with over 175 mills, has witnessed the shutdown of several factories, while those still operating are producing below capacity. The smuggling of textile materials into the country has undermined local production. The consequence of this development is that many textile companies have closed, resulting in the loss of jobs for many Nigerians. Most of the textile materials smuggled into Nigeria across the Nigeria–Benin border originates from China.

In the last two decades, several Chinese textile factories have spent time studying Nigeria's fabric, which they are now successfully imitating. These imitation materials are shipped to West Africa's entrepôt states, such as the Benin Republic, where the consignments are loaded onto trucks and either driven straight across the land border between Benin and Western Nigeria or up through Niger. The World Bank estimates that the value of textiles smuggled

70 *Ibid.*

into Nigeria through Benin is $2.2bn a year, compared to local Nigerian production that has shrivelled to $40m annually.[71]

7 Loss of Revenue

The Nigerian government suffers huge annual revenue losses due to the activities of smugglers operating at the Nigeria–Benin border. The ability of the smugglers to navigate the border area in and out of Nigeria with smuggled goods has enabled them to rob the Nigerian Customs of Duty Paid Value (DPV) on contraband. Citing a World Bank report on smuggling in West Africa, Gateway Nigeria claims that about ₦750 billion ($5 billion) worth of assorted goods are smuggled into Nigeria through Benin every year.[72] The report claims there is "enough evidence" that over $400 million (₦6 billion), representing about 25% of the total current annual revenue collected by the Customs Service, is lost through smuggling across the sub-regional borders. In other words, more than $400 million in import duty revenue is lost to smugglers and their collaborators in the Nigeria–Benin border region.[73]

Between 1999 and January 2010, the Nigeria Customs Service (NCS), Badagry Area Command made a massive seizure of smuggled goods. The head of the command, Comptroller Aliu Barbriel Toba, put the value of goods seized at ₦573.3 million. Among the seizure were (*tokunbo*) vehicles, bags of rice, wines, textile materials, and vegetable oil as well as pharmaceutical products[74] In 2004, the Manufacturers Association of Nigeria (MAN) declared that the country lost $6.3billion (about ₦800 billion) in 2003 to unwholesome trade practices such as smuggling and product counterfeiting through the trafficking of contraband goods.[75] In the same vein, in 2013 PRAN (Patriotic Rice Association of Nigeria) submitted that the Nigerian government "lost revenue from imported rice from Cotonou amounting to ₦10 billion monthly but the Nigerian Customs

71 Tom Burgis, "Nigeria unravelled", *The Financial Times ,13 February 2015*, www.ft.com/stream (retrieved 28 August 2016).

72 Gateway NigerianNews (2011), "Smuggling and the Nigerian Economy", www.gatewaynigeriatv/relocate/category/nigeria-news (accessed 12 January 2016).

73 *Ibid.*

74 Ahmed, L.E. & Chilaka, F.C., "The Political Economy of Criminality Along Nigeria-Benin Republic Borders And Worsening Insecurity in Nigeria", *Journal of Social Sciences and Public Policy*, 5: 2 (2013), p. 65.

75 Dauda S. Garuba, "TransBorder Economic Crimes, Illegal Oil Bunkering and Economic Reforms in Nigeria", Policy Brief Series, no. 15, October, Global Consortium on Security Transformation, (2013), www.securitytransformation.org/gc_publications.ph, (accessed 12 July 2013).

Service's figure puts this at ₦27 billion in four months [...]".[76] Rice stakeholders in Nigeria under the aegis of the Nigeria Rice Development Association (NRDA) affirmed that the country loses ₦110 billion every year because of rice smuggling.[77] They added that when other smuggled commodities, apart from rice, are computed, Nigeria's losses will run into billions of dollars annually. The group stressed that the country was losing a huge ₦9.7 billion monthly from an estimated 80,000 metric tonnes of rice smuggled into the country from Benin alone.[78]

Other groups that have suffered from the nefarious activities of smugglers include the Chemical and Non-metallic Products Employers Federation (CANMPEF). The group has accused the Beninois government of state-sponsored smuggling, which has taken a devastating toll on Nigerian businesses and it has called on the Nigerian government to take urgent action to address the situation.[79] According to the President of the Association, Devakumar Edwin, the activities of smugglers in the Nigeria–Benin border area has led to the closure of 53 companies in Nigeria.[80] The National Union of Textile Garment and Tailoring Workers (NUTGW) has also suffered from the smuggling of cheap and counterfeit textile materials into Nigeria, through the Nigeria–Benin border. The union lamented that smuggling has led to the shutdown of several textile industries and loss of its members jobs.

The Nigerian government has also recorded huge losses due to the smuggling of its petroleum products across the border into the Benin Republic. The International Monetary Fund (IMF) estimated, as far back as 1986, that smuggled petroleum products from Nigeria form 20% of Benin, with this consumption rising to 68% by 1991.[81] Also in 1991, 17% of Cameroon's fuel consumption comprised smuggled petrol and diesel from Nigeria, despite the fact that Nigeria was a net oil importer. Officially recorded sales of petroleum products in the Benin Republic fell from 134,800 tonnes in 1986 to 63,300 tonnes by 2001, suggesting that the volume of smuggled products increased during the 1990s.[82] The increase in the smuggling of petroleum products in the mid-1980s, across

76 Sunny Ikhioya & Godwin Oritse "Smuggled rice floods Nigerian market, as merchants suffer losses", *Vanguard*, 7 October 2013, p. 5.

77 "Nigeria's Economic Survival under Smuggling Threat", *Thisday*, 30 April 2013.

78 *Ibid.*

79 "Informal Illegal Trade & Arms/Smuggling menace across Nigeria-Benin border", *Daily Independence*, 12 September 2012, p. 14.

80 *Ibid.*

81 "How To Stop Fuel Scams In West Africa", *African Business Magazine*, 20 July 2012.

82 *Ibid.*

Nigeria's borders into her immediate neighbours, was partly a response to the damaging effects of the Structural Adjustment Programme (SAP) on the country and the attendant rise in the crime rate.

Similarly, investigations into illicit oil trade in the Benin Republic in December 2005 by Action Sociale, a Beninese non-governmental organisation, revealed that about 80% of consumers in Benin buy from the informal market.[83] Interestingly, a report from an extraordinary meeting of the Beninese Cabinet on illicit oil trade, held on 2 November 2012, states that there was a predominance of the informal market in the supplies of petrol products in the country. Specifically, the informal or black oil market supplies more than 90% of the oil in the petroleum sector. Claude Allagbé, Director General of Internal Trade Promotion of the Beninese Ministry of Trade estimates that the petrol sold in the informal sector accounts for at least seven times the level of sales in the duly accredited filling stations. Taking into consideration the sales figures of the said accredited stations based on statistics from the Benin's Ministry of Trade, the legally imported fuel into the country was estimated at about 2.5 million litres per month. According to Allagbé, that means "more than 17 million litres of fuel are introduced every month into Benin by fraudulent means, which is more than 200 million litres a year".[84]

8 Smuggling Threatens the Implementation of Nigeria' Trade Policy

Nigeria's trade policy provides the blueprint that regulates the country's tariff regime, particularly those charged by the Nigerian Customs on the importation of goods and also clearly stipulate goods banned under the import prohibition list.[85] Unfortunately, the criminal activities of smugglers operating along the Nigeria–Benin border have been a major threat to the implementation of Nigeria's trade policy. The continued smuggling of contraband from the Benin Republic into Nigeria has not only violated the country's import prohibition list and tariffs on import duty across her borders, but denied the Nigerian government the realisation of its trade policy objectives. Most of the contraband smuggled from Benin into Nigeria feature on Nigeria's importation prohibition list (see tables 3.3. and 3.4).

83 Nigeria Infos: L'actualitenigeriane en Français, (The Nigerian news in French) "Fuel Smuggling in Nigeria, Benin and Togo: an intractable trade".

84 *Ibid.*

85 Mr. Ambrose Obeji, (Director of Economic Manufacturing Association of Nigeria (MAN), 77 Awolowo Way, Ikeja, Lagos).

TABLE 3.3 Nigeria's Import Prohibition List, (Contraband Goods) October 2008

Items	
Frozen poultry	Meat (beef, pork, lamb, etc.)
Eggs	Vegetable oils and fats
Spaghetti – noodles	Fruit juice in retail packs
Waters without added sugar	Waters with added sugar
Bagged cement	Medicaments (various ones)
Used pharmaceuticals	Tooth picks
Mosquito repellant coils	Plastics
Electric generators sound proof casings	Used car tyres
Corrugated paper, paper boards, and boxes	Toilet paper and facial tissues
Textile fabrics of all types and articles of clothing	Furniture
Hollow glass bottles for beverage	Gaming machines
Footwear and bags of leather and plastic	Ball point pens
Used air conditioners and compressors	Telephone re-charge cards
Used motor vehicles over 10 years old	Finished soaps

SOURCE: NIGERIAN CUSTOMS, PROVIDED BY THE WORLD BANK, CITED IN STEPHEN S. GOLUB, "ENTREPOT TRADE AND SMUGGLING IN WEST AFRICA: BENIN, TOGO AND NIGERIA", *THE WORLD ECONOMY* (2012).[a]

a Stephen S. Golub, "Entrepot Trade and Smuggling in West Africa: Benin, Togo and Nigeria".

In 2016, the Nigerian Ministry of Finance circulated a list of items banned from entering the country either through its seaports or land borders. This is part of ongoing efforts to control importation and protect Nigeria's local industries.

The smuggling of the listed items, particularly through the Nigeria–Benin border, has continued to weaken the production capacity of Nigerian manufacturing companies. The contraband goods find their ways onto the Nigerian market and, because of their low price compared to locally produced goods, they have an advantage over similar goods made for the Nigerian market. The effect of this development is that, due to low sales, some manufacturing companies have been forced to downsize their staff in order to remain in business, or, in a worst case scenario, have closed down completely.

TABLE 3.4 List of Prohibited Items by the Nigerian Government in 2016

1	Live or dead Birds, including poultry
2	Pork, Beef
3	Bird's eggs, excluding hatching eggs
4	Refined vegetable oil excluding refined linseed, castor and oil. Crude vegetable oil are however not banned
5	Cane or beet sugar and chemically pure sucrose, in solid form containing added flavouring or colouring matter
6	Cocoa butter, powder and cakes
7	Spaghetti/noodles
8	Fruit juice in retail pack
9	Water, including mineral waters and aerated waters, containing added sugar or sweeting matter or flavoured, ice snow
10	Bagged cement
11	Waste pharmaceuticals
12	Soaps and detergents
13	Sanitary ware made from plastic
14	Rethreaded and used pneumatics tyres, excluding used truck tyres for rethreading of size 11.00 x 20 and above 40 12. 20. 10 00
15	Corrugated paper and paper boards
16	Carpets and other textile floor coverings failing
17	Used motor vehicles 15 years
18	Furniture
19	Ball point pens and parts, including refills
20	Hollow glass bottles with a capacity exceeding 150 ml (0.15 litres) of all kinds used for packaging beverages from breweries and other beverages and drinks companies

SOURCES: OLADEINDE OLAWOYIN, "25 ITEMS BANNED FROM IMPORTED INTO NIGERIA (FULL LIST)", *PREMIUM TIMES*, 6 JANUARY 2017, P. 12.

9 Conclusion: Tackling the Menace of Smuggling

The Nigerian government has made several attempts, some in collaboration with the Beninois government, to curtail smuggling along the Nigeria–Benin border. On two occasions, 1984 and 2003, the Nigerian government closed its border with the Republic of Benin in a bid to curb smuggling.[86] The Nigerian

86 Ehikioye, A., "Why Nigeria moved against Benin Republic", *The Comet*, 17 August 2003, p. 5.

government has also approved joint border patrols by Nigerian and Beninois security personnel in order to reduce the scale of smuggling along their common border.[87] In the same vein, the two governments have signed cross-border cooperation treaties aimed at addressing smuggling and other border-related challenges. In 1984, Nigeria signed the Quadrupletite Agreement with her neighbours, partly aimed at bringing an end to smuggling. Nigeria's then head of state, General Ibrahim Babangida, expressed optimism that the cooperation would be fruitful. "We are better prepared to combat criminals, incapacitate smugglers, and defeat the traffickers in arms, drugs and currencies", he said.[88] Before the reopening of the border in 2003, Nigeria and the Republic of Benin established the Joint Committee on Commerce (JCC) with the aim of encouraging Benineois to take advantage of the huge Nigerian market to bring their goods legally into Nigeria, rather than through the back door.[89] These efforts have produced mixed results, but have not succeeded in putting an end to smuggling across the Nigeria–Benin border or in reducing the effect on Nigeria's economic development. However, to date, the Nigeria government has yet to consider the use of incentives to discourage smuggling into the country and to dissuade Nigerian importers from patronising the Beninois seaport. Moreover, the Nigerian government must evolve a more realistic border management policy that would effectively and efficiently address border-related problems, including smuggling. The government can learn a lot from the SMART border policy of the United States in relation to Mexico, for example. Measures could include donating equipment to the Republic of Benin to fight the menace of smuggling, prompt information exchange, and ensure the full implementation of the ecowas Protocols on the movement of goods imported through the seaport of a neighbouring country. The regulation stipulates that the custom personnel of the country in question will accompany the consignments to the land border of the receiving country with the appropriate custom papers to prevent the loss of revenue. The Nigerian government must adopt a holistic approach and a broader border policy that not only addresses smuggling, but other border-related problems with its immediate neighbours. Finally, the Nigerian government should re-examine its foreign policy, which has been exploited by smugglers wanting to turn Nigeria into a dumping ground for all manner of imported items.

---

87 Folusho Aileru, "Nigeria, Benin for joint border patrol", *New Nigerian*, 22 June, 1992, p. 1.

88 "Nigeria, 3 Others Sign Pact", *New Nigerian* 11 December 1984, pp. 1, 12.

89 Yemi Akinsuyi, "FG Lifts Ban on Beninois Goods", *Thisday*, 31 May 2005, p. 17; Oluyinka Akintunde, "FG lifts ban on textiles from Benin Republic", *The Punch*, 29 November 2004, p. 29.

Bibliography

Adamoli, S., et al., *Organised Crime Around the World Helsinki*, European Institute for Crime Prevention and Control, 1998.

Ahmed, L.E., and F.C. Chilaka, "The Political Economy of Criminality Along Nigeria-Benin Republic Borders And Worsening Insecurity in Nigeria", *Journal of Social Sciences and Public Policy*, 5: 2 (2013), p. 65.

Aileru, F., "Nigeria, Benin for Joint Border Patrol", *New Nigerian*, 22 June 1992, p. 1.

Akinsuyi, Y., "FG Lifts Ban on Beninoise Goods", *Thisday*, 31 May 2005, p. 17.

Akintunde, O., "FG lifts ban on textiles from Benin Republic", *The Punch*, 29 November 2004, p. 29.

Akinwumi, A., and R. Musa, "Smuggling Import N7trn worth of Goods Annually, say Senate", *Daily Independent*, 18 July 2017, p. 2.

Albert, I.O., "Smuggling Second-Hand Cars through the Benin-Nigeria Borders", in A.I. Asiwaju et al. (eds.), *Cross Border Crimes and Community Policing: Prospects and Challenges in Nigeria-Benin Cross-Border Areas of Ogun State*, Imeko: African University Institute, 2006.

Andreas, P., "Gangster's Paradise: The Untold History of the United States and International Crime", *Foreign Affairs* (March/April 2013), pp. 23–24.

Anene, J.C., *The International Boundaries of Nigeria 1885–1960: The Framework of an Emergent African Nation*, London: Longman Group Limited, 1970.

Asiwaju, A.I., *Boundaries and African Integration: Essay In Comparative History and Policy Analysis*, Lagos: Panaf Publishing, 2003.

Blum, C., *Cross-Border Flows Between Nigeria and Benin: What Are the Challenges for (Human) Security?*, Abuja: Friedrich-Ebert-Stiftung, 2014.

Burgis, T., "Nigeria Unravelled", *The Financial Times*, February 13, 2015. Retrieved from www.ft.com/stream (accessed 28 August 2016).

Collins, J.D., "The Clandestine Movement of Groundnuts across the Niger–Nigeria Boundary", *Canadian Journal of African Studies*, 10:2 (1976), pp. 262–267.

Commons.wikimedia.org/wiki/File:Dahomey-Nigeria_boundary_LOC_76696106jpg.

Cooke, J.J., "Anglo-French Diplomacy and the Contraband Arms Trade in Colonial Africa, 1894–1897", *African Studies Review*, 17: 1 (1974), pp. 34–35.

Day, A.J. (ed.), *Border and Territorial Disputes*, London: Longman Group Limited, 1982.

Dioka, L.C., *Lagos and Its Environs*, Lagos: First Academic Publishers, 2001, pp. 201–202.

Domínguez, J.I., "Smuggling", *Foreign Policy*, 20 (1975), p. 87.

Donna, F.K., "'We Are the Border': Identity, Exchange, and the State along the Bénin Nigeria Border", *American Ethnologist*, 24: 2 (1997), p. 328.

Ehikioye, A., "Why Nigeria Moved against Benin Republic", *The Comet*, 17 August 2003, p. 5.

Ering, S.O., "Trans-border Crime and Its Socio-economic Impact on Developing Economies", *Journal Sociology and Anthropology*, 2: 2 (2011), pp. 73–80.

Felsen, D. & A. Kalaitzidis, "A Historical Overview of Transnational Crime", in P. Reichel (ed.), *Handbook of Transnational Crime & Justice*, London: Sage Publications, 2005.

Garuba, D.S., "Trans-Border Economic Crimes, Illegal Oil Bunkering and Economic Reforms in Nigeria", Policy Brief Series, no. 15, (October 2013), Global Consortium on Security Transformation. Retrieved from www.securitytransformation.org/gc_publications.ph (accessed 12 July 2013).

Gastrow, P., "African Actors in International Organized Crime", in J.T. Picarelli (ed.), *International Organized Crime: The African Experience*, Courmayeur Mont Blanc: International Scientific and Professional Advisory Council of the United Nations Crime Prevention and Criminal Justice Programme ISPAC, 2010.

Gateway Nigerian News, "Smuggling and the Nigerian Economy", (2011). Retrieved from www.gatewaynigeriatv/relocate/category/nigeria-news (accessed 12 January 2016).

Golub, S.S., "Entrepot Trade and Smuggling in West Africa: Benin, Togo and Nigeria", *The World Economy* (2012), p. 1.

Hansen, N., *The Border Economy: Regional Development in the Southwest*, Austen, TX: University of Texas Press, 1981.

Hargreaves, J.D., "The Making of the Boundaries: Focus on West Africa", in A.I. Asiwaju (ed.), *Partitioned Africans: Ethnic Relations across Africa's International Boundaries 1884–1984*, London: C. Hurst & Company, 1985.

"How To Stop Fuel Scams In West Africa", *African Business Magazine*, 20 July 2012, p. 14.

Igué, O.J., "Clandestine Trade Developments between Dahomey and Nigeria since the Biafra War", *Canadian Journal of African Studies / Canadian Journal of African Studies*, 10: 2 (1976), pp. 235–257.

Igué, J.O. and B.G. Soulé, *L'Etat Entrepôt au Benin: Commerce Informel ou Reponse ala Crise?* Karthala: Paris, 1992.

Ikhioya, S., and G. Oritse, "Smuggled Rice Floods Nigerian Market, as Merchants Suffer Losses", *Vanguard*, 7 October 2013, p. 5.

"Informal Illegal Trade & Arms/Smuggling Menace across Nigeria–Benin Border", *Daily Independence*, 12 September 2012, p. 14.

McEwen, A.C., "The Establishment of the Nigeria/Benin Boundary, 1889–1989", *The Geographical Journal*, 157: 1 (1991), p. 62.

"Nigeria, 3 Others Sign Pact", *New Nigerian*, 11 December 1984, pp. 1, 12.

"Nigeria's Economic Survival under Smuggling Threat", *Thisday*, 30 April 2013, p. 4.

Nigeria Infos: L'actualite nigeriane en francais, (The Nigerian news in French) "Fuel Smuggling in Nigeria, Benin and Togo: an intractable trade", Retrieved from nigeriainfosblog.com.ng (accessed 28 January 2015).

Nwokedi, E., "Nigeria-Benin Relations: The Joys and Anguish of Bilateralism", in B.E. Ate and B. Akinterinwa, *Nigeria and its Immediate Neighbours: Constraints and*

Prospects of Sub-Regional Security in the 1990s, Lagos: Nigerian Institute of International Affairs (NIIA), 1992.

Olawoyin, O., "25 Items Banned from Imported into Nigeria", *Premium Times*, 6 January 2017, p. 12.

Olorunfemi, A., "The Liquor Traffic Dilemma in British West Africa: The Southern Nigerian Example, 1895–1918", *The International Journal of African Historical Studies*, 17: 2 (1984), pp. 240–241.

Olson, E.L., et al., "Introduction", in E.L. Olson, D.A. Shirk, and Andrew Selee (eds.), *Shared Responsibility: US–Mexico Policy Options for Confronting Organized Crime*, Washington, DC: Mexico Institute, Woodrow Wilson International Center for Scholars, 2010.

Olukoshi, A.O. and C.I. Obi, "The State of Nigeria's Trade Relations with its Neighbours: Issues and Problems", in G.A. Obiozor, A.O. Olukoshi, and C.I. Obi (eds.), *West African Regional Economic Integration: Nigerian Policy Perspectives for the 1990s*, Uppsala: Nordiska Afrika Institute, 1996.

Onyekpe, N., "The Nature and Problems of Nigeria's Dependent Economic Status", in Y. Akinyeye (ed.), *Nigeria and the Wider World in the 20th Century: Essay in Honour of Professor Akinjide Osuntokun*, Ibadan: Davidson Press, 2003.

Passas, N. "Cross-Border Crime and the Interface between Legal and Illegal Actors", in P.C. Duynevan, K. Lampevon, and N. Passas (eds.), *Upperworld and Underworld in Cross-Border Crime*, Nijmegen: Wolf Legal Publishers (WLP), 2002.

Raballand, G., and E. Mjekiqi, "Nigeria's Trade Policy Facilitates Unofficial Trade but Not Manufacturing", in Volker Treichel (ed.), *Putting Nigeria to Work A Strategy for Employment and Growth*, Washington, DC: The International Bank for Reconstruction and Development / The World Bank, 2010.

Shah, A., "Structural Adjustment – A Major Cause of Poverty", *Global Issues* 24 March, 2013 Retrieved from www.globalissues.org (accessed 20 December 2015).

"Structural Adjustment Programme", Washington, DC: The World Bank Group 2003, p. 5.

"The Benin Border Closure", *The Tribune*, 25 August 2003, p. 10.

Touval, S., "Partitioned Groups and Inter-State Relations", in A.I. Asiwaju (ed.), *Partitioned Africans, Ethnic Relations across Africa's International Boundaries* 1884–1984, London: C. Hurst & Company, 1985.

United Nations Security Council, "Report of the Secretary General on Illicit Cross-Border Trafficking Movement", New York: Security Council Report, 19 October 2012, p. 2.

UNODC, "United Nations Convention against Transnational Organized Crime and the Protocols Thereto", Vienna: United Nations Publications, 2004.

Van Duyne, P.C., "Organized Crime Markets in a Turbulent Europe", *European Journal on Criminal Policy and Research*, 1: 3 (1993), pp. 10–29.

Vorrath, J., "On the Margin of Statehood? State-Society Relations", in I.W. Zartman (ed.), *Understanding Life in the Borderlands: Boundaries in Depth and in Motion*, Athens, GA: The University of Georgia Press, 2010.

Wilson, T.M., and H. Donnan, "Border and Border Studies", in T.M. Wilson and H. Donnan (eds.), *A Companion to Border Studies*, Oxford: Blackwell Publishing Ltd, 2012.

Zartman, I.W., "Identity, Movement and Response", in I.W. Zartman (ed.), *Understanding Life in the Borderlands: Boundaries in Depth and in Motion*, Athens, GA: The University of Georgia Press, 2010.

Private Communications

Algbierere, O.B., interviewed by Jackson Aluede, 2015, Lagos, National Drug Law Enforcement Agency (NDLEA) Lagos Office.

Amosun, M., interviewed by Jackson Aluede, 2015, Owode/Yewa South Local Government Area of Ogun State, Nigeria.

Obeji, A., interviewed by Jackson Aluede, 2015, Manufacturing Association of Nigeria (MAN), Head Office77 Awolowo Way, Ikeja, Lagos.

Omolade, P.O. interviewed by Jackson Aluede, 2015, Owode/Yewa South Local Government Area of Ogun State, Nigeria.

Sule, L.S., interviewed by Jackson Aluede, 2015, Nigerian Customs Headquarters, Abuja, Nigeria.

CHAPTER 4

Changing Patterns of Crime and Malfeasance in Nigerian Port Environments since the 1990s

Edmund Chilaka

1 Introduction

This chapter examines the phenomenon of crime and criminal activities in Nigerian port environments with the aim of tracing the patterns and changes in the trend since the 1990s. Nigerian ports constitute a major part of global sea trade, which accounts for 92% of the transportation of goods and cargo generated by international trade; the remainder is carried by air, rail, road and pipeline modes. The Nigerian economy is the destination for nearly 70% of West Africa's sea trade and crime rates within its port environments are very high despite the security rules governing regional sea trade.

Port environments are special locations where sailing ships make contact with people ashore after voyages that have lasted for days, weeks, or months. In security parlance, a port is technically defined as any location with an established ship-to-shore interface. Many activities take place in port environments although the primary goal is the loading and offloading of goods or cargo. The predominance of seaborne international is due to the relatively low cost of sea freight compared to air, road, rail, and pipeline modes. Since the new millennium, the demands of world trade, compelled by the new trends of globalisation, security, and computer cybernetics (i.e. the worldwide web/internet), have forced port industries in developing countries to catch up fast with the benchmarks of speed and efficiency previously set by mostly developed maritime nations. Part of this efficiency is the security benchmark aimed at reducing crime and criminality to a minimum.

2 Overview of Criminality in the Global Port Industry

The literature on criminal activities within and around port environments globally shows some interesting dimensions. Due to the huge proportion of international trade conveyed by sea, a high propensity of criminal activities has been logged by police and security forces in almost all maritime jurisdictions all

 | DOI:10.1163/9789004396289_006

over the world. However, the variety and scope of the crimes usually conform to the specific indices of development or underdevelopment of the countries surveyed. For example, illegal migration, people smuggling, illicit drug rings, and tax evasion dominate the crime scenes in the United States, the ports of Canada, Europe, and advanced Asian countries, whereas pilfering, piracy, container broaching, vandalism, robbery, and document frauds are typically reported in most ports in Africa, Latin America, and developing Asian nations.[1]

Clinard and Abbott have shown that the high rate of crime in most developing nations, of which port crimes constitute an aspect, is a reflection of the phenomenal development taking place there, and that the advanced nations of today recorded similar occurrences at the nascent stages of their developmental strides.[2] In fact, Clinard and Abbott asserted that higher crime rates ultimately indicate rapid advancement in a Western-style development of society, including the establishment of democratic or representative governments, fast-paced construction of schools, universities, city and intercity expressways, hospitals, electricity provision, higher living standards of the citizenry, and substantial provision of legal and police security infrastructure for the enforcement of law and order. According to Clinard and Abbott, it is within these ambits of development that the capacity for criminal legislation, crime detection, reporting and processing, could be empowered through the establishment of appropriate regulatory institutions and monitoring machinery. Thus, we can see the changing patterns of criminality in developing countries' port environments as episodic features of socio-economic and political progress in the port industries in particular.

Although a recent review shows that crime is on a downward trend in Europe and North America, one of the major crimes in British ports is the smuggling of people and hard drugs.[3] Many criminals have made fortunes from the increasing illegal migration by small boats of Africans, poor Asians, and Middle Easterners fleeing the wars in Syria, Iraq, and Libya. Charging as much as $10,000 per head to ferry the migrants, the traffickers use wooden boats, polypropylene dinghies, or rigid-hulled inflatable boats, equipped with high-powered outboard engines. These boats are then filled beyond capacity for the risky sea voyage to thirteen landing sites on UK shores, including Calais and Dover, where the migrants are assisted in entering into the country by whatever

1 "9 Types of Maritime Crimes", *Marine Insight*, 21 July 2016.

2 Marshall B. Clinard and Daniel J. Abbott, *Crime in Developing Countries: A Comparative Perspective*, (New York: John Wiley & Sons, 1973).

3 "The curious case of the fall in crime", *The Economist*, 408: 8845, 20 July 2013, p. 9.

means possible.[4] The arrangement of passports, fake or genuine, processing of applications for asylum, etc. are other aspects of this illegality, which involves operators from several sectors of society.

Tax fraud and evasion is another crime common in British ports. It often occurs with collusion from abroad. For example, the EU Anti-Fraud Office (OLAF) has claimed that "systematic failures by UK customs officials have allowed criminal gangs to defraud the European Union of at least £2bn in just four years plus billions more in lost Value Added Tax [VAT] [and] the failures by Customs and Excise has cost at least 5.2bn Euros (£4.5bn) in lost duties and VAT".[5] According to the agency, this fraud was perpetrated with the collusion of Chinese partners who shipped clothing and footwear into the UK ports of Dover and Felixstowe and utilised warehousing arrangements co-owned by the colluding partners in a series of transactions that pitted the UK authorities against the EU's OLAF in unending fraud investigations. UK ports and small beaches now targeted in such crimes include Dymchurch in Kent, Chichester Marina, Whitstable in Kent, Hull, Immingham in North East Lincolnshire, Tilbury, Purfleet in Essex, and Newhaven and Portsmouth on the south coast.[6]

In fact, the work of Clinard and Abbot serves as a general theoretical framework for this study because it profiled a global coverage of various crime cases in several US, African, Asian, Latin American, and European countries revealing data that highlights the diversity of their socio-economic and political heterogeneity to explain the crime statistics.[7] Their coverage of developing countries, for example, implicates poverty, lack of reporting procedures or policing infrastructure, as well as poor human development indices as determinants of the perceived levels of criminality in their communities.[8] With reference to Nigeria, this framework explains the fluctuation in actual port crime conditions, both in the recorded incidences and the associated social development in the sector. After the 2001 port reforms and concession programme, for example, the pattern of criminality in the ports changed significantly. It became highly reduced in most terminals. In one of the new greenfield developments in Lagos, Ports and Terminal Multiservices Limited (PTML) built and operated by Grimaldi Line on a Build, Operate and Transfer (BOT)

4 Peter Dominiczak, Steven Swinford, and Laura Hughes, "Britain's border weakspots: The areas identified by criminal gangs smuggling hundreds of migrants into the UK", *The Telegraph*, 1 June 2016.

5 Andrew Hosken, "Criminal gangs use UK ports to defraud EU customs", BBC, 5 April 2017.

6 *Ibid.*

7 Clinard and Abbott, *Crime in Developing Countries*, pp. 35–69.

8 *Ibid.*

basis, one importer who had suffered pilferages at other terminals reported that the incidence of pilfering there had reduced to zero.[9]

According to him, this was in sharp contrast to his experience at another Lagos terminal, a roll-on, roll-off (RoRo) port, where he complained of pilferage from a second-hand Mack tanker lorry, which he imported and was shipped aboard *MV Morning Charlotte* in July 2017. After initial checks and confirmation by his agent that the lorry was intact, when the vehicle was leaving the port some days later, it was found that the diesel in the tank had been siphoned and the fuel tank cover and ignition battery had been stolen.[10] The usual report to the terminal's management was made but the missing items were not recovered. He attributed the differential crime rates to the management and ownership structures of the concessions, implying that the traditional weaknesses of the Nigerian Ports Authority (NPA)-built terminals might still be dogging their concessionaires, whereas BOT operators such as Grimaldi Line appear to have a firmer grip on their investments and activities. Thus, in comparative analysis using Clinard and Abbot's framework, the ports in different parts of the world are now coping better with the variegated anomies in line with the levels of national socio-economic development.

For Asian ports, such as those in China, port crimes tend to assume a multinational dimension. For example, the rampant distribution of narcotic drugs through several nations where Chinese dealers have established networks inspired the UN Office on Drugs and Crime to call for China to sign up to the Global Container Control Programme, which "would allow container shipments from the two countries [China and Australia] to be risk-profiled to other places, greatly improving the security of the container trade".[11] The decision was made following a complaint by Jeremy Douglas, the regional representative for the UN Office on Drugs and Crime, about the illegal flood of narcotics, crystal meth, also known as "ice", during a seizure worth A$1.26 billion (HK$7 billion) in Sydney and the arrest of three Hong Kongese and a mainland associate.[12] The Global Container Control Programme, which was introduced in 2004, is now effective in 52 countries where major drug seizures, including "23 metric tonnes of cocaine, around 6 metric tonnes of cannabis and 1.2 metric tonnes of heroin worldwide were made in 2013". The success of this programme can be attributed to "basic procedures such as investigating cargo manifests

9 Interview with Mark Khima by author, 15 July 2017.

10 *Ibid.*

11 Danny Lee, "Hong Kong, China cargo ports crucial to stopping transnational drug smuggling: UN request to sign up to global crackdown", *South China Morning Post*, 21 February 2016.

12 *Ibid.*

and invoices to spot red flags".[13] According to the UN Office, the major Southeast Asian ports in Thailand, Indonesia, the Philippines, Vietnam, Malaysia, Karachi (Afghanistan's port-of-call in the massive exporting of heroin), and the Panama Canal are all covered in the programme.

In the Americas, the situation in Canadian ports concerns the smuggling of "...precursor chemicals, illegal drugs and counterfeit goods", according to Canada's official releases.[14] The most common items of crime include stolen cars and synthetic drugs exported through Canadian ports by organised crime groups. They conceal the materials in containers, engage in the false declaration of shipping documents, and use transit countries to try and frustrate tracing by customs authorities. To the south of the border, port crimes in the US mainland is mirrored by the situation at the busiest port in the country, the Ports of New York and New Jersey, where, with the expansion of facilities in the mid-1980s, "more robberies, assaults, thefts and other crimes than ever", such as rape and muggings, were reported over a five-year period; in fact, 3,300 crimes were reported in 1983.[15] Despite an operating history of nearly 500 years since 1524, crimes levels at this port, as at other frontline US ports, has continued to escalate with the advances in human development and technology, especially with the heightened interconnectedness of the global maritime community. Thus, in addition to conventional crimes, the scourge of cyber attacks now afflicts ports on a global scale. Based on Clinard and Abbot's hypothesis, it might be that the higher level of human development index in the US accounts for both the higher reported figures of conventional crimes and the deadlier effects of new crimes such as cyber attacks. For example, in one such incident, a "cyber attack in Europe [on a particular] Tuesday morning closed operations at the Maersk shipping terminal at Pier 400 in the Port of Los Angeles ", the following day and grounded shipping movements and operations for two straight days, "... provoking concerns from Congress over the vulnerability of American ports".[16] The global attack knocked out the carrier's computer network, which controlled cargo operations and ship programming. Thus, the characteristics of port crimes are highly environmental in nature and, in some cases, culture-bound.

---

13 *Ibid.*

14 "Marine Ports and Organized Crime", Organized Crime Research Brief no. 25, accessed https://www.publicsafety.gc.ca/cnt/rsrcs/pblctns/rgnzd-crm-brf-25/rgnzd-crm-brf-25-eng.pdf on 11 July 2017.

15 William R. Greer, "As Port Authority Bus Terminal has Expanded, so has Problem of Crime", *The New York Times*, 11 June 1984.

16 Rachel Uranga, "LA port's largest terminal remains closed after cyberattack", *Long Beach Press Telegram*, 28 June 2017.

3 The Peculiarity of Crimes, Criminality, and Malfeasance in Port Environments

Crime, criminality, and malfeasance of all sorts within port environments attract special attention because of their peculiarity. Ports are the physical meeting points between international seafarers and trading ships, and peoples and authorities of the maritime nations involved in international trade. Consequently, crimes committed within port environments are more likely to involve or impact foreigners and foreign business interests directly. This situation can provoke diplomatic consequences, tit-for-tat or international court actions by virtue of prevailing admiralty laws to which the maritime nations are signatories. For example, a fire incident aboard a foreign ship berthed at Apapa Port in Nigeria will immediately activate global news alerts by the world wire news services because of the possibilities of terrorism and due to other implications such as marine insurance claims, locally and overseas.

In such a situation, the embassy of the flag state of registration and countries of the ship's crew might be notified to stand ready in case of emergency procedures for rescue, hospitalisation, repatriation, or other essential measures, depending on the seriousness of the fire. Of course, the ship's agent, as a rule, would act on these notifications as the chief coordinator of the remedies and responses. Likewise, any serious attack on a berthed ship or her crew, either by an individual or a group of criminals, would elicit a set of reactions, also depending on the intensity and scope of the incident. Conversely, a bigger fire raging at a 25-storey office building in the same city, even if a few poles from the port gate, would result in barely half the international stir as the burning carrier! Thus, a significant port crime has the potential to trigger a chain of reactions that could traverse the globe within a matter of hours, especially with the speed of today's wireless telecommunication and information superhighway. This justifies the very high or critical level of security rating usually assigned to port crimes, criminality, and malfeasance.

4 The History of Port Crimes in Nigeria

The scope of this study covers Nigeria's system of six major ports, located along the Atlantic shoreline between the two coastal borders at Lagos and Calabar. These ports serve Africa's most populous and largest economy of nearly 200m people. For administrative purposes, the ports were zoned into two, namely, Eastern and Western Zones, under the control of the Nigerian Port Authority

(NPA) until August 2017 when the Board announced changes to the structure.[17] The Eastern Zone, with headquarters in Port Harcourt, was composed of the Rivers Port Complex, Onne Port Complex, Calabar Port, and Warri Port. The Western Zone, with headquarters at Apapa, comprised the Lagos Port Complex and Tin Can Island Port Complex. Other significant port facilities under the management of the NPA include the Kirikiri Lighter Terminal, Phases 1 and 2 (located at Kirikiri near Apapa), the Lily-Pond Container Terminal (Ijora), and the Ikorodu Port at Ikorodu, all in Lagos. Many other wharves and jetties (public and private), including the crude oil loading jetties in the Niger Delta region dot the country's coastal waters, some at inshore locations, others along the shoreline or within the exclusive economic zone (EEZ (see map 4.1)).

Since port crimes and malfeasance are offences perpetrated mainly against goods in transit, they are closely monitored, detected, and controlled by the authority responsible for cargo handling at each point in time. In Nigerian ports, from the inception of the Port Act of 1955, cargo handling was managed by the NPA until the port reforms ushered in the concessionaires in 2006. The

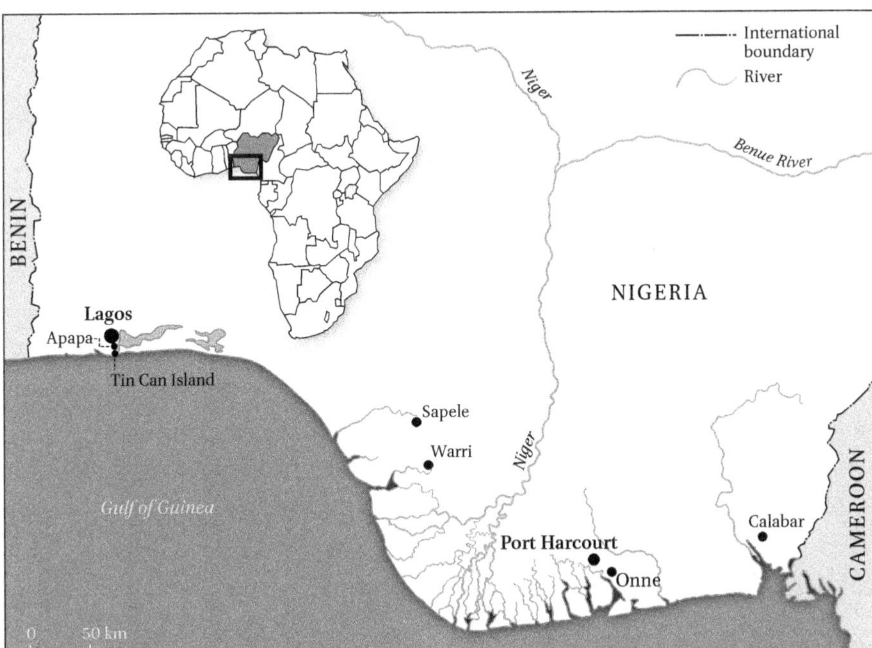

MAP 4.1 Sketch map of the major port locations in Nigeria
NEL DE VINK (DEVINK MAPDESIGN)

17 "NPA Board Approves New Structure", email message to author, 25 August 2017.

patterns of crimes and criminality in the port environments can, therefore, be studied under the two analytical periods of pre- and post-concession eras. Before the advent of seaport reform and the concession programme in the new millennium, the trajectory of crimes in Nigerian ports reflected the general level of crime and corruption in the wider society, where armed robbery was adjudged the dominant crime in the country.[18] In the post-concession period, however, there has been a remarkable reduction of port crimes in terms of scope, intensity, and frequency. As analysed below, the pre-concession era of port crimes reflected the spate of crimes in the wider society, which was increasing annually and seemingly intractable (See Table 4.1). According to

TABLE 4.1 Volume of Cargo Pilfered within Nigerian Seaports from 1995–2013

Year	Volume of Cargo Pilfered (Metric Tons)	% Volume of Cargo Pilfered
1995	2,177	
1996	3,570	
1997	5,213	
1998	3,817	
1999	2,411	1.53
2000	5,369	27.9
2001	3,415	13.8
2002	6,009	23.8
2003	6,842	24.5
2004	8,741	32.5
2005	9,322	31.9
2006	4,151	12.3
2007	3,322	8.0
2008	4,981	10.9
2009	4,981	10.9
2010	3,093	6.6
2011	2,111	4.1
2012	1,112	2.4
2013	2,915	

SOURCE: NPA OPERATIONAL STATISTICS DATABASE 2013.

18 Ukoji Vitus Nwankwo and Okolie-Osemene James, "A Study of Crime Reporting in Nigeria", *Nigeria Watch Project* 2016, in www.nigeriawatch.org>html>ukoji2016, (accessed 25 August 2017).

Transparency International, Nigeria was rated as one of the world's most corrupt nations, in the same league with Ethiopia, Somalia, Indonesia, and Nicaragua.[19] Topping the list of common crimes in Nigerian ports during the study period was the pilfering of goods, followed by container broaching, robbery, and bribery and corruption at the gates and offices where goods were cleared. There were also cases of fraud, arson, burglary, drug trafficking, gun running, vehicular break-ins, intimidation of port users by security personnel on duty, stowaways, illegal fishing, illegal bunkering, smuggling, and assault.[20]

Stowing away is a crimes with international ramifications. For example, ships in which stowaways have been caught are liable to be detained by the maritime authorities and can face the financial implications of repatriating the individuals to their countries of origin, including their one-way air tickets and any other associated expenses. They could also be subjected to other punishments depending on the legal codes of the nations where they are caught. In view of this, ship captains and terminal management in Nigeria take extra measures to ensure that stowaway checks are conducted in every part of the vessel where stowaways could hide before the vessel leaves the port.

However, as a recent case of seven Nigerian stowaways caught at Tema port shows, the lure to travel abroad continues to push those desperate enough to take such risks. According to Paul Ansah Asare, the Marketing and Public Relations Manager of Tema Port, "the suspects were arrested on 25 August 2015 on board *MV Guo Tuo 108*, after two of them disembarked, thinking that they were in South Africa instead of Ghana".[21] The criminals had hidden in the ship's hatch, intent on making their way to South Africa, not knowing that the vessel was programmed to call at other ports before the final destination. When two of them emerged from their hideouts at Tema, thinking that the ship was in Johannesburg, officials of the Ghana Ports and Harbours Authority arrested them and searched the ship to discover their five accomplices. They were handed over to the Ghana Immigration Services officials who took them to the Nigerian High Commission for repatriation. Whether they were processed for the Ghanaian currency, Cedi, GHc250 fine stipulated by Ghana law was not stated. Generally, however, incidences of such crimes have drastically reduced during the post-concession era, following the implementation of international-standard security measures. Nevertheless, the International Maritime Bureau

19 "Nigeria Corruption Rank 1996–2017", *Trading Economics*, 2017.

20 Extract from the study's survey, August 2017.

21 Della Russel Ocloo, "Seven Nigerian stowaways arrested at Tema Port", *Graphic Online*, 5 September 2015.

(IMB) still categorises Nigeria together with India as being among the top five spots in sea crime reporting for 2015.[22]

Other examples of crimes include a reported attack against *MV Cool Aster*, which was loading palm kernel cake for export at Berth 19A at the Apapa Port about 2100 hours on 1 July 2009. The hoodlums gained entrance to the ship but were chased by the crew, jumped overboard, and escaped in their boat; nothing was stolen from the ship. Again, on 27 December 2009 at about 0500 hours, hoodlums suspected to have come with a speedboat from Ogogoro Village, Apapa attempted to board *MV Canarsie Princess*, which was laden with raw bulk sugar. Nothing was stolen from the ship and no arrest was made.[23]

The crimes committed against containerised goods also included pilfering, with the containers broken and their contents stolen. Sometimes, whole containers were declared missing in what became known as "flying containers" out of the port. This was usually facilitated by collusion between port criminals, called "wharf rats", and the security agencies guarding the port premises. Some of the importers and exporters also indulged in: under-declaration (e.g. stating that 50 bales of cotton materials were imported instead of 350 bales); false declaration (e.g. stating that a 40-ft container with two vehicles contained only household furniture); non-declaration (e.g. tampering with the manifest to show that the goods imported were not imported at all); MO (that is "machined outside", a practice where the customs certificate of duty-payable value (DPV) was printed outside of the port and with very low tariff), etc. At other times, the importation of contraband was perpetrated by the collusion of the customs and other security officials at the port, which resulted in all import documents being "arranged" and huge kickbacks being paid, as well as much less DPV being paid by the importer than was due.

Explaining the intricacy of under-declaration, non-declaration, and such malfeasances in the port, the National Publicity Secretary of ANLCA, Kayode Farinto, fingered "retired senior customs officers" as the arrowheads of sharp practices in cargo clearance. According to him, these retired officials employed the young customs officers when they were in service. After their retirement, those of them who registered clearing and forwarding companies to practice in the ports would lean on these protégés by extracting IOUs of some sort, such as " [...] us[ing] these young officers to evade outright payment on cargoes".[24]

22 Girija Shettar, "India, Nigeria in top five sea crime hotspots, says IMB 2015 report", *IHS Fairplay*, 2 February 2016.

23 Dangote Greenview Terminal, (Lagos) 2009, 3rd Annual Report.

24 Tola Adenubi, "661 Pump Action guns destined for Festac Town – Customs", *Nigerian Tribune*, 4 February 2017.

In fact, the depth of the revelation justifies the verbatim quotation of his narration below:

> It is very difficult for many of these young customs officers to say "No" to their benefactors. These young officers owe their enlistment into the Customs Service to these now retired senior officers. So, when such containers belonging to the retired senior customs officers arrive ports manned by the young officers, such containers are skipped from examination, and allowed to leave the ports, like the case of the 440 pump action rifles container. Since the onus to call for cargo examination rests majorly on the Customs, many cargoes have exited the ports in this manner without anybody knowing [...]. Meanwhile, in most cases, similar containers filled with banned or dangerous products have exited the ports in the past without trace. Until the scenario of the pump action rifles, I am sure many did not know that some containers, when they arrive the ports, are granted privileged status by not being stemmed down for examination, and allowed to exit the ports without any form of payment [...]. In the case of under-declarations, cargoes are not totally exempted from examination. They are surface-checked and assumed to be what they are not, thereby allowing the owner pay cheaply what he or she should have paid heavily for. Imagine a container carrying series of maybe 2016 SUV jeeps. On the Customs duty payment regulation, such vehicles ordinarily are expected to pay maybe 20million Naira as duty paid value. To beat the system, the owner of such container approaches the inspecting customs officers and gives such officer maybe 2million Naira. To ensure there is no hiccup, the officer informs the owner about his colleagues who are also on the same inspection chain. The customs officer who has pocketed 2million Naira knows that if he fails to inform his colleagues in that unit, he is bound to be exposed along that inspection line. So the cargo owner just ends up spending around 5million Naira to silence a chain of Customs cargo inspectors, thereby depriving the nation around 20million Naira that could have accrued into the government coffers.[25]

Such revelations from insiders are hard to refute and no dissenting voice has been heard since Farinto made the claim.

Criminal activities can also be traced to officials at the Harbours Department of the NPA. Sometimes, high-value vessels with extra-size products, such as gigantic factory machinery, can be brought by ships that are purposely cleared by the harbour master to sail into port during the late evening hours for

25 *Ibid.*

a quick and discrete midstream discharge of their cargo. In this case, the operation is concluded well before daybreak and the ship sails away from the port environment either en route overseas or to lay by at anchorage, well away from the prying eyes of day officials. Thus, the entire port charges, royalties, and all due payments normally charged to calling ships are shared by the colluding officials. In fact, the Nigerian Senate recently raised an alarm that 282 ships were missing from the record of NPA ship calls, an allegation that certainly fits the aforementioned mode of criminal activity.[26] The Senate alleged that "[w]e are looking for these vessels. We have the dates of arrival, the ports of discharge and manifest. Everything is with us, but from information available to us, no money was collected by either (sic) the Customs, the NPA or any other person".[27] In reality, the numbers rarely get as high as that. The NPA management later debunked the allegation and challenged the Senate to look into its logs or produce their own data to prove the allegation. A statement released by the NPA's Principal Manager, Public Affairs, insisted that of the 29 items listed by the Senate Committee on Customs, Excise and Tariff, "only five vessels were identifiable while the other 24 items are repetitions of the five vessels that were identified. A report to this effect with relevant supporting documents evidencing payment of all charges for the five vessels has been forwarded to the Senate Committee as requested".[28] This exchange illustrates the far-reaching effects of port crime on the socio-economic and political life of a maritime nation.

Aside from outright criminal activity, some of the operations of the stevedores and dockworkers during the study period were criminal in nature. For example, under an infamous practice called "*akube*", gangs of workers supplied by stevedores to work the ships are deliberately reduced, sometimes from 16-men gangs to as low as nine- or eight-men gangs. This spreads the workmen thinly on the ground, thereby prolonging the stay of ships in port, with the effect that more money for man-hours is demanded by the stevedore union leaders and contractors. In this case, the shipping lines, ship owners, and cargo interests are the ultimate losers. In fact, the scheme was so pervasive that even the former President of the Maritime Workers Union of Nigeria, Comrade Uzoije Ukaummunna, was caught red-handed in a bribery scheme targeted at the Transport Minister, Ojo Maduekwe and subsequently sacked at the height of the scandal.[29]

---

26 Damilola Oyedele, "Senate Alleges N30tn Leakage in Customs, Others, Queries NPA over 282 Missing Vessels", *Thisday* (Lagos), 22 July 2017.

27 *Ibid.*

28 Anthony Nwachukwu, "No verifiable facts on alleged missing 282 vessels – NPA", *The Authority* (Lagos), 27 July 2017.

29 "Nigeria: Former Transport Minister, Ojo Maduekwe, dies at 71", *Maritime Matters*, 1 July 2016.

As a result of the permissive atmosphere created by "*akube*", many other nefarious activities of Nigerian dockworkers goes unsanctioned. Palpable fear seized most port users because the rank and file of the port labour force at the quayside is too compromised. Thus, loading and offloading of dry bulk goods such as rice, sugar, wheat, or other edibles, such as fish, milk, apples, and wine, is done with massive pilfering by the stevedores to the chagrin of the cargo owners. This atmosphere has contributed to the bad name given to Nigerian ports as foreign seafarers, perched in their cabins or around the deck, witnessed the open display of indiscipline, pilfering, assaults against port users, bribery, and stealing perpetrated by dock workers working on their ships, with little control or sanction from higher authorities. Frequently, armed robbers would gain access to ships and assault the foreign sailors, robbing them of objects such as telephone handsets, wrist watches, or money, day or night. Unlike the ramped up security at the ports after the concession era, the presence of law enforcement agents in Nigerian ports in those days was very weak and ineffectual.

Other crimes include gun running and drug importation. The recent illegal importation and clearance of a container load of contraband pump action guns, which passed into the country through the AP Moller Terminal without the necessary papers from the relevant quarters is a case of high-profile malfeasance by prominent men in society.[30] Similar manoeuvres by criminal gangs operating in the ports reflect the persistence of smuggling and false declarations that dog the port industry. In fact, smuggling through Nigerian ports and land borders usually requires collusion as such ventures are at a high risk of being discovered due to the presence of multiple agencies involved in the customs clearance process and the use of scanners to search containers and other imports. Table 4.2 demonstrates a clear pattern of port crimes recorded in one Nigerian port location during the study period.

Presently, the architecture of port security is modelled on that of the Nigerian Police Force (NPF), which facilitates the process of legal enforcement such as arrest of suspects, trial, and imprisonment or acquittal. Police constables man the port gates and sensitive areas jointly with operatives from other security agencies, including: the Nigerian Drug Law Enforcement Agency (NDLEA); the Nigerian Customs Service (NCS); Nigeria Immigration Services (NIS); the Nigerian Agency for Food and Drug Administration and Control (NAFDAC); the State Security Services (SSS); the National Intelligence Agency (NIA); and the Nigerian Ports Authority Security Department. However, the integrity of operatives of these agencies is highly suspect as some of them have been

30 Tola Adenubi, "661 Pump Action Guns", *Nigerian Tribune, 4 February,2017.*

TABLE 4.2 Crime incidents reported at Berths 19 and 20, Apapa Port, 2006–2016

Month/Year	Incident /Crime	Location	Action taken
Nov 2006	Cable theft by 6 men	Drainage tunnel, GDNL	Handed over to the Police
Jan 2009	Unstated crime, 1 person	GDNL	Arrested, discharged.
Feb 2009	Unstated crime, 2 persons	GDNL	Arrested, discharged.
March 2009	Unstated crime, 2 persons	GDNL	Arrested, discharged.
April 2009	Unstated crime, 1 person	GDNL	Reprimanded.
May 2009	Unstated crime, 2 persons	GDNL	Arrested, discharged.
June 2009	Unstated crime, 3 persons	GDNL	Arrested, discharged.
July 2009	Unstated crime, 7 persons	GDNL	Arrested, discharged.
Aug 2009	Stowaways, 6 persons	Aboard ship	4 prosecuted, 4 convicted, 2 discharged.
Sept 2009	Unstated crime, 2 persons	GDNL	Arrested, discharged.
Oct 2009	Unstated crime, 5 persons	GDNL	3 prosecuted, 3 convicted, 2 discharged.
Nov 2009	Unstated crime, 2 persons	GDNL	Arrested, discharged.
Dec 2009	Unstated crime, 2 persons	GDNL	1 prosecuted, 1 convicted, 1 discharged.
Jan–Dec 2010	Theft case, 4 persons.	GDNL	4 arrested, charged to court, remanded at Kirikiri Prison.
	Cases of stealing, assault, and illegal access into terminal. 7 persons.	GDNL	7 arrested, handed over to Port Police Command for investigation and prosecution.
Jan–Dec 2011	2 stowaway attempts, 3 persons	Aboard ship	3 arrested and handed to Nigerian Immigration Services for further processing.
	Cases of stealing, illegal access into terminal and other “affrays”. 20 persons	GDNL	Some suspects were prosecuted, convicted and serving jail terms at Kirikiri Prison.

Month/Year	Incident /Crime	Location	Action taken
Jan–Dec 2012	Cases of assault, motor boys attacking dock workers, 2 incidents.	GDNL	Suspects handed over to Police and remanded in Kirikiri Prison.
	3 stowaway attempts, 4 persons.	Aboard ship	4 persons handed over to Nigerian Immigration Services for processing.
	Theft cases, 6 persons	GDNL	6 arrested and handed over to Port Police. 6 charged to court and remanded in prison.
	Other crimes such as illegal access into terminal, etc.	GDNL	13 arrested. 3 charged, acquitted, 3 granted bail, 2 reprimanded and released, 5 convicted and serving prison terms.
Jan–Dec 2013	3 attempted stowaway incidents, 13 persons.	Aboard ship	13 arrested and handed over to Nigerian Immigration Service for investigation and prosecution.
	2 cases of assault, motor boys against dock workers during cargo discharge.	GDNL	Suspects handed over to Port Police, charged and remanded in prison.
	2 Theft cases, 7 persons	GDNL	7 arrested and charged to court, remanded in Kirikiri Prison.
	3 cases damage to property: security barrier damaged by third party trucks.	GDNL Main Gate.	Nascon Plc truck and Dangote Transport truck impounded until repairs were effected by offenders.
Jan–Dec 2014	Cases of theft, assault, and damage to property, 6 persons	GDNL	6 arrested,6 charged to court, convicted and jailed in Kirikiri prison.
Jan–Dec 2015	2 cases of Burglary and Theft	GDNL	Suspects handed over to Port Police.

TABLE 4.2 Crime incidents reported at Berths 19 and 20, Apapa Port, 2006–2016 (*cont.*)

Month/Year	Incident /Crime	Location	Action taken
	Narcotics, 1 person smoking Indian Hemp	GDNL	1 arrested and handed over the Port Police.
	Bribery and corruption	GDNL	1 arrested and handed over to the Police.
	Case of assault, involving a driver and security guard.	GDNL	Suspects handed over to Port Police.
	2 cases of traffic offences	GDNL	2 drivers cautioned for over-speeding.
	3 incidents of damage to property: security barrier, LPFO pipeline, and main gate.	GDNL	Processed by Terminal Security.
	Hawking	GDNL	1 arrested.

SOURCE: DANGOTE GREENVIEW TERMINAL ANNUAL REPORTS 2007–2016.

indicted for complicity or collusion with criminals operating in the ports. Although the responses to our questionnaire for this paper varied markedly, that of the NPA Police Command is reproduced here. According to their submission, the aggregated statistics of principal offenders in port crime are as follows: dockworkers 15%; employees of terminal operators 15%; employees of government and security agencies 15%; and other miscreants from outside the port environment 55%. Of the action taken on reported crime incidents: 60% of all reported cases were processed by the police and investigated; 60% of all reported cases were charged and sent to court; 30% of all reported cases received a conviction; and 30% of all reported cases were dismissed due to lack of evidence. The modes of crime reporting were as follows: across the counter in person 60%; by telephone 20%; and by email, SMS, or social media 20%. In terms of the source of the crime incident reports, importers and exporters made the most reports at 50%, followed by other port users and stakeholders 25%; shipping lines and shipping companies 15%, and government and security agencies 10%. In terms of the national ranking of ports on the percentage of crime incident reported, Lagos was rated at 40%, Port Harcourt and Calabar port at 30% each, Onne at 20%, while Warri port had the least crime incident reports. The police assessment also put the average crime incident reports over the last three years at six per week, 40 a month, and 107 per year. Perhaps, the low ranking of Warri Port in crime reporting can be explained by the lower level of operations at the port because of the sand shoal at Escravos bar, which restricts the entrance of big vessels into the port.

5 Port Facility Security Assessment Report Prior to ISPS Code Implementation

Prior to the implementation of the International Ships and Port Facility Security (ISPS) Code in 2004, teams of security officers from all terminals were mandated, in view of the dimension of criminal activities, to undertake a tour of port facilities in their jurisdictions and to submit a security assessment report for consideration by the authorities. Some of their observations included:

(i) Fishermen caught on camera climbing on top of buoys along the Port Harcourt channel to lie down and rest and moor their canoes, thereby vandalizing the critical navigational aid and jeopardizing their functionality.[31]

(ii) Owing to the sensitivity of the cargo discharged at this berth [Berth 19, Apapa Port, Dangote Sugar Refinery], hoodlums always attack the ship even when at berth.[32]

(iii) By the side of GM Western Operation's office [Lagos] is a mini-market where stolen goods [especially food items] from the port are sold to standby market women; Creek Road / Wharf Bus Stop which is the entrance to the Apapa Port is very rowdy and crowded and market women waiting for stevedoring workers to bring stolen goods are there.[33] Goods on display at this street market included fish, rice, sugar, tinned foods, etc.

(iv) The Old Works Yard Gate block fence at the Port Harcourt Port was breached through a large hole made by miscreants popularly called wharf rats for the purpose of creating illegal access into the port premises.[34]

---

31 Port Facility Security Assessment Report for Rivers Ports Complex 2003, p. 10.

32 Port Facility Security Assessment for Lagos Port Complex and Container Terminal 2003, p. 13.

33 *Ibid.*, p. 17.

34 Port Facility Security Assessment Report for Rivers Ports Complex, 2003, p. 62.

6 The Legacy of Security Loopholes and Vulnerabilities in the Late 1990s and the New Millennium

The mounting security problems, which fuelled crimes and criminal behaviour in the operation of the Nigerian ports, derived from the legacy of running the terminals as part of the federal civil service, in which ineptitude, inefficiency, and lawlessness went mostly unchallenged. The legacy of loopholes that were exploited by criminals to commit maritime crimes was enumerated by the Port Facility Security Assessment Reports of the various committees set up to tour the ports. Some of the identified loopholes include the porous nature of the entrance and exit gates at the ports and the use of empty containers and soft-sided body trucks by criminal gangs as a means of conveying unauthorised persons into the ports.[35] They noted that although vehicles going in and out of the ports were checked, manpower shortage and the lack of electronic screening devices to assist the few security operatives on duty meant that sometimes they were slack in carrying out adequate or thorough checks.

Moreover, the presence of administrative offices or police posts within port grounds made the environment vulnerable to unwanted guests. Apart from the NPA Colonial Administrative Block, the new structures such as the Export Building and Marketing Hall housed the Nigerian Customs Services, NPA's Export Department, and some banks. As centres of daily commercial activities, they generated a multiplicity of activities and a high volume of human and vehicular traffic, thereby inhibiting the assessment of bona fide port users. Also, the "Anyman" Canteen house behind the sheds of "A" Warehouse opened the area to an influx of people from all walks of life, including the cooks, their assistants, and patrons of the eating house. Again, two mosques were located behind the former Port Manager's Administrative Block at Apapa Port and were attended by worshippers from within and outside the port gates, especially on Fridays. Their movements created substantial traffic that was unrelated to port activities and created a loophole in port security.

To worsen the situation, some of the administrative offices were inoperative for bureaucratic reasons. An example was Tugwell House at Apapa Port, which was formerly a seamen's mess. When this building came under renovation, the long period of disuse was exploited by miscreants and hoodlums who turned it into a hideout for anti-social behaviour, including using it as a place to smoke Indian hemp and as a hiding place for goods stolen from Flour Mills Nigeria Ltd.[36] Another facility equally abused by "wharf rats" was the stacking areas

35 Port Facility Security Assessment for Lagos Port Complex and Container Terminal 2003, p. 18.

36 *Ibid.*

"A" to "G" behind transit sheds 1 to 20 at Apapa Port. Ordinarily, the spaces were reserved for the stacking of laden and empty containers and for the carrying of export produce. Over time, however, some of the long-abandoned empty containers were taken over by illicit oil sellers (for illegal bunkering) and hoodlums, who converted the empty containers into escape joints. Indeed, all disused or abandoned warehouses and sheds were put to similar use by port criminals.

Moreover, according to the report, in all port terminals where flour milling berths had erected conveyor belts for the offloading of dry bulk goods such as wheat, corn, clinkers, gypsum, or other grainy chemicals, the installations were at risk of being exploited by daredevil criminals seeking access to the quays or the berthed vessels. The affected ports include: Apapa Port (Berths 1–4); Tin Can Island Port (Berths 1 and 1A); and Port Harcourt Port (Berths 3, 4 and 8). Poor illumination around installed port infrastructures adds another dimension to the problem. This was a general condition of many of the port terminals across the country for which the port reform and concessions were expected to offer remedies. Crimes were usually perpetrated under cover of darkness or poor illumination. In one of the terminals, some of the high-level "restricted access" points were vulnerable to crime, including oil pipelines, ship "unloaders", ships at berth, conveyor belts, high-perimeter wire security fences, and the power house (for electric power generators). Although the security arrangements outlined in this paragraph are specific to Greenview Development Nigeria Ltd, operator of the Dangote Ports concession at Apapa Port, many other terminals maintained similar structures.

The report revealed that at Tin Can Island Port, the massing of commercial motorcycles popularly called "okada" and the indiscriminate parking of loaded trucks and used cars along the port's access roads constituted vulnerabilities to port safety, security, and anti-crime monitoring.[37] In the same vein, villages and forests on the opposite banks of the port grounds were adjudged security risks. These villages or large forests constituted serious vulnerabilities as the abode of criminals who preyed on ships and port users. Apapa Port, Tin Can Island, and the RORO Port Complex were directly opposite Ogogoro Island and Snake Island, respectively. At Port Harcourt Hard Quays (Abonema Wharf), there is a large swathe of mangrove swampy forest, as there is at the New Calabar Port and Warri Port. In the case of Federal Lighter Terminal (FLT) Onne, although Ikpokiri village across the Bonny River was not there *ab initio*, it later developed as a thriving community of local peoples where some of the

37 Port Facility Security Assessment for Tin Can Island Port Complex and RORO Port 2003, p. 6.

port workers live. In fact, the denizens of Ikpokiri village use the port grounds as a thoroughfare to the city, even though the situation has rendered security planning a nightmare.

Furthermore, the channels of Nigeria's river ports traverse scores of nautical miles inshore with mangrove forests on both sides of the roads leading to the port terminals from the Fairway Buoy (FB) or the open sea. Calabar port lies 45 nautical miles (NM) from the FB; Port Harcourt 41 NM; Onne Port 31 NM; and Warri Port 46 NM. Only the Lagos ports are closer to the FB: Apapa Port is about 8 nautical miles, while Tin Can Island is about 11 nautical miles from the FB, with the channel passing through open waters and built-up environments on the right-hand side. Thus, the report noted that the "boat people", men and women in canoes of various sizes, emerged daily from the uncharted localities and rowed across international shipping traffic, sometimes as "harmless" fishermen and -women or vegetable hawkers and cooked edibles or fruits. However, it is also widely believed that this traffic is exploited by criminals who approach berthed ships or vessels underway as robbers or stowaways or perpetrators of other crimes against the maritime and port community.

7 ISPS Code and the Changing Patterns of Crime and Malfeasance in Nigerian Ports

Certain local and international events converged to reduce the scope, frequency, and pattern of crime and criminality in Nigerian port environments in the new millennium. First, with the onset of the new civilian administration of President Olusegun Obasanjo in 1999, there was a groundswell of negative commentary about the persistent ills of the Nigerian ports' system. By 2001, these complaints had motivated the Federal Ministry of Transport, under the leadership of Chief Ojo Maduekwe, to order fundamental changes that crystallised in the port reform agenda that swept across the nation's ports. It reduced the role of the NPA to solely that of landlord status and introduced the port concession agenda allowing the private sector to take over terminal operations and curtail the erstwhile inefficiencies and poor governance. Second, imperatives of global maritime security dictated by the fallout of the terrorist attack on the twin towers of the World Trade Centre in New York on September 11, 2001 revolutionised the security apparatus of international port facilities. Concurrently, this strengthened the enforcement of security codes and protocols whereby crimes and malfeasance in Nigerian ports were greatly reduced.

In sequel to the September 11 terrorist incident in New York and a subsequent bombing of the French oil tanker, Limburg, the International Maritime Organization (IMO) acceded to pressures from the US Coast Guard for special protection for US maritime trade and sea trade in general.[38] Consequently, the IMO organised the Diplomatic Conference on Maritime Security, held in London in December 2002, where the Contracting Governments adopted an amendment to Chapter XI of the Safety of Life at Sea (SOLAS) Convention. The convention thereafter encompassed additional protocols known as the International Ship and Port Facility Security Code (ISPS Code). The major aim of the new convention is to include "minimum security arrangements for ships, ports and government agencies" and it prescribes responsibilities to governments, shipping companies, shipboard personnel, and port/facility personnel to detect security threats and take preventative measures.[39] To fast-track Nigeria's compliance with these urgent global changes, the federal government set up the Presidential Implementation Committee on Maritime Safety and Security (PICOMSS) to help meet the July 2003 compliance deadline.

With regards to Nigeria's beleaguered ports system, this new dispensation of maritime security architecture overtook the erstwhile ramshackle anti-crime control measures. In fact, the rigorous procedures introduced by the ISPS Code and, lately, the port concession programme, have proved a sufficiently robust deterrent against the criminal community. The Code's guidelines stipulate controls for access to the ports. All persons not authorised to enter the ports with individual vehicles were bussed in and out of all port facilities. Stricter monitoring of the ports was extended to the ship berthing areas, which are now designated as "restricted" for unauthorised persons. There are guidelines for supervising the handling of cargo and ships' stores. Readily available security communication is now mandatory. Stowaway searches are also mandatory before a ship sails from the berth.

At every port terminal, the standard reporting procedures for crime and safety issues stipulate that all staff, visitors, contractors, transport representatives, and canteen operators are encouraged to report crimes or suspicious movements to the Security Department. Dedicated telephone lines are provided by each facility for this purpose. The Code has made it mandatory for a Declaration of Security (DoS) to be signed between the ship and the terminal immediately the ship berths and before any other activity takes place. The

38 *Handbook on ISPS Code Implementation and Governance*, 2013, p. 7. Nigeria: Legal Notice No 102.

39 *Ibid.*

DoS is an exchange of security information between the Ship's Security Officer (SSO) and the Port Facility Security Officer (PFSO) detailing their respective security responsibilities during the vessel's time in that port. The captain of the ship is also given a contact phone list and GSM phones are handed over to the crew so that immediate contact can be made with the terminal or their agent in the event of any incident affecting the berthed ship. All reported incidents are handled immediately by the terminal's security department and subsequently passed on to the Port Authority Security Department on a weekly basis.

This reporting regime also includes monitoring by the PICOMSS and the US Coast Guard. For example, in January 2009, a typical PICOMSS verification and inspection exercise (VIE) team, led by Engineer O.C. Ogbuagu, visited the Greenview Development Nigeria Ltd Terminal in the company of Messrs Ignatius Uche, Mike Oyebanji, and Engineer John Okoh.[40] Their mission was to ascertain the level of ISPS Code compliance by the GDNL Port Facility. After the first visit by the VIE team in January 2009, the Terminal Management was also invited to Abuja for further consultations on the compliance process. Moreover, the US Coast Guard team also visited GDNL Terminal on 20 October 2009 accompanied by Col. Ajunwa, the PICOMSS representative, and a representative of the US Embassy in Nigeria.[41] On 28 August 2013, Mr. Tivo Romero of the US Coast Guard also led a VIE team to verify ISPS Code compliance at GDNL.[42] These visits are typical of the supervisory role of the international, multi-layered authorities at all the ports and terminals in the country, in line with the reporting procedures of the ISPS Code following Nigeria's signing of the protocol.

8 The Security Force for Each Port, Terminal, or Facility

As already stated, the security template adopted by all Nigerian ports, terminals, and jetties, (public or private) is governed by the guidelines issued by PICOMSS. These guidelines conform to the ISPS Code for all ports hosting ships of 500 Gross Registered Tons (GRT) and above. In addition to this security architecture for the entire maritime domain, the Nigerian Police Force created the Nigerian Ports Authority Police Command, which oversees the Marine Police detachment in all ports and terminals where it must erect police posts. A parallel force structure is maintained and controlled by terminal operators

40 Dangote Greenview Terminal (Lagos) Annual Report 2009, p. 16.

41 *Ibid.*

42 Dangote Greenview Terminal Annual Report 2013, p. 27.

formed with the aid of private security firms. For purposes of harmonisation, the PICOMSS directed all prequalified security organisations interested in providing services in the ports to obtain port operating licences. Thus, the security apparatus of port terminals in Nigeria is multi-layered and compliant with IMO standards.

In the case of GDNL's Apapa terminal, for example, which the study is using as a reference point, safety and security matters are supervised by the terminal's Head of Security Department, Mr. Kwaling Pakka Zipya, who is also the Port Facility Security Officer (PFSO). He is assisted by two others, all trained and certified by the IMO as ISPS Code-compliant security officers. Their retained security firm is Interfalcon Security Services Nigeria Ltd, which provides 48 security guards and two resident supervisors. To complement this, the Port Authority Police Command assigned 18 regular police officers and four Marine Police personnel to the terminal throughout the year to work at designated points inside the premises and installations. At the main gate of Apapa Port, which is a common-user area, the Port Authority Police Command stations a Special Squad of regular policemen and a detachment of Mobile Police Force (MOPOL 22) on standby for quick intervention to arrest any threat to the security of the complex's five terminal operators and other ports users. This security template is similarly maintained at all the six major port complexes in Nigeria.

The security and anti-crime infrastructure in port terminals is a dynamic feature of port operations, often tailored to meet the perceived threat levels and security budgets. For example, despite the touted advantages of close-circuit television (CCTV) and other video-based security system solutions, they are not a mandatory feature of the ISPS Code and are only deployed by the terminals at such times as deemed necessary. Greenview Development Nigeria Ltd only installed CCTV cameras in 2010, after over three years of operation. In 2015, the CCTV coverage was upgraded from four to 12 cameras to augment the efforts of the security guards by spreading the searchlight to identified blind spots in the facility. Other terminals have taken similar measures. Generally, the number of turnstile gates installed by all operators has increased with the passage of time. Common security measures adopted by terminal operators industry-wide include the delimitation of "restricted access" zones, which require higher level authorisation, frisking or body scanning by mounted security guards before entry is allowed into the terminal and the use of radio frequency identification (RFID)-controlled automatic gates to disallow passage to restricted areas. Others are under-vehicle scanners/mirrors, regular foot and vehicle patrols of port grounds, VHF Walkie-Talkie handsets, physical barriers, and search of bags, persons, and vehicles.

The scope of anti-crime measures varies according to the special needs of each terminal operator. For example, GDNL procured a twin-engine patrol boat for its Marine Police personnel's regular patrol of the waterfront at Berths 19 and 20. It is operated by two experienced quartermasters. Such arrangements are the outcome of the peculiar security situations observed by operators in their concessions. In fact, terminal security assessments and plans are further strengthened by high-level networking in joint security committee meetings where industry stakeholders discuss and share security-related information with Port Force Security Officers (PFSOs), State Security Officers (SSOs), Chief Security Officers (CSOs), Police, and other security officers. These meetings take place under the auspices of Zonal Security Committees, Joint Security Committees, and Port Working Committees. Furthermore, the Port Facility Security Officers' Forum, composed of all certified officers, meets monthly that are routinely attended by security officers in all the port zones in Lagos, Warri, Calabar, Port Harcourt, and Onne.

9 The ISPS Code in Operation

As noted earlier, the levels of crime and malfeasance before the port reform and concession programme varied markedly from the state of affairs after that period. This was the outcome of the imposed security benchmarks dictated by the IMO as the UN organ in charge of global maritime trade. Following the security challenges arising from the September 11, 2001 terrorist attack, procedures for safeguarding international shipping trade were reorganised. Consequently, Nigeria's port security infrastructure after the 2001 reforms became hinged on the ISPS Code, which was enforced worldwide from July 2004. In this section, we shall examine how port crimes and malfeasance in Nigerian ports came to be overwhelmed by measures originally targeted against serious crimes.

The ISPS Code established minimum standards and guidelines for securing assets of the shipping and maritime industry against terrorism and similar crimes in any jurisdiction. The major aim was the protection and security of trading ships and their cargo, ports, wharves, jetties, and personnel on duty. For the special protection of US-bound cargo, the US Department of Homeland Security (DHS) was mandated by the Safe Port Act – another outcome of the terrorist attack – to ensure 100% scanning of all US-bound cargo, a target the agency is yet to fully achieve. The DHS maintains the scanning operations in 750 ports around the world.[43] As a starting measure, preparations for the

43 Mark Szakonyi, "100 Percent Container Scanning for US-Bound Cargo Remains Elusive", *JOC.com*, 27 February 2014.

introduction of the ISPS Code saw the IMO establish an updatable "white list" comprising maritime nations whose ports had complied with the stringent procedural security checks.

A major complement of the security measures is the "IMO Ship Identification Number", a permanent seven-digit identification number given to every seagoing cargo ship above 300 Gross Registered Tons (GRT) and every passenger ship of 100 GRT and inserted into the ship's registration documents.[44] This number is mandated to be written in very bold letters on the ship's hull or superstructure, for passenger ships, made visible from the air. Introduced in 1987 to enhance maritime safety, pollution prevention, and to check fraud, it has since been strengthened as part of the security architecture of the ISPS Code and the reporting of incidents aboard ship would include this detail. The code also stipulates that all port premises should be secured by impregnable perimeter fencing. On-duty personnel in all terminals are mandated to wear clear ID tags at all times while at work and their movements and that of port users around the port premises are strictly guided by delimitation so that "high-security" areas such as stacking or goods storage sections, quay aprons, and ship berthing areas are off-limits to all but authorised personnel. Every terminal is mandated to appoint a trained Port Facility Security Officer (PFSO) as the responsible officer for security and health, safety and environment (HSE) in the facility. On the arrival of any ship to any facility, the PFSO must establish contact with the captain as a mandatory protocol to harmonise the security arrangements between the ship and the terminal until she concludes cargo or other operations and sails away.

Despite all these rigorous procedures, however, crimes of various kinds persist, albeit at a much lower rate than during the pre-concession era. As the terminals deal in different cargo morphologies, so the associated criminalities against their operations differ, also from zone to zone. Common persistent crimes include pilfering, broaching containers, stowaways, vandalism and stealing of vehicle parts, under-declaration of duty-payable value (DPV), and bribery and extortion at the entrance and exit gates by police and port security officials.

10 Conclusion

The study on the changing patterns of crime and malfeasance in Nigerian port environments has discussed the various epochs of the port industry in the country and analysed the fluctuating trends. The dimensions of the problem support the theoretical framework, which established a causal relationship

44 IMO Circular No. 1886/Rev.5.

between the status of socio-economic and political development in the country and the types of crimes observed during the study period. Of particular significance is the role played by the interdependency and interconnectedness of sea trade in the causation and amelioration of the problem. Thus, whereas, on the negative side, international criminal actors were implicated in some malfeasances, on the positive side, the insistence by the IMO on the implementation of the ISPS Code in all maritime nations has reduced the spate of port crimes drastically. Doubtless, a remarkable change was caused by the port reforms and concession programme at the turn of the century, which radically changed the theatre of operation such that wharf rats and criminal gangs lost their turf to the technology-driven security installations that barred access to their former rendezvous inside the ports.

Nevertheless, due to a combination of human factors, especially human error, collusion, entrenched interests in the goods clearance industry, and the mass poverty in the land, common port crimes such as stealing, pilferage, robbery, frauds, and stowaways persist. The frequency is, however, manageable as it appears that the PFSOs and their security departments in all the ports and facilities have redoubled their efforts to stamp them out. The implementation of ISPS Code and other multi-layered security procedures have become an unrelenting daily operation, supervised by the US Coast Guards and the Nigerian Maritime and Safety Agency (NIMASA). With the steady introduction of electronic gates for human and vehicular access, televideo monitoring devices, and CCTV cameras mounted in port and at the decks and hatches of RoRo ships carrying cars, the noose on pilferage and similar malfeasances is increasingly being tightened. With the simultaneous effect of forensic auditors, container scanners, and inter-agency goods clearance procedures, such as the Single Window Trade Portal, port crime control is now receiving priority attention, especially because terminal operators see port crimes as a major threat to their operations.

Bibliography

Adenubi, T., "661 Pump Action guns destined for Festac Town – Customs" accessed https://www.latestnigeriannews.com/news/4017265/661-pump-action-guns-destined-for-festac-town-customs.html on 25 August 2017.

Clinard, M.B. and D.J. Abbott, *Crime in Developing Countries: A Comparative Perspective*. New York: John Wiley & Sons, 1973.

"Dangote Greenview Terminal 3rd Annual Report", Lagos: Dangote Corporation, 2009.

"Dangote Greenview Terminal Annual Report 2013", Lagos: Dangote Corporation, 2013.

Dominiczak, P., S. Swinford and L. Hughes, "Britain's border weakspots: The areas identified by criminal gangs smuggling hundreds of migrants into the UK" accessed https://www.telegraph.co.uk/news/2016/06/01/criminal-gangs-using-more-than-a-dozen-ports-on-britains-coastli/ on 22 July 2017.

Greer, W.R., "As Port Authority Bus Terminal has Expanded, so has Problem of Crime" accessed https://www.nytimes.com/1984/06/11/nyregion/as-port-authority-bus-terminal-has-expanded-so-has-problem-of-crime.html 12 July 2017.

Hosken, A., "Criminal gangs use UK ports to defraud EU customs", accessed https://www.bbc.com/news/business-39502316 on 2 May 2017.

International Maritime Organisation, "Circular Letter No.1886/Rev.5", London: IMO, 2014.

Lee, D., "Hong Kong, China cargo ports crucial to stopping transnational drug smuggling: UN request to sign up to global crackdown" accessed https://www.scmp.com/news/hong-kong/law-crime/article/1914651/hong-kong-china-cargo-ports-crucial-stopping-transnational on 12 July 2017.

Maritime Matters, "Nigeria: Former Transport Minister, Ojo Maduekwe, dies at 71" accessed http://maritimematters.com.ng/nigeria-former-transport-minister-ojo-maduekwe-dies-at-71/ on 12 July 2017.

MI News Network, "9 Types of Maritime Crimes", accessed https://www.marineinsight.com/marine-safety/9-types-of-maritime-crimes/ on 15 July 2017.

Nigerian Maritime Administration and Safety Agency, *Handbook on ISPS Code Implementation and Governance*, Lagos: NIMASA.

Nwachukwu, A., "No verifiable facts on alleged missing 282 vessels – NPA", Lagos: *The Authority*, 27 July, 2017.

Nwankwo, U.V. and O. James, "A Study of Crime Reporting in Nigeria" accessed http://www.nigeriawatch.org/media/html/Ukoji2016.pdf on 12 July 2017.

Ocloo, D.R., "Seven Nigerian stowaways arrested at Tema Port", accessed https://www.graphic.com.gh/news/general-news/seven-nigerian-stowaways-arrested-at-tema-port.html on 17 July 2017.

Oyedele, D., "Senate Alleges N30tn Leakage in Customs, Others, Queries NPA over 282 Missing Vessels", Lagos: *Thisday*, 22 July, 2017.

"Port Facility Security Assessment Report for Rivers Ports Complex, 2003".

"Port Facility Security Assessment for Lagos Port Complex and Container Terminal, 2003".

"Port Facility Security Assessment for Tin Can Island Port Complex and RORO Port, 2003".

Presidia Security Consulting Inc., "A Study of the Vulnerability of Marine Port Operations to Organized Crime". Ottawa, ON: Public Safety Canada, 2011.

Shettar, G., "India, Nigeria in top five sea crime hotspots, says IMB 2015 report", accessed https://fairplay.ihs.com/commerce/article/4261521/india-nigeria-in-top-five-sea-crime-hotspots-says-imb-2015-report on 27 June 2017.

Szakonyi, M., "100 Percent Container Scanning for US-Bound Cargo Remains Elusive", accessed https://www.joc.com/regulation-policy/import-and-export-regulations/us-importexport-regulations/100-percent-container-scanning-us-bound-cargo-remains-elusive_20140227.html on 27 June 2017.

The Economist, "The curious case of the fall in crime", London, vol. 408 no. 8845, July 20, 2013.

Trading Economics, "Nigeria Corruption Rank 1996–2017", *Trading Economics* accessed https://tradingeconomics.com/nigeria/corruption-rank?continent=america on 22 July 2017.

Uranga, R., "LA port's largest terminal remains closed after cyberattack" accessed https://www.sbsun.com/2017/06/29/la-ports-largest-terminal-still-closed-three-days-after-cyberattack/ on 15 July 2017.

CHAPTER 5

Nature and Management of Human Trafficking: The Nigerian Edo People's Experience

Leo Enahoro Otoide

1 Introduction

Trafficking in human beings, aptly described as modern slavery, is one of the most tragic human rights issues of our time. It is a global scourge of phenomenal proportion that has grave implications for national and international security. It has been estimated that annually, about 2.5 million people are trafficked globally.[1] The International Labour Organisation (ILO) has estimated that 24.9 million victims are presently trapped in modern-day slavery: 16 million (64%) exploited for labour; 4.8 million (19%) sexually exploited; and 4.1 million (17%) in state – imposed forced labour. The statistics also shows that 71% of trafficked victims worldwide are women and girls, while 29% are men and boys.[2]

Bizarre as it is, human trafficking is extremely lucrative; after drugs and weapons, it is the third biggest source of revenue of organised crime, generating an annual profit of roughly $150 billion.[3] Traffickers and syndicates are in a complex and invidious network that has defied international coalition efforts. The victims are intricately trapped in a web that looks like an octopus with a ubiquitous mode of operation that defies local and international coalitions to disentangle them. Its dimensions and damaging consequences are mind-boggling. The United Nations has several conventions against transnational crimes and methods of enforcement, with the General Assembly resolution 55/25 of 15 November 2000 as the main instrument in the fight against transnational organised crime. Globally, individual governments are complementing the United Nations. For instance, the United States government, which is at the forefront of the global fight against human trafficking, recently passed the Human Trafficking Prioritization Act 2014, to enable it to effectively fight human

1 B.S. Seker & D. Dalakis, "Contemporary Maritime Security Challenges: Human Trafficking and Migrant Smuggling at Sea", June 2016 https://www.researchgate.net (accessed 20/10/17) p. 135.

2 ILO Report 2017: Human Trafficking and Walk Free Foundation, www.ilo.org (accessed 20/08/17).

3 *Ibid.*

 | DOI:10.1163/9789004396289_007

trafficking worldwide. The United Kingdom, which, like the United States, is a destination for trafficked persons from all over the world, has, through the provisions of the Modern Slavery Act enacted in 2015, strengthened existing laws to pursue perpetrators, increase protections for victims, and established the UK's first Independent Anti-Slavery Commission. Similarly, Italy has several laws in place to combat human trafficking, the main one being the Criminal Code 1930, amended in 2003 and 2016). Japan, which is a destination for trafficked persons from Philippines, Taiwan, Thailand, Columbia, among others, has, since October 2003, commissioned the Japan Network against Trafficking in Persons (JNAPTIP). In April 2004, the Japanese government established the Inter-Ministerial Liaison Committee on Trafficking in Persons and proposed the Action Plan to Cope with Trafficked Persons in December 2004. This has since metamorphosed into a law against Crimes of Capture and Kidnapping in the Penal Code, a revised immigration law to strengthen the fight against human trafficking.[4] In spite of these measures, there were only 14,894 prosecutions and 9,071 convictions globally in 2016, representing an infinitesimal proportion of the victims.[5] For instance, in Africa, out of the 18,296 victims identified in 2016, only 1,251 were prosecuted with 1,119 convictions.[6] Current global indices indicate that Nigeria, Brazil, China, Vietnam, and Russia constitute the top five non-European Union countries of origin of victims of human trafficking. In Nigeria, Edo State, an inland community in the central southern region, with Benin City as capital, has been identified as the hub for human trafficking. The currency and complexity of this phenomenon, in relation to the Edo people, compel intense study.

This study focuses on the nature and management of human trafficking in Edo State, with particular emphasis on the societal and institutional responses. However, in order to situate the discussion in a proper context, it is important also to examine the origins and prevalence of the phenomenon. The paper begins with the historical background and conceptual clarifications. Next, it attempts to provide an overview of the wider Nigerian experience as the basis for understanding the Edo phenomenon. In analysing the Edo case, this writer has worked from the vantage position of being a citizen of Edo State, a keen observer of the phenomenon of human trafficking for decades, and a witness to the interrogation of some of the victims. This present study has benefited

4 See Minoru Yokohama, "Measures Against Human Trafficking in Japan" *Women and Criminal Justice 1–2,* (2010), pp. 27–39.

5 US Department of State. NAPTIP Trafficking in Person Report Country Narrative: Nigeria(2017), https://www.state.gov/j/tip/rls/tiprpt/2017/271114.htm (accessed 21 August 2017).

6 *Ibid.*

from the existing literature in addition to primary data sourced from the Benin offices of the National Agency for the Prohibition of Trafficking in Persons and Other Related Matters (NAPTIP), Idia Renaissance, Committee for the Support of Dignity of Women (COSUDOW), Sisters of Charity, Edo Government House, and the Edo Ministry of Women Affairs.

2 Historicism and Conceptual Clarifications

The term *human trafficking* (HT) or *trafficking in persons* (TIP) has been defined and conceptualised in different ways.[7] A common thread that runs through the concept and various definitions of human trafficking is the movement of one or more human beings by one or more human beings from point A to point B for the questionable purposes of exploitation. The UN Protocol against Organised Transnational Crime (2000), quoted in a 2006 UNESCO document comprehensively defines human trafficking as:

> The recruitment, transportation, transfer, harbouring or receipt of persons, by means of the threat or use of force or other forms of coercion, of abduction, of fraud, of deception, of the abuse of power or of position of vulnerability or of giving or receiving of payments or benefits to achieve the consent of a person having control over another person, for the purpose of exploitation.
>
> Exploitation shall include, at a minimum, the exploitation of the prostitution of others or other forms of sexual exploitation, forced labour or services, slavery or practices similar to slavery, servitude or the removal of organs. The consent of a victim of trafficking in persons to the intended exploitation...shall be irrelevant where any of the...aforementioned means ...have been used.

7 Christiana.Okojie, Obehi Okojie, Kokunre Eghafona, Gloria Vincent-Osaghae, Victoria Kalu, "Trafficking of Nigerian Girls to Italy", *United Nations Interregional Crime Justice Research Institute* 2004: pp. 33–38; Yokohama M., "Measures Against Human Trafficking in Japan", Women in Criminal Justice,20 (2010): pp. 32–33; Linus Akor, "Trafficking of Women in Nigeria: Causes, Consequences and the Way Forward", *Lorvinus Journal of Sociology and Social Policy*, 2 (2011): pp. 94–95; T.S. Braimoh, "Sex Trafficking in Edo State: Causes and Solutions", Global Journal of Human & Social Science Research,13:3 (2013), p. 4, https://socialscienceresearch.org (Accessed 20/07/17); R.N. Pati and Y.B. Shaik, "Socio-Cultural Dimensions of Trafficking Among Women in Ethiopia: An Anthropological Appraisal", *Sacha Journal of Policy and Strategic Studies* 5: 1 (2015), p. 14; Saheed Aderinto, "Journey to Work: Transnational Prostitution in Colonial British West Africa", *Journal of History and Sexuality* 24: 1 (2015), pp. 99–124.

> The recruitment, transfer, harbouring or receipt of a child for the purposes of exploitation shall be considered "trafficking in person", even if it does not involve [any of the above-listed means].
>
> "Child" shall mean any person under eighteen years of age. (Art. 3)[8]

The UN definition clearly and purposefully delineates the nature, instruments, types, and purposes of trafficking in persons and appropriately makes it a crime against humanity.[9]

Trafficking of human beings is as old as mankind. From the very early stage to this age of globalisation and ICT, human trafficking has remained a recurrent phenomenon. Although its forms and stratagems change from era to era, its nature, essence, and purpose have remained the same. The Bible records the insightful experience of Joseph, whose brothers sold him to migrant Egyptian merchants, who then trafficked him to Egypt and into slavery. The trafficking of able-bodied persons was central to the trans-Atlantic slave trade, just as taking prisoners of war for domestic slavery characterised the early history of several communities. The abolition of the trans-Atlantic slave trade in 1896 did not really put a stop to human trafficking and slavery. Today, human trafficking is another form of slavery, riding on the back of capitalism, which is the real cause and sustainer of all forms of trafficking and exploitation. The dynamics and dimensions of the problem have made the search for a practical solution incredibly challenging.[10]

Victims of human trafficking are often recruited from harsh economic backgrounds, particularly from the poor and lowest class of people, who are at the mercy of the manipulative propensities of the rich middle- and upper classes. The target is generally children and women in their prime, although young men are also victims of the scourge.[11] In terms of destination for trafficked

8 United Nations Convention against Transnational Organised Crime https://www.unodc.org/ cited in Bisi Olateru-Olagbegi et al., *Haman Trafficking in Nigeria: Root Causes and Recommendations*, Policy Paper Poverty Series No 14.2(E) (Paris, 2006), p. 19.

9 This is also extensively discussed in Olateru-Olagbegi et al., pp. 19–62.

10 See details in Olateru-Olagbegi, 2006; MinoruYokohama "Measures against Human Trafficking in Japan", *Women and Criminal Justice*, 20 (2010), pp. 26–29; Autunes das Neves, "Women Trafficking for Sexual Exploitation in Portugal: Life Narratives", *International Journal of Humanities and Social Science*, 1: 17 (2011), pp. 186–191; UNICEF, Child Trafficking in West Africa: Policy Responses, UNICEF Innocent Research Centre, (Florence, 2002), pp. 1–25; A.L Hastings, "Human trafficking in the United States: Overview of Domestic Trafficking, Department of State Trafficking in Persons Report", 2007.Retrieved from, https://alceehastings.house.gov/ (accessed 20/08/17).

11 UNESCO/IPPE Policy Paper Poverty Series 14:2(2006); Pati, R.N. and Y.B Shaik, "Socio-Cultural Dimensions of Trafficking Among Women in Ethiopia: An Anthological

persons, two types of human trafficking are identifiable: intra-national trafficking, which involves the movement of victims from one part of a country to another. For instance, a victim taken from Calabar in Southern Nigeria could be transported by a boss to Lagos in Western Nigeria to work as a domestic servant. On the other hand, the movement could transcend national and intercontinental boundaries, such as the trafficking of women from Nigeria to Europe and Asia for prostitution and unskilled labour.[12] Human trafficking can also be classified according to gender and age. Accordingly, there is trafficking in minors (children) and trafficking in women (women trafficking), both of which have been recognised as the worst types of trafficking in Nigeria and other parts of the world.[13] In all cases, the overriding purpose of trafficking is exploitation.

It is now widely recognised that certain socio-economic and historical conditions nourish the growth of human trafficking. In Africa, as in other regions of the world, there are push- and pull factors that encourage people to indulge in human trafficking.[14] The push and pull factors that instigate potential victims to surrender themselves for trafficking are rooted in stifling socio-economic and political conditions, such as abject poverty, unemployment, greed, and political instability in sub-Saharan Africa. Socio-cultural factors, such as a lack of parental care and support, gender bias, and oppression have also played a role. It is important to add that the problem has persisted because of the lack of effective legal, social, and governmental machineries to prevent the incidence of human trafficking. The internet has increasingly facilitated the global business of trafficking in women and children.[15]

Human trafficking, like drug trafficking, is a highly organised crime whose patrons and sponsors operate underground and deploy ingenious methods to frustrate anti-trafficking measures that may be put in place. Members of the

---

Appraisal"*Sachal Journal of Policy and Strategic Studies, 5* (2015), pp. 14–16; Akor, L "Trafficking in Women in Nigeria: Causes, Consequences and the Way Forward" *Lorvinus Journal of Sociology and Social Policy,*2 (2011), pp. 90–94.

12 *Ibid.*

13 UNICEF, Child Trafficking in West Africa: Policy Responses; 2002; ILO, Eradication of Forced Labour, Promoting Decent Work for All Retrieved from www.ilo.org 20August 2017.

14 National Agency for the Prohibition of the Trafficking in Persons (NAPTIP) *Communication policy and strategy abridged version.* (Abuja, 2017); UNICEF, 2002; Pati, R.N., and Y.B. Shaik, "Socio-Cultural Dimensions of Trafficking Among Women in Ethiopia: An Anthropological Appraisal", *Sacha Journal of Policy and Strategic Studies*, 5 (2015), pp. 13–28.

15 See details in Okojie et al., pp. 33–38; Yokohama,2010; Akor, 2011; Braimoh, 2013; Aderinto, 2015; C.A. Osezua, "Changing status of women and the phenomenon of women trafficking for transactional sex in Nigeria: A quantitative analysis",*Journal of International Women's Studies*, 14: 3 (2013), pp. 14–30.

international syndicate include law enforcement agents, sponsors, embassy officers in source, transit, and destination countries, "spiritualists" as they are called in Nigeria, voodoo masters, charm and talisman "fabricators", who, with the active collaboration of human traffickers, solemnise the business with orgies of blood and the oaths of secrecy and loyalty that put the victims in docile servitude and prevent them from divulging the identity of the traffickers whenever they are being interrogated.[16]

The scourge is global with the involvement of virtually every country either as a source of supply, transit, or destination ground. Russia, together with some of its former federating units of the defunct USSR, constitute a major source particularly to Europe, Israel, the United Arab Emirates, Saudi Arabia, the Scandinavian countries, China and North America; and more recently a destination from Kyrgyzstan, Tajikistan, and Uzbekistan into Russia," for sex trade and "slave labor in construction work, fisheries, fieldwork and shops".[17] France is destination to about 2.5 million trafficked victims, ninety per cent of whom are women, mainly from French-speaking African countries, Asia, and other European countries; and Portugal is source, transit, and destination country for trafficked persons from Brazil, Ukraine, Nigeria, etc. The first Portuguese official attention to the scourge was in the mid-2000s, when Boaventura Sousa Santos and others conducted research on women trafficking for sexual exploitation in Portugal.[18] Millions of people, particularly children and women, are trafficked yearly across intra-national and international boundaries for the purposes of mindless exploitation and crude labour. Similarly, Japan is a destination for trafficked persons from the Philippines, Taiwan, Thailand, and Columbia. In Africa, Nigeria is a notorious recruiting ground for traffickers and a seemingly safe destination and transit country for trafficked persons. Italy, popularly called *I-taa-lee* in Edo language, is the most notorious destination for trafficked victims from Edo State as well as victims from other African, Asian, Eastern European, South American countries and even from poor Western European countries.[19]

---

16 *Ibid.*

17 M. Buckley " Human trafficking in and out of Russia", 8 September 2013. Retrieved from *Fair Observer*. https://www.fairobserver.com/region/europe/human-trafficking-and-out-russia/ 24 August 2017.

18 Antunes das Neves. "Women trafficking for sexual exploitation in Portugal: Life Narratives", *International Journal of Humanities and Social Sciences* 1: 17 (2011), pp. 186–192.

19 US Department of State, Trafficking in Persons Report Narrative: UK. 2017 https://www.state.gov/j/tip/rls/tiprpt/countries/2017/271308.htm (Accessed 21/8/17).

3 The Experience of Edo People in the Context of the Nigerian State

Nigeria is the most populous country in Africa, hence it is often called the Giant of Africa. The last national census of 2006 put Nigeria's population at 140, 003,542. At present, its population is estimated at 186 million people. Its oil-rich Niger Delta makes it one of the richest oil-producing countries of the world. The country is also blessed with other abundant natural and human resources. However, these resources have not been harnessed to improve the lives of the citizenry. Rather, the enormous wealth has been hijacked by foreign multinationals companies and the greedy Nigerian ruling class, who have made themselves stupendously rich while the majority of Nigerians are wallowing in abject poverty. Nigeria is the sixth poorest country in the world in terms of per capita income and standard of living. The official monthly minimum wage is 18,000 Naira, which is 36 US dollars, where a dollar exchanges for 500 Naira. Consequently, the bulk of its people eke out a living against great odds in an environment riddled with, among others, organised crime, endemic corruption, high unemployment, and insecurity. This socio-economic character of Nigerian society provides fertile ground for horrible crimes such as kidnapping, armed robbery, ritual killings, human and drug trafficking, etc., which flourish untamed.

Nigeria is a source of trafficked persons to other destinations. The country also serves as transit or destination for persons successfully trafficked from other parts of Africa. In 2006, UNESCO listed human trafficking as the third most common crime in Nigeria, after economic fraud/corruption and drug trafficking. The BBC reported in June 2011 that at least ten children are sold daily across the country. The 2014 Global Slavery Index estimated that close to one million Nigerians were living in slavery outside the country. The document put the average age of trafficked children at fifteen and added that Nigerians constitute between 60–80 per cent of the girls trafficked for the sex trade in Europe, while about eight million Nigerian children are involved in exploitative child labour.[20]

Many scholars are of the view that the phenomenon of human trafficking originated in the 1980s when the economic fortunes of Nigeria changed, ushering in depression and hard times.[21] However, it has been established that

20 NAPTIP *Situation assessment of child trafficking in eleven southern Nigerian states.* Abuja, 2004; E. Madueke, (2015). "Human trafficking in Nigeria: Sisters provide services, seek greater justice for all" *Global Sisters Report* http://globalsistersreport.org/column/justice-matters/trafficking/human-trafficking-nigeria-sisters-provide-services-seek-greater.

21 O.S.B. Ekundayo & O.A. Ikediugwu, "Poverty and greed as negative catalysts of social scourges", in Felix Ogoanah (ed.), *The Return of Ameze. Okike: An African Journal of New*

human trafficking for sex exploitation and other organised crimes existed at certain levels in colonial Nigeria.[22] Although the cases may have appeared to be few and isolated, they were serious enough to generate public concern. Aderinto documents the experience of one Nigerian child prostitute trafficked to Gold Coast (Ghana) in 1939 and the fate of her trafficker, Bassey Assor, who was later sentenced to eighteen months in prison. More horrendous is the fate of another child prostitute whom one Mary Eforghere of Warri trafficked to Gold Coast in 1943 and subsequently murdered for refusing to sleep with a white sailor. Eforghere was found guilty and sentenced to death in Gold Coast. There is also evidence that the British colonial administration made concerted efforts to prevent the trafficking of young girls from Owerri, Ogoja, and Calabar to the Gold Coast for prostitution.[23]

In post-colonial Nigeria, specifically between 1960 and 1979, trafficking of Nigerians to other destinations was unpopular, as were other dastardly crimes that are now common. Then, the Nigerian economy was more vibrant and sanguine and the social fabric more stable and orderly. It was the era of the discovery of oil and its consequent boom that so enriched the coffers of the Nigerian government in the early 1970s that General Yakubu Gowon, the then Head of State, made the paradoxical declaration that "the problem of Nigeria is not money but how to spend it".[24] Nigeria, in that hopeful era, possessed a promising economy and a Naira was at par with the British Pound Sterling, and stronger than the American Dollar. Consequently, Nigeria played host to many migrants who engaged in all sorts of unskilled jobs, including trafficked persons who indulged in manual labour, prostitution, and whatever else they could do to keep body and soul together. They included Europeans, Ghanaians, citizens of Republic of Niger, and Cameroonians, many of whom also worked in the rural areas. Some Europeans and American women were involved in prostitution in Nigeria's urban centres in the 1960s and 1970s. For instance, the red-light district of Ugbague and Reservation Road in Benin City were actually founded by foreign prostitutes, not Edo women Today, Edo women have acquired notoriety for the prostitution trade. For Nigeria, the prosperous era came to an abrupt end in the closing years of the 1970s. Austerity set in and persisted, forcing the

---

Writing 54, (2015), pp. 136–150; E.T. Egbon, "Socio-cultural correlates of perception on human trafficking in Edo state: A study of Oredo and Egor Local Government Areas". MSc thesis, Sociology and Anthropology. University of Benin, 2014.

22 S.Ellis, *This Present Darkness: A History of Nigerian Organized Crime*. (London: Hurst &Company, 2016).

23 Aderinto, 100–123.

24 Collins Olayinka "Nigeria: At 80 Gowon Explains Nigeria's Problems is Not Money, but How to Spend it" The Guardian 19 October 2014 in https://www.nairaland.com> money-not-our-problem-but-how-to-spend-it (accessed 26 November 2018.

Nigerian government of President Shehu Shagari (1979–1983) to evict illegal foreigners, particularly Ghanaians who constituted the largest group, from the country. The mass deportation, which was popularly tagged "Ghana-must-go", however, did not ameliorate the hard times that had inevitably set in.

Nigerians responded to the economic recession in different ways. Some took to stealing, while others began to traffic young girls for prostitution. Ritual murders for money making became widespread and ever more people became involved in fraudulent activities now popularly called "419". By the 1990s, the scourge of intra-national and international human trafficking had become a national epidemic, spreading like an outbreak of a deadly infectious disease. Syndicates and merchants emerged, purchasing and recruiting human beings and trafficking them to places within and outside Nigeria.[25] Children and women were trafficked from the rural areas of western, southern and northern Nigeria to the cosmopolitan cities of Lagos, Abeokuta, Ibadan, Kano, Kaduna, Calabar, Benin, and Port Harcourt. At the international level, Nigerians were sourced from every part of the country and trafficked to other African countries and Western Europe. The popular European destinations were Italy, Spain, Belgium, the Netherlands, Greece, Germany, and the United Kingdom. The northern states of Nigeria supplied the victims who were trafficked to the North African countries of Morocco and Algeria, Mali, Uganda, Egypt, Saudi Arabia, and United Arab Emirates. The southern states of Edo, Delta, Cross River, Imo, etc. supplied children and young girls who were trafficked mainly to Europe and America.[26] Of all the states of Nigeria involved in the international trafficking of women for the sex trade, Edo State has been the most notorious. This raises the fundamental question: What has been the response of individuals, government, and local institutions to the social malady known as human trafficking?

The regime of General Ibrahim Gbadamosi Babaginda (August 1985 to August 1993) created Edo State in August 1991 from the defunct Bendel State (see maps 5.1 and 5.2). The other half was promptly renamed Delta State. The ancient City of Benin is the capital of Edo State. Benin is among the eight largest cities in Nigeria. The population of Edo is about four million people. The lastcensus of 2006 put its population at 3,233,366.[27] It consists of five major ethnic groups and other smaller groups. The largest group is Bini, who constitute more than 50 per cent of the total population. Benin is popularly believed to be the place of origin for other groups in the state who dispersed to their current

25 UNICEF. (2002). Child trafficking in West Africa: Policy response. Florence: Unicef Innocenti Research Centre; Ellis, *This present darkness...2016;* US Department of State, 2015.

26 *Ibid.*; also see Ellis, 2016.

27 Edo State Government Gazette, 2006.

abode. Esan is the second largest ethnic group, followed by Etsako, Owan-Ora, and the Akoko Edo group, an assemblage of diverse people speaking Edo, Ebira, and Yoruba dialects and the admixture of people from the neighbouring states of Ondo and Kogi. These groups spread across the eighteen Local Government Areas of the state. Benin City, the capital, had its first contact with the Portuguese in the sixteenth century and later with British adventurers.

The history of Edo people, at least up till the 1970s, had little or no records of prostitution or sexual promiscuity. Rather, stories of female heroism depicting their moral rectitude abound, the Princess Imaguero in Bini history is a classic example. Princess Imaguero had asked her husband, Chief Oliha, to execute her for falling victim to an organised adultery in the royal circle. When Chief Oliha hesitated to execute her as tradition stipulated, because of the love he had for her, she committed suicide. Although the ancient Edo people were patrilineal, women of substance had a chance to prove their mettle. They include Queen Idia, Queen Ede, Imaguero, Emotan, Itohan, etc. Bini is renowned not only for the extensive empire that it built in the pre-colonial

MAP 5.1 Map of Nigeria showing the 36 states and Federal Capital Territory (FCT)
NEL DE VINK (DEVINK MAPDESIGN), RETRIEVED FROM HTTPS://WWW.GOOGLE.COM/SEARCH?Q=THE+MAP+OF+NIGERIA+AND+EDO+STATE&CLIENT

MAP 5.2 Map of Edo State showing the Local Government Areas
NEL DE VINK (DEVINK MAPDESIGN), BASED ON HTTPS://WWW.RESEARCHGATE.NET/FIGURE/278017631_FIG1_FIGURE-1-MAP-OF-EDO-STATE-SHOWING-THE-LOCAL-GOVERNMENT-AREAS

period, and for the works of art that have achieved world acclaim, but also for the importance Edo people attach to their culture and tradition, whose influence remains strong today.[28]

However, since the 1980s, the notoriety of Edo girls for international prostitution has smeared the glorious and inspiring historical records of the great Edo people. Now, Edo and Benin City are the epicentre of women trafficking

28 See Okojie et al. 2003; also see C.A. Osezua, pp. 16–17.

in Nigeria. Records from the National Agency for the Prohibition of Trafficking in Persons and other Related Matters (NAPTIP) indicates that, "[m]ore than 90 percent of the girls trafficked from Nigeria are believed to come from the southern part of the country with Edo State leading with 90%".[29] The NAPTIP summary of convictions of traffickers from 2004–2012 for eight states and their capitals – Abuja, Lagos, Kano, Uyo, Benin, Sokoto, Enugu, and Maiduguri – shows Edo leading with 34 (23%) out of 149 convictions. In the 1990s and at the turn of the new millennium, the Western Union Money Transfer, operated by the First Bank of Nigeria, appeared to have had its busiest offices in Benin City, because it was a means by which migrants and trafficked persons of Edo origin who were "working" overseas remitted money to their relations in Benin City.[30] The majority of the Nigerians repatriated from Europe, Libya, Morocco, etc. are Edo citizens.[31]

NAPTIP assessment of child trafficking in eleven southern Nigerian states in 2004 also placed Edo State as number one in the trafficking of teenagers (14–18 years) for international prostitution. Furthermore, NAPTIP's Victims of Human Trafficking from Edo State from 2004 to 2017 is statistically revealing. Table 5.1 is a summary of the one-page tabular report for the 18 Local Government Areas in the state.

TABLE 5.1 A Summary Table for Victims of Human Trafficking for Edo 2004–2017

S/N	Name of Local Government Area	Headquarters	Figures	Senatorial District and Sub-Ethnic Group
1	Oredo LGA	Benin	121	Edo South Senatorial District
2	Orhionmwon	Abudu	186	Core Edo and capital of
3	Ikpoba Okha	Idogbo	207	ancient
4	Uhunmwode	Ehor	88	Benin Empire
5	Egor	Uselu	81	
6	Ovia South West	Iguobazuwa	40	
7	Ovia North East	Okada	65	
		Total	788 =63%	

29 Akor:2011.

30 Osezua,2013:25.

31 *Ibid.*, p. 15.

TABLE 5.1 (*cont.*)

S/N	Name of Local Government Area	Headquarters	Figures	Senatorial District and Sub-Ethnic Group
8	Igueben	Igueben	33	Edo Central
9	Esan Central	Irrua	37	Migrated from ancient Edo
10	Esan South East	Ubiaja	56	
11	Esan North East	Uromi	114	
12	Esan West	Ekpoma	74	
		Total	314=25%	
13	Etsako Central	Fuga	11	Edo North Senatorial District
14	Etsako	Auchi	27	Etsako sub-ethnic group also
15	Etsako East	Agenebode	20	Migrated from ancient
		Total	58=4.69%	Benin.
				Esan sub-ethnic group
16	Owan West	Afuze	25	Edo North Senatorial District
17	Owan East	Sabo	19	Ora and other Edoid language groups
		Total	44=3.56	
18	Akoko Edo	Igarra		Edo North Senatorial District Edoid language, Yoruboid, and Ebira language groups
		Grand Total	31=2.511235	

The above table, collated from NAPTIP office in Benin City, shows that the southern area of Edo State, with seven local government areas populated primarily by core Bini people, constitutes the bulk of the victims (63%), the Esan sub-ethnic group trailing behind with 25%. It should be noted that these figures represent only the cases that NAPTIP handled between 2004 and 2017. Several cases go unreported and uninvestigated annually. Similarly, Stephen Ellis, who has documented the story of organised crimes in Nigeria in an unprecedented style, says that "the trade in sex workers from Nigeria to Europe is dominated by people from Edo State, just one of Nigeria's 36 states with an amazing 98 percent of those trafficked from Nigeria coming from the State of Edo".[32]

32 Ellis, 2016, p. 182.

Italy has been a popular destination for trafficked victims from Edo State. Indeed, it is estimated that about 80 per cent of girls and women trafficked into Italy from Nigeria are from Edo State.[33] The Edo community is saddled with tales of rich, young traffickers called *akatarians*, *awayrians*, *Italian Mamas*, or *sponsorers* returning to live in affluence; poor parents striving to send their daughters to Italy willy-nilly; young men and women selling their parents' houses and land with or without their consent to raise money to fly abroad, and defiant parents writing "This House is not for Sale" boldly on the walls of their houses to warn unsuspecting buyers. There is also the sordid reality of victims perishing en route, suffering on the streets of alien cities and languishing in jails overseas, having to undergo grimy sexual experiences to pay their ineluctable debts or for repatriation and returning with strange terminal illnesses.[34] Morality, self-esteem, and national pride are being dealt a great blow and marriages and family cohesion are being torn apart. By the year 2000, it was difficult to find a Bini family in Benin City that did not have a relation "working" in Italy or another part of Europe.[35]

Numerous explanations have been advanced for this plunge into international prostitution.[36] It has been contended that the dominance of Edo women in international prostitution might be a rebellion against or reaction to the strong patriarchal cultural system of the Edo people; that is, the socio-economic domination of women by men, gender inequality, and oppression and the fact that women in Edo culture are not allowed to inherit property.[37] It is doubtful if this theory can explain the existing phenomenon. Until adequate studies are conducted to validate it, it is questionable to assert that it is the dominant patriarchal culture of the Edo people that pushes their young girls massively into the sex trade. While an oppressive patriarchal culture may be a contributing factor, it may not convincingly explain the dominance of Edo women in the trade. Some studies[38] show that Edo men travel abroad in great

33 Okojie et al. citing E. Aghatise, "Trafficking for prostitution in Italy". Concept paper presented at the "Expert Group Meeting on Trafficking in Women and Girls", 18–22 November 2002, Glen Cove, New York.

34 Ellis, 2016, p. 182.

35 Ekundayo and Ikediugwu, 2015; Ellis, 2016.

36 See UNICEF Policy Response, 2002; Akor, 2011; Osezua, 2013; Osimen Uwa, Pedro Okor, and Ahmed Titilade", Human Trafficking and Interface of Slavery in 21st Century in Nigeria" *Research on Humanities and Social Sciences*, 4: 21 (2014), pp. 10–19; Aderinto, 2015.

37 Hughes, S. (2000). "The Natasha trade: the transnational shadow market of trafficking Women" *Journal of International Affairs* 53 (2) 2000: 1–18; O.T.Oshadare, "The past and present dimensions of slavery in Nigeria".*Paper presented in the Faculty of Arts and Humanities at Kogi State University, Anyigba* 28th to 30th April 2004. Akor, 2011; Osezua, 2013; Egbon, 2014; and NAPTIP, 2017a).

38 NAPTIP, 2004.

numbers for menial and degrading labour. Besides, people of other ethnic groups are also in the business. And, as is well known, Edo is not the only patriarchal, male-dominated society in Nigeria or Africa. So, why has the factor not propelled women of other male-dominated societies to flood the international sex market as Edo women do?

The involvement of Edo girls in international prostitution can best be rationalised as an accident of history caused by harsh economic conditions, the desperation to make money on the part of the victims, and greed on the part of the traffickers. Some studies of the phenomenon confirm that Edo victims go into international prostitution and other forms of servitude abroad in order to escape poverty and hard times, improve their income or get rich quick, and that the perceptions of the phenomenon differ according to people's educational and socio-economic backgrounds.[39] The first-comer or pioneer factor may also be relevant. Edo women were the first in Nigeria to go into the international sex trade in large numbers. Before the onset of economic austerity in Nigeria in the early 1980s, a number of Binis were already engaged in international businesses: men and women who were importing finished goods like clothes, electronics, jewellery, etc and exporting foods and artifacts to Europe and America. In the process, they veered into the lucrative business of prostitution. Trafficking of relatives abroad, under some kind of agreement or Memorandum of Understanding (MoU) became attractive. The initial experimental victims returned home wealthy and then started to recruit and encourage others: the success factor. Soon, it became a way of life and before other Nigerian ethnic groups could catch up, Edo women had populated the streets of European cities for the sex trade. A people once renowned for moral rectitude soon became a symbol of carnal pleasure.

This was exacerbated by the fluctuation of the currency exchange rate. Countries strong currencies, such as those in Western Europe and America often attract immigrants and trafficked persons from countries with devalued currencies. When the Naira, Nigeria's currency, was very strong in the 1960s and 1970s, at par with the British Pound and stronger than many other currencies, foreigners migrated to or were trafficked to Nigeria to work. The Naira they earned translated into large sums of money in their local currencies. In the 1980s and 1990s, when the value of the Naira plummeted in the international market, Nigerians started migrating and trafficking fellow Nigerians to countries with superior and stable currencies, such as the US, the UK, the Netherlands, and Italy.

39 Egbon, 2014; F.Ozoeme, "The perception of parents towards human trafficking: A study of Oredo Local Government Area of Edo State", MSc Thesis Social Work, University of Benin,2017.

There is also the spiritual/mystical factor, which has become an important catalyst in the dominance of Edo women in international prostitution. This is the oath-taking ritual, which is ingrained in the culture, religious beliefs, and worldview of the Edo people. Edo people, like many other groups in Africa, are deeply religious and spiritual. The religion of the people can be described as pantheism, the worship of many deities. At the helm in the pantheon is the supreme God called *Osa* (God), *Osanobua*, *Osalobua* (God Almighty), the One who formed the universe and is believed to be somewhere in the vast sky watching everyone. Below Osa are many lower deities whom the people worship as divine intermediaries. Some of these deities are listed below:

i. Osa(nobua). Supreme God (Deity);
ii. Olokun: one of the most popular deities, the water (sea, river, ocean) god of good luck, wealth, and fertility;
iii. Obiemwen: Mother goddess of fertility and children;
iv. Esu: devil-like god of war, anger, confusion, cunning, oath, and power;
v. Orunmila: god of divination, protection, and wisdom;
vi. Esango: god of revenge, rain, lightning, and thunder;
vii. Eziza: god of the land;
viii. Ogun: god of iron, violence, and war;
ix. Asigidi: god of protection made of earth and herbs, which some individuals have at home;
x. Owegbe: a secret cult and an awesome spirit god;
xi. Osun: god of medicine and herbalism;
xii. Oguega: god of wisdom
xiii. Ayelala: awesome god of protection, destruction, and revenge, etc.[40]

These deities are invoked during oath-taking rituals for critical ventures and agreements, such as: in marriage, where women are asked to take oaths of fidelity; during inter-tribal war, when warriors swear not to betray their people; during land disputes and land sharing; and when lending and borrowing money, etc. The established use of these structures for ensuring peace and order, preventing and curbing betrayal, and life-threatening treachery was later hijacked by Edo human traffickers. Taub rightly noted that:

> In Benin City, important agreements are often sealed with an oath, administered by a juju priest. The legal system can be dodged or corrupted, the thinking goes, but there is no escaping the consequences of violating

40 S.T. Dawodu. (2008). Edo religion www.edonation.net/religion,htm 8 September, 2017 Otedo News Update.2013, May. Ebho (Edo deities) and Spirituality.

> a promise made before the old gods. Many sex traffickers have used this tradition to guarantee the obedience of their victims. Trafficked-girls' Madams in Italy have their surrogates in Nigeria who take the girls to a local shrine, where the juju priest performs a bonding ritual, typically involving the girl's fingernails, pubic hair, or blood, which the priest retains until she has repaid her debt to her trafficker.[41]

Some other personal charms and spiritual powers are usually employed for the oath-taking rituals. Some so-called "spiritual churches" are also culpable, operating just like traditional priests in local shrines, the difference being that they have modernised their activities and they chant from spiritual or magical literatures.

The oath and rituals are done in three stages: the pre-ritual preparations; the oath and rituals themselves; and the post-oath-taking results. In the first stage, the traffickers or his/her trusted agents source willing, forced, or deceived victims and weird ritual materials that nearly always include animals such as cocks, snakes, hens, gin, wine, kola nut, alligator pepper, etc.[42] Stage two is the administration of the oath itself, which involves all kinds of bizarre rituals.[43] Obaji succinctly explains the nature of the rituals as follows, which has also been corroborated by victims of trafficking:

> Before they leave, they are taken to traditional shrines where they are often forced to undergo a juju oath-swearing ritual that commits them to repaying the money they owe to their smugglers on pain of death or insanity, and not to denounce them to the police. In what has become a very common ritual in Benin City, girls are made to undress. They have been told to wear underwear stained with menstrual blood, and that is taken from them. Their pubic hair and toenails are cut, and they are forced to swear over the blood of an animal, usually a chicken, that they would never betray their "benefactor". According to traditional beliefs,

41 B. Taub, "The desperate journey of trafficked girl". *The New Yorker* [2017, April, 10]. Retrieved from https://www.newyorker.com/magazine/2017/04/10/the-desperate-journey-of-a-trafficked-girlust 8 August, 2017.

42 P.Collins", A Nigerian Voodoo priest make women trafficked into sex work eat snakes". Retrieved from *Daily Mail* online. www.dailymail.co.uk/ 8 September, 2017. This was confirmed in a group interview (names withheld) with Victims of Trafficking (5), Benin City, 07/08/2017.

43 Interview Victims of Trafficking (5), Benin City, 07/08/2017.

> which are strong in Benin City, this gives the priests power to punish erring women wherever they are in the world.[44]

The oath-taking carries with it elements of blackmail and scandal, while exaggerating the omnipotence and omniscience of these gods and their priests. It is nurtured by the reality of a society where fertile human minds are not cultivated with the healthy seeds of education, enlightenment and scientific thinking; thus allowing ignorance, superstitions, and all manner of beliefs to hold sway. The fear of violent and painful death compels victims into surrender and shields human traffickers from the arms of the law and exposure.[45]

4 Organised Response to Human Trafficking in Edo State

An organised official response to the phenomenon of human trafficking appears to have been delayed until the mid 1990s. It received a boost at the end of that decade and at the turn of the twenty-first century in Nigeria. At the national level, the government of President Olusegun Obasanjo (May 1999–May 2007) proposed a bill entitled Trafficking in Persons Prohibition and Administrative Act to the National Assembly, which was passed into law in July 2003. The new law gave legal backing to the establishment of the National Agency for the Prohibition of Trafficking in Persons (NAPTIP), which defines and criminalises human trafficking. Accordingly, the Agency was established on 8th August 2003 with branches set up later in all the state capitals. The law was amended in 2005 and several other amendments have followed, the latest being in 2015. Apart from preventing human trafficking, NAPTIP is empowered to identify, investigate, and prosecute human traffickers as well as collaborate with other government agencies in the campaign against people trafficking. The Nigerian Police Force (NPF), Nigerian Immigration Service (NIS), Nigeria Customs Service (NCS), Ministry of External Affairs, etc. have all been involved in this regard. The Agency also undertakes undercover investigations and organises enlightenment campaigns on the evil of human trafficking and other related social ills.[46]

---

44 P.Obaji The Juju Curse on Italy Sex workers. Daily Beast 3/10/15. Retrieved from. *Daily Beast*.3/10/15 Assessed 7/8/17 http://www.thedailybeast.com/the-jujucurse-on-italys-sex-workers.; also see Collins, 2016:1–2.

45 Interview Victims of Trafficking (5), Benin City, 07/08/2017.

46 NAPTIP: Operational guide for monitoring and evaluating protection and assistance services for trafficked persons in Nigeria. Abuja 2014.

In 2008, the Federal Government of Nigeria followed up with the enactment of a National Policy on Protection and Assistance to Trafficked Person in Nigeria, upon which NAPTIP developed a Strategic implementation Framework (SIF). Succinctly put, "[t]he Strategic Implementation Framework (SIF) is a roadmap for fast tracking the implementation of the National Policy on Protection and Assistance to Trafficked Persons. Its goal is to ensure uniformity in standards and to provide a benchmark to drive implementation".[47] The primary goal of the policy is to empower trafficked persons to become functionally reintegrated into society. The NAPTIP Strategic Implementation Framework is scientific, delineating twelve key procedural areas of assistance and reintegration for victims of human trafficking. These are reception, "identification, sheltering, health, counselling, family tracing, return/reparation, integration, empowerment, follow-up/after care, disengagement and preventive measures".[48] The federal government also formulated the National Policy on Child Labor and National Plan of Action for the Elimination of the Worst Forms of Child Labour in 2013.

Since its inception in 2003, NAPTIP, together with other government agencies in Nigeria, has arrested and prosecuted several traffickers, raised the consciousness of the people, campaigned against the scourge in public places: schools, market centres, worship houses, and on the streets, thereby making the business difficult for traffickers and preventing individuals from falling for the traffickers' bait. The 2017 human trafficking report by NAPTIP shows that 654 cases were investigated, 24 prosecuted, and 23 persons were convicted under the 2003 and 2015 amended anti-trafficking law and sentenced to various terms in prison ranging from eighteen months to fourteen years. NAPTIP identified 1,128 potential trafficking victims, which it categorised as: "529 sex trafficking victims, 426 child labor victims – some of whom were forced, including 261 children in domestic servitude – and 173 adult forced labor victims, an increase from 943 victims identified in the previous reporting period".[49]

Between June and August, 2017, NAPTIP made a number of arrests and rescued many victims, particularly from Edo State. On 8 July 2017, NAPTIP Rapid Response Squad arrested a notorious trafficker in the Upper Sakponba area of Benin and rescued some of his victims. The Nigerian Immigration Service

47 NAPTIP: Strategic implementation framework for the national policy on protection and assistance to trafficked persons in Nigeria. Abuja 2011: viii.

48 NAPTIP: Operational guide for monitoring and evaluating protection and assistance services for trafficked persons in Nigeria. Abuja: 2014.

49 US Department of State. (2017a). NAPTIP trafficking in person report country narrative: Nigeria.https://www.state.gov/j/tip/rls/tiprpt/countries/2017/271255.htm) Accessed 20 August, 2017.

handed over 21 victims aged between eighteen and 34 to NAPTIP, and on 26 July 2017, NAPTIP arrested another notorious lady trafficker who lured girls in Benin into international prostitutions. On 23 August 2017, NAPTIP arrested six persons who trafficked victims to the United Arab Emirates for the sex trade. In the same period, the agency agreed to collaborate with Italian Law Enforcement Agents in curbing human trafficking from Nigeria to Italy. This was followed by a meeting of the NAPTIP delegation with the heads and officials of key security agencies handling trafficking, smuggling, and migrant issues: the Italian Anti-Mafia and Terrorism Department; the Public Safety Department; Italian Police; and Prosecutors of Palermo and Catania Sicily.[50] NAPTIP, as well as other agencies, has limitations, essentially arising from poor funding and infrastructural decay. Facilities to implement the arrest, detention, and prosecution of offenders are inadequate and at times non-existent. Matters are made worse by the prevalence of corrupt officials who sabotage the process at every point. The result is that Nigeria has been downgraded to Tier 2 Watch List, which translates to the fact that the government of Nigeria does not fully meet the minimum standards for the elimination of human trafficking, despite significant efforts to do so.[51]

Early advocacy and awareness organisations were more focused on addressing political issues that affected human rights and were perhaps not so involved in matters relating to human trafficking. For example, the Committee for the Defence of Human Rights (CDHR), formed in 1989, was in response to the detention of a trade unionist. The organisation then evolved into a human rights organisation with objectives to: promote, defend, and sustain fundamental human rights; establish a system of prompt and efficient assistance for needy persons whose human rights are violated; and collaborate with other organisations committed to participatory democracy.[52] The earliest advocacy group in Nigeria with a focus on women, *Women in Nigeria* (WIN), was established in 1982 with a broad mandate to organise and improve the condition of Nigerian women in all areas: women's liberation, equality, and social justice. The organisation has offices across the country with each office determining its agenda and priorities in response to the environmental needs. WIN organises conferences and produces publications to increase awareness of issues affecting women. It also provides legal aid to indigent women. The issue of women

50 Nigeria: NAPTIP partners Italian Police against human traffickers. *Daily Trust.* Retrieved from http://allafrica.com/stories/201707250827.html on 20 August, 2017.

51 US Department of State. (2017b). Trafficking in Persons Report Narrative: UK. Retrieved from https://www.state.gov/j/tip/rls/tiprpt/countries/2017/271308.htm.

52 Committee for the Defense of Human Rights. http://www.achpr.org/network/ngo/54/ Assessed 8/10/17; also see Okojie et al., pp. 83–87.

trafficking may not have been prominent in its agenda, but it raised awareness regarding the plight of women in Nigeria.[53] NGOs emerged in Edo State to raise public awareness about devastating issues concerning women and children. These NGOs increased the consciousness of Nigerians and emboldened them to confront the monster of human trafficking and other social ills of the time. The Women's Health and Action Research Centre (WHARC), founded in 1993 by Prof. Friday Okonofua, conducted a major survey of human trafficking in 2002. It was a community-based study aimed at estimating the extent of sexual trafficking in Benin City. A special edition of its journal, *Women's Health Forum*, was also devoted to sexual trafficking as part of its advocacy agenda.[54] The International Reproductive Rights Action Group (IRRAG) also came on board. In addition, The Girls Power Initiatives (GPI) was established in 1993 by the Marxist feminist-activist, Mrs. Ben Madunagu, and Mrs. Grace Osakue, a Benin-based women rights defender. GPI undertakes community social works on sexuality, family life, HIV/AIDS, gender oppression and draws public attention to the invidious flourishing of trafficking in women and teenagers for prostitution.[55] In 2002, GPI examined sex trafficking in four Nigerian states: Edo, Delta, Akwa Ibom and Cross River. The study inquired into the plight of trafficked girls and the available services to assist them. The sessions engaged stakeholders, including victims, traffickers, NGOs, traditional and religious leaders, policymakers, and government representatives.[56] The emergence of three non-governmental organisations established by the wife of a Vice President and a State Governor, respectively, as well as some Catholic Christians in 1999 gave further impetus to the fight against human trafficking and child labour. Mrs. Amina Titi Atiku Abubakar, wife of Alhaji Atiku Abubakar, the then Vice-President of the Federal Republic of Nigeria, established Women Trafficking and Child Labour Eradication Foundation (WOTCLEF). The organisation has handled over 500 cases of human trafficking and child labour. In 2015, WOTCLEF rehabilitated 20 trafficked victims between the age of eighteen and 22. They were empowered and reintegrated into society.[57] The Committee for the

53 Women in Nigeria https://en.wikipedia.org/wiki/Women_in_Nigeria Accessed 8/10/17; also see Okojie et al., 83–87.

54 Women's Health and Action Research Centre: WHARC http://www.wharc-online.org/ Accessed 8/10/17; also see Okojie et al., pp. 83–87.

55 E. Madunagu (ed.) (2017). *Bene Madunagu at 70: Tributes to revolutionary commitment, struggle and service.* Calabar: Itrophy Publishers.

56 *Ibid.*

57 Women Trafficking and Child Labour Eradication Foundation (WOTCLEF) https://en.wikipedia.org/wiki/Women_Trafficking_and_Child_Labour_Eradication_Accessed 8/8/17.

Support of Dignity of Women (COSUDOW) was established in 1999 by Reverend Sisters of the Roman Catholic Church in Nigeria. COSUDOW "has continued to raise the consciousness of many Nigerians to the evil of human trafficking". The sisters trace victims' families, reunite victims with their families, provide "victims with both spiritual and emotional healing", and reintegrate them into society. They protect trafficked persons and their families and work with NAPTIP to bring known traffickers to justice. COSUDOW manages the shelter "built by the Episcopal Conference of Italian Catholic Bishops in Benin City and the house acquired in Lagos, which is "a welcoming home, rehabilitation and a skill training center for international trafficked victims".[58]

Mrs. Eki Igbinedion, wife of Chief Lucky Nosakhare Igbinedion, former Edo State Governor, established Idia Renaissance in Edo State specifically in response to the massive trafficking of Edo women for international prostitution in European countries. Its mission and vision are clearly articulated as: "to challenge society to be more responsive to the needs and aspirations of the less privileged with a view to restoring hope and dignity to the lives of children, youth and women" and "to promote positive cultural values and restore human dignity through education, information, communication, advocacy, mobilization and counseling".[59] The name Idia Renaissance invokes positive memories of the famous Bini amazon: Queen Idia, the greatest Queen of the ancient Benin Empire, who was renowned for vigour, moral principles, great insight, courage, and love for the people of the ancient Edo Kingdom. She symbolises dignified womanhood.[60] Idia Renaissance confronts sex trafficking and child labour mainly by investigating the plight of children, youths, and women, and the scourges of human trafficking, prostitution, and cultism. It advocates mobilisation and education by liaising with religious institutions, focal groups, and local/international organisations and agencies, garnering their understanding, cooperation, and support. It engages in lobbying for and sponsoring appropriate legislation to protect and empower vulnerable victims of trafficking and to criminalise the events of trafficking. The organisation empowers youths through the Idia Renaissance Youth Resource Centre, established in 2004 in collaboration with the United Nations Children's Fund

58 E. Madueke, Human trafficking in Nigeria: Sisters provide services, seek greater justice for all. Retrieved from *Global Sisters Report* 2015 http://globalsistersreport.org/column/justice-matters/trafficking/human-trafficking-nigeria-sisters-provide-services-seek-greater.

59 *Idia Renaissance: Restoring Hope and Dignity to Humanity*, Idia Renaissance, Benin City, n.d, p. 3.

60 *Ibid.*, p. 5.

(UNICEF) with support from the Swedish International Development Agencies (SIDA). It builds local capacity through free skills acquisition training in vocations such as computer studies, fashion design and tailoring, catering and hotel management, and hairdressing, cosmetology and beadwork. The centre also provides life skills training in reproductive health education, social and health counselling services, including access to AIDS/HIV testing, counselling, and intervention.[61]

Idia Renaissance collaborates with NAPTIP in Edo State, international organisations, and the Ministry of Women Affairs, which the Edo State Government established "to advise government on gender and children issues, matters affecting persons with disabilities and the aged; initiate policy guidelines and lead the process of gender equality and mainstreaming at both the national and international levels, and cater for women and enhance their development". Furthermore, Idia Renaissance has assisted in rehabilitating and reintegrating hundreds of youths and girls repatriated from Europe, and is the first NGO to establish a "shelter" for returnees and other survivors of human trafficking in Nigeria. It provides psychosocial and health counselling as well as vocational skills and/or other empowerment packages before they are reintegrated into society. It has trained many victims of trafficking, mostly young girls repatriated form European and African countries, particularly Italy, the Netherlands, Libya, and Morocco, in such skills as fashion design and accessories, hairdressing, catering, cake baking, soap making, and computer operation and repairs.[62] Between 2000 and 2012, the Centre rehabilitated and reintegrated over 500 victims of human trafficking and trained over 3,500 youths in various skills and vocations. Under the ALNIMA-TAMPEP Italy Project, designed to help vulnerable and socially discriminated persons to reintegrate into the society, it trained 50 victims of human trafficking, and arranged micro-credit loans for them from the United Nations Office on Drugs and Crime (UNODC) and the United Nations Interregional Crime and Justice Research Institute (UNICRI) micro-credit project executed by a coalition of NGOs in Edo State. From 2012 to 2017, no fewer than a thousand youths have been trained at the Centres shown in Table 5.2.[63]

61 *Ibid.*, pp. 3–19.

62 *Ibid.*, pp. 11–23.

63 The Centre has expanded its scope to offer vocational skills to empower interested youths and women. Individuals and associations are taking advantage of the opportunities provide by the Centre. In 2016, the centre enrolled candidates from the Army Wives Association for skill acquisition. Interview with Administrator, Idia Renaissance Youth Resource Centre, 24/10/17.

TABLE 5.2 Figures of Graduates from Idia Renaissance Training Centre

S/N	Skills	2012	2013	2014	2015	2016	2017	Total
1	Fashion	52	61	116	52	39	51	371
2	Hairdressing	35	32	65	29	09	18	188
3	Catering	113	131	33	87	42	43	449
4	ICT (Computer)	28	42	31	12	04		117
5	Photography & Videography		08					08
Total		**228**	**274**	**245**	**180**	**94**	**112**	**1,133**

SOURCE: CORPORATE HEAD OFFICE, IDIA RENAISSANCE, BENIN CITY.

A close examination of these figures reveals that compared to the period 2000 to 2012, in which the Centre rehabilitated and trained over 4,000 victims and trainees, only 1,133 youth were trained at the Centre from 2012 to 2017. In the period shown in the Table 5.2, catering had the highest number of students in the Centre, closely followed by fashion design and hairdressing. Programme number five with eight graduates, was a pilot scheme innovated in 2013, but has stalled due to inadequate funding for equipment.[64] The totals from both the vertical and horizontal axes reveal a sharp drop in the intake figures and the number of graduates. The percentages of progressive decline are presented in Table 5.3 below, with a reordering of the totals in the horizontal axis, which presents the sum total for each year.

Table 5.3 shows a clear line of decline from 2013 to 2017. While the figure increased by 4% from 20% to 24% in 2013, it progressively declined thereafter, from 22% in 2015, and 16% in 2015 to only 8% in 2016

This is an indication of dwindling financing which has characterised several self-funding NGOs. This portends a serious threat to the sustenance of NGOs that provide platforms for the empowering of women and youth generally and continued intervention in the unrelenting scourge of human trafficking, particularly in Edo State.

The inauguration of Mr. Godwin Nogheghase Obaseki as Edo State Governor in November 2016 was accompanied by renewed hope. Mr. Obaseki's body language and utterances inferred zero tolerance for the trafficking menace. He appears determined to reduce it to a minimum. Mr. Obaseki has set out to curb human trafficking in the State through international diplomatic

64 *Ibid.*

TABLE 5.3 Percentages of Decline in the Figures of Graduates of the Centre

	2012	2013	2014	2015	2016	2017	Total
Total	228	274	245	180	94	112	1,133
Percentages	20%	24%	22%	16%	8%	10%	100%

collaborations, economic empowerment, education, job creation, and other initiatives. Consequently, the Strategic Planning Unit (SPU) established by the government organised an anti-human trafficking workshop in Benin City on 6 May 2017. The Honourable Laura Boldrini, the President of Italy Chambers of Deputies, led a delegation of Italian government officials to the well-attended workshop.

Addressing participants at the workshop, Mr. Godwin Obaseki declared:

> My Government takes the issue of human trafficking very serious. For us it is a major crime, it is the modern day slavery. This is threatening the survival of our people when the people who benefit from this trade are not from Edo State but they have a well-developed worldwide system to exploit innocent people. We got a data recently that about 37,000 illegal immigrants were arrested in Europe and about 15,000 of them are from Edo and Delta States. Those are even the people who survived the journey because people go through the sea, some go through the Sahara and so many must have died in the process. So, I think it is an issue we can no longer trivialise. This is an issue that has to do with the survival of our people, it is an issue we must deal with urgently. So I am not afraid politically to talk about it, it is not a political issue any more, everybody is affected. The greatest challenge is to deal with the god fathers of trafficking and this is where we need the help of the international community and security agents to help us. These are business people, they have bank accounts in Europe, they have agents who come here to recruit people, we should be able to establish who these people are and prosecute them.
>
> We in Edo state are prepared to give our best to fight this wicked act. We are going to domesticate the law so that we will make it effective that human trafficking is as bad as kidnapping if not worst. And for those who survived it, we will give them opportunity to be rehabilitated. We are going to strengthen our institutions to work with the Federal government on this issue. At the political level we will do what we need to do and make the relevant appointment. We will train these victims, rehabilitate

> them and integrate them into the society. *And the Edo State Government is ready to pay the money which these so-called traffickers have demanded from their victims so we can free them* [emphasis added by author]. Trafficking is a threat that I think we all must deal with, it is not something we should be ashamed of anymore. Those victims will be first priority in our job creation initiative. Religious institutions and traditional institutions must now rise up to be part of this. When religious institutions were praying for people to get visas to Europe, we thought it was a right thing to do, now look at the problem it has created. The Church, the Mosque, royal fathers, now need to make this a priority because they know what we are talking about and we must fight it together.[65]

The Governor's statement reflected the wish of the good and conscientious people of Edo State and his resolve to combat human trafficking. He further revealed that the Edo State government is refurbishing technical institutions in the state to provide vocational and technical education and skills acquisition to the large numbers of youth in the state, commencing with a pilot scheme at Benin Technical College. Technical/vocational education and employment opportunities, as the Governor rightly believes, will provide employment opportunities for Edo's restive youths and reduce or stop the tide of human trafficking and illegal migration to foreign countries through dangerous and costly routes for prostitution and forced labour. Obaseki's government has promised provide 200,000 Edo people with employment. In addition, the government has embarked on a massive enlightenment programme and invested in the reorientation of deportees and potential migrants. Jobs centres for youths and special youth employment initiatives, such as the Lady Mechanic Initiative, have been established. The Lady Mechanic Initiative is located in Government House in Benin City, and trains mainly young women, and some young men, in automobile mechanism and repairs. Above all, Obaseki believes that the cardinal programmes of his government will enhance the people's welfare and effectively uproot the causes of illegal migration and other social abnormalities. His government's main objectives are economic recovery, agricultural revolution, social welfare enhancement, tourism and environmental sustainability, infrastructural expansion, and technical and vocational education.

Beyond theories, there are practical indications that the government is goal driven. On 16 August, 2017, Mr. Obaseki inaugurated an Anti-Human Trafficking

65 "Government policy toward curbing illegal human trafficking". An address by Mr. Godwin Obaseki, Governor of Edo State, at the Workshop on Human Trafficking, Benin City, 6 May 2017.

Task Force at Government House in Benin City to generate a comprehensive action plan to combat human trafficking in the State. The inauguration address to the members of the Task Force and the press was instructive:

> Clearly, we cannot as Edo people afford to be stigmatised and taunted anymore on the issue of human trafficking. It is like human trafficking is synonymous with the people of Edo State, and this is unacceptable. It is unacceptable. [...] we have decided to take the bull by the horns and take action ourselves [...] I received a letter from NAPTIP which I thought was really really annoying, telling me that what we are trying to do was unnecessary [...] that there is a federal law on human trafficking and therefore, we should adopt and work with it. If all of those worked, why do we have a crisis? May be Abuja does not understand the issue of trafficking the way we do...it has become a social scourge for us, apart from the humiliation. So, for us in Edo State, we have decided to work through the constitutional provisions to deal with this matter [...] we will domesticate the national law on human trafficking and we will prosecute [...] we have special courts in this town to prosecute those involved [...] and even if federal government officials are involved, we will prosecute them because we cannot accept this disgrace anymore [...].[66]

Among other terms of reference, the Task Force has the mandate to generate an action plan against human trafficking, combat and eradicate human trafficking in the State, establish and promote contacts with other internal and external bodies in the fight against the menace, gather intelligence on human traffickers, draft and promote laws to complement existing ones, and ensure that victims of human trafficking are not stigmatised. The Governor directed the Committee/Task Force to produce and submit a draft law and action plan on or before 29 September 2017. He assured the Committee that special budgetary allocations would be provided to facilitate the operations and activities of the Committee:

> The feeling of the Edo State Governor captured in the tone of his address at the inauguration of the Task Force are understandable especially when viewed against the backdrop of his provenance as a decent and well-educated Edo-Bini man. A major obstacle in the fight against the

66 An address by Mr. Godwin Obaseki, the Executive Governor of Edo State, during the inauguration of the Task Force on Human Trafficking at Government House, Benin City, 16 August 2017.

> menace in Nigeria is the overlapping nature of the duties of the government agencies, which the Governor has suddenly ran into, but is determined to overcome. Governor Obaseki asked a relevant question: "If all of those laws worked, why are we still having the crisis?" One thinks that any effort to confront human trafficking at any level by anyone or by any tier of government should not be regarded as "unnecessary". Rather, it should be accommodated in the mainstream of efforts to combat the inhumanity of global human trafficking. As the saying goes, "you do not drive away someone who has come out energetically to join you in killing a boa yawning to swallow you up". The action-plans envisioned by Edo State Government, if doggedly executed and replicated in other Nigerian states, will make "human trafficking a thing of the past".[67]

The dimensions and damaging consequences of human trafficking in Edo State are mind-boggling, testing the strongest resolves and policies of concerned international organisations, governments, and individuals. The prayer featured in a flyer by the Sisters of Charity, a religious group in Nigeria devoted to, among others, the abolition of trafficking in persons, captures the monstrosity, dastardly stratagems, and sad effects of human trafficking:

> Creator of us all, our words cannot express what our minds can barely comprehend and our hearts feel when we hear of children and adults deceived and transported to unknown places for the purposes of sexual exploitation and forced labour because of human greed. Our hearts are saddened and our spirits angry that their dignity and their right are being transgressed through threats, deception and force. We cry out against the degrading practice of trafficking and seek ways for it to end. Strengthen the fragile-spirited and broken-hearted. Make our promises to fill these sisters and brothers with a love that is tender and good and send the exploiters away empty-handed. Give us the wisdom and courage to stand in solidarity with them, that together we will find ways to the freedom that is your gift to all of us. Amen.

5 Conclusion and Recommendations

This chapter has examined the phenomenal scourge of human trafficking, tracing its origin and highlighting the Nigerian-Edo people's experience. The

67 *Ibid.*

origin of the social epidemic has been traced to the pre-colonial time and the dimensions in the colonial and contemporary Nigeria highlighted. The efforts by the Nigerian government, Edo State government, and NGOs to combat human trafficking from the 1990s to the present time have been examined. It is established that in Nigeria, Edo is indeed the largest suppliers of victims of women trafficked for prostitution in Europe, although all the states of Nigeria have enhanced the trade as supplier, transit, or destination. When engaging with this discussion, Edo cannot be taken outside the Nigerian context. Its predominance is perhaps an accident of history. In any case, the trend in Nigeria is that victims from the northern part of the country are trafficked to North African and Asian countries, particularly the Middle East, while victims from southern Nigeria are regularly trafficked to European countries, South Africa, Morocco, Libya, America, Russia, etc. This makes a conclusive assertion of its trend and prevalence difficult.

Nigerian NGOs, government, and religious bodies have risen to the challenge, using the tools of advocacy, enlightenment, reorientation, rehabilitation, reintegration, punishment, and jail terms for traffickers. Thus, it can be asserted that the Nigerian society has not left the evil to fester or subsumed it in its character and culture. While some measure of success has been recorded, the menace continues to defy organised efforts to dismantle its network and operations. The global predicament of human trafficking has continued to defy solution because scholars, NGOs, government functionaries and religious bodies involved in the fight somehow concentrate on the socio-economic causes without taking time to look at the very deep socio-political cause that fuel this global issue and the agony that people experience as a result of it. Poverty, unemployment, hunger, hard times, etc, which are regularly presented as the root causes, do not just occur: circumstances often generate them. To fight the menace, therefore, humanity must first engage the socio-political system, which engenders mass corruption, thus giving rise to poverty, exploitation, and servitude for a majority of the peoples of the world and absolute wealth and pleasure for a minority who hardly labour to produce the wealth. So long as the advanced capitalist and imperialist countries of the world conspire against the less developed countries of the world, particularly the ones in Africa and Asia; so long as the leaders of these poor countries, as in Nigeria, connive with foreign capitalists to exploit and cheat their peoples, social scourges like human trafficking, destitution, prostitution, kidnapping for ransom, armed robbery, etc., will continue to flourish as extreme reactions to the invidious global socio-political capitalist machinery and their local collaborators that generate and fuel them.

In Nigeria, for example, the minimum monthly wage is 18,000 Naira (36 US dollars) in sharp contrast to the absurd wages of the ruling class and the stupendous amounts accumulated through corruption, thereby depriving many Nigerians of employment, healthcare, education, and basic social amenities. Advanced western countries deliberately manipulate the socio-political structures and the minds of the ruling class in Africa to initiate and execute programmes that facilitate foreign exploitation and the devaluation of their currencies. This invariably escalates the cost of living and impoverishes the people. According to World Bank reports, African countries consistently top the list of the world's poorest countries, with African countries dominating the list of 25–30 poorest countries in the world in 2016 and 2017. Only four of the countries listed are not in Africa.

Pushed against a wall, people react in desperate ways in order to survive, enrolling in advance fee fraud, indulging in local and foreign prostitution, begging in open and clever ways and, of course, migrating abroad to earn hard currency. Unless the socio-political system that glorifies greed, and is mired in wickedness, corruption, and exploitation by the ruling class is dismantled, and until the philosophy which believes that exploitation is the order of nature and society is obliterated, there will always be hunger, unemployment, and hard times that will push victims into the seamy sides of life, in this case human trafficking. During the 2017 Trafficking in Persons Report Launch Ceremony in June 2017, US Secretary of State Rex Tillerson enthused: "It is our hope that the 21st century will be the last century of human trafficking, and that's what we are all committed to". The end of the 21st century is some long 83 years from now!

However, some of Edo State's cardinal programmes of infrastructural expansion, agricultural revival, creation of massive job opportunities, and welfare enhancement as well as the inauguration of an anti-human trafficking Task Force to confront, head on, the anomy of human trafficking, if well monitored and executed, will certainly curb the scourge. In addition, the following recommendations may assist in hindering the activities of human traffickers:

i. **The use of an "octopus" multi-media approach.** This is a comprehensive multi-media approach that considers all the possible options of aggressively attacking the challenge from all directions, like an octopus. The approach includes the use of the print and electronic (radio and television) and social media, ICT-driven multimedia, the use of artistic and semiotic images, film shows, dramatic pieces, etc. to reach target groups and effectively weaken and discredit human trafficking.

ii. **The Jehovah Witnesses' approach.** A sub-committee of the Task Force should be set up and empowered to take enlightenment to the grassroots:

families, public primary and secondary schools, mosques and churches, traditional and other worship centres with multimodal materials as suggested in (i) above, as the Jehovah Witnesses do.

iii. **Application of the four R's: Repatriation, Reparation, Rehabilitation, and Reintegration.** The sub-committee, or another special sub-committee of experts and undercover spies should be empowered and sent to Italy and other European destination countries to identify, round-up, and repatriate victims trapped there. Having been repatriated, Edo State government should make efforts to give victims reparations and organise reorientation and rehabilitation programmes and packages for them before reintegrating them into society.

iv. **Criminalisation of oath-taking and rituals.** NAPTIP and the newly established Task Force against Human Trafficking in Edo State should call a congress of all *babalawo, obo* (native doctors, voodoo priests) and enlighten them on the dangers and implications of the oaths they administer to trafficked victims; their actions could be criminalised and sanctioned. This will reduce the powers that human traffickers wield over their victims. Edo traditional rulers, like the Oba of Benin, who are revered as the custodians of traditions and culture of their people, should not relent in condemning such practices.

v. **Enlightenment and access to education.** Public information and enlightenment about the ills of the crime are to be included in school curriculum and taught in Edo State and Nigerian schools. Some studies of the Benin metropolis have shown that education plays a key role in the perceptions and attitudes of Edo-Bini people towards the phenomenon. Highly educated women and parents should be encouraged to come out publicly to condemn the illicit enterprise. They should discourage children from considering the sex trade as an option for getting rich.[68]

vi. **Family planning and family unit restructuring.** Family planning campaigns and family unit restructuring will also strengthen the fight against human trafficking. Families should be made to understand the implications of producing too many children that they cannot adequately cater for. Family planning campaigns and methods should be utilised for this purpose. Society will then be better organised to eliminate or reduce social vices. In some developed countries, like China, Denmark, Finland, etc., the size of the family is generally very small compared with other countries.

vii. **Stigmatisation.** Apart from facing the full wrath and weight of the law, (convicted) traffickers should be exposed and stigmatised. Known

68 Egbon, 2014; Ozoeme, 2017.

traffickers who benefit directly from the proceeds of human trafficking should also be stigmatised and prevented from holding important positions in government and taking titles and honorary awards.

viii. **Reparation.** The bank accounts of known traffickers should be frozen and the savings used to pay reparations to the girls and their families, as well as to non-governmental organisations and institutions facilitating the continued rehabilitation and reintegration of victims. The properties amassed through human trafficking should be confiscated and nationalised by the state, turned into rehabilitation centres, or sold to generate money for the rehabilitation of victims.

ix. **Institutional Cooperation.** All agencies involved in the drive to eradicate human trafficking should be encouraged to cooperate and exchange information willingly. Government and financial institutions should give financial assistance to NGOs involved in the fight against human trafficking.

x. Lastly, the response of Edo State Government to human trafficking, in addition to suggestions (i) to (viii) should be replicated in other states of Nigeria.

Acknowledgement

I am grateful to Steve Bode Ekundayo and Prinye G. Otoide for helping to source materials for this work, going through the final draft, and offering very useful advice. I also appreciate Iziengbe Omoregie giving me access to some of her papers.

Bibliography

Aderinto, S., "Journey to Work: Transnational Prostitution in Colonial British West Africa", *Journal of History and Sexuality*, 24: 1 (2015), pp. 99–124.

Aghatise, E., "Trafficking for prostitution in Italy", Concept paper presented at the "Expert Group Meeting on Trafficking in Women and Girls", 18–22 November 2002, Glen Cove, New York.

Akor, L., "Trafficking of Women in Nigeria: Causes, Consequences and the Way Forward", *Lorvinus Journal of Sociology and Social Policy*, 2 (2011), pp. 89–110.

Autunes, das Neves, "Women 'Trafficking for Sexual Exploitation in Portugal: Life Narratives'", *International Journal of Humanities and Social Science*, 1: 17(2011), pp. 186–192.

Braimoh, T.S., "Sex Trafficking in Edo State: Causes and Solutions", *Global Journal of Human & Social Science Research*, 13: 3 (2013), pp. 17–29, p.4.

Buckley, M., "Human Trafficking in and Out of Russia", 8 September, 2013. Retrieved from:https://www.fairobserver.com/region/europe/human-trafficking-and-out-russia/ (accessed 24 August 2017).

Collins, P. "A Nigerian Voodoo Priest Makes Women Trafficked into Sex Work Eat Snakes", 8 September 2017, *Daily Mail*. Retrieved from: www.dailymail.co.uk (Accessed 8 September 2017).

Committee for the Defense of Human Rights, *Nigeria: 6th Periodic Report,* 56th Ordinary Session, 21 April–7 May 2015 Retrieved from: http://www.achpr.org/network/ngo/54/ (accessed 8 October 2017).

Dawodu, S.T. "Edo Religion" Retrieved from www.edonation.net/religion,htm (Accessed 8 September, 2017).

Egbon, E.T., "Socio-Cultural Correlates of Perception on Human Trafficking in Edo State: A study of Oredo and Egor Local Government Areas", MSc thesis, Sociology and Anthropology. University of Benin, 2014.

Ekundayo, O.S., and O.A. Ikediugwu, "Poverty and Greed as Negative Catalysts of Social Scourges" in Felix Ogoanah's, *The Return of Ameze* in *Okike: An African Journal of New Writing,* 54 (2015), pp. 136–150.

Ellis, S., *This Present Darkness: A History of Nigerian Organized Crime*, London: Hurst & Company, 2016.

Hastings, A. "Human Trafficking in the United States: Overview of Domestic Trafficking, Department of State Trafficking in Persons Report", 2007, Retrieved from: https://alceehastings.house.gov/ (accessed 20 August 2017).

Hughes, S, "The Natasha Trade: The Transnational Shadow Market of Trafficking Women", *Journal of International Affairs*, 53: 2 (2000), pp. 1–18.

Idia Renaissance, *Restoring Hope and Dignity to Humanity*, Benin City: Idia Renaissance (n.d.).

International Labour Organisation, "International Labour Organization and Walk Free Foundation to collaborate on Global Estimate of Modern Slavery", Geneva (ILO News), 17 March 2017.

International Labour Organisation, "Global Estimates of Modern Slavery" Retrieved from https://www.ilo.org/wcmsp5/groups/public/.../wcms_575479.pdf (Accessed 20 August 2018).

Leo, R., "Nigeria: NAPTIP Partners Italian Police against Human Traffickers", *Daily Trust,* 25 July, 2017 Retrieved from: http://allafrica.com/stories/201707250827.html (accessed 20 August 2017).

Madueke, E., "Human Trafficking in Nigeria: Sisters Provide Services, Seek Greater Justice for All", Global Sisters Report, 2015, Retrieved from: *globalsistersreport.org* (Accessed 20th August, 2017).

Madunagu, E. (ed.), *Bene Madunagu at 70: Tributes to Revolutionary Commitment, Struggle and Service*. Calabar: Itrophy Publishers, 2017.

National Agency for the Prohibition of the Trafficking in Persons (NAPTIP), "Situation Assessment of Child Trafficking in Eleven Southern Nigerian States", Abuja: NAPTIP, 2004. Retrieved from: http://globalsistersreport.org/column/justice-matters/trafficking/human-trafficking-nigeria-sisters-provide-services-seek-greater (Accessed 18 July 2017).

NAPTIP, "Strategic Implementation Framework for the National Policy on Protection and Assistance to Trafficked Persons in Nigeria, viii", Abuja: NAPTIP, 2011.

NAPTIP, "Operational Guide for Monitoring and Evaluating Protection and Assistance Services for Trafficked Persons in Nigeria", Abuja: NAPTIP, 2014.

NAPTIP, "Communication Policy and Strategy: Abridged version", Abuja: NAPTIP, 2017.

Obaji, P., "The Juju Curse on Italy Sex Workers", *Daily Beast*, 3 October 2015.

Obaseki, G., "Government Policy toward Curbing Illegal Human Trafficking". An address by Governor Godwin Obaseki at the Workshop on Human Trafficking, Benin City, 6 May, 2017.

Obaseki, G. "Address at the inauguration of the *Task Force on Human Trafficking*" at Government House, Benin City, 16 August 2017.

Okojie, C. et al., "Trafficking of Nigerian Girls to Italy", Turin, Italy: United Nations Interregional Crime Justice Research Institute, 2004.

Osezua, C.A., "Changing Status of Women and the Phenomenon of Women Trafficking for Transactional Sex in Nigeria: A Quantitative Analysis", *Journal of International Women's Studies*, 14: 3 (2013), pp. 14–30.

Oshadare, O.T., "The Past and Present Dimensions of Slavery in Nigeria", Paper presented at the 1st National Congress of the Faculty of Arts & Humanities, Faculty of Arts and Humanities, Kogi State University, Anyigba, 28–30 April 2004.

Otedo News Update, "Ebho (Edo Deities) and Spirituality", May 2013.

Ozoeme, F., "The Perception of Parents towards Human Trafficking: A Study of Oredo Local Government Area of Edo State", MSc Thesis Social Work, University of Benin, 2017.

Pati, R.N., and Y.B. Shaik, "Socio-Cultural Dimensions of Trafficking Among Women in Ethiopia: An Anthropological Appraisal", *Sacha Journal of Policy and Strategic Studies*, 5 (2015), pp. 13–28.

Seker, B.S., and D. Dalakis, "Contemporary Maritime Security Challenges: Human Trafficking and Migrant Smuggling at Sea", Research Gate: June 2016, pp. 135–142 Retrieved from: https://ww.researchgate (Accessed 20 October 2017).

Taub, B., "The Desperate Journey of a Trafficked Girl", *The New Yorker*, 10 April 2017. Retrieved from: https://www.newyorker.com/magazine/2017/04/10/the-desperate-journey-of-a-trafficked-girlust (Accessed 8 August 2017).

UNICEFie, "Child Trafficking in West Africa: Policy Responses", Florence: UNICEF Innocent Research Centre, 2013.

"United Nations Convention against Transnational Organised Crime", Palermo, Italy, December 2000. Retrieved from: https://www.unodc.org/ (Accessed 20 August 2017).

US Department of State, "NAPTIP Trafficking in Persons Report, Country Narrative: Nigeria" (2013). Retrieved from: https://www.state.gov/j/tip/rls/tiprpt/countries/2017/271255.htm (accessed 20 August 2017).

US Department of State, "Trafficking in Persons Report, Country Narrative: UK" (2017). Retrieved from: https://www.state.gov/j/tip/rls/tiprpt/countries/2017/271308.htm (accessed 21 August 2017).

US Department of State, "NAPTIP: Trafficking in Person Report, Country Narrative: Nigeria" (2017). Retrieved from: https://www.state.gov/j/tip/rls/tiprpt/countries/2017/271255.htm (Accessed 20 August 2017).

Uwa, Osime et al., "Human Trafficking and Interface of Slavery in the 21st Century", *Research on Humanities and Social Sciences*, 4: 21 (2014), pp. 10–20.

UNICEF, "Child Trafficking in West Africa: Policy Responses", UNICEF Innocent Research Centre, Florence, Italy, 2013.

Wikipedia "Women in Nigeria" Retrieved from: https://en.wikipedia.org/wiki/Women_Trafficking_and_Child_Labour_Eradication (Accessed 8 August 2017).

Women's Health and Action Research Centre: WHARC, "About Us" Retrieved from: http://www.wharc-online.org/ (accessed 8 October 2017).

Women Trafficking and Child Labour Eradication Foundation (WOTCLEF), Abuja, Nigeria, 1999 https://en.wikipedia.org/wiki/Women_Trafficking_and_Child_Labour Eradication. (Accessed 8 October 2017).

Yokohama, M., "Measures against Human Trafficking in Japan", *Women and Criminal Justice*, 20 (2010), pp. 26–29.

Private Communications

Group Interview (names withheld) with Victims of Trafficking (5), Benin City, 7 August 2017.

Interview with Administrator, Idia Renaissance Youth Resource Centre, 24 October 2017.

CHAPTER 6

Militancy and Criminality in the Niger Delta Region of Nigeria

Abiodun Oluwadare

1 Introduction

Nigeria's Niger Delta is of significant economic value. According to a World Bank Report, it is one of the world's largest wetlands, and Africa's largest delta formed by the accumulation of sedimentary deposits transported by the Niger and Benue Rivers.[1] In 2006, the Federal Government of Nigeria classified the Niger Delta as the part of Nigeria situated in the southern part of the country bordered to the south by the Atlantic Ocean and the east by Cameroon. The Niger Delta has a land area of about 112,100 square kilometres, representing twelve per cent of Nigeria's total surface area, and a population of 28 million inhabitants (in 2006). Situated in the region are the nine states of Abia, Akwa-Ibom, Bayelsa, Cross-River, Delta, Edo, Imo, Ondo, and Rivers, representing one quarter of Nigeria's 36 states.

Ibaba provides a scientific, historical, and political description of the present-day Niger Delta.[2] According to him, the Niger Delta could be scientifically described as the location in Nigeria where the River Niger splits into its major tributaries of the River Nun and the Escravos, which originates in the Benin Basin in the West, goes up to Agbor in the north, and then to the Imo River. Ibaba identifies the historical Niger Delta as the conglomeration of people who canvassed for special recognition before the Henry Willinks Minorities Commission in 1958. They were the people from Ogoni province, Degema province, and others from the current South-South geo-political zone excluding the present Port Harcourt and Warri.

The political Niger Delta is a recent phenomenon, associated with the Niger Delta Development Commission (NDDC). Politically, the Niger Delta is synonymous with oil production and assumes that all oil-producing communities

1 World Bank Report Defining an Environmental Development Strategy for the Niger Delta, Vols 1 and 2 (Washington, DC: World Bank, 1993).

2 B.A. Fubara, "The Politics of the Niger Delta", in P.I Ozo-Eson & U. Ukiwo (eds.) *The Niger Delta Development Commission: towards Development Blueprint*, (Port-Harcourt: Centre for Advanced Social Science, 2011). Retrieved from https://eujournal.org/index.php/esj/article/viewFile/8015/7712 on 20/01/17.

 | DOI:10.1163/9789004396289_008

are part of the Niger Delta. The defunct Oil Minerals Producing Areas Development Commission consequently viewed the Niger Delta as including at least the seven states of Rivers, Bayelsa, Delta, Akwa Ibom, Cross Rivers, Edo, and Ondo.[3] Some of the ethnic groups in the Niger Delta area include the Igbo, Ibibio, Annang, Efik, Itsekiri, Isoko, Ogoni, Urhobo, Ukwuani, Abua, Ijaw, and Yoruba. It is estimated that the Niger Delta region has about 60 ethnic groups that are primarily engaged in fishing, farming, and trading. In spite of the importance of the oil companies, over 80 per cent of the people are still dependent on traditional agriculture and petty trade.

Despite its abundant natural resources, the Niger Delta represents a situation of extreme poverty and underdevelopment.[4] As Ajanaku rightly points out, the Niger Delta is a land of great wealth but, sadly, of high inhuman poverty.[5] Secondly, it is an area of strategic importance to international and the domestic economy of Nigeria. Nigeria is the largest oil producer in Africa and the seventh largest in the world. Consequently, signs of unrest in the area can easily affect the global oil price. The insecurity pervading oil exploration activities in the Niger Delta has adversely affected the socio-economic well-being of the people and the political stability of Nigeria. The failure of successive governments to find an acceptable solution to the neglect of the Niger Delta and its environmental degradation has resulted in the restiveness that characterises the region.[6] The task of this paper is to relate how the initial agitation for improved material conditions of the people of the Niger Delta has progressed into agitation for resource control that has, in turn, degenerated into militancy and criminality.

2 Theoretical and Conceptual Framework

The theory of relative deprivation partly explains the nexus of insurgency and criminality in the Niger Delta of Nigeria. As already indicated, the protracted agitation against government neglect laid the foundation for the insecurity in the area. Townsend's seminal work on poverty shows that there is a vital connection between poverty and subjective deprivation on the one hand, and protracted and intractable violence on the other, transmuting into

3 The Defunct Oil Minerals Producing Areas Development Commission. was created in 1993.

4 L.C. Nwachukwu & S.J. Pepple, "Disarmament of Niger Delta Militants and Nigeria's National Security: A critical APPRAISAL", *Journal of International Politics and Development Studies*, 7 (2011), pp. 90–120.

5 L. Ajanaku, "The Squandering of Riches". *Tell*, 18 February 2008, pp. 36–38.

6 R.O. Dode, "The Political Economy of Resource Curse and the Niger Delta Crisis in Nigeria: Matters Arising", *European Journal of Sustainable Development*, 1: (2012), pp. 235–248.

criminality.[7] Extant research also shows that the history of societies is replete with endemic class struggle between the exploiters and the exploited groups.[8] The situation in the Niger Delta of Nigeria is not an exception, as the multinational oil companies, in connivance with the ruling class, use government apparatus to explore oil resources from the region without ploughing back a substantial part of the revenues to develop the people and the area. The long struggle of the Niger Delta people for redress resulted in the formation of militia groups, beginning from the Niger Delta Volunteer Force founded by Isaac Adaka Boro in 1966. The militarisation of the Niger Delta also encouraged the upsurge of crime both as a weapon of prosecuting the "war" against the Nigerian State and as a means of securing their own share of the national cake or booty, particularly by those who could brave the odds. The militancy in the Niger Delta can be differentiated from criminality in terms of motive and objectives. While the goal of the militancy is essentially to fight for the group right of the people of the Niger Delta within the Nigerian federation, the goal of criminality in the area is to satisfy the selfish material desire of the militants.

According to Gottfredson and Hirschi, criminality is characterised by self-centeredness and indifference to the suffering and needs of others. They further explain that criminality can be attractive to an impulsive group of people because of the immediate gratification received through easy or simple strategies.[9] Admittedly, violent agitations are not new dimensions to the political development in the Niger Delta. What is intriguing and a source of concern, however, is the criminalisation of the struggle by cult groups and unscrupulous individuals, especially since the return to civil rule in the country in 1999. It is, therefore, imperative to distinguish between insurgency and criminality, and differentiate genuine agitation from mere criminal acts.

Different schools of thought have analysed the typologies of militancy in the Niger Delta. The intellectual ideologists believe that the struggle in the Niger Delta should be resolved through peaceful dialogue. Most of the militants believe that only the use of violence can persuade the government to end the injustice in the Niger Delta. They concluded that since the government has been insensitive to their plight, it is only the barrel of the gun that can force the government to respond to their situation. The failure of the government to keep its

7 Peter Townsend, *Poverty in the United Kingdom. A Survey of Household Resources and Standards of Living*. (Harmondsworth, Penguin Books 1979).

8 Karl Marx & Frederick Engels, *Selected Works in One Volume* ,Moscow: International Publishers, 1970.

9 Michael R. Gottfredson & Travis Hirschi. *A General Theory of Crime.* (Stanford, CA: Stanford University Press, 1990).

promise to find a lasting solution to the problem invariably encouraged a growing number of Niger Delta youths to join the militants' ranks. While it is true that some joined because of lack of employment, many simply exploited the situation to amass financial wealth, not minding the cost. The criminality associated with this transition heightened the insecurity in the Niger Delta and the country. While many people explained the insecurity in the Niger Delta with the frustration aggression theory, the government considered the situation serious enough to deploy soldiers to enforce peace in the troubled region. The involvement of the soldiers became a double-edged sword, which, although it helped to keep the oil companies working, also encouraged the militants to begin to acquire their own weapons to confront the soldiers. As could be expected, leadership tussles and disagreements about the mode of operation led to the emergence of splinter groups and the proliferation of arms in the area. To sustain themselves, many of the groups embarked on illegal oil bunkering, kidnapping, pipeline vandalisation, and the assassination of political figures.

3 Dimensions of Militancy and Criminality in the Niger Delta Region

The first attempt to defend the rights of the Niger Delta using violence was in February 1966 when Isaac Jasper Adaka Boro, who is regarded as the father of Niger Delta activism, proclaimed the independence of region. The Niger Delta Republic lasted only a few months before Boro and his associates surrendered to the federal government. Convicted for treason and subsequently pardoned, Boro died on the battlefront, defending the federal side during the Nigerian civil war. In latter years, the struggle was internationalised by Ken Saro Wiwa and the Ogoni youths, who formed the Movement for the Survival of Ogoni People (MOSOP). This group started the practice of harassing oil workers as a way of alerting them to their corporate social responsibility. The development later resulted in the hanging of Saro Wiwa and eight others in 1995. This extra-judicial murder did not deter the youth from disrupting the oil exploration in the Niger Delta particularly through the vandalisation of pipelines.

3.1 *Vandalisation of Petroleum Infrastructure*

The formation of the Movement for the Emancipation of the Niger Delta (MEND) in 2004 led to the systematic disruption and destruction of petroleum infrastructure in the Niger Delta. For instance, on 4 February 2012, the militant group bombed a trunk pipeline belonging to Italy's Eni SPA, at Brass in

Bayelsa State, where the company lost "about 4,000" barrels per day of "equity production" from the incident.[10] Another militant group, the Niger Delta Avengers (NDA) blew up the Nigerian National Petroleum Corporation (NNPC) pipeline in Oruk Anam on 16 June 2016. The group also claimed responsibility for the explosion of Agip Brass crude oil pipelines in Bayelsa State on 10 February 2016, the Chevron valve platform on 4 May 2016 as well as the NNPC Gas and Crude trunk line close to Warri despite the presence of soldiers guarding the facility.[11] The militant groups even extended the attacks to government facilities outside the Niger Delta and to local elites perceived as collaborators of the oppressive federal government. For instance, MEND set off two car bombs on 15 March 2010 in Warri, the Delta State capital, where a post-amnesty dialogue was holding. This incident left one person dead and several others injured.[12] The 1 October 2010 car bombing that killed twelve people and disrupted the Nigeria 50th anniversary celebrations is believed to have been masterminded by the MEND leader Henry Okar. The group further claimed responsibility for the bombing of the Ogbogbabene country home of the Minister for Niger Delta, Elder Godsday Orubebe in Burtutu Local Government Area of Delta State on 28 January 2012.[13]

All these bombings took place in spite of the presence of the government's Joint Task Force (JTF) in many parts of the Niger Delta.

3.2 *Kidnapping and Hostage-Taking*

The kidnapping and taking hostage of foreign nationals working with oil companies has been a major tactic of the militant groups. Generally speaking, criminals from within and outside the region have cashed in on the agitation and insecurity to perpetuate different social and economic crimes.[14] Kidnapping for ransom of parents and children of political leaders, rich individuals, and traditional rulers in the Niger Delta states has been on the rise since 2007.

10 E. Mamah & E. Amaize, "Nigeria: MEND Resumes Hostilities: Blows Up Agip Trunk Line in Bayelsa", *Vanguard* (2012). Retrieved 06/03/2017 from http:/allafrica.com/stories/201202060224.html.

11 See David Adetula, "Here is a list of attacks by Niger Delta Avengers so far", *Ventures*, 16 June 2016.

12 S. Ofehe, "Features on Niger Delta Amnesty", *Ex Ponto Magazine* 6 August 2010. Retrieved 11 May 2010 from www.expontomagazine.com/nl/reportages/2279-features-on-Niger-Delta-amnesty.

13 E. Mamah & E. Amaize, "Nigeria: MEND Resumes Hostilities-Blows Up Agip Trunk Line in Bayelsa" *Vanguard*, 26 May 2016. Retrieved from http:/allafr (accessed 6 March 2017).

14 A. Ikelegbe, "The Economy of Conflict in the oil-rich Niger Delta Region of Nigeria", *Nordic Journal of African Studies* 14:2 (2005): pp. 208–234.

This is a clear example of criminal violence in the name of the struggle.[15] The number of cases recorded in the first four years when the issue began to generate national concern is cited in table 6.1.

The kidnappers were hiding behind the popular struggle for the political and economic emancipation of the Niger Delta to commit crime and to collect different categories of ransom depending on the political and economic standing of the victims. The lucrative nature of this crime has encouraged its extension to other parts of Nigeria, particularly on the major highways.

3.3 *Illegal Oil Bunkering*

The operations of militants in the Niger Delta and the spate of insecurity in other parts of the country have overstretched the Nigerian military and made it impossible to provide adequate protection for all the oil facilities in the Niger Delta. Illegal oil bunkering, a euphemism for oil theft, has assumed critical dimensions in the Niger Delta. This criminal but economically lucrative act involves the illegal siphoning of oil from Nigeria's petroleum infrastructure into barges, which then transport it from the creeks to standby ships offshore for sale and refining in other countries. It is well known that many of the militant groups used the proceeds from oil thefts to finance their operations. Some of them even set up their own crude oil refineries in the

TABLE 6.1 Kidnapping and hostage-taking 2009–2011

Year	No. of cases	Remarks
2009	960	Annual Record
2010	579	Annual Record
2011	441	Annual Record
2012	285	Jan 01–Jun 30 only
Total	2,184	

SOURCE: POLICE REPORTS AS CITED IN ALEMIKA.[a]

a E.E.O. Alemika, "Corruption and Insecurity in Nigeria", in R.A. Dunmoye, E.A. Unobe & A.R. Sanusi (eds.), *Proceedings of the ABU@50* (Humanities' International Conference). Zaria: Ahmadu Bello University Press, 2012, pp. 35–50.

15 Anayochukwu Agbo "Hostage economy: Oil Firms flee Niger Delta", *Tell* 9 June 2008, pp. 5–7.

creeks. The militancy in the Niger Delta and oil bunkering have increased the incidence of piracy in Nigerian territorial waters and created insecurity in the Gulf of Guinea.

The negative impact of oil bunkering on the Nigerian economy cannot be over-emphasised. Among others, it leads to loss of revenue, environmental degradation from explosions, and the proliferation of illegal arms in the Niger Delta. In February 2016, the NNPC was reported to have incurred N24.23 billion operational deficits. In March 2016, a report indicated that it had declared a N18.89 billion loss. The insecurity associated with bunkering creates a corridor for international collaborators and gives a bad image to the country.[16] Oil bunkering has become the most profitable illegal private business in Nigeria. Over the years, it has evolved from the rather small-scale practice of local people tapping small quantities of oil for personal use or the local market into an extensive and sophisticated business involving transnational criminal networks.[17]

3.4 *Intra-/Inter-Gang Confrontation*

Intra- and inter-gang turf wars constitute a major factor of instability in the Niger Delta. According to Ikelegbe, factionalisation, leadership crises, and conflicts among youth groups have resulted in violent and bloody clashes.[18] In an attempt to outdo one another, cult groups are involved in violence over the control of space. In August 2004, the clash between the supporters of Asari Dokubo of the Niger Delta People Volunteer Force and Tom Akele of the Niger Delta Vigilantes, on the Njemanze waterfront in Port Harcourt resulted in the death of six people and the burning of about fifty houses. In the same River State, a community called Bodo witnessed a violent inter-cult clash between rival Deebam and Deewell groups that resulted in the death of over 42 people in 2007.[19] The criminal aspect of these clashes is that the cultists use the opportunity to loot innocent people's property, especially stores, shops, and houses.

16 A.E. Duru, "Addressing Oil Theft, Illegal Bunkering in Niger Delta", *Daily Independent*, 29 November 2013. Retrieved from http://www.dailindependent.com/2013/1 15 November 2016.

17 K.U. Omoyibo & Osunde Omoruyi, "Political Economy Diagnosis of Crude Oil Theft in Nigeria: The Way Forward", *Mediterranean Journal of Social Sciences*, 5: 2 (2014), pp. 297–302.

18 A. Ikelegbe, "The Economy of Conflict in the Oil-Rich Niger Delta Region of Nigeria".

19 B.S. Owonikoko & U. Ifukor, "From Campuses to Communities: Community-Based Cultism and Local Responses in the Niger Delta Region, Nigeria", *International Journal of Arts and Humanities*, 5: 4 (2016), pp. 16–32 .

4 The Proliferation of Illicit Small Arms and Light Weapons

One of the consequences of criminality in the Niger Delta is that large quantities of small arms and light weapons (SALW) have found their ways into the wrong hands in the Delta Region. The Proliferation of arms has indirectly encouraged insurgency and criminality in the Niger Delta. Virtually all the militant groups are armed. The types of weapons possessed by the armed groups include AK-47s and other assault rifles, automatic and semi-automatic rifles, general-purpose machine guns, RPG-7, shotguns, and handguns. The larger groups appear to have more sophisticated weapons. The sources of the arms include illegal importation from neighbouring countries, purchase from local dealers, seizures from opponents, retired military and police officers, soldiers returning from peacekeeping missions, and politicians and patrons.[20]

It is difficult to give a precise figure for illicit weapons in the Niger Delta, not to mention the country as a whole. However, at the UN Small Arms Convention in 2001, the Nigerian Minister of Defence stated that approximately one million SALW were possessed illegally in the country.[21] For example, *Tell Magazine* reported that the Niger Delta Volunteer Force under Asari Dokubo had a membership of 566 in September 2004. The paper added that Dokubo promised to surrender 3,000 guns even though he has the capacity to produce 10,000 rifles at short notice. It has also been reported that Asari Dokubo received N300 million for the guns he returned to the government under the guns-for-cash programme of the River State government in 2004. It was rumoured that the state government was paying as much as $8,000 for each AK-47 returned by the gang members.[22] The situation was so threatening that scholars asserted that some of the armed groups operating in the Delta were even better equipped and trained than the Nigerian security forces.[23] Oil bunkering finances arms acquisition either directly, as part payment for the stolen oil, or indirectly as payment for providing security services for oil bunkering operations.[24] The

20 J.M. Hazen & J. Horner, *Small Arms, Armed Violence, and Insecurity in Nigeria: The Niger Delta in Perspective, Small Arms Survey,* Graduate Institute of International Studies Small Arms Survey Occasional Paper 20, (Geneva: 2007), p. 82.

21 A. Vines, "Combating light weapons proliferation in West Africa", *International Affairs* 81: 2 (2005), pp. 341–360.

22 See Okechukwu Ibeanu & Fatimah Kyari Mohammed, *Oiling Violence: The Proliferation of Small Arms and Light Weapons in the Niger Delta* (Lagos: Friedrich Ebert Foundation, 2005), pp. 39 & 68.

23 J.M Hazen & J. Horner, *Small Arms, Armed Violence, and Insecurity in Nigeria.*

24 S. Davies, "The Potential for Peace and Reconciliation in the Niger Delta", in Cyril Obi & Siri Aas Rustad (eds.), *Oil and Insurgency in the Niger Delta: Managing the Complex Politics of Petro-violence* (London: Zed Books, 2009), p. 66.

continuation of the struggle in the Niger Delta region does not give room for the control of the circulation of illicit arms and the attendant ills. To say the least, the proliferation of weapons has also encouraged the high rate of armed robbery in the Niger Delta

5 Issues in the Niger Delta Conflict

One major instrument of the disempowerment of the communities in the Niger Delta is the several laws enacted by the Nigerian government to govern the oil industry in the country. These laws constrain the development of Niger Delta in two ways. One, it deprives the people of the ownership of the oil and gas resources found in their land. Second, the law fails to adequately protect the Niger Delta environment from environmental pollution that has negatively affected their traditional occupations. Some of the Acts or laws include:

- The Petroleum Act of 1969 (CAP 350) by which the federal government appropriated all minerals in the continental shelf of the coastal or littoral states. In other words, this piece of legislation vests the ownership of all onshore and offshore revenue derived from these resources in the federal government.
- Lands (Title, Vesting, etc.) Decree recognises the federal government as the sole proprietor of any land within 100 metres of the coast, water course, or river throughout the country. This implies that most of the riverine communities of the Niger Delta have become tenants of the federal government.
- The National Inland Waters Authority Decree 13 of 1977 makes all navigable waters the property of the federal government. The implication of this law is that the federal government has not only usurped the ownership of all oil minerals, but it has also taken over the region's water resources. The implication for the Niger Delta is huge when one considers the central role water plays in the lives of inhabitants of the region.
- Land Use Act of 1978 expropriated the ownership and control of all lands in Nigeria and vested it in the federal government.[25]

Through these enactments, the Nigerian state has effectively dispossessed the Niger Delta people of their lands and the benefits that could be derived from them. The Land Use Act stripped the Niger Delta communities of the right to grant permission to Multi National Oil Companies (MNOCs) for the use of their

25 S.I. Ibaba, *Understanding the Niger Delta Crisis.* (Port Harcourt: Amethyst and Colleagues Publishers, 2005).

land, and to participate in the determination of type and rates of compensation for their destroyed resources.[26] In the final analysis, Nigerians from the non-oil producing region dictate the management of land in the Niger Delta. The reading of the situation led one Niger Delta activist, Douglas Oronto, to say that:

> Now you can be given licence in Abuja, and that licence immediately translates to a decree that you can go and uproot houses and pollute land, and take away the oil, that's what it amounts to. Nobody given a licence can just walk in and say we discuss, there's no discussion. An oil licence is equal in effect to the military decree, backed by military action, to take away whatever land that you have and take the oil and return to Abuja. That is unjust, that is dispossession that is denial, that is deprivation and it has to stop. We are saying the best way to go about it is to sit down and let us discuss.[27]

The devastating effect of the Land Use Act on the very existence of the Niger Delta people becomes more apparent when one considers the sociological relevance of land to the society. The relationship of individuals with their land ultimately frames their identities, especially in Africa, where each group occupies an identifiable homeland. By the provisions of the Land Act, the people of the Niger Delta have become tenants as well as subjects of the Nigerian state. This is an act of injustice, deprivation, and colonisation that the people of Niger Delta have vehemently opposed and challenged over the years.

The second major issue in the Niger Delta crisis is the failure of the government interventionist programmes to solve the problems of the Niger Delta. The agencies and boards include the Niger Delta Development Board (NDDB) of 1961, which later metamorphosed into Niger Delta Basin Development Authority (NDBDA) in 1976. There was also the Oil Minerals Producing Areas Development Commission (OMPADEC) that allocated 1.5 per cent of the national budget to the oil producing communities; the Petroleum Trust Fund (PTF) and the current Niger Delta Development Commission (NDDC). Although it could be said that the government had good intentions in setting up these bodies, their achievements fell short of expectations due to poor implementation and

26 K. Okoko & S.I. Ibaba, "Oil spillages and community disturbances: The SPDC and the Niger Delta experience", *Nigerian Journal of Oil and Politics*, 1 (1997), pp. 56–69.

27 O. Douglas, "A community guide to understanding resource control", retrieved from www.waado.org/NigerDelta/Essays/Resource-Control/Guide_Douglas.html, accessed on 14 December 2016.

corruption. It has also been argued that they failed to address the developmental needs of the people because the structures were created on faulty foundations.[28] All the institutions operated a top-down approach devoid of inclusive participation from the affected communities. It has also been observed that even the NDDC master plan was drawn up by a German company, with the approval of the vested authorities in Abuja, and effectively forced down the throats of the Niger Delta people.[29] The short comings of the programmes encouraged the youths of the Niger Delta to take laws into their own hands. Reprisals by the federal government resulted including the army invading several communities in the Niger Delta,. Examples include the invasion and massacre of innocent Niger Deltans in Umuechem in 1990, Ogoni in 1994, Kaiama in 1998, Odi in 1999, and Choba in 2000.[30]

The Nigerian state took these military measures against the people because it perceived the Niger Delta crisis as a security issue. This explains why the government of President Yar'dua allocated N446 billion in the 2008 budget to security in the Niger Delta. This huge sum would have yielded more benefits if it had been used to provide amenities for the deprived and abused people of the region. As Oronto Douglas, one of the Niger Delta activists argued, insecurity is not a cause but the symptom of several fundamental issues:

> Insecurity in the Niger Delta is directly proportional to poverty, directly proportional to the denial of the rights of the local people, directly proportional to corporate arrogance and dominance of the means of survival and existence. It is directly proportional to the denial of access of our people and communities to natural wealth.[31]

The awareness that the military option alone cannot resolve the crisis led to renewed efforts to address the problem differently by dangling the carrot of a presidential amnesty before the militants. Consequently, a presidential panel was created in May 2009 to work out the modalities for granting pardon to repentant militants, and disarming and reintegrating them into the society. As expected, the exercise ran into several problems, which led to agitations for the dissolution of the Presidential Amnesty Committee. The people of the

---

28 L. Edigin & I.E. Okonmah, "Mystifying Development Policy Strategies in the Niger Delta: The Unending Mistake", *Journal of Research in National Development*, 8: 2 (2010), 173–181.

29 D. Dafinone, "The Niger Delta Crisis: Genesis, Exodus and Solution", *The Vanguard Daily*, 16 November 2007, p. 25.

30 P.K. Inokoba & D.L. Imbua, "Vexation and Militancy in the Niger Delta: The Way Forward"Kamla-Raj Journal of Human Ecology, 29:2 (2010), pp. 101–120.

31 *Newswatch*, Newspaper 13 August 2007.

region alleged that the amount devoted to the exercise was too little. They also protested against the continued detention of ex-militants and the adding of fictitious names to the register of ex-militants. They were equally not happy with the conditions in the rehabilitation centres designed to host ex-militants, which they described as falling short of the international standard.[32] One of the greatest challenges of the amnesty package is its top-down approach. The decisions that informed the process and procedure were derived from consultations at Abuja with top government officials of Niger Delta origin, top politicians, and leaders of a few militant groups who are believed to have used the opportunity to enrich themselves. The argument is that a more inclusive approach that allows for the active participation of all stakeholders, including people at the grass-roots, would have been more appropriate.[33]

Nevertheless, the situation has improved considerably in recent years. For instance, more than 30,000 ex-militants are placed on a monthly salary of N65,000, hundreds of them have been trained locally in different forms of agriculture, a large number of them have been trained abroad as artisans who can work in the oil industry, while some recently graduated as automobile engineers. Statistics from the office of the Presidential Amnesty Programme show that the office had a budget of N63.28 billion in 2014, and that in 2013, 2,400 ex-militants were deployed to vocational training centres within and outside the country. The Special Adviser to the President on the Amnesty Programme said, "Of this number, 671 delegates have since graduated, earning globally recognised certificates in such fields marine technology, commercial driving, agriculture, drilling, boat building, oil and gas technology, automobile technology, and, of course, aviation".[34] He added that in 2013, 834 ex-militants were admitted to about 100 universities across the world. The benefits of the Amnesty Programme have encouraged more militants to surrender their weapons, in particular since President Muhammadu Buhari assumed office in May 2015. The vision of the Amnesty Programme is to create a Niger Delta Region with

32 C. Obi & S.A. Rustad, "Conclusion: Amnesty and Post-Amnesty Peace, is the Window of Opportunity Closing for the Niger Delta?", in Obi, C. & S.A. Rustad (eds.), *Oil and Insurgency in the Niger Delta: Managing the Complex Politics of Petro-Violence* (London/New York: Zed Books, 2011).

33 R. Ako, "The Struggle for Resource Control and Violence in the Niger Delta", in C. Obi & S.A. Rustad, (eds.), *Oil and Insurgency in the Niger Delta: Managing the Complex Politics of Petro-Violence* (London/New York: Zed Books, 2011).

34 See "Amnesty Programme: FG to spend N35.83bn on Ex-Militants in 2014, Says Kuku", *Information Digest*, 28 Feb. 2014 , retrieved from https://www.informationng.com/2014/02/amnest-programme-fg-to-spend-n35-83bn-onex-militants-in-2014-says-kuku.html on 30/03/2017.

modern cities, with cutting-edge environmental management practices, economic prosperity, and populated by skilled and healthy people living in social harmony. The realisation of the objectives will remain elusive until the fundamental issues in the Niger Delta crisis are first understood and addressed appropriately. As has been seen, coercion cannot achieve this goal.[35]

6 Conclusion

The current dynamics of militancy in the Niger Delta, and the transition of the insurgency from popular to criminal violence, are complicated. There are complex relations between patrons and militias, between ethnic minorities and petro-elites, between oil MNCs and militias, between oil communities and militias, and between armed groups and gangs. Even within the militia formations, there are complex relations and tensions within the alliance(s) and between the diverse groups, armed bands, cultists, and pirates.

The tendency for criminal violence is traceable to state repression and trust deficits. The infiltration of the legitimate struggle by self-seeking elites has compounded this situation, thus propelling the popular struggle towards criminal self-enrichment by a few through illicit trade in arms, kidnapping, and oil bunkering. The high levels of poverty and youth unemployment and the proliferation of arms have also aggravated the situation immensely. The tragedy is that what began as a genuine struggle has been hijacked by the elite and oil theft syndicates who now manipulate and deploy several militias for the perpetration of crimes in the Niger Delta.

Firstly, the Land Use Act 1978 is controversial not only in the Niger Delta, but in Nigeria as a whole. The best solution is for the government to lessen the direct dependence of the people on the land, in particular through the establishment of small-scale industries and the provision of infrastructural facilities. It is time to adopt the simple method already used for the rapid development of Abuja to develop the Niger Delta. The state and local governments should also be encouraged to contribute meaningfully to the development of the region. The government should establish a credible institution to check the corrupt practice of governors, local government chairmen, chiefs, community leaders, and youths in the Niger Delta region. This will ensure that the people enjoy the dividends of democracy and erode the material basis for the allegation of marginalisation.

35 Fidelis Mbah, "Niger Delta Promises", 12 February 2008,, retrieved from http://nwaokonaku.blogspot.com.ng/2008/02/niger-delta-promises.html?m=0 on 30/03/2017.

The Nigerian economy should be diversified in order to reduce dependence on the petroleum sector. The success of this diversification will reduce the rising incidence of oil theft and oil pipeline vandalisation and guarantee national security. It has been observed elsewhere that the most feasible economic plan would be one that calls for an integrated development in the mould of a Marshall Plan for the region. The NDDC master plan seems adequate, but the plan for its financing has over the last few years has continued to fall short of expectations. This must be addressed.

The government must take seriously the destruction of the Niger Delta environment by MNOCs. Although the current government embarked on a cleaning up of the region in February 2017, beginning with Ogoniland, a report by the United Nations Environmental Programme indicates that it will cost $1bn and take up to 30 years to achieve.[36] The ecosystem can be protected by enacting laws that will regulate the activities of MNOCs and agencies to monitor such activities and enforce compliance. Market-based instruments like pollution taxes and effluent charges should be utilised. Revenue obtained from pollution taxes should be ploughed back into developmental projects or used to compensate inhabitants of the Niger Delta who have suffered as a result of environmental damage. An attempt should be made to mainstream environmental concerns in national economic policies to promote the visibility and sustainability of environmental policies.

The government must ensure, immediately, that oil-producing companies comply with international standards by stopping gas flaring in the Niger Delta. The country has a National Gas Policy that seeks to end gas flaring by 2020. The problem is the lack of political will to achieve this goal. For instance, the Nigerian Extractive Industries Transparency Initiative (NEITI) indicated the reluctance of the government to enforce its own regulations on the penalty to be paid by companies flouting the gas flaring regulation. The group noted that, as a result, the country lost $14.298 billion between 2008 and 2016.[37] Today, Nigeria is ranked seventh among the world's worst gas flaring nations. The Gas Master Plan should be implemented in a way that will encourage the gas that is currently flared to be converted into industrial and domestic use.

In order to halt the proliferation of illicit SALW in the Niger Delta, there is a need to address the core issues underlying the demand for these deadly

---

36 John Vidal, "Niger Delta Oil Spills Clean-up will Take 30 Years, says UN", *Guardian Newspaper*, 4 August 2011, retrieved from https://www.theguardian.com/environment/2011/aug/04/niger-delta-Oil-Spill-clean-up-on.30/03/2007.

37 Michael Eboh, "Non-Implementation of gas flare penalties costs Nigeria N2.9 trn", *Vanguard Newspaper*, 10 January 2017.

weapons, such as high rates of unemployment, social disintegration, unequal revenue distribution, political manipulation, and corruption. The short-term issues related to the supply of these tools of violence also need to be addressed, since their prevalence has an impact on the prospects for peace and justice in the Delta region. The guns-for-cash policy is not a viable solution, since militants can always use the proceeds to buy more guns.

The disarmament, demobilisation, and reintegration (DDR) process accompanying the amnesty and post-amnesty programmes needs a comprehensive and sustainable development strategy that addresses the root causes of the conflict, otherwise, the self-reinforcing cycle of arms proliferation and violence will continue. At the same time, the international community must enforce strict arms export control and put in place an effective juridical framework capable of halting illegal arms trafficking.

Finally, adequate compensation should be paid wherever there is an oil spill and the pollution should be cleaned up within a stipulated time. If these measures are taken, it may ultimately be possible to achieve peace and development in the Niger Delta.

Bibliography

Ajanaku, L., "The Squandering of Riches", *Tell Magazine*, 18 February 2008, pp. 36–38.

Ako, R., "The Struggle for Resource Control and Violence in the Niger Delta", in C. Obi and S.A. Rustad (eds.), *Oil and Insurgency in the Niger Delta: Managing the Complex Politics of Petro-violence*, London: Zed Books, 2009, p. 66.

Alemika, E.O., "Corruption and Insecurity in Nigeria", in R.A. Dunmoye, E.A. Unobe.

Bassey, N., "The Oil Industry and Human Rights in the Niger Delta: Being his Testimony before the United States Senate Judiciary Sub-Committee on Human Rights and the Law". US Senate Judiciary Sub-Committee on Human Rights and the Law, 24 September 2008. Retrieved from http://www.earthrights.org/sites/default/files/documents/Nnimo-testimony-9-24-08.pdf (accessed 24 December 2016).

Chukwuemeka, E.E.O. and V.N.O. Aghara, Niger Delta Youth Restiveness and Socio-Economic Development of Nigeria. Newswatch, August 13, 2007, pp. 40–43.

Dafinone, D., "The Niger Delta Crisis: Genesis, Exodus and Solution", *The Vanguard Daily*, 16 November 2007, p. 25.

Davies, S., "The Potential for Peace and Reconciliation in the Niger Delta", in C. Obi and S.A. Rustad (eds), *Oil and Insurgency in the Niger Delta: Managing the Complex Politics of Petro-violence*, London: Zed Books, 2009, p. 142.

Dode, R.O., "The Political Economy of Resource Curse and the Niger Delta Crisis in Nigeria: Matters Arising", *European Journal of Sustainable Development*, 1: 2 (2012), pp. 235–248.

Douglas, O., "A Community Guide to Understanding Resource Control", Urhobo Historical Society, 3 July 2001. Retrieved from www.waado.org/NigerDelta/Essays/Resource-Control/Guide_Douglas.html (accessed 14 December 2016).

Duru, A.E., "Addressing Oil Theft, Illegal Bunkering in Niger Delta", *Daily Independent*, 29 November 2013 Retrieved from http://www.dailyindependent.com/2013/1 (accessed 15 November 2016).

Edigin, L., and I.E. Okonmah, "Mystifying Development Policy Strategies in the Niger Delta: The Unending Mistake", *Journal of Research in National Development*, 8: 2 (2010), pp. 173–181.

Fubara, B.A., "The Politics of the Niger Delta", in P.I. Ozo-Eson, and U. Ukiwo, *The Niger Delta Development Commission: Towards Development Blueprint*, Port-Harcourt: Centre for Advanced Social Science (CASS), Port-Harcourt. Retrieved from https://eujournal.org/index.php/esj/article/viewFile/8015/7712 (accessed 20 January 2017).

Gottfredson, Michael R., and Travis Hirschi, *A General Theory of Crime*, Stanford, CA: Stanford University Press, 1990 (E-Book Library).

Hazen, J.M., and J. Horner, "Small Arms, Armed Violence, and Insecurity in Nigeria" The Niger Delta in Perspective, Geneva: Small Arms Survey Graduate Institute of International Studies Small Arms Survey Occasional Paper 20, 2007, p. 82.

Ibaba, S.I., *Understanding the Niger Delta Crisis*, Port Harcourt: Amethyst and Colleagues Publishers, 2005 (E-Book Library).

Ikelegbe, A., "The Economy of Conflict in the Oil-Rich Niger Delta Region of Nigeria", *Nordic Journal of African Studies*, 14: 2 (2005), pp. 208–234.

Inokoba, P.K., and D.L. Imbua, "Vexation and Militancy in the Niger Delta: The Way Forward", *Kamla-Raj J Hum Ecol*, 29: 2 (2010), pp. 101–120.

Mamah, E., and E. Amaize, "Nigeria: MEND Resumes Hostilities-Blows Up Agip Trunk Line in Bayelsa", *Vanguard* May 26 2016. Retrieved from https://www.vanguardngr.com/2016/05/militants-blow-agip-shell-trunk-line-bayelsa/ (accessed 6 March 2017).

Marx, Karl, and Frederick Engels, "*Selected Works in One Volume*", Moscow: International Publishers, 1970.

Mbah, Fidelis, "Niger Delta Promises", Port Harcourt: FidelisMbah, 12 February, 2008. Retrieved from http://nwaokonaku.blogspot.com.ng/2008/02/niger-delta-promises.html?m=0 (accessed 30 March 2017).

Nwachukwu, L.C., and S.J. Pepple, "Disarmament of Niger Delta Militants and Nigeria's National Security: A Critical Appraisal", *Journal of International Politics and Development Studies*, 7 (2011), pp. 90–120.

Obi, C., and S.A. Rustad, "Is the Window of Opportunity Closing for the Niger Delta?", in C. Obi and S.A. Rustad (eds.), *Oil and Insurgency in the Niger Delta: Managing the Complex Politics of Petro-Violence*. London/New York: Zed Books, 2011.

Ofehe, S., "Features on Niger Delta Amnesty", *Ex Ponto Magazine*, 6 August 2010. Retrieved from http://www.expontomagazine.com/nl/reportages/2279-features-on-Niger-Delta-amnesty (accessed 11 May 2017).

Okoko, K., and S.I. Ibaba, "Oil Spillages and Community Disturbances: The SPDC and the Niger Delta Experience", *Nigerian Journal of Oil and Politics*, 1 (1997), pp. 56–69.

Oil Minerals Producing Areas Development Commission (OMPADEC), "Quarterly Report", 1: 1 (October 1993). [NB. OMPADEC is now defunct].

Omoyibo, K.U., and O. Omoruyi, "Political Economy Diagnosis of Crude Oil Theft in Nigeria: The Way Forward", *Mediterranean Journal of Social Sciences*, 5: 2 (2014), pp. 297–302.

Owonikoko, B.S., and U. Ifukor, "From Campuses to Communities: Community-Based Cultism and Local Responses in the Niger Delta Region, Nigeria", *International Journal of Arts and Humanities*, 5: 4 (2016), pp. 16–32.

Sampson, Robert J., and John H. Laub, *Crime in the Making: Pathways and Turning Points through Life*, Cambridge, MA: Harvard University Press 1993 (E-Book Library).

Stouffer, Samuel A., *Adjustment During Army Life*, Princeton, NJ: Princeton University Press, 1949, p. 125.

Tell Magazine, "Hostage Economy: Oil Firms Flee Niger Delta", 9 June 2008, pp. 5–7.

Townsend, Peter, *Poverty in the United Kingdom. A Survey of Household Resources and Standards of Living*, Harmondsworth: Penguin Books, 1979.

Udama, R.A., "Understanding Nigeria Terrorism, Its Implications to National Peace, Security, Unity and Sustainable Development: A Discussion", *Journal of Humanities and Social Sciences*, 8: 5 (2013), pp. 110–115.

Vines, A., "Combating Light Weapons Proliferation in West Africa", *International Affairs*, 81: 2 (2005), pp. 341–360.

World Bank, "World Bank Report Defining an Environmental Development Strategy for the Niger Delta, vols 1 & 2", Washington, DC: World Bank, 1993.

CHAPTER 7

Crime at the University of Lagos: Insights from Akoka Campus

Franca Attoh

1 Introduction

This chapter interrogates the phenomenon of crime at the University of Lagos (UNILAG), Nigeria using the Akoka campus as a case study (see map 7.1 in the appendix to chapter 7). The chapter is premised on the assumption that the rising criminality in the external environment of the campus, for example in the slums of neighbouring Bariga and Ilaje, is likely to affect the prevalence of crime on the university campus. The data for the chapter were generated through the triangulation of a cross-sectional survey, in-depth interviews, and key informant interviews. Anchoring the discourse on the Broken Window and Defensible Space theories, the chapter avers that the phenomenon of crime on UNILAG's Akoka campus is still insignificant even though crimes such as theft and drug use are rampant in the hostels. Other places where crime is relatively high are the walkways, the classrooms, and the offices. The most secure place on campus is the staff quarters, where the members of staff reside. The architectural designs of the Jaja, Mariere, and New Halls were found to be facilitating theft in the student hostels and allowing cult members to hang out in front of the halls, in spite of the university's zero tolerance of cultism. In addition, leaving hostels unrepaired gives the impression that no one cares, and encourages criminals, especially cult members, to hang out in such places. The data from the survey show that the time of crime is usually between 12.00 am and 6.00 am. Evidence from the qualitative data shows that the presence of security personnel on campus has reduced the incidence of crime. However, members of the security unit believe that a higher level of security could be achieved with the recruitment of more personnel and provision of logistics such as lamps and more telephone lines within a closed user group (CUG) to aid communication and facilitate the apprehension of criminals. In addition, they have called for the provision of vehicles to increase motorised patrols on campus. Finally, it is suggested that prompt prosecution and sanction of convicted criminals will serve as a deterrent to potential criminals on campus.

 | DOI:10.1163/9789004396289_009

The University of Lagos, established in 1962, was specifically created to offer day and evening courses to meet the increasing demand for workers in the newly independent Nigeria. At inception, an unusually large number of candidates applied to the evening and day programmes to study courses in commerce, business administration, economics, and higher management studies. However, of the 3,000 candidates who applied for admission, only 72 were offered a place.[1] The number of students grew progressively to the point that, annually, an average of 1,000 candidates apply to study at the University of Lagos. Presently, the University has a student population of about 45,000 and offers both full- and part-time courses at its College of Medicine, twelve Faculties and via its Distance Leaning Institute. The total staff is about 4, 000, comprising both academic and non-teaching staff.[2]

The University of Lagos is fully accredited by the National University Commission (NUC) and with the Webometrics ranking of universities placing UNILAG in first place in Nigeria, there is increasing pressure on the facilities and built environment at UNILAG as the student population continues to rise. Significantly, the growth in Nigeria's urban crime rate, a major social problem facing the country in recent times, is also impacting built environments such as universities, which have not been spared this social malaise and are reporting incidences of theft, burglary, armed robbery, drug use and cultism. In the case of UNILAG, the main campus is surrounded by a ghetto and a slum, Bariga and Ilaje, where crimes are commonplace. The work of Newman and Jeffrey has examined the physical characteristics of the built environment that promotes or impedes criminal behaviour.[3] They found that specific characteristics of the built environment were associated with higher crime rates. These observations centre on the crime prevention through environmental design (CPTED) movement, which advocates making changes in the physical characteristics of a place to reduce crime. The contradictions that stem from a growing urban population characterised by a rising urban criminality have inspired this chapter to ascertain whether external environments such as the sprawling Bariga and Ilaje ghetto, where crimes such as cultism, drug use, and peddling,

1 See, A.B. Aderibigbe, "Emergence of the University, 1962–1967", in R.T Akinyele & Olufunke Adeboye (eds.), *A History of the University of Lagos, 1962–2012* (Lagos: University of Lagos Press, 2013), p. 13.

2 For statistics regarding the expanding numbers of students and staff expansion, see "Appendix", in Akinyele and Adeboye, *A History of University of Lagos*, pp. 667–668.

3 O. Newman, *Defensible Space: Crime Prevention Through Urban Design.* (New York: Macmillan, 1972), cited in E.R. Groff (2005), "Simulating Crime Prevention Strategies: A Look at the Possibilities". Retrieved from https//www.researchgate.net/publication/228817396 on 10/11/16.

including armed robbery, are rife, could affect a built environment such as the University of Lagos' Akoka Campus. The goal of this chapter is to ascertain the spatial distribution of crime on UNILAG's Akoka CampusThe specific objectives are:

- To identify architectural defects of the study environment that promote crime and fear of crime on campus;
- To design a specific crime prevention strategy through environmental design and tactical responses that can be deployed in the study environment to improve security;
- To suggest policy directions for a more secure campus environment.

To achieve the set objectives, the chapter is divided into five sections. Section 1 discusses the establishment of the University of Lagos and how the rapid increase in population has created some social problems on the campus. Section 2 anchors the discourse on two environmental theories, namely the Broken Window Theory and the Defensible Space Theory. Section 3 discusses the triangulation method deployed to generate the data for the study, namely a cross-sectional survey, in-depth interviews, and key informant interviews. Section 4 discusses the results of the generated data, while Section 5 concludes with recommendations to help secure the built environment.

2 Theoretical Underpinnings

The Broken Window Theory is an environmental theory of the causation and prevention of crime developed by James Wilson and George Kelling in 1982.[4] They argued that physical deterioration results in anxiety about personal safety, which, in turn, leads to further deterioration and higher rates of victimisation in an area. The implication is that certain architectural and environmental characteristics can heighten and engender increased crime in a community. It avers that a broken window, left unrepaired, is a sign that no one cares and thus impels other windows to be broken, leading to environmental disorder and degradation. The theory further posits that the prevalence of disorder creates fear in the minds of citizens, who are convinced that the area is unsafe. This withdrawal from the community weakens social controls that previously kept criminals in check. Once this process begins, it feeds itself. Disorder causes crime, and crime causes further disorder and crime. Scholars often define two

4 J.Q. Wilson & G.L. Kelling, "Broken Windows: The Police and Neighbourhood Safety", in E. McLaughlin, J. Maurice & G. Hughes (eds.), *Criminological Perspectives: Essential Readings* (2nd Edition), (London: Sage Publications, 2003).

different types of disorder. The first is what is referred to as physical disorder, typified by vacant buildings, broken windows, abandoned vehicles, and vacant lots filled with trash. The second type is social disorder, typified by aggressive panhandlers, noisy neighbours, and groups of youths congregating on street corners. The line between crime and disorder is often blurred, with some experts considering such acts as prostitution and drug dealing as disorder, while many others classify them as crimes. Within the Akoka Campus of the university, hostels such as Jaja Hall, a predominantly male hostel, Sodeinde in New Hall, also a male hostel, Elkanemi which the university has now pulled down, and female hostels such as Amina and Makama-Bida lack modern amenities and are in a state of deterioration. They are also housing a large population of both bonafide and illegal (squatters) residents and have been identified as crime infested areas on campus.

The Defensible Space Theory was postulated by Oscar Newman in 1972. It consists of a range of mechanisms that combine to bring an environment under the control of its residents. According to Newman, crime can be prevented by deploying good architectural designs that eliminate the opportunity for criminality.[5] Defensible Space Theory is a crime prevention model that posits that crime victimisation and the fear of crime are the fallout of an environment where residents have lost control, but that crime can be prevented by once more bringing the environment under the control of residents through a systematic manipulation of the architectural designs in a built environment. The theory avers that crime is a product of spatiality, an outcome of the interaction between a (potential) criminal and the architectural designs of a built environment. The Defensible Space Theory is traced to the Chicago School of Criminology, founded by Robert Part and Ernest Burgess in their quest to find a solution to the social disorganisation that characterised the city of Chicago in the 1920s. Defensible space, therefore, is a range of real and symbolic barriers, strongly defined areas of influence, and improved opportunities for surveillance that help residents own their environment.[6] According to Özkan Gök , the theory is anchored on two models, namely the situational model and the community model. He argues that the situational model prevents crime by eliminating the opportunities for crime, whereas the community model brings the environment under the control of the residents who defend their space to achieve greater security. This is achieved by deploying three main strategies,

5 L.J. Sigel & J.J. Senna, Introduction to Criminal Justice. (Cengage Advantage Books) 12th Edition, (Boston:Wadsworth, 2009).

6 O. Newman, *Defensible Space: Crime Prevention Through Urban Design*. New York, Macmillan, 1972; S. Emitt, *Architectural Technology*, (London: Blackwell Science, 2002).

namely natural surveillance, natural access control, and territoriality. Natural surveillance is the ability to see into or out from the space.[7] Surveillance is the close observation of persons and events. For instance, when buildings are designed with doors and windows that look onto streets, parks, and parking lots, and pedestrian friendly streets are equipped with adequate lighting etc., crime is thus deterred by increasing the offender's perception of greater risk of recognition or apprehension. Natural access control consists of symbolic and real barriers that prevent crime by increasing the risk of apprehension when a criminal enters a building. By using particular architectural landscape, access to private or privatised areas is denied. This is achieved by placing entrances, exits, perimeter fencing, lighting, landscaping, and boundary markers to increase the possibility of apprehension or recognition. Territoriality is the use of architectural and landscape structural elements to create a sense of ownership in residents and legitimate users. Territoriality enables residents to recognise fellow residents from strangers and to determine what constitutes acceptable norms of behaviour within the sphere of influence. The territorial space is further reinforced through environment laundry, i.e. improving the physical appearance of a space by cleaning and cleansing it from criminal elements. A dignified environment increases the risk of apprehension while simultaneously reinforcing residents' confidence and interest in controlling their space. Residents could also deploy technological devices such as CCTV and burglar alarms. For built environments such as university campuses, the Defensible Space Theory is appropriate for determining the spatial causes of crime and modelling intervention programmes. This becomes significant as some forms of victimisation may occur on campus in addition to issues of drugs, petty theft, and cultism.

3 Method

3.1 *Study Population and Sample Size*

The data for the chapter were generated from the cross-sectional survey, in-depth interviews (IDIs), and key informant interviews (KIIs). The questionnaires used in the survey were administered to members of the university community, comprising students, members of staff, vendors, service providers, and residents. The IDIs were conducted among top officials of the academic and non-academic staff. Vendors, service providers, and residents were also interviewed. The KIIs were conducted among principal officers of the university, top

7 Baskanligi, P.A "The Role of Opportunity in Crime Prevention and Possible Threats of Crime Control Benefits", *Turkish Journal of Police Studies*, 13: 1 (2011), pp. 77–114.

security officials, and security officers posted to strategic locations on campus such as hostels, staff school, and other strategic areas. The reason for selecting these groups of people for the qualitative data was their ability to share their experiences and the fact that their views about the spatial distribution of crime at the University of Lagos reflect the general perception of people in the study area.

3.2 *Sampling Techniques*

For the cross-sectional survey, a quota sampling technique was adopted. A quota sampling technique is one in which certain proportions of the sample are reserved for certain groups or categories of respondents. When using a quota sampling technique, the researcher first decides how many of the elements in different classes or categories will be included in the sample. Having decided this, the subjects who match the quota factors are selected (this is a non-random process). By adopting this technique, the UNILAG population was categorised into students, members of staff, and others. The "others" category included traders, artisans, vendors, and other persons who are on campus. A sample size of 550 respondents was selected, comprising 400 students, 100 members of staff and 50 individuals categorised as "others".

3.3 *IDI and KII*

The In-Depth Interview (IDI) and Key Informant Interview are two qualitative research methods adopted to complement the generated quantitative data from the cross-sectional survey. KII and IDI are research methods that involve every stakeholder identified by the researcher being asked specific questions in a discursive atmosphere about his/her perception and opinion on spatial distribution of crime on campus, how environmental and architectural designs on campus influence crime, and the general security situation of the university community. The essence of the KII and IDI is to allow respondents to share their divergent views about the subject matter of the study. Unlike the questionnaire, which may not allow respondents to provide detailed information about their experiences or witnessing of crime or their views about the architectural designs and crime on campus, the KII and IDI give respondents an opportunity to air their views freely and elaborately. Thus, a total of 30 IDIs and eighteen KIIs were conducted in the context of this research.

4 Discussion of Findings

Returned survey questionnaires were edited prior to the digital data-entering process and the results of the IDIs and KIIs were transcribed from the tapes in preparation for the final analysis. Survey data were analysed using descriptive statistical methods. This involved the use of percentages and frequency tables. A content analysis method was adopted after the data had been described for the analysis of the KIIs and IDIs. The responses to each question were summarised and important quotations and phrases were reported verbatim to complement the survey findings. Table 7.1 contains the socio-demographic characteristics of the respondents.

TABLE 7.1 Socio-demographic characteristics

Sex	**Frequency**	**Percentage**
Male	273	52.7
Female	245	47.3
Total	**518**	**100.0**
Age	**Frequency**	**Percentage**
Less than 15 years	3	.6
15–19	130	25.1
20–24	119	23.0
25–29	50	9.7
30–34	16	3.1
35–39	15	2.9
40–44	16	3.1
45–49	31	6.0
50 years and above	17	3.3
No Response	121	23.4
Total	**518**	**100.0**
Religion	**Frequency**	**Percentage**
Christian	403	77.8
Islam	105	20.3
Traditional	2	.4
Others	8	1.5
Total	**518**	**100.0**
Ethnic Group	**Frequency**	**Percentage**
Hausa	16	3.1
Igbo	87	16.8

TABLE 7.1 Socio-demographic characteristics (*cont.*)

Ethnic Group	**Frequency**	**Percentage**
Yoruba	371	71.6
Others	44	8.5
Total	**518**	**100.0**
Educational level	**Frequency**	**Percentage**
Primary	6	1.2
Secondary	37	7.1
Undergraduate	336	64.9
Graduate	75	14.5
Postgraduate	60	11.6
No response	4	.8
Total	**518**	**100.0**
Marital Status	**Frequency**	**Percentage**
Single	399	77.0
Married	111	21.4
Divorced/Separated	1	.2
Widow/Widower	5	1.0
No response	2	.4
Total	**518**	**100.0**
Employment Status	**Frequency**	**Percentage**
Employed	157	30.3
Unemployed	64	12.4
Retired	2	.4
Student	295	56.9
Total	**518**	**100.0**
Monthly Income (Naira)	**Frequency**	**Percentage**
Less than 50,000	105	20.3
50,000–100,000	18	3.5
101,000–150,000	19	3.7

Monthly Income (Naira)	Frequency	Percentage
151,000–200,000	12	2.3
201,000–250,000	3	.6
No Response	361	69.7
Total	**518**	**100.0**

Status on Campus	Frequency	Percentage
Student	359	69.3
Staff	94	18.1
Vendor	18	3.5
Artisan	15	2.9
Others	32	6.2
Total	**518**	**100.0**

Place of Stay on Campus	Frequency	Percentage
Hostel	258	49.8
Office Area	52	10.0
Business/Shopping Complex	25	4.8
Staff Quarters	25	4.8
Others	17	3.3
No Response	141	27.2
Total	**518**	**100.0**

The socio-demographic characteristics considered are: sex; age; religion; ethnic group; educational level; marital status; employment status; monthly income; status on campus; and place of stay on campus.

4.1 *Sex*

The indication is that 52.7% (273) of the respondents were men, while 47.3% (245) were women. The table shows a higher percentage of male respondents than female respondents in the study.

4.2 *Age*

Table 7.1 shows the age range of respondents in the study. It indicates that: 6% (3) of the respondents were less than fifteen years old; 25.1% (130) were between the age range of 15–19; 23.% (119) were between the age range of 20–24; 9.7% (50) were between 25–29 years; 3.1% (16) were between the age range of

30–34; 2.9% (15) were between 35–39 years old; 3.1% (16) were between 40–44; and 6.% (31) were between the age range of 45–49 years and 3.2% (17) were 50 years and above.

4.3 *Religious Affiliation*

Data on the religious affiliation of respondents reveal that: 77.8% (403) are Christian; 20.3% (105) practice Islam; 0.4% (2) practice traditional religion; and 1.5% (8) practice other forms of religion.

4.4 *Ethnic Group*

The distribution of respondents by ethnic group shown in Table 7.1 reveals that: 3.1% (16) of the respondents were from the Hausa ethnic group; 16.8% (87) were from the Igbo ethnic group; 71.6% (371) were from the Yoruba ethnic group; and 8.5% (44) were from other ethnic groups. The table shows that most of the respondents were from the Yoruba ethnic group. This is not surprising given that the university is located in the south-west of Nigeria.

4.5 *Educational Level*

Data on the educational level of respondents show that: 1.2% (6) had completed their primary education; 7.1% (37) had secondary level education; 64.9% (336) were undergraduate students; 14.5% (75) had a first degree certificate; and 11.6% (60) had a postgraduate qualification. The table reveals that most of the respondents were undergraduate students and this is due to the fact that they constitute the majority of the university community.

4.6 *Marital Status*

The distribution of respondents by marital status shows that: 77% (399) of the respondents were single; 21.4% (111) were married; 0.2% (1) were divorced and 1% (5) were widowed. The table shows that the majority of the respondents was single. This can be attributed to the fact that most of them were undergraduate students.

4.7 *Employment Status*

With respect to the employment status of respondents, Table 7.1 indicates that: 30% (157) was employed; 12.4% (64) was unemployed; 0.4% (2) was retired; and 56.9% (295) were students.

4.8 *Monthly Income*

The distribution of respondents by monthly income reveals that: 20.3% (105) of the respondents earned less than ₦50,000; 3.5% (18) earned between ₦50,000–₦100,000; 3.7% (19) earned between ₦101,000– ₦150,000; 2.3% (12) earned between ₦151,000–₦200,000; and 0.6% (3) earned between ₦201,000–₦250,000.

4.9 *Status of Respondents on Campus*

Data on the status of respondents on campus shows that: 69.3% (359) of the respondents were students; 18.1% (94) were staff; 3.5% (18) were vendors; 2.9% (15) were artisans; and 6.2% (32) formed other categories such as service providers, such as cleaners, laundry staff, etc.

4.10 *Respondents' Place of Stay on Campus*

Table 7.1 shows the distribution of respondents by place of stay on campus. The table reveals that: 49.8% of the respondents stayed in the hostel; 10% (52) stayed in the office area; 4.8% (25) stayed in the business/shopping complex in school; and 4.8% (25) stayed in staff quarters, while 3.3% (17) stayed in other locations in the school, such as in their faculty.

TABLE 7.2 Experience of crime on campus

Experience of Crime on Campus	Frequency	Percentage
Experienced	104	20.1
Not Experienced	414	79.9
Total	**518**	**100.0**
Experience of Crime in the Hostel	**Frequency**	**Percentage**
Experienced	46	44.2
Not Experienced	58	55.8
Total	**104**	**100.0**
Experience of Crime in the Office	**Frequency**	**Percentage**
Experienced	9	8.7
Not Experienced	95	91.3
Total	**104**	**100.0**
Experience of Crime in the Shopping Complex	**Frequency**	**Percentage**
Experienced	7	6.7
Not Experienced	97	93.3
Total	**104**	**100.0**

TABLE 7.2 Experience of crime on campus (*cont.*)

Experience of Crime in the Classroom	Frequency	Percentage
Experienced	14	13.5
Not Experienced	90	86.5
Total	**104**	**100.0**
Experience of Crime on Road/Walkway	**Frequency**	**Percentage**
Experienced	15	14.4
Not Experienced	89	85.6
Total	**104**	**100.0**
Experience of Crime at Motor Park	**Frequency**	**Percentage**
Experienced	6	5.8
Not Experienced	98	94.2
Total	**104**	**100.0**
Experience of Crime in Staff Quarters	**Frequency**	**Percentage**
Experienced	5	4.8
Not Experienced	99	95.2
Total	**104**	**100.0**
Experience of Crime at Sport Complex	**Frequency**	**Percentage**
Experienced	1	1
Not Experienced	103	99
Total	**104**	**100.0**
Experience of Crime at Relaxation Centre	**Frequency**	**Percentage**
Experienced	1	1
Not Experienced	103	99
Total	**104**	**100.0**
Experience of Crime at Medical Centre	**Frequency**	**Percentage**
Not Experienced	104	100.0
Total	**104**	**100.0**

Table 7.2 gives information on respondents' experience of crime. The table shows that 20.1% (104) of the respondents had experienced crime on campus, while 79.9% (414) had not. The table also presents data on the location where crime was experienced.

4.11 *Experience of Crime in Hostels*

Table 7.2 indicates that of the respondents who had experienced crime, 44.2% (46) had experienced crime in student hostels, while 55.7% (58) had not. The table shows that almost half of the respondents who had experienced crime on campus had their experience in the hostels.

4.12 *Experience of Crime in the Office*

Data on experience of crime in the office shows that 8.7% (9) of the respondents had experienced crime in the office, while 91.3% had not. The data presents a relatively low percentage of experience of crime in the office. This implies that the office areas on campus are relatively secure compared to the student hostels.

4.13 *Experience of Crime in the Shopping Complex*

Table 7.2 shows that 6.7% (7) of the respondents had experienced crime in the shopping complex areas, while 93.3% (97) had not. This finding suggests that there is a relatively low incidence of crime in the shopping complex areas.

4.14 *Experience of Crime in the Classroom*

Data on experience of crime in the classroom shows that 13.5% (14) of the respondents had experienced crime in the classrooms, while 86.5% (90) had not. This shows that fewer students had experienced crime in the class rooms.

4.15 *Experience of Crime on the Road/Walkway*

Table 7.2 indicates that 14.4% of the respondents had experienced crime on the road/walkways, while 85.6% had not.

4.16 *Experience of Crime at the Motor Park*

The distribution of respondents based on experience of crime at the motor park shows that 5.8% (6) of the respondents has experienced crime at the motor park, while 94.2% (98) had not.

4.17 *Experience of Crime in Staff Quarters*

Data on experience of crime in staff quarters reveal that 4.8% (5) of the respondents had experienced crime in the staff quarters, while 95.2% had not.

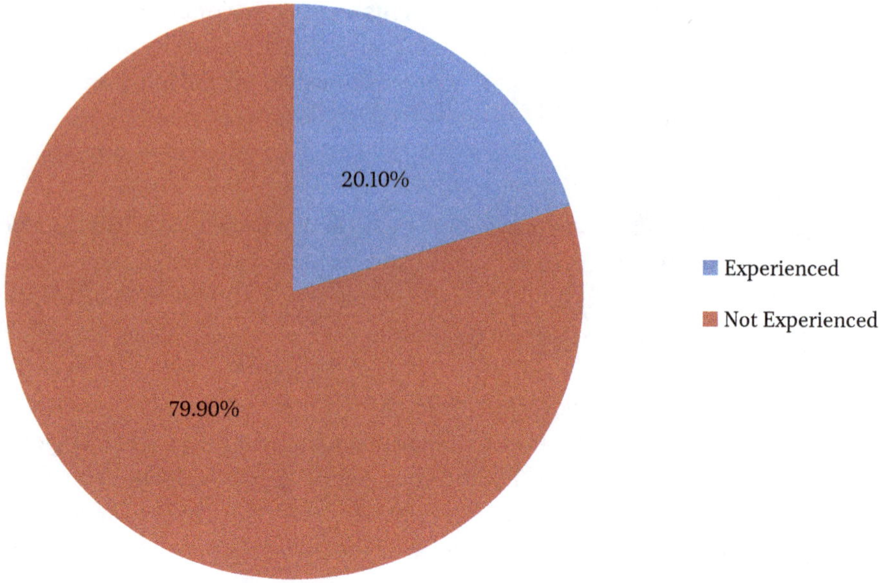

FIGURE 7.1 Experience of crime on campus
SOURCE: OWN RESEARCH

4.18 *Experience of Crime at Sports Complex*

Table 7.2 shows that 1% (1) of the respondents had experienced crime at the sports centre, while 99% (103) had not. This data indicates a very low incidence of crime at the campus sports centre.

4.19 *Experience of Crime at the Relaxation Centre*

The distribution of respondents on experience of crime at the relaxation centre shows that 1% (1) of the respondents had experienced crime at the relaxation centre, while 99% (103) had not.

4.20 *Experience of Crime at the Medical Centre*

Table 7.2 shows that none of the respondents had experienced crime at the university medical centre.

Figure 7.1, above, is a graphic representation of respondents' experience of crime on campus. The pie chart indicates that 20.1% of the respondents had experienced crime on campus, while 79.9% had not. It can be inferred from this graphic representation that the incidence of crime on the UNILAG campus is relatively low. Responses from the qualitative study also corroborate this observation. A cobbler interviewed during the study attested to the relative safety on campus:

> To me, the security personnel have been doing fine. I will score their performance level 80–85% because; for the past one year, we have not had cause to report missing or stolen properties. Personally, I have not experienced any form of harassment, nor theft.[8]

An official in the Faculty of Engineering also lent credence to the low incidence of crime on campus:

> I think cases of burglary occurred before I assumed my duty here. Since my resumption of office here, nothing of that nature has happened. This is probably because some lecturers usually stay late into the night to accomplish one or two academic works. Their presence may serve as deterrent to some bad boys who might want to burgle offices in those odd hours.

An official of the University Staff School also alluded to the low incidence of crime on campus:

> Not really. What we normally experience here is pupils' belongings getting missing. That usually happens when they go out to play and drop their bags on the floor. We don't experience the incidence of burglary here even during holidays as security officers are always present here.

An interview with a medical officer at the Medical Centre revealed that the incidence of crime is not as high as it used to be and it has been a long time since there had been any incidence of crime in the area:

> In the past, maybe 5–6 years ago, there used to be incidence of car burgling and vandalisation. But now, such a thing has not been experienced since the security officers are always on patrol day and night around this place.

Although there seem to be a consensus on the low incidence of crime on campus, there are still some instances of crime within the campus, especially in

8 The views of the respondents cited in this study are reported anonymously because of the security implications.

hostels and classrooms. In an interview with a porter in the Faculty of Arts, it was revealed that there had been cases of theft within the faculty:

> Some of them (students) have reported that their phones were stolen in the class rooms. We wonder at times when we meet students in the class rooms in the morning at the time the classrooms should have still been under lock and key. All the keys to the classrooms have been changed

Figure 7.2 provides a graphic illustration of the locations where crime has been experienced. The graph shows that hostels have the highest incidence of crime. Other locations with some incidences of crime are classrooms, road/walkways, and offices. A number of responses from the qualitative study (IDI and KII) with respect to locations on campus with incidence of crime corroborate the data from the quantitative survey. According to a top member of staff:

> The issue of petty theft is quite common in the students' hostels. They always come up with complaints like, "somebody stole my laptop", "somebody stole my wallet", "and somebody stole my phone". This is very common usually in the students' hostels. There is also the issue of breaking into people's cars. This is rampart around the sport centre, and occasionally in some faculties'. "People park their cars and go away, and come and discover that someone has broken into their cars. Of course, there is the issue of drug on campus. Quite a number of students have been apprehended smoking marijuana, been intoxicated by some other more potent

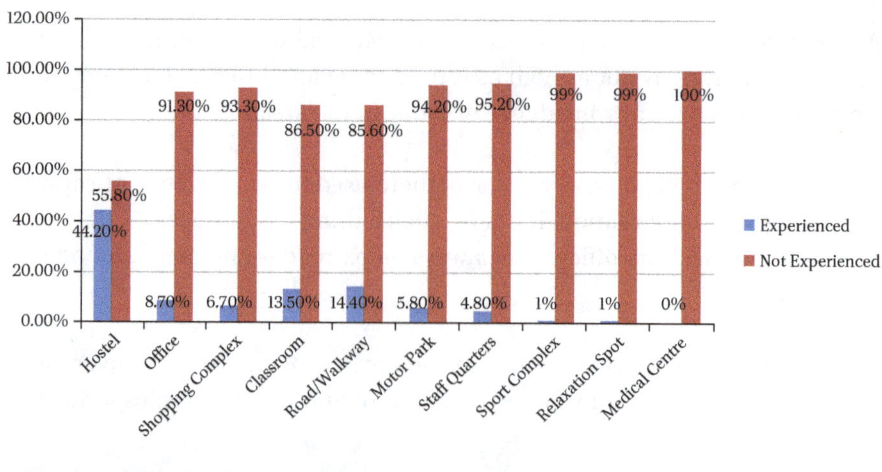

FIGURE 7.2 Location of crime experienced
SOURCE: OWN RESEARCH

> drugs. These are some of the challenges we face in terms of security on campus.

Similarly, an insider in the Faculty of Arts identified hostel areas as being prone to crime:

> Crime prone areas on campus are those close to the students' hostels, especially now that substance abuse is a common phenomenon among students'. And drug abuse is something perpetrated by cult boys and girls. On the surface it seems that cults are nonexistent because of the university zero tolerance on cultism. This has driven them underground. You find them hanging out in isolated places on campus.

According to a security officer in Sodehinde Hall, more security officers should be posted to hostels to ensure security within the hostels:

> You don't expect the security man monitoring the entrance of this hostel to know what is going on inside. And not two or three officers should be posted to this hostel; at least four at a time. Because when two officers are at the gate checking people in, the other two would be inside moving around, watching the movement of the students. In fact some students do challenge us when we move around telling us there is no problem. In female hostels, male security officers have limits to their movement around the hostel as some of them don't normally dress well and they can allege that you are peeping at them. That is the challenge in the female hostels. But crime is minimal in the female hostels'. We only record cases of theft of phones, dresses and occasionally a laptop.

In the same vein, a security officer in Jaja Hall expressed the view that more security personnel should be posted to hostels for effective security of lives and properties:

> You won't have issues with students once you know what you are doing. There is shortage of staff. Work that is supposed to be done by three people would be done by one person and you expect perfect performance. It is not possible. The work cannot be perfect. He would only try his best. If they can post to this Jaja Hall five persons in the morning, five in the afternoon, and five in the evening [, it] is not too much. The stress of checking people coming in alone is not something two persons can handle. We are just using our brain. How will two of us here be able to go round the hall to see what is happening inside? We just manage to do that and.

> mind you, Jaja and Sodeinde are places where you find some of these cult boys hanging out, but we accost them once we notice such movements.

For a top official in the Faculty of Engineering, the faculty and staff quarters are relatively secure. He also noted that proper identification of people in the university community would help reduce incidences of crime on campus:

> The staff quarters are relatively secure. The problem of security in this community is lack of proper identification of who is who. The University of Lagos is a public property where a large number of people visit every day. The University authority is trying to address the problem of identification through the introduction of bio metrics for both the staff and the students. But that gesture has not been extended to other members of the community like business owners on campus. And this I consider a big challenge.

In a key informant interview with a security officer at Jaja Hall, it was observed that the low incidence of crime could be attributed to the long period in which there was no students' union at the university; even though the management has since lifted the ban on the Student Union.

Crime has really reduced. Before, when there was a students' union, every crime committed would be defended by the union. If someone committed a crime, they would say he is a member of the students' union. Even the management could not do anything to them then. Until they burnt the VC Lodge during a crisis, [then] the union was suspended. So, those who used to commit crime hiding behind the students' union had to leave the school. But the ban on the union was just lifted last year. If you arrested somebody before, the students' union would come to say he is our person, release him. But now, [there is] nobody to defend you if you are caught. Even if you are a bad boy, you have to caution yourself as other students are too busy to come out and defend you.

Figure 7.3 presents a cross tabulation of experience of crime by sex. The figure shows that more men (22%) experienced crime on campus compared to females (18%). Despite this finding, the difference is not found to be statistically significant at a p-value of .254.

The cross-tabulation of experience of crime by status on campus is given in Figure 7.4. It shows that 21.4% of students who participated in the study had experienced crime, while 78.6% had not. For members of staff who participated in the study, 14.9% had experienced crime on campus, while 85.1% had not. The cross-tabulation in Figure 7.3 shows that 16.7% of vendors who participated in the study had experienced crime on campus, while 83.3% had not. For artisans who participated in the study, 13.3% had experienced crime, while

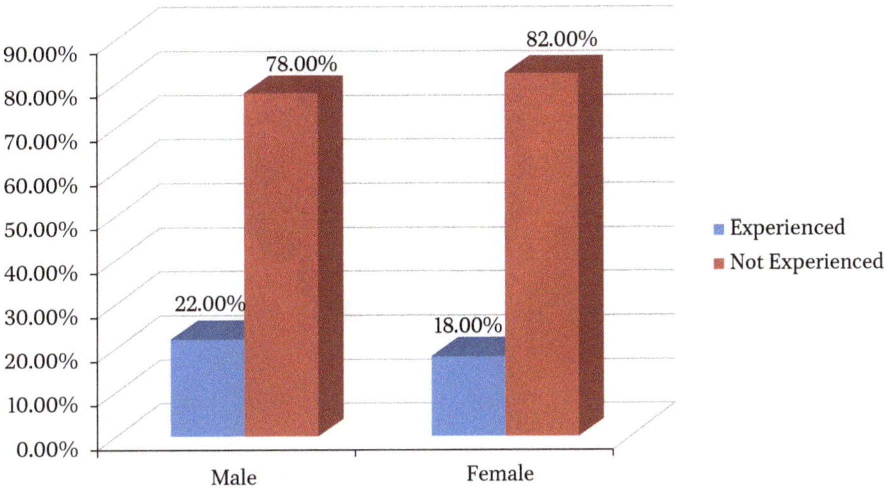

FIGURE 7.3 Experience of crime by sex
SOURCE: OWN RESEARCH

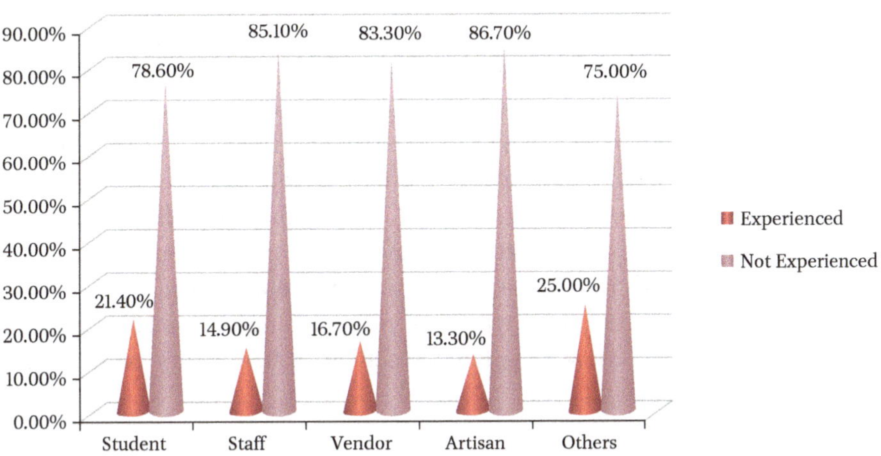

FIGURE 7.4 Experience of crime by status on campus
SOURCE: OWN RESEARCH

86.7% had not. The cross-tabulation also shows that for other participants in the study, 25% had experienced crime on campus, while 75% had not.

Experience of crime by age is given in Figure 7.5. It shows that: 33.3% of the respondents who are under fifteen years old had experienced crime on campus; 23.8% of respondents between the ages of 15–19 years had experienced crime on campus. Of those respondents between the ages of 20–24, 20% had experienced

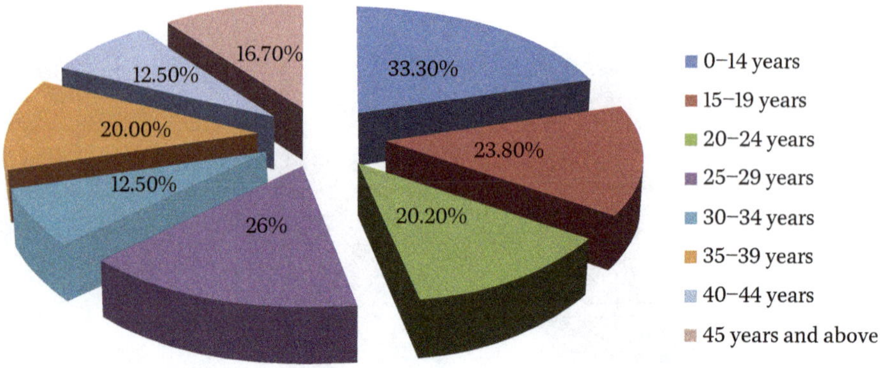

FIGURE 7.5 Experience of crime by age
SOURCE: OWN RESEARCH

crime on campus; 26% of respondents between the ages of 25–29, 12.5% of respondents between 30–34, and 20% of those between 35–39 years had experienced crime. Meanwhile, 12.5% of respondents between the ages of 40–44% and 16.7% of respondents that were 45 years and above had experienced crime on campus. The data presented in the graph shows that respondents under the age of fifteen had the highest percentage of experience of crime in the study; this is because only three respondents were in this age category, one of whom had experienced a crime at the UNILAG campus. This equates to 33.3% of this group. Thus, the high percentage of experience of crime among respondents under the age of fifteen is not necessarily indicative of a high prevalence of crime among young people on campus. Indeed, collaboratively, results from the chi square analysis shows that there is no significant relationship between age and experience of crime on campus as the p-value was 0.821.

Table 7.3 presents data on the type of crime experienced by the respondents in the study. Forms of crime experienced include theft, burglary, rape, harassment, and physical assault.

4.21 *Experience of Theft*

Table 7.3 shows that 69.2% (72) of the respondents had experienced theft, while 30.8% (32) had not experienced theft. The data suggest that theft is a very prevalent form of crime experienced on campus.

4.22 *Experience of Burglary*

Table 7.3 shows that 12.5% (13) of the respondents had experienced burglary, while 87.5% had not. The data indicates that a relatively low number of respondents had experienced burglary. This can be attributed to the fact that most of the respondents live in the student hostel.

TABLE 7.3 Type of crime experienced

Experience of Theft	**Frequency**	**Percentage**
Experienced	72	69.2
Not Experienced	32	30.8
Total	**104**	**100.0**
Experience of Burglary	**Frequency**	**Percentage**
Experienced	13	12.5
Not Experienced	91	87.5
Total	**104**	**100.0**
Experience of Rape	**Frequency**	**Percentage**
Experienced	2	1.9
Not Experienced	102	98.1
Total	**104**	**100.0**
Experience of Harassment	**Frequency**	**Percentage**
Experienced	21	20.2
Not Experienced	83	79.8
Total	**104**	**100.0**
Experience of Physical Attack	**Frequency**	**Percentage**
Experienced	10	9.6
Not Experienced	94	90.4
Total	**104**	**100.0**
Time of Experience of Crime	**Frequency**	**Percentage**
12.00 am–3.00 am	17	16.4
3.00 am–6.00 am	18	17.3

TABLE 7.3 Type of crime experienced (*cont.*)

Time of Experience of Crime	Frequency	Percentage
6.00 am–9.00 am	13	12.5
9.00 am–12.00 pm	6	5.8
12.00 pm–3.00 pm	15	14.4
3.00 pm–6.00 pm	12	11.5
6.00 pm–9.00 pm	11	10.6
9.00 pm–12.00 am	12	11.5
Total	**104**	**100.0**
Experience of Intervention by security Officers		
Experienced	17	16.3
Not Experienced	87	83.7
Total	**104**	**100.0**

4.23 *Experience of Rape*

Data on experience of rape among respondents show that 1.9% (2) of the respondents had experienced rape, while 98.1% (102) had not experienced rape. This information indicates that either rape is a relatively less prevalent form of crime on campus, or that victims of rape are not willing to discuss their experiences.

4.24 *Experience of Harassment*

Table 7.3 shows the distribution of respondents who have experienced harassment. It shows that 20.2% (21) of the respondents had experienced harassment, while 79.8 (83) had not.

4.25 *Experience of Physical Attack*

The data on respondents' experience of physical attack show that 9.6% (10) of the respondents had experienced physical attack, while 90.4% (94) had not.

Figure 7.6, below, shows the type of crime experienced as revealed by the respondents, while Figure 7.7 depicts the time of the day when crime was experienced.

Figure 7.6 presents a graphic illustration of types of crime experienced by respondents. The graph shows that majority of the respondents (69.2%) had

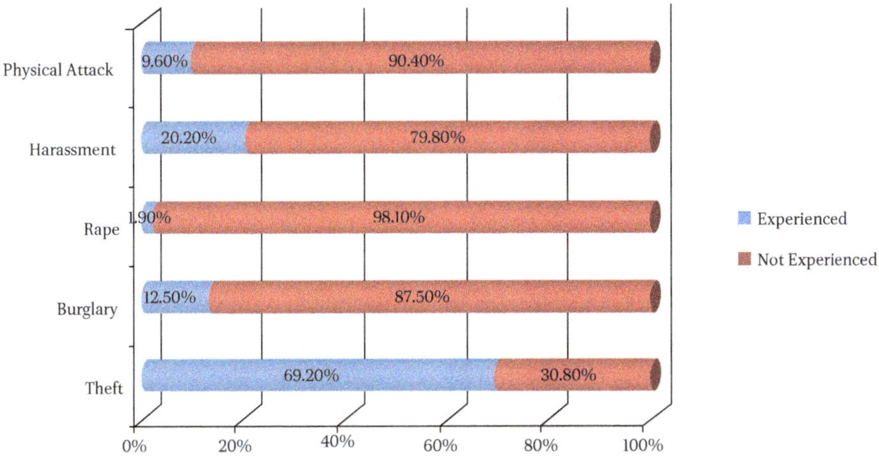

FIGURE 7.6 Type of crime experienced
SOURCE: OWN RESEARCH

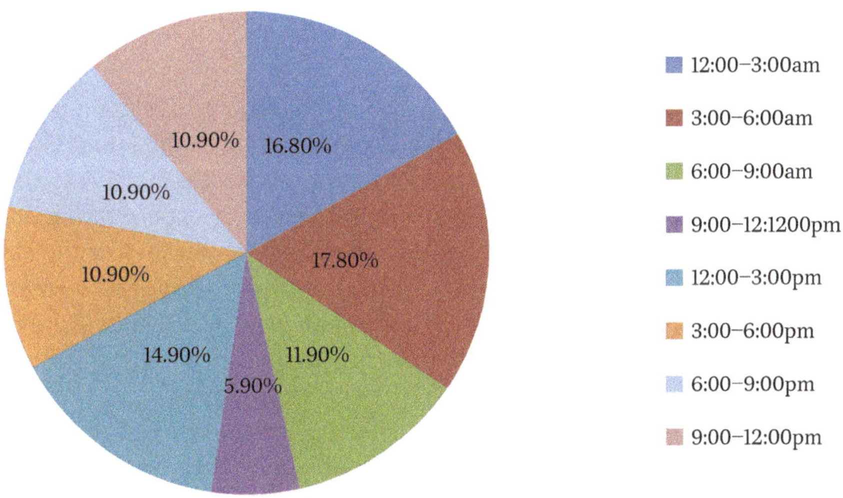

FIGURE 7.7 Time of experience crime
SOURCE: OWN RESEARCH

experienced theft on campus. Findings from the qualitative study corroborate the quantitative study as responses from respondents revealed that theft is the most commonly experienced form of crime on campus. It was also found that students engage in drug abuse on campus. A student who participated in the in-depth interviews identified theft and drug abuse as common crimes among students:

> I think theft should be one and also guys consume drugs here as there are some bushes into which they go to smoke and things like that. I cannot

> tell what kind of drugs they take. I have once heard of a guy who tried to force a lady into sex along the road here in the day break. The lady screamed and the security men around came to arrest the situation.

A medical officer at the Medical Centre alluded to cases of assault and drug abuse among students:

> I have been working here for the past fifteen years. Here, we have received victims of assault and all that. When we are to compare the level of security in the university with the surrounding environments, we may conclude that some areas need to be addressed here. The area of substance abuse needs to be addressed. Whenever a patient is brought here, we normally run urine tests and the results are always amazing.

With respect to incidences of drug abuse, a principal officer of the University stated that measures are put in place to deter students from getting involved in this risky behaviour:

> There is a lot of enlightenment on campus especially in relation to drug abuse by students, and the university has also acquired some testing equipment at the Medical Centre. What they do there is that, if a student is suspected to have been taking marijuana etc. they expose the student a critical test and the result comes out positive or negative as the case may be. These are things to have a check on the students, and once you are found to have been engaging in such practices, it now enters into the social misconduct panel; you face the university panel.

Data on time of experience of crime is shown in Figure 7.7. The data reveal that: 16.8% (17) of the respondents experienced crime between 12:00 am–3:00 am; 17.3% (18) experienced crime between 3:00 am–6:00 am; 12.5% (13) experienced crime between 6:00 am–9:00 am; 5.8% (6) experienced crime between 9:00 am–12:00 pm; 14.4% (15) of the respondents experienced crime between 12:00 pm–3:00 pm; 11.5% (12) experienced crime between 3:00–6:00pm; 10.6% (11) experienced crime between 6:00 pm–9:00 pm; and 11.5% experienced crime between 9:00 pm–12:00 am. It can be seen that most of the crime experienced on campus occurred at night, between the hours of 12:00 am to 6:00 am. Responses from the qualitative study confirm the findings of the quantitative study. In an interview with a member of staff in the Faculty of Engineering, it was revealed that students in the faculty had been victims of crime very early in the morning:

> When I assumed duty here, I discovered that no security officer is being posted to the faculty both day and night. We only have porters whose duty is to keep and release keys to members of the faculty to gain access to their various offices. Some times last year when I just assumed duty, I received the report of students being robbed of their belongings by some boys around the car park in the early hours of the morning precisely around 6:00 am.

Another reason given for the high rate of crime during these hours is that during examination periods, students go to their faculties and some selected areas within the campus to read for their examinations and some criminal elements take advantage of unwary students. They steal students' phones, laptops, and other valuables. Some students doze off while reading and by the time they wake up their belongings are gone. It was also found that some students are targeted when returning to their hostels in the morning.

Apart from students, members of staff also experience crime in these odd hours. For instance, a member of staff in the Faculty of Law shared his experience:

> I have had time to invite the security officers and they were cooperative. My house has been robbed three times in three years at the Ransom Kuti staff quarters. One of the robbery happened around 3:00 am. The robbers came into the house but couldn't get into my room. So I was hearing their voices from inside my room. The burglary experience took place 4 months ago. The security officers were called and they investigated everywhere in the house and asked if there was any suspect. I didn't really have any suspect.

The results from both the quantitative and qualitative data show that despite the low incidence of crime on campus, there are some areas, such as the hostels, where the crime rate is worrisome, as evidenced by the qualitative data. According to some of respondents, such places could do with more policing and logistics to deter potential criminals.

5 Conclusions and Recommendations

The findings from the survey show that theft is the most commonly reported crime on the UNILAG campus and this stems from the fact that the designs of some buildings on campus offer criminals the appropriate cover to commit crime. Significantly, leaving hostels unrepaired gives the impression that the environment is not owned by anyone, thus allowing cult members to hang around places such as Jaja, Mariere, and the New Halls, especially Sodeinde Hall. Moreover, some faculty buildings, notably the Education and Arts buildings, were designed with too many entrances and exits, which hinders surveillance to stem crime. The above findings corroborate the postulations of Newman,Baskalingi, and Gök that increased guardianship would encourage residents to feel they own their environment.

Certain fundamentals are imperative to increase security in a built environment such as a university campus. These include adequate personnel, communication equipment, vehicles and other logistics to aid the work of the security unit. Evidence from the qualitative data revealed that there are some areas on campus that are not well lit. Some faculties experience power outages at night, while some faculties are yet to install CCTV. In the light of this, the following recommendations are made:

- The introduction of motorised and foot patrols around the hostel areas to deter criminals, especially the Amina Hall axis, Jaja, Mariere, and New Halls between the hours of 12.00 am and 6.00 am;
- All hostels to be fitted with CCTV cameras in order to capture daily activities in the hostel areas;
- The road from the AP filling station to the ISL roundabout should be well lit and patrolled from 12.00 am to 6.00 am as there are reports of isolated assaults on that road;
- The university should provide telephone lines within a "Closed User Group" (CUG) to all security personnel, who have complained of inadequate logistics to facilitate their work;
- There is an urgent need to prosecute and sanction arrested criminals in order to deter others. Security education should be incorporated into the orientation programme for freshmen, to create security consciousness among students.

Finally, the security unit should go beyond orthodox policing and embrace twenty-first-century policing, which is anchored on intelligence gathering.

Appendix

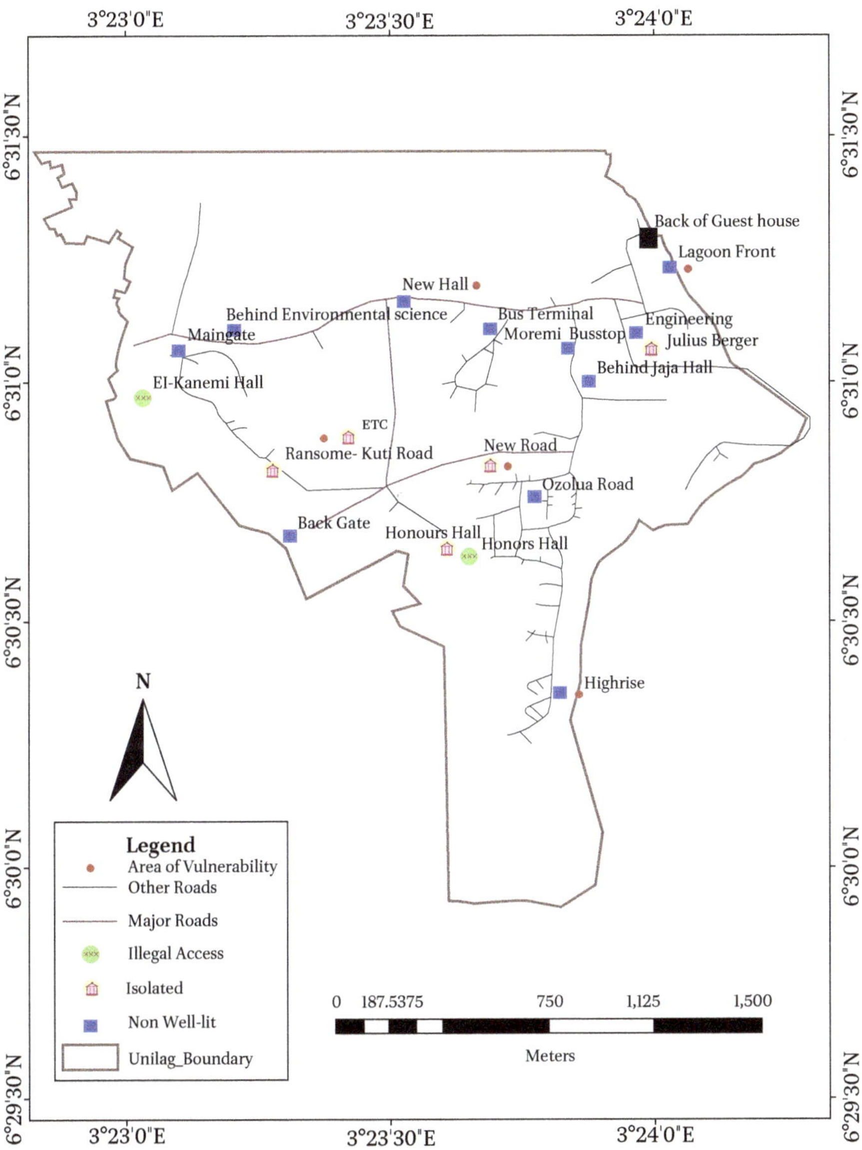

MAP 7.1 Map of the Akoka Campus at the University of Lagos, Nigeria
MAP DRAWN BY AUTHOR

Bibliography

Aderibigbe, A.B., "Emergence of the University, 1962–1967", in R.T. Akinyele and A. Olufunke (eds.), *A History of the University of Lagos*, Lagos: University of Lagos Press, 2013, p. 13.

Akinyele, R.T., and A. Adeboye, *A History of University of Lagos*, Lagos: University of Lagos Press, 2013, pp. 667–668.

Baskanligi, P.A., "The Role of Opportunity in Crime Prevention and Possible Threats of Crime Control Benefits", *Turkish Journal of Police Studies*, 13: 1(2011), pp. 77–114.

Emitt, S., *Architectural Technology*, London: Blackwell Science Ltd, 2002.

Newman, O. *Defensible Space: Crime Prevention Through Urban Design*, New York: Macmillan, 1972.

Sigel, L.J., & J.J. Senna, *Introduction to Criminal Justice*,Boston: Cengage Advantage Books, 12th Edition, 2009.

Wilson, J.Q., and G.L. Kelling, "Broken Windows: The Police and Neighbourhood Safety", in E. McLaughlin, J. Maurice, and G. Hughes (eds), *Criminological Perspectives: Essential Readings* (2nd Edition), London: Sage Publications, 2003.

Private Communications

The views of the respondents cited in this study are reported anonymously because of the security implications.

CHAPTER 8

Reporting Crime in Contemporary Lagos

Samson Folarin

Crime is a phenomenon that is not peculiar to Nigeria. There is crime in every part of the world. In fact, according to Clements Worldwide, a US-based company that provides security information to foreigners, the top five countries with the highest crime rates are South Africa, Venezuela, Honduras, Belize, and India.[1] In the United States, crime and criminality abound. The point here is that no country is insulated from crime; what varies is the rate of crime.

Lagos is unique because it is a microcosm of Nigeria. Lagos is home to all manner of conmen and criminals. It attracts people of all natures and cultures, who adopt all kinds of vices and devices. It is not for nothing that Lagos is called *Eko Akete, Ilu Ogbon*, that is 'Lagos, the city of the wise'. There is a popular saying that if one comes to Lagos and remains stupid and foolish, then the foolishness and stupidity is eternally incurable. In short, Lagos is a phenomenon.

This chapter is about two things: crime in Lagos and the reporting of it. In other words, I will be sharing my experience as a crime reporter for one of the most credible news organisations in Nigeria, the newspaper *PUNCH*.

The chapter is divided into four parts: the City; the Crime; the challenges of reporting; and the cost.

1 The City

Lagos State is one of the 36 states in Nigeria. It is located in the south-western geopolitical zone of the country and is arguably the most economically important state in the country. Lagos is one of the fastest-growing cities in the world. The population growth rate, as well as the diversity, is unique. Lagos was the first city in West Africa to attain a population of 1 million, a record achieved in 1963.[2] According to the 2006 census, the population rose to 9,019,534. By 2011,

1 See "The Clements World Wide Risks Index" in https://www.clements.com/resources/articles/Countries-with-the-Highest-and-Lowest-Crime-Rates Retrieved 25 April 2018.

2 P.O. Sada & A.A. Adefolalu, "Urbanization and Problems of Urban Development", in A.B. Aderibigbe (ed.), *Lagos: The Development of an African City*. (Lagos: Longman, 1975), pp. 79–102.

 | DOI:10.1163/9789004396289_010

the United Nations had estimated the population of the city to be 11.2 million. Today, the state government estimates Lagos to be home to 21 million people inhabiting an area of 3,577sq km. Significantly, too, Metropolitan Lagos, now covers 22 of the 27 Local Governments Councils of Lagos State, thus accounting for about 88 per cent of the total population of the state.[3]

Although the state covers less than four per cent of the total land area of Nigeria, it accounts for about 25 per cent of the country's total Gross Domestic Product. Lagos account for over 60 percent of industrial and commercial activities in Nigeria.[4] The major sea and air ports are also in Lagos. Thus, the city has remained the commercial nerve centre of Nigeria. The perception of Lagos being, like the United States, a land of opportunity is responsible for the influx of people into the city. Indeed, there are over 250 ethnic groups in Lagos.

Lagos is divided into two: Lagos Island and Lagos Mainland. Most of the population lives on the mainland, and most industries are located there as well. The mainland districts are: Ebute-Meta; Surulere; Yaba; Ikeja; Mushin; Maryland; Somolu; Oshodi; Oworonsoki; Isolo; Ikotun; Agege; Iju Ishaga; Egbeda; Ketu; Bariga; Ipaja; Ajah; and Ejigbo.

Lagos Island comprises a Central Business District, characterised by high-rise buildings, and also many of the city's largest wholesale marketplaces, such as the popular Idumota and Balogun markets. The neighbourhoods on Lagos Island are: Ikoyi; Obalende; Victoria Island; Eko; and Lekki. In addition, there are a number of coastal towns located on the outskirts of Lagos, including: Badagry; Ikorodu; Ibeju-Lekki; and Epe.

In view of the large and diverse population of Lagos, it is therefore not surprising that the crime rate of the state is on the high side, because the vultures always gather where there is food.

2 The Crime

Many crimes are being perpetrated in Lagos every day: burglary; rape/sexual violence; extortion; fraud; piracy; riots; civil unrest; bribery; murder and ritual killings; robbery; cultism; human trafficking; domestic violence and child abuse; and, recently, militancy and kidnappings are increasing (see figures 8.1 – 8.7 below).

According to Ayodele and Aderinto (2014), a 2013 National Crime Victimization Survey by the CLEEN Foundation that analysed experience of crime

3 R.T. Akinyele, "Lagos is Our Land: Indigeneship Associations and the Protection of the Rights of Lagosians since 1950", *Lagos Historical Review*, 15 (2015), pp. 89–110.

4 Ijeoma Nwagwu and Tamilore Oni "Lagos and Its Potentials for Economic Growth" https://ng.boell.org posted 2 July 2015, (accessed 19/12/2018).

FIGURE 8.1 Aerial view of Lagos Island
PHOTOS: CONNECTNIGERIA.COM

by region, Lagos was ranked as second in the states most vulnerable to kidnapping (4%), 20th for robbery, seventh for physical assault, fourth for mobile phone theft, a third for car theft in Nigeria.[5]

According to the same report, the Lagos police command said it had foiled 462 and 418 cases of robbery in 2012 and 2013, respectively. Out of the 1,448 and 1,263 vehicles stolen in Lagos in 2012 and 2013, respectively, 1,187 vehicles were recovered in 2012 and only 954 vehicles recovered in 2013.

Moreover, 270 people were murdered in different parts of Lagos, while a total of 32 policemen died in gun exchanges with armed robbers that also led to the death of 140 robbers.

Following repeated allegations that many of those involved in crime in Lagos were conveyed to the scene of the crime by commercial motorcyclists popularly called 'Okada riders', the Lagos State Government promulgated the State Traffic Law 2012, prohibiting commercial motorcycles and tricycles from 520 roads in Lagos. Despite the law that has led to the disappearance of commercial motorcycle operators from the major streets of the city, Lagos State

5 Johnson Ayodele & Adeyinka Aderinto, The Nature of Crime and Crime Reporting of Victims in Lagos, Nigeria, *International Journal of Criminology and Sociological Theory',vol. 7,no.1,2014, pp.1–14.*

FIGURE 8.2 Some criminal suspects arrested by Zone 2 Police Command, Onikan, Lagos
PHOTO: THE PUNCH NEWSPAPER

still ranks as one of the states with the highest crime rates in Nigeria, according to a 2016 survey released by the aforementioned CLEEN Foundation. In the survey, 67% of Lagos residents fear becoming victims of crime. The general public believes that crime is on the increase. This is supported by statistics which shows that crime rate in Lagos actually increased from 12% to 21% between 2011 and 2012, with robbery (28%) and theft of property (17%) the more prevalent crimes in the state.

The survey also shows that, unlike other parts of the south-west geopolitical zone of Nigeria, which have seen a reduction in assault-related crimes, assault cases in Lagos State rose sharply from 27% to 38% in 2012 and by 11% in 2011. Let me now turn to the most recent crimes reported by my media organisation, which have become topical issues.

2.1 *One Gang and a Series of Deaths*

According to the statistics from the Lagos State Police Command, 44 armed robberies took place in 2015.[6] That is the official figure, so the true number could be more. For example, that figure might not include those robbers who broke into cars early in the morning during traffic congestion on Oworonshoki Road, in Ketu, Obalende, and Ikorodu areas, among others.

It may also not include those who lured residents from their homes after turning off their generators, and when the the people came out to check what had happened, they were attacked and killed. During the year under review, a

6 Editorial Opinion "The Crime Statistics in Lagos", *The Guardian*, 31 December 2015, p. 18.

notorious robbery gang, which adopted the style of wearing police and military uniforms and blowing up targeted places with dynamite, attacked commercial banks in different parts of Lagos, including the neighbouring states of Ondo and Ogun, and killed eighteen people. The *PUNCH* newspaper of 29 December 2015 reported that the gang started with three banks in Lekki. The daredevil robbers killed two policemen and a hawker and carted away hundreds of millions of naira. Next, the gang went to Festival of Arts Village (FESTAC) and attacked the Diamond and Access banks there. During the robbery, the gang killed a mother and her baby, who were on the third floor of their house. They also injured two security men.

The next targets were the banks in Ikorodu Town. They arrived using the waterways and subsequently stopped all movements in the vicinity of the areas they wanted to operate. While a number of the group operated inside the bank, others waited outside. When they were done, they burnt their operational vehicles and zoomed off in the boats they had anchored by the shore. This was indeed a deadly gang.[7]

2.2 *Cultism and Street Gangs*

In 2015, I wrote a report in which I stated that, in the space of six months, about 80 people were killed by street gangs in different parts of Lagos State.[8] Every local government area in Lagos has its own cult group. Significantly, many of the leaders are members of the National Union of Road Transport Workers. The cultists bear strange and terrifying names such as Yellow, Eleye (witch), Black, Ibro, Elede (pig), Igbin (snail), and Oniposi (pall bearer).

In the Ebute Meta area, there are two cult factions: Skippo's boys and Segun's boys. The factions are named after their leaders who attracted followers due to the loyalty/disloyalty to the local council leader since the cult boys also generally have political affiliations and are often recruited as political thugs. However, some of Skippo's boys attacked and killed Segun and few years later, Skippo was also murdered by Segun's boys.

In Agege, the Awawa boys is a gang consisting mostly of teenagers. The name Awawa, means, 'we are there/we belong/we are invincible'. They rape, rob, and kill. Their mode of operation is to walk in groups and unleash havoc on whoever has the misfortune of getting into their midst.

In the Mushin/Fadeyi area of Lago State, Toba's boys and Toheeb's boys intimidate the local population. I know the two leaders and have spoken with them a number of times. As mild-mannered as they appear, no fewer than 50

7 Olalaye Aluko "One robbery gang, harvest of deaths and losses", *Punch* 30 December 2015, pp.14–15.

8 Samson Folarin, "Lagos Cult Kill 80 in Six Months" *Punch* 19 July 2015, p. 6.

FIGURE 8.3 Scene of a riot in Mile 12 Lagos
PHOTO: THE PUNCH NEWSPAPER

people have been killed because of them. And they keep count. They also have special ways of killing their rivals, including: beheading; burying alive; a hammer blow to the skull; and killing in front of the victim's parents. Mushin is probably the worst place in Lagos for a child to be born.[9]

In Mushin, a cult leader and hitman named Adigun Oriyomi accused of being responsible for at least thirteen murders, including those of pregnant women, children, and former allies who had left his camp. I have personally followed his case since 2013, when he was arraigned before a magistrate's court and mysteriously escaped, only to surface at the murder of his former best friend, whom he killed in the presence of his four-year-old daughter. He was sentenced to death by hanging on the strength of the testimony of the little girl.[10]

2.3 *Kidnapping and Militancy*

Kidnapping started in the South-South region of Nigeria and, before long, it shifted to Lagos and some border towns between Lagos and the neighbouring Ogun States like Arepo and Isheri. In the majority of kidnapping cases a

---

9 For the prevalence of the problem of cultism in Lagos, See Afeez Hanafi "500 youths renounce cultism, surrender guns" *Punch* 7 November 2017, pp. 4–5.

10 Samson Folarin "Gang Leader, Adigun Oriyomi to die by hanging" *Punch* 1 March 2016, p. 4.

FIGURE 8.4 Scene of a riot in Mile 12 Lagos
PHOTO: THE PUNCH NEWSPAPER

ransom is paid. Among the most publicised of these kidnappings was the 2016 kidnapping of three schoolchildren from Barbington College, Ikorodu, for which a ransom of about ₦5.6m was paid. The next high-profile kidnapping was that of the traditional ruler of Iba on the outskirts of Lagos. The family paid ₦3.5m in ransom before he was freed. The pipeline vandals, infamous for their nefarious activities in the Niger Delta, found a safe haven in the areas of Arepo and Isheri, where they combined bunkering with kidnapping. Initially, it was reported that five landlords in Isheri had been kidnapped and a ransom of about ₦3.6m was paid. The lucrative nature of the business seems to account for the spate of kidnapping in that axis. As recently as 25 May 2017, the kidnappers again struck at the Model College, Igbonla Epe, where some students were kidnapped for the second time within the space of six months. The capture of the kidnapping kingpin Chukwudumeme Onwuamadike, alias Evans, who was believed to be behind the abduction of wealthy individuals in the Ojoo – Alaba Axis of Lagos has not achieved a significant reduction in the spate of kidnappings in Lagos. Currently, the Lagos State Commissioner of Police is working on how to make the school environment safe.[11]

11 John Ameh and Afeez Hanafi "Police arrest three suspected kidnappers of Lagos pupils" *Punch* 1 June 2017, pp. 4–5; Afeez Hanafi "Kidnappers write to another school, vow to abduct pupils" *Punch* 22 June 2017, pp. 4–5.

FIGURE 8.5 Scene of a riot in Mile 12 Lagos
PHOTO: THE PUNCH NEWSPAPER

2.4 *Human Trafficking and Ritual Murder*

Human trafficking is another major crime in Lagos. Young girls from different parts for the country are brought to Lagos where they are kept in the custody of someone who provides shelter for them while they prostitute their bodies. I wrote a story about this phenomenon under the headline, "I slept with 400 men in five months: 22-year-old trafficking victim". It captures the travail of victims of human trafficking in Lagos State.[12]

Lagos State has had numerous cases of ritual murder, particularly in the Ikorodu area of the state. The Badoo cult group has been unleashing a reign of terror on the people here. To date, more than a hundred people have been killed in gruesome fashion. The common mode of execution is for members of the dreaded group to break into the homes of their victims in the middle of the night and smash their heads with a pestle or grinding stone, before wiping the blood of the female victims with a handkerchief, which is subsequently sold to ritualists for ₦500,000, that is about US$1,250. The blood of the victim is used to prepare medicine for those who want magical powers or those who want to acquire wealth quickly.

The dimension of the problem has forced landlords in the area to start building high fences, while local welders, who once grumbled about a lack of

12 Samson Folarin, "I slept with 400 men in five months: 22-year-old trafficking victim", *Punch*, 19 May 2016, p. 4.

FIGURE 8.6 Suspects arrested during a riot in Mile 12, Lagos
PHOTO: THE PUNCH NEWSPAPER

work, are now in demand for the making of burglar-proof and steel doors. The equally dreaded Oodua Peoples Congress (OPC), a militant Yoruba ethnic militia that once provided vigilante services for many parts of Yorubaland, is now being invited to lead the fight against the Badoo Cult in Ikorodu. The leaders of the African Traditional Religions in Ikorodu have also given the Badoo group an ultimatum to surrender or face the consequences.[13] How the whole thing will go is yet to be seen.

3 The Cost

Crime comes at a great cost to the state, individuals, and families. Since this study focuses on Lagos State, it is important to note that the government has spent billions of dollars in a bid to reduce the high rate of crime in the state.

Reports from 26 November 2015, indicate that the state governor, Akinwunmi Ambode, had spent ₦4.8 billion on buying: 100 saloon cars; 55 Ford Ranger pick-ups; 10 Toyota Land Cruiser pick-ups; 15 BMW power bikes; 100 Isuzu trucks; 3 helicopters; 2 gunboats; 15 armoured personnel carriers; revolving

13 Afeez Hanafi "Badoo Cult Killed 26 Lagos Residents in 12 Months" *Punch* 30 June 2017, pp.4–5; Kunle Falayi "Surrender or meet deadly end, Ikorodu traditionalists tell Badoo cult" *Punch* 1 July 2017, p. 10.

FIGURE 8.7 Vehicles donated by the Lagos State Government to the Rapid Response Squad to fight increasing crime
PHOTO: LTV

lights; a siren and public address system; vehicular radio communicators; and security paraphernalia, including bullet-proof vests, helmets, handcuffs, etc., just to improve the security situation in the state.[14] One can only imagine what might have happened if the same money had been invested in infrastructure, healthcare, or education. The state government is still spending billions of naira every year to tackle the rising crime rates in the city of Lagos. Although the visibility of the police has increased, the worsening employment situation has not helped matters. If anything, Lagos has a sizeable percentage of unemployed youths and a large floating population that will do anything to survive in Lagos.

4 Challenges of Reporting

From personal experience, there are different challenges reporters face when reporting crime in Lagos.

Firstly, there is the issue of security. I once interviewed a suspect during a parade at the State Criminal Investigation and Intelligence Department in Yaba. A few months later, I saw the same suspect when I was out and about. I did not recognise him, but he had called me over. Once I realized that I was face-to-face with a criminal suspect, I had to 'beg' for my life out of fear that he might have been offended by the negative publicity from my report. This

14 Kazeem Ugbodaga "Ambode Commissions 4.765b Copters, APCs, gunboats for Lagos Police" 27 November 2015, in pmnewsnigeria.com accessed 19 December 2018.

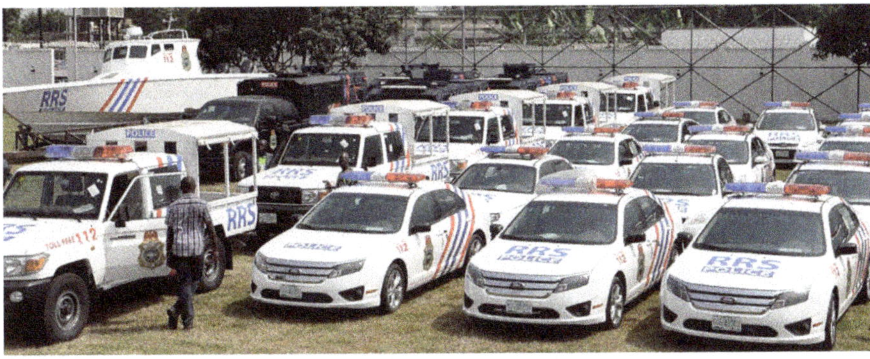

FIGURE 8.8 Vehicles donated by the Lagos State Government to the Rapid Response Squad to fight increasing crime
PHOTO: LTV

is because some of the criminals are powerful, once they are let off the hook, and they go out to fight those who they felt were behind their ordeal or did not treat them kindly.

Secondly, finding sources for criminal cases is difficult. Understandably, people are scared and afraid for their safety. It generally takes a long time for a reporter to gain their confidence or trust.

There is also the challenge of libel. A criminal suspect who has been released after being acquitted by a court of law can sue a reporter for 'damaging' his reputation while he was being accused of the crime. In sum, an investigative reporter is in no lesser danger than the police or the undercover detectives in a city like Lagos.

Bibliography

Akinyele, R.T 'Lagos is Our Land: Indigeneship Associations and the Protection of the Rights of Lagosians since 1950,' *Lagos Historical Review*, vol.15, 2015, pp. 89–110.

Aluko, Olalaye "One robbery gang, harvest of deaths and losses", *Punch,* 30 December 2015, pp. 14–15.

Ameh, John and Afeez Hanafi "Police arrest three suspected kidnappers of Lagos pupils" *Punch* 1 June 2017, pp. 4–5.

Ayodele, Johnson and Adeyinka Aderinto 'The Nature of Crime and Crime reporting of victims in Lagos, Nigeria' *International Journal of Criminology and Sociological Theory',* 7: 1 (2014), pp. 1–14.

Falayi, Kunle "Surrender or meet deadly end, Ikorodu traditionalists tell Badoo cult" *Punch* 1 July 2017, p. 10.

Folarin, Samson "Lagos Cult Kill 80 in Six Months" *Punch* 19 July 2015, p. 6.

Folarin, Samson "Gang Leader, Adigun Oriyomi to die by hanging" *Punch* 1 March 2016, p. 4.

Folarin, Samson "I slept with 400 men in five months: 22-year-old trafficking victim", *Punch*, 19 May 2016, p. 4.

Hanafi, Afeez "Kidnappers write to another school, vow to abduct pupils" *Punch* 22 June 2017, pp. 4–5.

Hanafi, Afeez "Badoo Cult Killed 26 Lagos Residents in 12 Months" *Punch* 30 June 2017, pp. 4–5.

Nwagwu, Ijeoma and Tamilore Oni "Lagos and Its Potentials for Economic Growth" https://ng.boell.org posted 2 July 2015, (accessed 19/12/2018).

Sada, P.O and, A.A Adefolalu 'Urbanization and Problems of Urban Development' in A.B. Aderibigbe, (ed.), *Lagos, The Development of an African City*. Lagos, Longman, 1975, pp. 79–102.

Ugbodaga, Kazeem "Ambode Commissions 4.765b Copters, APCs, gunboats for Lagos Police" 27 November 2015, in pmnewsnigeria.com accessed 19 December 2018.

CHAPTER 9

Currency Counterfeiting and "Substantial Justice" in Colonial Nigeria: *Rex vs Tijani Ali*, 1931–33

Ayodeji Olukoju

1 Introduction

The literature on law in colonial Africa has established the diversity of judicial systems, the non-compliance with strict canons of metropolitan law, and the role of context in the dispensation of justice.[1] According to the Nigerian law historian, Omoniyi Adewoye, Residents, who presided over provincial courts, the type analysed in this paper, were mandated to accelerate the judicial process without being burdened by "technicalities of law and procedure".[2] In many cases, colonial subjects were short-changed by the often bewildering interpretation and application of the law, especially where extraneous factors, such as the vested interest of the colonial government, were involved. In colonial Nigeria, criminal justice treated offences against property and the State, alongside homicide, with great severity. One such offence was the counterfeiting (and uttering) of colonial coinage and currency notes.[3] Counterfeiting struck a potentially mortal blow against the integrity of the colonial monetary

1 A pioneering collection on this subject is Kristin Mann & Richard Roberts (eds.), *Law in Colonial Africa*, (London: Heinemann, 1991). See also, Bonny Ibhawoh, *Imperial Justice: Africans in Empire's Court*, (Oxford: Oxford University Press, 2013); and Shaunnaugh Dorsett & John McLaren (eds.), *Legal Histories of the British Empire: Laws, Engagements and Legacies*, (Abingdon & New York: Routledge, 2014).

2 See, Omoniyi Adewoye, *The Judicial System in Southern Nigeria, 1854–1954*, (London: Longman, 1977), p. 139. A.I. Asiwaju notes that Frederick Lugard, the amalgamator of Nigeria, intended the provincial courts "to curb the tendency for 'useless litigation without good results' that characterized the Supreme Court". See, A.I. Asiwaju, "Law in African Borderlands: The Lived Experience of the Yoruba Astride the Nigeria-Dahomey Border", in Mann & Roberts (eds.), *Law in Colonial Africa*, p. 231.

3 The major publications are: Toyin Falola, "'Manufacturing Trouble:' Currency Forgery in Colonial Southwestern Nigeria", *African Economic History* 25 (1997), pp. 121–147; Toyin Falola & Akanmu Adebayo, *Culture, Politics and Money Among the Yoruba*, (New Brunswick, NJ: Transaction Publishers, 2000); M.E. Ochonu, *Colonial Meltdown: Northern Nigeria in the Great Depression*, (Athens, OH: Ohio University Press, 2009), pp. 93–98; Ayodeji Olukoju, "Self-Help Criminality as Resistance?: Currency Counterfeiting in Colonial Nigeria", *International Review of Social History* 45 (2000), pp. 385–407; and Ayodeji Olukoju, "The Adisi Case: Currency

 | DOI:10.1163/9789004396289_011

and financial systems. Hence, Governor Hugh Clifford opined that unless it was checked, there was "the gravest danger that the coinage system of Nigeria will prove unsound, for public confidence in it will speedily become shaken if ever a comparatively trifling proportion of spurious coins win its way into circulation".[4] Consequently, severe punishment was inflicted on convicts in the form of long prison sentences with hard labour. However, miscarriages of justice, disproportionate sentences, or lack of mitigation frequently characterised the dispensation of colonial justice.

This was particularly true in the Northern Provinces of the British West African colony of Nigeria, which operated the Penal Code, in contrast with the Criminal Code adopted in the Southern Provinces. Under the Penal Code, accused persons were presumed guilty and the onus of proving their innocence rested with them. Second, in both regions of Nigeria, colonial administrators (Residents), rather than regular judges, adjudicated even criminal cases, including appeals from lower courts, in the Provincial Courts. Third, legal representation by attorneys in the Provincial Courts was non-existent. It was in this setting – a trial presided over by a colonial administrator without legal representation for the accused in a criminal case that subverted the colonial regime – that one Tijani Ali was convicted at Sokoto in 1931.[5] Appeals against his conviction were pursued all the way to the Secretary of State for the Colonies in London.[6]

This case study is significant for the following reasons. First, for the light it sheds on the colonial justice system, with its emphasis on "law and order" and its inconsistencies, especially when a similar case in a sister colony (The Gold

Counterfeiting in Interwar Colonial Gold Coast", in C. Eagleton, H. Fuller, & J. Perkins (eds.), *Money in Africa* (London: The British Museum, 2009), pp. 68–74.

4 National Archives of Nigeria, Ibadan (NAI), CSO 1/32/78, 112 of 6 February 1925, Clifford to Lord Amery.

5 There is no mention of this episode in Ayodeji Olukoju, "The Colonial Monetary System in Northern Nigeria, 1903–1939", in Toyin Falola (ed.), *Nigeria in the Twentieth Century*, (Durham, NC: Carolina Academic Press, 2002), pp. 183–199. Ochonu, *Colonial Meltdown*, p. 95 only made a vague reference to the arrest of "a gang of counterfeiters at Gusau". But, contrary to his claim that the government "discovered their base to be Ijebu-Ode", no such connection or inference was made during the trial, as shown subsequently.

6 For a contemporary case (albeit for a capital offence) pursued to the apex of the imperial justice system, see Stacy Hynd, "*Benjamin Knowles v Rex*: Judging Murder, Race and Respectability from the Colonial Ghana to the Judicial Committee of the Privy Council", in Dorsett & McLaren (eds.), *Legal Histories of the British Empire*, pp. 77–91. Tijani Ali's case, too, would probably have been pursued to the Privy Council if it had gone to the Nigerian Supreme Court. The Privy Council and lower imperial appellate courts are examined in Ibhawoh, *Imperial Justice*.

Coast) was resolved differently.[7] Second, it illustrates the limitations of ad hoc judges in the adjudication of criminal cases during the colonial period.[8] Third, the Tijani Ali case highlights the pitfalls and perils of "substantial justice"[9] meted out to colonial subjects in the law courts and the limited opportunities for redress by aggrieved colonial subjects during the heyday of British colonial rule in Nigeria. "The concept of substantial justice", it has been observed, "is ill-defined in legal discourse [...] It refers to the administration of justice in a way that satisfies a community's sense of fairness while not necessarily adhering strictly to legal technicalities".[10] It delivers judgement based upon the merits of the case. Conversely, technical justice refers to the use of some legal technicalities to take advantage of loopholes to get reprieve for an accused person.[11]

Fourth, this study underscores the importance of context (local, regional, or global) in understanding and explaining the phenomenon under consideration. In this case, the context of the inter-war economic vicissitudes was critical to the events examined below. Fifth, it also demonstrates the need to focus on individual actors and to humanise crime and the criminals, to give a human face and voice to the accused persons. The latter are often presented as ciphers, statistics, and mere objects, rather than real persons with emotions, concerns, and their own narratives. Finally, this paper confirms that the criminal profiling of ethnicities and occupational groups (the Ijebu and goldsmiths, respectively, in this case) during the colonial period was the precursor to current practices of racial profiling in some Western countries. This study relies on the record of proceedings of the trial to provide details of the alleged offence and the differential roles of personalities involved in the saga.

---

7 This was the *Rex versus Amissah* (alias E. Reese) case, documented in National Archives of the United Kingdom, CO 554/95/7, "West African Currency Counterfeiting and Forgery Attempts".

8 As we shall see later in this essay (fn. 27), while Resident C.A. Woodward in Sokoto delivered a flawed judgement in his Provincial Court, his counterpart in Ijebu Province, P.A. Talbot, redressed a case of miscarriage of justice in a lower court in similar circumstances.

9 The concept of "substantial justice" was cited in justification of the admittedly fraught judgement against Tijani Ali in an anonymous Colonial Office bureaucrat's side comment, dated 5 May 1933, in CO 583/186/6, "Petitions – Liasu Alli Against Conviction of Tijani Alli".

10 Michael Bruce Goddard, *Substantial Justice: An Anthropology of Village Courts in Papua New Guinea*, (New York & Oxford: Berghahn Books, 2009), p. 1.

11 In the aforementioned *Rex versus Amissah* case, the accused won the appeal on a technicality.

2 The Context: Inter-War Colonial Northern Nigeria

The setting in which the Tijani Ali case unfolded was Northern Nigeria, with its peculiar indigenous and colonial political and economic systems. First, colonial rule had been firmly established in the region after the defeat of the precolonial Muslim emirates. The British then imposed their economic, administrative, and judicial systems on the people. The new order was underpinned by a judicial system that combined British and Islamic law, including the so-called Alkali (Al-Qadi) courts, with ultimate authority vested in the colonial officials.[12] Second, the economy was re-oriented towards the metropolis with the promotion of groundnut and cotton exports. Expatriate firms (European and Levantine) and indigenous merchants traded in foreign manufactures and local produce at Kano, Gusau, Zaria, and other important commercial centres in Northern Nigeria.[13] Third, colonial currencies were introduced with the ultimate aim of demonetizing local currencies, such as cowries, manillas, and Maria Theresa dollars.[14] A feature of the monetary system was recurring shortages, which contributed to the circulation of counterfeit coins.[15] Fourth, colonial rule facilitated peaceful social and economic exchanges, and the movement of people and merchandise between different parts of Nigeria. As we shall see in this paper, Southern Nigerian traders, artisans, employees of expatriate firms, and railway workers settled in various Northern Nigerian communities. The Yoruba from southwestern Nigeria had had commercial relations with the region for several centuries and their settlement in Kano has been dated to the

12 Allan Christelow, "Theft, Homicide, and Oath in Early Twentieth-Century Kano", in Mann & Roberts, *Law in Colonial Africa*, pp. 205–223, provides some insights into the administration of the two legal systems in colonial Northern Nigeria. He notes (p. 206) that the Alkali or Muslim judge adjudicated marriage and business disputes only.

13 Studies of the economy of inter-war colonial Northern Nigeria include R.W. Shenton, *The Development of Capitalism in Northern Nigeria* (Toronto: University of Toronto Press, 1986); and Ochonu, *Colonial Meltdown*.

14 Details in Olukoju, "The Colonial Monetary System in Northern Nigeria, 1903–1939". See, also W.I. Ofonagoro, "From Traditional to British Currency in Southern Nigeria: Analysis of a Currency Revolution, 1880–1948", *Journal of Economic History*, 39: 3 (1979), pp. 623–654.

15 Olukoju, "Self-Help Criminality as Resistance", p. 404; Ochonu, *Colonial Meltdown*, p. 74. Other factors in the rise and persistence of counterfeiting, ranging from personal greed, societal changes, economic uncertainty, and desperation, to resistance, have been highlighted in Falola, "Manufacturing Trouble", pp. 122–123, 128, 144; Falola and Adebayo, p. 20; Olukoju, "Self-Help Criminality as Resistance", pp. 386, 404; and Ochonu, *Colonial Meltdown*, p. 71.

eighteenth century.[16] It was from this community that the main protagonists in the episode considered in this paper were drawn.

3 The Trial of Tijani Ali and Others, 1931

On Friday, 19 June 1931, four suspects were arraigned before C.A. Woodhouse, the Resident of Sokoto Province in Northern Nigeria, at the Provincial Court, Sokoto. They were E.J. Otobushin (correctly, Otubusin), a 64-year old native of Ijebu-Ode, a former employee of the United Africa Company (UAC), and Gusau-based businessman; E.A. Otobayo, aged 26, also from Ijebu-Ode; I.A.A. Gonsalo (correctly, Gansallo), an indigene of Ijeshaland; 49-year old W.M. Morgan from the Colony of Sierra Leone, and Tujane Bali (correctly, Tijani Ali), a 25-year old goldsmith, who hailed from Ijebu-Ode. All but Morgan were Yoruba from Southern Nigeria.[17] The five men faced the following two-count charge:

> (i) Making counterfeit silver coin with respect to current coin of Nigeria, contrary to Section 147 of the Criminal Code ("Silver" as defined in Section 146 of the Criminal Code) (ii) As regards the First Accused (that is, Otubusin) – Having in his possession a mould, which is adapted to make the resemblance of a silver coin, knowing the same to be such a mould [Criminal Code Section 143(c)].

The particulars of the charge stated that one Onadipe (or Balogun) supplied information that led to the arrest by the Native Authority (N.A.) Police[18] of Otubusin in his office on June 7. Counterfeit coins (Exhibit "A") were found in his pocket and a mould (Exhibit "B") was found on the ground, which presumably dropped from his hand at the time of arrest. A search of his residence the next day yielded another mould (Exhibit C.1), various chemicals (Exhibit C.2), and sundry tools (Exhibit "D"). Information supplied by Onadipe also led to the arrest of the other four accused persons.

16 Adamu Mohammed Fika, *The Kano Civil War and British Overrule, 1882–1940*, (Oxford: Oxford University Press, 1978), pp. 133, 158 (fn. 182).

17 CO 583/186/6, Donald Cameron to Cunliffe-Lister, 25 February 1933, enc. 4: "Proceedings of the Trial". The names "Alli" and "Ali" appeared in the title and content of the file, respectively.

18 A history of the N.A. Police is Kemi Rotimi, *The Police in a Federal State: The Nigerian Experience*, (Ibadan: College Press, 2001). See also, T.N. Tamuno, *The Police in Modern Nigeria 1861–1965: Origin, Development and Role*, (Ibadan: Ibadan University Press, 1970).

Altogether, the following exhibits were assembled after a police investigation: five unfinished counterfeit shillings; a mould for making counterfeit coins, dated 1928; another mould, dated 1924; a cardboard box containing a bottle of cyanide of potassium, two empty tubes of gold salts, a pair of scales and a tin of black powder; sundry tools – one anvil (consisting of a block of wood and flat iron), one hammer, a pair of bellows, five files, a forge (bucket), a ladle, two crucibles, two pieces of lead and two zinc matchbox covers – and an envelope containing ten-shilling alloy coins, all dated 1924, and one mutilated five-franc silver coin. All the items, except the envelope, were found in the house or on the person of Otubusin. The envelope was found in the house of Tijani Ali.[19] All the accused persons pleaded "Not Guilty" to the charge.

During the trial, four witnesses testified against the accused persons. The first witness, Benedictus Adekoya Onadipe, nicknamed "Balogun", was a 31-year old indigene of Ijebu-Ode, where three of the suspects hailed from. He was a road contractor, based at Zaria, who had been seconded to Gusau by the expatriate Assistant Engineer of the Public Works Department. Incidentally, Onadipe claimed to have known Otubusin since 1928, when the latter was a UAC employee at Rigachikun. Otubusin had also visited him at Zaria, when he came to make some purchases. Onadipe testified that Otubusin confided in him that he had come to Zaria to buy material for making counterfeit coins, and had even shown him some "white shillings" that he was attempting to turn to brown. On that occasion, he invited him (Onadipe) to be an accomplice in counterfeiting. The latter deferred a decision till his next visit to Gusau. But a few days after returning to Gusau, Onadipe approached a fellow Ijebu-Ode man, one Emmanuel, a general contractor at Gusau, to warn Otubusin and his accomplice, Otobayo, to desist from their illegal activity. However, when Emmanuel confronted the two men, they retorted that "everyone came to Gusau to make money and that [...] [Onadipe should] mind ... [his] own business". The two men then reported him to his landlady at Gusau to the effect that he had been impugning their character. When her intervention yielded no results, as the two accomplices asked him to mind his business, he reported the matter to the Galadima, the local Head of the N.A. Police (Yan Doka). It was decided to bide the time and lull the accomplices into complacency before useful arrests could be made.

19 It is significant, as we shall see later, that Tijani's house was searched in his absence. Hence, he could claim that any incriminating evidence was planted in his house. Even so, all the alloy coins, totalling ten shillings, were actually genuine, thus nullifying the material evidence against him.

After a while, Otubusin and his accomplice reportedly renewed acquaintanceship with Onadipe and requested him to "help them by paying [his] [...] labourers with their counterfeit coins". They offered to supply him fake £50 for genuine £30 and in the meantime asked him to advance them £2 10s to complement the sum of £7 in their possession to procure "medicine" (chemicals) with which to turn the counterfeits to brown. Onadipe played along by requesting to see the mould as a condition for joining the gang. On a subsequent visit, he learnt that the forgers had sent an assistant to Kaura Namoda to utter the counterfeits that they had produced. He, therefore, arranged a meeting for a Sunday evening when he would deliver his contribution of £2 10s after sighting the mould. The police and N.A. authorities were duly notified so that the counterfeiters could be caught red-handed. Otobayo, Gonsalo, and Morgan arrived Otubusin's residence at various times but Otubusin excused himself to retrieve the mould from a certain "big man" in town where he claimed to have kept it. He returned with Morgan, who brought a mould dated 1928 out of his pocket for Onadipe to see.[20] They also showed him samples of their forged coins and stated that there was another mould, dated 1924, in their possession. Having seemingly been convinced, Onadipe, too, excused himself to fetch the money, which was a decoy to invite the police. However, other accused persons had left Otubusin's residence at 7.30 pm when Onadipe returned with three N.A. policemen, who accosted Otubusin outside his house. It was revealed during cross-examination that Otubusin had uttered £50 at Kaura Namoda and had approached another laterite contractor named Mayegun to assist in injecting the fake coins into circulation.

A second prosecution witness, Mayegun, a 52-year old indigene of Lagos, testified that when he met Otubusin four months before, he was shown a mould and asked to participate in the Otubusin-Tijani counterfeiting project. He claimed that Tujane (Tijani) demanded £5 in return for £10, which Tijani said he raised "not by trading but by coining money". Mayegun spurned the offer and alerted the District Head to Tijani's attempt to escape after Otubusin had been arrested. The third witness, Johnson Babagunde (Babatunde?) Jariogbe, a 25-year old native of Abeokuta, worked for the European firm of Messrs G.B. Ollivant. He claimed to have known Tujane (Tijani) at Zaria well before he came to Gusau in November 1930. According to him, Tijani visited him and offered to give him money with which to pay people who brought in produce for sale to his firm. When Tijani produced two shillings, he pointed out to him that

20 Yet, as we shall see, Morgan was acquitted and Tijani, on whom nothing was found, was convicted.

they were "'Ijebu' money", another name for counterfeits.[21] Tijani reportedly retorted: "Do you not know that I am an Ijebu man and a Goldsmith and that I make money?"[22] Jariogbe claimed that he declined to join the gang of counterfeiters even when a repeated overture was made a few days later. Jariogbe testified that in February 1931, he resigned from G.B. Ollivant to set up his own "*gari*" (cassava flour) merchandise enterprise. He claimed that when Tijani's wife bought a bag of "*gari*" worth 22 shillings from his shop, she included fake coins worth ten shillings, which Tijani redeemed when he went to his shop to complain.

The fourth witness, John Ayemeiaope Williams, a 41-year old indigene of Warri (Southern Nigeria), was a Gusau-based contractor and trader. He testified that he first encountered Otubusin in March 1931, while he was an employee of the UAC. Otubusin had visited him at Gusau, where he stayed with Onadipe, the first prosecution witness. It was on that visit that Otubusin promised him cheaper beans and pepper at six shillings instead of 7s 6d in the market. He then confided that he was getting cheaper supplies from the villages by paying them in "Ijebu" money (counterfeits).[23] Perhaps to impress, Otubusin allegedly produced "white-coloured" five-shilling coins. He reportedly promised Williams fake £150 for genuine £100. Williams promised to give £100 if he was shown the mould. He claimed to have met at Otubusin's residence Otobayo and Tijani, as well as "one of the rich Ijebu men of Gusau", one Emmanuel Ojashigun, popularly known as "Olowo Pashele Laru".[24] Williams asserted that Ojashigun himself was also involved in the illicit activity but the lead was not followed by the court. Williams said he rebuffed Tijani's demand that he should be sworn to secrecy. Though he was prevailed upon not to divulge the secret, he duly reported the matter to Onadipe and informed the Galadima, who was head of the N.A. Police.

21 Counterfeit coinage had been dubbed "Ijebu-Ode money" since the late 1920s. See, Olukoju, "Self-Help Criminality as Resistance", p. 388, for the discussion and supporting oral and archival sources.

22 There was indeed a widespread association of the Ijebu and the goldsmith's craft with counterfeiting during this period. See, Olukoju, "Self-Help Criminality as Resistance", pp. 388, 400, 404–406. There was allusion to Tijani's craft in the judge's summing up as shown below.

23 In 1929, the Resident of Ondo Province in Southern Nigeria had directed colonial officials and native courts to keep "extra careful watch on markets frequented by Ijebus". See, NAI, CSO 26/1 03447, "Counterfeit Coins", Secretary, Southern Provinces to Chief Secretary to the Government, 14 November 1929.

24 The meaning of this praise name is obscure but it acknowledges him as "*olowo*" (literally, "owner of money", meaning, "rich man" in Yoruba).

Otubusin defended himself against Onadipe's testimony on the grounds of revenge over gambling and other matters. Tijani hinged his innocence on the bitterness that Jariogbe nursed against him following his seduction of the latter's wife. This claim was given credence by the fact that the woman, Abeke, had filed for divorce with Tijani's financial support. Tijani called one Busari, a fifteen-year old fellow native of Ijebu-Ode, who claimed that, while giving Jariogbe a haircut, the latter threatened that if Tijani was not careful, he (Jariogbe) would get him into trouble for cavorting with his wife. Busari stated that he duly informed Tijani of Jariogbe's threat.

4 The Provincial Court's Verdict

After due consideration of the evidence, the testimony and cross-examination of the accused and witnesses, C.A. Woodhouse summed up and delivered his verdict. He quickly dealt with the charge against the second, third and fourth accused – Otobayo, Gonsalo, and Morgan. The judge noted that Onadipe was the only witness that testified against Gonsalo and Morgan, and none of the other witnesses even mentioned their names in their testimony. As for Otobayo, though he was mentioned as being present at meetings attended by two prosecution witnesses, the judge considered that his role was "practically passive". No evidence was adduced to prove that he took part in producing fake coins or sharing the profit of the illicit enterprise.

The case against Otubusin, in the judge's opinion, was overwhelming. First, he was mentioned by the first and fourth witnesses, and the second witness testified that he showed him a mould for counterfeiting coins. Moreover, a mould apparently dropped from his hand and counterfeit coins were found on his person. Incriminating evidence – another mould and various items associated with counterfeiting – was found in his house. His defence of being in financial straits, rather than the wealthy man that a counterfeiter was supposed to be, appeared supported by his current financial status. The judge surmised that he was "taking up, or probably resuming, an occupation to which he was unaccustomed in a locality new to such transactions on a larger scale and that he had to go slowly until he had sounded and enlisted [...] persons [...] who would be useful as agents for the distribution of his manufactures". It seemed to the judge that Otubusin could have experienced temporary financial embarrassment having just invested heavily in the enterprise. He noted that the accused had only recently sent his servant, Gajere, to "plant" a consignment of fake coins at Kaura Namoda.

In contrast, Woodhouse admitted that the case against Tijani, the fifth accused, presented "the greatest difficulties". The first and fourth witnesses identified him as present during meetings where negotiations for the uttering of fake coins took place. The second witness also testified that Tijani had approached him on the same subject. The testimony of the third witness was wholly focused on him. "The evidence against him", the judge admitted, "is accumulative rather than corroborative", but that seemed to him damning enough. To be sure, Tijani had sought to portray the witnesses as biased against him for one reason or another. Moreover, no incriminating evidence was found on his person or premises, unlike Otubusin. The ten-shilling coins found in his house were genuine even though they bore the date of one of the moulds. The judge surmised – and this amounted to speculation – that he might have taken advantage of the time lag between Otubusin's arrest and his own apprehension to get rid of incriminating evidence.

Woodhouse then made "legitimate deductions from the evidence [...] [as] proof of his guilt, i.e. that he used his trade as a goldsmith for the purpose of making counterfeit coins and approached various persons with a view to disposing of his manufactures". Even so, the evidence against Tijani, the judge admitted, was "not so amply conclusive as against [...] [Otubusin], but in my opinion he must be considered equally culpable". Finally, on 6 July 1931, Woodhouse delivered the following verdict: the second, third, and fourth accused were discharged, but both the first and fifth were found guilty and given the maximum sentence of fourteen year's imprisonment with hard labour on both counts. The sentences were to run concurrently.

5 The Judgement Aftermath: Petitions by Liasu Ali

The judgement raised a number of issues, especially in relation to Tijani, who was convicted on the basis of evidence that, as Woodhouse himself admitted, was neither wholly conclusive, nor corroborative. Accordingly, Liasu Ali, Tijani's elder brother, forwarded a strong appeal to higher authority for justice. Liasu, a trader resident at Idepo Street, Ijebu-Ode, was in Gusau for his brother's trial.[25] Having made a futile appeal to the Governor of Nigeria to free Tijani, a "disgusted and perplexed" Liasu approached the Secretary of State for the Colonies to order the re-trial of Tijani "in the Court of Law of Nigeria, or

25 CO 583/186/6, Donald Cameron to Cunliffe-Lister, 25 February 1933, enc. 3: Affidavit by Liasu Ali, 6 September 1933, signed by E.C. Clegg, Ag. D.O., Ijebu-Ode.

the Great Assize", or quash his sentence.[26] The comprehensive petition was written on Liasu's behalf by one Ramos A. Oshintade, who charged a fee of £1:1, instead of the £2:4 payable, for the original and three copies of the document.

Liasu described Tijani as a victim of a "false and malicious sentence", instigated by one Mr. J.B. Johnson inflamed by "a malicious mind and bitter hatred". He stressed the "grave dissension" between Tijani and Johnson over the former's seduction of Johnson's wife, Abeke.[27] Though Abeke was still "the legal wife" of Johnson "by native law and custom", the woman had already transferred "some of her properties" to Tijani's residence. She had also proceeded to Abeokuta, where both Johnson and herself hailed from, to "obtain judicial separation" from Johnson. Liasu claimed that Tijani funded and underwrote the cost of her journey and the refund of her dowry. A letter written in the Yoruba language by Abeke was enclosed as proof of this liaison.[28] According to Liasu, Johnson's anger knew no bounds and he determined to frame up Tijani to extirpate the amorous liaison between Tijani and Abeke.

Liasu also reinforced his plea by emphasising that no incriminating evidence was found in the possession or premises of Tijani to warrant his conviction. Even so, his house was searched in his absence (while in police custody), contrary to the law. It was alleged that ten shillings were found in his house out of which counterfeit three shillings were allegedly detected. The claim that Tijani had once tried to pass off bad coins to Johnson was debunked on the grounds that the bitter enmity between both men foreclosed such a transaction *ab initio*. Liasu asserted that Tijani was convicted on the strength of the "perjurative (sic) evidence and false prosecution [...] of the prisoner's

26 CO 583/186/6, Donald Cameron to Cunliffe-Lister, 25 February 1933, enc. 1: LiasuAlli c/o The "Reliable" Office (Registered in Nigeria), 75a Ita Affin Street, Ijebu-Ode to His Lordship, The Right Honourable, The Secretary of State for the Colonies, Downing Street, London, 29 August 1932. The points raised in the petition indicate an impressive level of awareness of fine legal points and the resolve to pursue justice to a logical conclusion even in the heyday of colonial rule. The Ijebu, Egba, and Lagos Yoruba already produced British-trained lawyers by the 1930s.

27 Liasu's contention that Tijani was framed by an adversary was probably informed by a similar case in Ijebu Ode in 1928. The paramount ruler, *Awujale* Adenuga, and the Judicial Council had convicted an anti-establishment figure, Joseph Oludaini Igu (popularly known as "Frugality"), on the trumped-up charges of possessing a mould for counterfeiting coins, attempting to sell it to one Tijani and for manufacturing counterfeits. It took the Resident's intervention and a re-trial by a colonial official to secure Igu'sacquittal. Details in Tunde Oduwobi, *Ijebu Under Colonial Rule, 1892–1960: An Administrative and Political Analysis*, (Lagos: First Academic Publishers, 2004), pp. 74–75.

28 CO 583/186/6, Donald Cameron to Cunliffe-Lister, 25 February 1933, enc. 2: Abeke of Oluwo House, Gbagura Ija Offa, Abeokuta, c/o Sanni Babalola, Aro Station to Tijani, 14 June 1931 (Yoruba and English translation).

enemy". He decried the falsehood, malice and hatred that underlay Johnson's testimony. More damning was the evidence that the presiding judge, who was also the Resident of Sokoto Province, had remitted via his counterpart in the Ijebu Province a postal order of ten shillings, which was cashed by Tijani's wife, Abusatu, at Ijebu-Ode on 23 September 1931. Liasu then asserted that if the entire sum was remitted, it meant that no fake three shilling coins were found in the said sum of ten shillings found in Tijani's house, contrary to the evidence adduced against him.

Liasu's petition was forwarded to London by Donald Cameron, Governor of Nigeria in February 1933, six months after it was received in Lagos.[29] The governor had reduced the initial sentence to ten years' imprisonment with hard labour. This was based upon a review of the proceedings by both the Attorney-General and the Acting Solicitor-General. The former had noted that Tijani was in all probability "not himself coining money but was acting as the distributor of money coined by the 1st accused (Otubusin)", whom he appeared to be shielding. Consequently, he hinged Tijani's conviction on Section 152 of the Criminal Code as amended by Section 7 of the Criminal Code (Amendment) Ordinance, 1924–1930, which stipulated that "in special cases an utterer of coin may get 10 years imprisonment", which was the maximum sentence. The mitigation appeared to have encouraged Liasu to petition for the transfer of the case to the Supreme Court. However, the application was "out of time" (filed too late) and the governor declined to reduce Tijani's sentence any further.

The governor dismissed the points raised in the petition as follows. First, Tijani was not convicted, as claimed, of being in possession of counterfeit shilling coins. He was "in fact convicted of making counterfeit coin".[30] Second, on the alleged bias of the witness, Johnson, the governor claimed that the "trial judge had taken this into consideration in his decision". However, he noted that the trial judge erred in his summing up by referring to the testimony of the first witness against Tijani. Yet, the Attorney-General was convinced that there was "nevertheless sufficient evidence otherwise to corroborate the story of the 4th witness and to sustain the conviction". The governor attributed the long delay between the submission of the petition and its transmission to London to the "protracted attempt by the Lieutenant-Governor, Northern Nigeria to trace Johnson and confirm that Tijani did seduce his wife". The petition was held up for "some time" in the office of the Secretary to the Government and "further unavoidable delays (took place) owing to the necessity of referring to Sokoto

29 CO 583/186/6, Donald Cameron to Cunliffe-Lister, 25 February 1933.

30 This claim was false, as no evidence was adduced linking Tijani to the making of counterfeits.

regarding the accuracy of the copy of the Court proceedings which had been supplied".[31]

6 Debate in the Colonial Office and the Secretary of State's Verdict

As was the practice in the Colonial Office in London, the governor's dispatch and its enclosures – Tijani's petition and the proceedings of the trial – were commented upon by the key advisers to the Secretary of State. The most insightful and most comprehensive of the minutes (comments) was the one by F.J. Pedler. He alluded to the error in the judge's summing up in claiming that the four witnesses mentioned Tijani in their testimony. Such a fundamental error, he claimed, was at variance with the governor's "statement that Mr. Woodhouse's judicial work has been well and carefully done".[32] Another official commented in the margin as follows: "Nor does a fair sprinkling of inadmissible evidence".[33]

Pedler also noted "other evidences (sic) of omissions from the account of the trial". He surmised that the "apparent error may possibly be due to an omission in the summary of the evidence of the 1st witness". Pedler noted that the governor had thus knocked out the phantom testimony of the first witness against Tijani while both himself and the Attorney-General had jettisoned the testimony of the third witness "for obvious impartiality". Even if the evidence of the second and fourth witnesses against Tijani stood, the case against him was "just as strong as the case against the 2nd accused [...] [who had been] heavily incriminated by the second witness". Both the second accused and Tijani had been shown by the fourth witness "to have taken passive part during the discussion of a coining deal, although Tijani's part was not quite so passive as that of the 2nd accused".

Pedler added that he could "find in the record of the trial no evidence to corroborate the story of the 4th witness". This, he stressed, was "a very important point, since with regard to the 2nd accused, the 4th witness was apparently discredited". Pedler was "the more surprised" at the Attorney-General's opinion regarding corroboration since Mr. Woodhouse stated that the evidence against Tijani was "cumulative rather than corroborative". The only person who could

31 CO 583/186/6, Donald Cameron to Cunliffe-Lister, 25 February 1933. Tijani was thus a victim of red tape.

32 CO 583/186/6, Minute by Pedler, 24 March 1933. Top advisers to the Secretary of State for the Colonies habitually made scathing comments about governors and other colonial officials.

33 CO 583/186/6, Anon, n.d. (March, 1933).

have corroborated the evidence of the fourth witness against Tijani was Emmanuel, the Ijebu wealthy trader at Gusau during meetings cited by the fourth witness. Ironically, that rich man played "a part about equal in importance to that played by Tijani" but was not apprehended or called as witness. Pedler surmised that, on the one hand, Emmanuel was not arraigned because there was no other witness to testify against him apart from the fourth witness. On the other hand, he was not called as a witness by the prosecution "presumably [...] because he would be unable to testify truthfully without incriminating himself".[34]

Pedler stated that Tijani was "convicted of making counterfeit money. It is now considered that he did not make any, but that he was an accomplice in attempting to pass counterfeit coins into circulation". Yet, he contended, under Clause 152 of the Criminal Code no punishment was prescribed for "any person who attempts to utter any counterfeit coin; the offence is only the actual uttering".[35] The only actual uttering alleged against Tijani, he insisted, was the third witness' story, which was, however, discredited because he was "known to have been biased against Tijani". Pedler remarked that "[t]he element of doubt in this case is so great that Mr. Browne advocated Tijani's release and the Attorney-General [recommended] [...] ten years' hard labour". Pedler concluded his submission that legal opinion be sought on the following issues:

First, whether the account of the trial was complete. Second, whether the evidence was sufficient to convict Tijani of (a) counterfeiting (b) uttering of false coin. Third, "whether Tijani was not guilty of the offence for which he was convicted but of a different offence and that his sentence be reduced to tally with the offence".[36] Pedler's detailed and forensic analysis elicited reactions from other officials in London.

One official stated that he "agreed generally with Mr. Pedler's criticisms but though there might have been grounds of appeal e.g. the admission of hearsay evidence, I do not think that this is such an exceptional case as to warrant intervention".[37] Another cautioned that it was:

> an established principle that the Secretary of State is not a revising authority for the findings of Colonial Courts. Only in exceptional cases, e.g.,

34 CO 583/186/6, Minute by Pedler, 24 March 1933.

35 *Ibid.*, emphasis in the original. Another CO official inserted an undated margin comment: "But see Section 4 of the Criminal Code". We shall compare this with the Amissah case in the Gold Coast in a subsequent discussion.

36 An anonymous official made an undated side comment: "This seems to be 'administrative interference.'"

37 CO 583/186/6, Minute by Roberts Wray, 24 March 1933.

> where there seems to have been a miscarriage of justice, will the Secretary of State intervene. I can see no grounds for such intervention here.[38]

He advised that Governor Cameron should inform Liasu Ali of the Secretary of State's "unpreparedness to intervene". In other words, his non-intervention did not detract from the merit of the case.

That was the final word on the matter. In an anonymous comment, a top official acknowledged that, though there were "some unsatisfactory features about [the trial] […], I am satisfied that *substantial justice* has been done".[39] Consequently, he did not consider that it was a case in which the Secretary of State should intervene. This verdict was duly conveyed to Governor Cameron and from him to the petitioner.[40] That was the end of the matter.

Ironically, while Tijani's sentence was reduced to ten years and Otubusin's original sentence retained, similar offenders in Southern Nigeria had their sentences reduced from fourteen to seven years' imprisonment with hard labour. The governor defended his decision as follows: "I have never heard of a sentence as high as 14 years for this offence".[41] The Acting Chief Justice acknowledged that while 14-year sentences had been confirmed in the past, "the particular facts of the case […] did not seem to me to warrant such a severe sentence as 14 years".[42]

7 The Tijani Ali Case in Perspective

The trial of five men accused of counterfeiting and uttering of colonial coinage in Northern Nigeria sheds significant light on several issues of colonial order and legal administration, commercial struggles and social relations in inter-war Nigeria. The plight of Tijani, rather than that of the principal culprit, Otubusin, has thrown up several issues for discussion.

First, is the context of entrepreneurship in which the entire saga took place. The alleged counterfeiters and their traducers were all businessmen, some of whom had a shared background as employees of European trading firms. Second is the factor of the inter-war depression, which precipitated the collapse

38 CO 583/186/6, Minute by S. Hazlerigg, 29 March 1933.

39 CO 583/186/6, Anon, 5 May 1933, italics added for emphasis.

40 CO 583/186/6, Secretary of State to Governor of Nigeria, no. 513 of 10 May 1933.

41 NAI, IjeProf2 C.12, vol.1, "(1) Counterfeiting (2) Counterfeit Coining", Chief Registrar, Lagos to Resident, Ijebu Province, 25 September 1933.

42 NAI, IjeProf2 C.12, vol.1, Chief Registrar, Lagos to Resident, Ijebu Province, 20 October 1933.

of many indigenous enterprises and, even, expatriate firms. This heightened competition among the struggling entrepreneurs in a shrinking market. There is, therefore, the possibility of business rivalry among the contending personalities (Otubusin, Onadipe, and Mayegun), especially for laterite contracts in the road construction business. Third, the context of the depression also put pressure on small businessmen trying to survive in an environment of economic desperation. This seemed to have tempted some of them to consider illicit schemes for making extra money, which entailed cutting corners. By the same token, group survival and self-preservation could have informed the decision to witness against Otubusin lest his scheme ruined all Southern Nigerian businessmen in Northern Nigeria. Fourth, all the actors, except Morgan, hailed from Southern Nigeria. Most of them, both accused and prosecuting witnesses, were of Yoruba stock, mainly from Ijebu Province. Tijani's nemesis, Johnson, was of Egba stock and it is suggested that, in addition to the problem of seduction, sub-ethnic rivalry between the Egba and Ijebu may have played some role in the bitter rivalry between them. Such an argument can be countered, however, by the fact that the chief witness against Otubusin was a fellow Ijebu-Ode man. Moreover, the lovers Tijani and Abeke were Ijebu and Egba, respectively.

After all is said and done, this episode presents its main protagonist, Tijani Ali, as a victim of several forces that were beyond his control. First, as has been documented in the literature, the imperial and colonial governments were paranoid about counterfeiting, which was a direct threat to the integrity of the colonial monetary, fiscal, and commercial systems. Hence, any whiff of it was to be squashed with utmost severity. Tijani was an unfortunate victim of this prevailing sentiment in colonial officialdom. Second, allied to this was the peculiar judicial and administrative systems in Nigeria (the "Lugardian system").

A major feature of that system was the anomaly of adding judicial functions to the primary administrative duties of colonial officers. In fact, this was a common feature of the quasi-military politico-judicial structures of colonial rule in its first two decades (the 1890s–1910s) and reforms did not take effect till 1934. While effecting cost savings, the concentration of administrative and judicial powers in colonial officials imposed additional burden on officials. They were also unlikely to be as detached and professionally competent as the lawyer-judges that adjudicated in the Lagos Colony. The great defects in the colonial judicial system were laid bare by the handling of the Tijani case. Flaws in the judgement – factual errors and wrong attribution in the summing up, admission of hearsay evidence, and inconsistency in the decision-making – were easily spotted in both Lagos and London.

However, as we have seen, the unfair verdict was retained possibly to save the face of a bungling official-judicial system in Northern Nigeria. Ironically, in the same year that Tijani's fate was sealed, a Gold Coast man, T. Biney Amissah, who allegedly initiated a counterfeiting scheme under the alias of "E. Reese", was discharged when his lawyers argued before the West African Court of Appeal that he had only attempted, and had not yet consummated, uttering fake currency. This was precisely the point that Pedler raised in his dissenting comment cited above. Fortunately for Amissah, the extant Gold Coast Law contained such a loophole – that an attempt did not amount to actually committing a crime – which did not exist in the Nigerian legislation against counterfeiting. The Gold Coast law was subsequently amended to match the tougher Nigerian legislation, which stipulated that an intent or attempt to counterfeit was as punishable as the act itself. Still, the case against Tijani was not conclusive – a fact that the judge admitted – but he ended up a notable sacrificial lamb, and there may well have been several other victims, of a justice system that refused to err on the side of circumspection and benefit of doubt.

8 Conclusion

The fate of Tijani vividly illustrates the overwhelming importance attached to the preservation of order (whether against the scourge of counterfeit currency or the loss of face that could result from quashing or reducing a sentence[43]) in colonial Nigeria. Consequently, Tijani, by no means an entirely innocent man, became collateral damage. He was only fortunate that counterfeiting was not a capital offence. It may be said that while the conflation of judicial and administrative functions saved the "Lugardian" colonial government money on personnel expenses, this was often at the expense of justice or the rights of the colonial subjects. Tijani might also have been a victim of the cloud of suspicion and resentment that hung over Southerners in the North and the reputation of his fellow Ijebu for making and uttering "Ijebu money".[44] To be sure, prejudice against Southern Nigerians or the Ijebu did not feature overtly during the trial

43 The Resident of Ijebu Province was "apprehensive that the Ijebu will regard [...] reductions as indication that offences against the currency are no longer regarded by Government so seriously as they have been in the past". See, NAI, IjeProf2 C.12, vol.1, Resident to Chief Registrar, Lagos 10 October 1933. Such an official was most unlikely to harbour, much less consider, any thought of quashing a wrong sentence.

44 "This does not suggest", as has been pointed out elsewhere, "that all Ijebu were counterfeiters, or that all counterfeiters were Ijebu". See, Olukoju, "Self-Help Criminality as Resistance?", p. 407, fn. 112.

or even, in officials' confidential comments. That said, Tijani did not get a fair hearing. He was convicted for the wrong offence (making counterfeit money) but sentenced for (uttering), as "an accomplice in attempting to pass counterfeit coins into circulation". Yet, the testimony for his conviction was obtained from a discredited witness, his romantic rival, Jariogbe. Even so, the delay that forestalled his appeal to the Supreme Court might not have been deliberate. However, the tardiness in his trial and the handling of his petition conveniently aligned with the official resolve to make an example of counterfeiters.

In sum, Tijani lost on all fronts: his amorous escapade ended in disaster, his business was ruined, and, for a young man in his mid-20s, the best years of his life were spent in jail. It is likely that he survived the jail term (especially with a reduced sentence) but returned home a broken man. Even so, he was luckier than his supposed principal, the 64-year old Otubusin, who probably did not survive the ordeal. In the final analysis, Tijani was essentially a victim of double profiling: he was both an Ijebu and a goldsmith. His ethnicity and occupation were the prime suspects in the crime of currency counterfeiting in colonial Nigeria. In that event, Tijani was dealt substantial injustice in the absence of substantial evidence by a flawed administration of "substantial justice" in colonial Nigeria.

Bibliography

Adewoye, Omoniyi, *The Judicial System in Southern Nigeria, 1854–1954*, London: Longman, 1977.

Asiwaju, A.I., "Law in African Borderlands: The Lived Experience of the Yoruba Astride the Nigeria-Dahomey Border", in Kristin Mann and Richard Roberts (eds.), *Law in Colonial Africa*, London: Heinemann, 1991, pp. 224–238.

Christelow, Allan. "Theft, Homicide, and Oath in Early Twentieth-Century Kano", in Kristin Mann and Richard Roberts, *Law in Colonial Africa*, London: Heinemann, 1991, pp. 205–223.

Dorsett, Shaunnaugh, and John McLaren (eds.), *Legal Histories of the British Empire: Laws, Engagements and Legacies*, Abingdon/New York: Routledge, 2014.

Falola, Toyin, "'Manufacturing Trouble:' Currency Forgery in Colonial Southwestern Nigeria", *African Economic History*, 25 (1997), pp. 121–147.

Falola, Toyin, and Akanmu Adebayo, *Culture, Politics and Money Among the Yoruba*, New Brunswick, NJ: Transaction Publishers, 2000.

Fika, Adamu Mohammed, *The Kano Civil War and British Overrule, 1882–1940*, Oxford: Oxford University Press, 1978.

Goddard, Michael Bruce, *Substantial Justice: An Anthropology of Village Courts in Papua New Guinea*, New York/Oxford: Berghahn Books, 2009.

Hynd, Stacy, "*Benjamin Knowles v Rex*: Judging Murder, Race and Respectability from the Colonial Ghana to the Judicial Committee of the Privy Council", in Shaunnaugh Dorsett and John McLaren (eds.), *Legal Histories of the British Empire*, Abingdon/New York: Routledge, 2014, pp. 77–91.

Ibhawoh, Bonny, *Imperial Justice: Africans in Empire's Court*, Oxford: Oxford University Press, 2013.

Mann, Kristin, and Richard Roberts (eds.), *Law in Colonial Africa*, London: Heinemann, 1991.

Ochonu, M.E., *Colonial Meltdown: Northern Nigeria in the Great Depression*, Athens, OH: Ohio University Press, 2009.

Oduwobi, Tunde, *Ijebu Under Colonial Rule, 1892–1960: An Administrative and Political Analysis*, Lagos: First Academic Publishers, 2004.

Ofonagoro, W.I., "From Traditional to British Currency in Southern Nigeria: Analysis of a Currency Revolution, 1880–1948", *Journal of Economic History*, 39: 3 (1979), pp. 623–654.

Olukoju, Ayodeji, "Self-Help Criminality as Resistance?: Currency Counterfeiting in Colonial Nigeria", *International Review of Social History*, 45: 3 (2000), pp. 385–407.

Olukoju, Ayodeji, "The Colonial Monetary System in Northern Nigeria, 1903–1939", in Toyin Falola (ed.), *Nigeria in the Twentieth Century*, Durham, NC: Carolina Academic Press, 2002, pp. 183–199.

Olukoju, Ayodeji, "The Adisi Case: Currency Counterfeiting in Interwar Colonial Gold Coast", in C. Eagleton, H. Fuller, and J. Perkins (eds.), *Money in Africa*, London: The British Museum, 2009, pp. 68–74.

Rotimi, Kemi, *The Police in a Federal State: The Nigerian Experience*, Ibadan: College Press, 2001.

Shenton, R.W., *The Development of Capitalism in Northern Nigeria*, Toronto: University of Toronto Press, 1986.

Tamuno, T.N., *The Police in Modern Nigeria 1861–1965: Origin, Development and Role*, Ibadan: Ibadan University Press, 1970.

CHAPTER 10

Class Based Criminal Justice Regime, Supermarket Courts, and Illicit Interests: The Nigerian Criminal Justice Administration System in Critical Perspective

A.E. Akintayo

1 Introduction

The class-based nature of Nigerian politics and political economy, like that of a number of other African states, have been well documented.[1] There are also works interrogating the class character of some aspects of the Nigerian legal regime and jurisprudence and its impact on the agency and freedoms and rights of the poor.[2] There appears, however, to be scant literature interrogating the nature of the Nigerian criminal justice system vis-à-vis its class relations and status and the impact of this on the malaise of bribery, corruption, and organised crime which is currently bedeviling the Nigerian state.

In a recent and popular book, Prof. Stephen Ellis traced the roots of organised crime and corruption in Nigeria to the closing years of colonial rule, when Nigerian nationalist politicians expended political patronage in exchange for personal and ethnic loyalties, which worked to fuel general disrespect for law and due process in the country.[3] Unfortunately, Ellis is not alone in his observation of Nigeria being an organised criminal state. Adesanmi, another notable Nigerian commentator, recently opined, following several instances

1 C. Boone, "The Making of a Rentier Class: Wealth accumulation and political control in Senegal", *The Journal of Development Studies*, 29: 3 (1990), pp. 425–449; R.A. Joseph, *Democracy and Prebendal Politics in Nigeria* (Ibadan: Spectrum Books, 1991); P. Lewis, "From Prebendalism to Predation: The political economy of decline in Nigeria", *The Journal of Modern African Studies*, 34 (1996), pp. 79–103.

2 O. Chinedu, "Between Elite Interests and Pro-Poor Resistance: The Nigerian courts and labour-led anti-fuel price hike struggles (1999–2007)", *Journal of African Law*, 54: 1 (2010), pp. 95–118; A.E. Akintayo, "Planning Law Versus the Right of the Poor to Adequate Housing: A progressive assessment of the Lagos State of Nigeria's Urban and Regional Planning and Development Law of 2010", *African Human Rights Law Journal*, 14: 2 (2014), pp. 553–579.

3 Stephen Ellis, *This Present Darkness: A history of Nigerian organised crime* (London: C. Hurst & Co, 2016).

 | DOI:10.1163/9789004396289_012

of the Nigerian presidency covering up high-profile crimes by well-connected wealthy elites and their cronies, that the Nigerian Presidency is a foster parent of crimes.[4] Adebamwi and Obadare have also made a clear link between the illicit interests of elites and corruption in Nigeria; a view shared by Agbigboa among many others.[5] The crucial question, then, becomes, how did Nigeria get to this pass?

Although Ellis and a few others have sought to provide answers to this most important question by tracing the origin of avarice, bribery, and corruption in Nigeria to certain sources, I suggest in this essay that those analyses and sources are incomplete without an examination of the impact and contribution of the inherited class-based criminal justice system in Nigeria. I argue here that the inherited class-based criminal justice system is complicit and is therefore also to be blamed for the present rot in Nigeria, as it contributed significantly to and fostered the illicit interests of the political and ruling elites and their cohorts in Nigeria. The analysis and explanation of how this came about is the focus of this essay.

This essay advances four main arguments: First, that Nigeria's criminal justice system is class-based, in the sense that it is for the protection of the propertied and the powerful and skewed against the poor. Second, that in a regime based on class and money, the rich and the propertied determine the basic standard of justice and it is expected that those in the privileged class with requisite resources will frequently use the judicial process to further their illicit interests, as is presently the case in Nigeria. Third, that the class-based and monied character of Nigeria's criminal justice system is derived from its colonial legal heritage, which continued after independence. Finally, that there is a symbiotic relationship between the class-based criminal law regime, the illicit interests of the wealthy or monied class, and corruption by some members of the Nigerian judiciary.

In this contribution, I intend to validate the aforementioned arguments by first examining the class and propertied nature of the seventeenth- and eighteenth-century criminal law regime of England, which formed the basis of present-day Nigeria's criminal justice system in Section 2 below. This is followed by an interrogation and broad exposition of the class and monied

4 P. Adesanmi, "The Nigerian Presidency as a Foster Parent of Crimes", *Sahara Reporters*, 15 April 2017 Retrieved from http://saharareporters.com/2017/04/15/nigerian-presidency-foster-parent-crimes-pius-adesanmi (accessed on 17-04-2017).

5 W. Adebamwi & E. Obadare, "When Corruption Fights Back: Democracy and elite interest in Nigeria's anti-corruption war", *Journal of Modern African Studies*, 49: 2, (2011), pp. 185–213; D.E. Agbiboa, "Between Corruption and Development: The political economy of state robbery in Nigeria", *Journal of Business Ethics*, 108: 3 (2012), pp. 325–345.

character of Nigeria's criminal law regime in Section 3. Thereafter, I examine how Nigeria's class-based regime, the illicit interests of elites, and the Nigerian judiciary legitimate and further each other's interests by analysing the symbiotic relationship between the class-based criminal law regime, the illicit interests of rich elites, and a corrupt judiciary in Section 4. Section 5 concludes the essay.

2 Class and Propertied Nature of Seventeenth- and Eighteenth-Century Criminal Justice System in England

Before the advent of capitalism, complex relations and use rights existed over land in pre-capitalist England, which equitably distributed land and resources there between stakeholders and citizens and saw to it that no person or group was economically disadvantaged. The advent of capitalism, however, removed the pillars upon which this social organisation and use rights, which hitherto guaranteed the economy and livelihood of the poor, were hinged. Capitalism gradually erased the pre-capitalist rights and claims of the poor over land and redefined them as crime under many new laws enacted for that purpose as times progressed.[6]

One of the most notorious statutes in this era of the dispossession of the poor was the Black Act. The Black Act punished with death persons armed and disguised and committing infractions as outlined in the Act against property. Many of the prohibited infractions, however, had been hitherto legitimate pre-capitalist use rights of the poor. A detailed examination, analysis, and assessment of the impact of the Black Act was ably undertaken by E.P. Thompson. Suffice it to say here that, as Thompson rightly concluded, the Act punished with death not only legitimate attempts by the poor to make a living, but also malice against the gentry.[7] Thus, the Black Act not only protected the property, but also the persons of the rich from the poor.

Although other studies exist in addition to Thompson's seminal work, which directly or indirectly interrogates the class-based nature of England's eighteenth-century criminal law regime, it is Douglas Hay's popular work that stands out among the pack. In his well-known work, *Albion's Fatal Tree: Crime and society in eighteenth-century England*, Hay points out that eighteenth-century

6 E.P. Thompson *Whigs and Hunters: The origin of the Black Act.* (London: Penguin Books, 1975), pp. 200–241.

7 *Ibid.*, 256.

England's criminal justice regime was rooted in and revolved around terror.[8] According to him, the system both mystified and operated against the poor through the three principal illusions of majesty, justice, and mercy.[9]

Regarding the illusion of majesty, Hay points out that criminal justice of the that era in England presented a majestic, dignified, righteous, and above board outlook through, among others, the procedure of the courts, the attire of the judges and their mannerisms, the judges' statement of the law and their direction to juries, and the arguments of counsels. In fact, the pomp and pageantry associated with the system at that time were calculated to overawe the poor and compel them to the law's obedience while masking the class character of the system as a whole.[10]

In terms of the regime's illusion of justice, Hay is of the view that England's eighteenth-century criminal justice system promoted the illusion of justice and equality before the law by occasionally punishing the rich and the powerful, who infrequently ran afoul of its provisions and by also being intermittently of use to the poor. He rightly observed, however, that:

> It was easy to claim equal justice for murderers of all classes, where a universal moral sanction was more likely to be found, or in political cases, the necessary price of a constitution ruled by law. The trick was to extend that communal sanction to a criminal law that was nine-tenths concerned with upholding a radical division of property.[11]

The contradictions and ambiguities of the bourgeois criminal law system come to the fore in times of need and economic stress, when the poor are wont to lay claim to property that has been appropriated by the rich for sustenance and survival. At such times, the bourgeois criminal law regime bared its fangs, prohibited and punished most harshly, even with the death penalty, any slight challenge or infraction by the poor to the proprietary interest of the rich and propertied; prohibitions and punishment judges of the time, who were also from the propertied class, were too happy to inflict with panache.

The class character of the criminal law regime of that era was again made apparent in the operation of the jury system, whose membership "had a sharp

8 D. Hay. "Poaching and the Game Laws on Cannock Chase", in D. Hay *et al.* (eds.), *Albion's Fatal Tree: Crime and society in eighteenth-century England* (London: Pantheon, 1975), p. 17.

9 *Ibid.*, pp. 26–49.

10 *Ibid.*, pp. 26–31.

11 *Ibid.*, p. 35.

property qualification".[12] The rationale for choosing members of the jury from the property class, according to Hay,

> was that the common Englishman could not be trusted to share in the operation of the law. A panel of the poor would not convict a labourer who stole wood from a lord's park, a sheep from a farmer's fold, or corn from a merchant's yard.[13]

Despite its equality and justice outlook, England's eighteenth-century criminal law system proved to be nothing but a cloak for class domination by the rich and the propertied.

Turning to the third principal illusion, the illusion of mercy pervaded the criminal justice administration of the day.[14] Private prosecution of crimes, which was the norm at the time and which placed the destiny and fate of the accused entirely in the hands of the accuser, usually a man of property, in terms of what offences to charge and whether to bring any charge at all, as well as how rigorously to conduct the prosecution, made nonsense of the reality of mercy for accused persons who were not men of property.[15]

More importantly, even where the accused did go to trial, whether or not he would be pardoned was largely dependent on finding a man or men of property provide a character reference; the fact that the judges who exercised this discretion were men of property did not ameliorate the situation.[16] Hay identified three different ways that class and property made nonsense of eighteenth-century royal pardon mechanisms: firstly, the rich and the propertied generally only stood as character references for one of their own, i.e. relatives or descendants; only a couple of the many pleas for pardon were for the poor and vulnerable; secondly, it became a system of patronage, influence-peddling, and exchange of favours among the rich and the propertied to the total exclusion of the poor; and thirdly, the system of royal pardon was used by the rich and the propertied to further the ideology of mercy, which presented the royal pardon as an act of grace by the English sovereign to the poor, rather than a system steeped in class interests and connections.[17] In this light, Hay concludes that eighteenth-century English law allowed the ruling class to make the courts "a selective instrument of class justice".[18]

12 *Ibid.*, p. 38.
13 *Ibid.*, p. 38.
14 *Ibid.*, p. 40.
15 *Ibid.*
16 *Ibid.*, pp. 43–45.
17 *Ibid.*, pp. 44–49.
18 *Ibid.*, p. 48.

Not all scholars, however, agree with Hay on the class nature and character of the eighteenth-century criminal justice system in England. One of the better known critiques of Hay's proposition originates from Langbein, whose response to Hay has been referred to as the "most robust".[19] For Langbein, Hay's notion of a class-based criminal justice system is mistaken because the system of the period applied equally to the rich and the poor, without any class distinction and bias. While he concedes that criminals, in fact, tend to be poor, his conclusion is that "[t]o turn these little crooks into class warriors one must wear rose-coloured glasses of the deepest hue".[20] Langbein also took issue with Hay's characterisation of eighteenth-century criminal prosecution in England as a class process.[21] While he, for instance, admits that class lines are often crossed when one moves from someone who has committed a crime to the victim, he argued that the difference in class did not amount to a gulf and that prosecutions by propertied elites in the terms narrated by Hay were few and far between. Langbein also argued that Hay underplayed the role of English juries in mitigating the supposed class effect of the criminal law regime of the time.[22] In addition, Langbein disputed that the pardon process was a class contraption used to serve class connections and interests, as Hay claimed.[23] In Langbein's view, what available evidence revealed was a pardon process based on principles rather than the predilections of propertied elites.

Perhaps the weightiest of Langbein's criticisms of Hay's thesis, in my view, is the "legitimation trick", which Langbein called "[a] staple of Marxist argumentation for dealing with contrary evidence".[24] In Langbein's view, Hay's proposition of a class conspiracy in the criminal justice system of eighteenth-century England cannot be tested by evidence. According to Langbein, Hay's main thesis is that the occasional equality in the application of the criminal law or the formal safeguards provided therein, which appear to protect the interests of both the poor and the rich alike, only serve to legitimate the class character of the system in the eyes of the lower strata of society by appearing to be neutral and objective. Langbein argues that the result would be the same even in a criminal justice system that is patently and blatantly class biased and that favours the rich over the poor – this would fit Hay's class bias thesis just as well.

19 J. Beatie, "Looking Back at Property, Authority and the Criminal Law", *Legal History* 10:1–2 (2006), pp. 10, 15–20.

20 J.H. Langbein, "Albion's Fatal Flaws, Past and Present", Faculty Scholarship Series. Paper 545, Harvard, (1983), pp. 100–101 Retrieved from http://www.law.harvard.edu/faculty/cdonahue/courses/lhsemelh/materials/Mats9F.pdf.

21 *Ibid.*, pp. 101–105.

22 *Ibid.*, pp. 105–108.

23 *Ibid.*, pp. 108–114.

24 *Ibid.*, p. 114.

Langbein therefore concludes that Hay's thesis "[...] is simply not testable. It floats above the evidence, it is self-proving".[25]

Despite the weighty nature of some of Langbein's and other's criticisms of Hay's proposition, Phillips has argued that Hay should be praised for not only provoking critical thinking and immense scholarship on the study of criminal law and society, but also for, in his view, getting a good deal of the arguments right.[26] Hay's essay has therefore been acknowledged as not only provoking a burgeoning literature in the study of the history of the criminal law of eighteenth-century England and elsewhere, it is also acknowledged as useful in understanding the political and ideological underpinnings of modern-day criminal justice systems and, consequently, remains relevant and applicable today.[27]

3 The Class and Monied Character of Nigeria's Criminal Justice Regime

It is a notorious fact, confirmed by robust studies, that British colonial Africa, including Nigeria, inherited most of its laws and procedure from eighteenth- and nineteenth-century England. Moreover, English penal laws and procedure were received into British colonial Africa without any concession to the African context and without regard to changes in substantive criminal law and criminological thinking taking place in England and elsewhere at the time.[28] After gaining formal independence, the penal laws and policies of post-colonial Africa remained largely as they were during colonial times. Colham aptly describes the post-colonial African penal context thus:

> The penal policies of independent African governments show a remarkable continuity with those of their colonial predecessors. In spite of the stress that many governments place on African values, African traditions, African socialism and the like, there has been little attempt to incorporate these values in the penal system. Penal policies continue to be characterized by their harshness, by their emphasis on retribution and

25 *Ibid.*, p. 115.

26 J. Phillips, "Albion's Empire: Property, authority and the criminal law in eighteenth-century Canada", *Legal History*, 10:1–2 (2006), pp. 10, 24.

27 J. Beatie, "Looking Back at Property, Authority and the Criminal Law", pp. 15–20; J. Phillips, "Albion's Empire: Property, Authority and the Criminal Law in Eighteenth-Century Canada", pp. 21–27.

28 S. Coldham, "Criminal Justice Policies in Commonwealth Africa: Trends and Prospects", *Journal of African Law*, 44: 2 (2000), pp. 218–219.

> general deterrence rather than on the individualization of penalty and the rehabilitation of offenders.[29]

In other words, British post-colonial Africa adopted the penal laws and policies they inherited during colonialism unamended.

With specific reference to Nigeria, the history of the introduction of the Criminal Code into Nigeria by the British colonists mirrored that of other British colonial African states, as examined by Colham. The history of the imposition of the Criminal Code in Nigeria has been comprehensively examined elsewhere.[30] Suffice it to say here that the Criminal Code was proclaimed by Lord Lugard in the northern part of Nigeria in 1904; this was after several failed attempts in the southern part of the country. The Code was extended to the whole country with minor amendments in 1916.[31] Modelled on the state of Queensland of Australia Criminal Code of 1899, the Code was rightly acknowledged to represent the "criminal law of England practically unadulterated".[32]

However, as a result of agitation by the Muslim community in northern Nigeria and the problem of the application of English criminal law to a community underpinned by a different moral and religious code, a Penal Code based on the Sudan Penal Code was thought to be more suited for the Muslim community and was introduced to northern Nigeria in 1960.[33] Karibi-Whyte has rightly observed that the division and application of two different codes in the North and South of Nigeria may falsely suggest that there are substantive differences between the two Codes; this is not the case as both Codes have a shared origin in the English common law of crime.[34]

The introduction of the Queensland based Criminal Code in the whole of Nigeria in 1916 was followed by a consolidation of the then existing Criminal Procedure Codes in the North and South of Nigeria by the Nigerian Criminal Procedure Ordinance of 1914.[35] The two procedure codes from which the Ordinance derived were themselves based on eighteenth-/nineteenth-century

29 *Ibid.*, p. 223.

30 F.H. Morris, "How Nigeria Got Its Criminal Code", *Journal of African Law*, 14: 3 (1970), pp. 137–154; *Idem*, "A History of the Adoption of Codes of Criminal Law and Procedure in British Colonial Africa, 1876–1935", *Journal of African Law*, 18: 1 (1974), pp. 6–23.

31 *Idem*, "How Nigeria Got Its Criminal Code", pp. 137–154.

32 *Ibid.*, p. 150.

33 C. Okonkwo. *Okonkwo and Naish on Criminal Law in Nigeria* (2nd. edn.), (Ibadan: Spectrum Law Publishing, 1980), pp. 9–10.

34 A.G. Karibi-Whyte, *Groundwork of Nigerian Criminal Law*, (Lagos: Nigerian Law Publications, 1986), p. 1.

35 F.H. Morris, "A History of the Adoption of Codes of Criminal Law and Procedure in British Colonial Africa, 1876–1935", p. 9.

English criminal procedure laws. In the final analysis, therefore, Nigerian criminal laws and procedure statutes, which formed the bedrock of criminal justice administration in Nigeria, were based on eighteenth-/nineteenth-century English criminal laws and procedure.

Having established that the foundation of criminal justice administration in Nigeria rested on eighteenth-century English criminal law regime, it is left to interrogate the extent to which present day criminal justice administration in Nigeria exhibits the class bias and character of eighteenth-century England. Critical analysis reveals that the Nigerian criminal justice system mirrors the class bias of eighteenth-century England in at least four different ways. Each of the four ways will now be examined in turn.

The first noticeable feature of the Nigerian criminal law regime is the similarity and close affinity of its offences and prohibitions with those of eighteenth- or nineteenth-century England. As is now clear, the provisions of the Nigerian criminal justice administration regime are a substantial reflection of the law of that time in England save for very minor amendments or adaptations. This point of view has been confirmed by a plethora of studies on the subject. As rightly pointed out by Colham, for instance, "[t]he Penal Codes were, of course, based closely on nineteenth-century English criminal law, and the principles of criminal liability, the definition of offences and the type and scale of penalties that they contained made no concession to the African context".[36]

The result of this state of affairs is that Nigerian criminal law regime imposed foreign morality and mores while prohibiting the conduct and morality in tune with the majority of Nigerian people. Thus, like other post-colonial African states, the Nigerian criminal justice regime suffers from cultural incompatibility.[37] But what has this got to do with the alleged class-based character of the regime? The link lies in the fact that the mores and morality of the regime were those of England's white elites and, in turn, became the morality and mores of African elites who had been socialised into the colonists' way of life. As noted by Seidman, the belief system underpinning the criminal codes in Africa are the belief systems and mores of a tiny European minority and the Westernised segment of African society, which primarily constituted the ruling class, while the vast majority of Africans subject to the codes live by a morality and mores foreign to the codes and therefore find the law socially and culturally incompatible.[38] In essence, the tenets of the imposed regime

36 S. Coldham, "Criminal justice policies in Commonwealth Africa", p. 219.

37 R.B. Seidman, "Mens Rea and the Reasonable African Man: The pre-scientific world-view and mistake of fact", *The international and Comparative Law Quarterly*, 15: 4 (1966), pp. 1135–1164.

38 Ibid., pp. 1136–1137.

are tenets of the imperial predecessor's ruling class and that of the African ruling elites after them.

The second important feature of Nigeria's criminal law regime is its protection of property as individual rights. Although the protection of property and the propertied is a key feature of all liberal legal orders, it appears to have enjoyed an unusually heightened status in eighteenth-century England. Indeed, according to Hay, property was deified in the legal regime of eighteenth-century England and was a measure of all things, including human life.[39] In Hay's words, "[a]gain and again the voices of money and power declared the sacredness of property in terms hitherto reserved for human life",[40] and the parliaments of that era were not shy in taking human life in the process of protecting property.

This deification of property and the preparedness of the state to sacrifice human life for it are clearly discernible in the Nigerian legal regime. Under the Nigerian Criminal Code Act, property is categorised into two types for the purposes of its protection – real or immovable property, and movable property. For immovable property, Section 282 of the Criminal Code Act allows owners of immovable property (dwelling house) to use lethal force to defend their property from intruders intent on committing a felony or misdemeanour therein. This was given judicial sanction in a case where the court held that a man who shot and killed a rioter throwing missiles at his house is entitled to defend his property under Section 282 of the Criminal Code Act (*R v Ebi*, 1936).

For movable property, Sections 289 to 294 of the Code allow a person in possession of movable property to use reasonable force to defend his or her possessions provided he or she does not harm the trespasser. The Criminal Code Act therefore appears to privilege the protection of landed over other types of property. This is a spillover from the thinking and climate prevalent in eighteenth-century England, when the interests of the landed gentry predominated and enjoyed heightened protection. The heightened protection enjoyed by landed property against other types under the Criminal Code Act therefore comes as no surprise, since the Code is a derivative of the legal norms and thinking of eighteenth-century England.

Beyond the provisions of the Criminal Code Act, however, individual property rights enjoyed constitutional protection and privilege. The Constitution of the Federal Republic of Nigeria, 1999 provides for an individual right to own or acquire immovable property in any part of Nigeria (Section 43 of the Nigerian Constitution, 1999). It also states that, save for recognised exceptions, no right or interest in any movable or immovable property shall be compulsorily

39 D. Hay, "Poaching and the game laws on Cannock Chase", p. 19.

40 *Ibid.*

acquired by the state without the payment of adequate compensation (Section 44 (1)). In addition, defence of property is one of the recognised grounds under which a person can legally deprive another of his or her right to life (Section 33 (2) (a)). Thus, the Nigerian legal order also privileges the individual right to property over human life.

The class-based nature or bias of the individual guarantee of property becomes more apparent when the regime is contrasted with, for instance, the corporate protection of property under African customary law. Unlike the English notion of ownership, which emphasises individual ownership and protection, under African customary law, land is the property of the tripartite pillar of African societies: the dead, the living, and the unborn members of the community.[41] Under the African customary law regime, a distinction is made between the ownership and the protection of land as against other types of property. Land is corporately protected to safeguard the interest of other members of society, as outlined above, while personal and other types of property are subject to individual ownership and protection.[42]

According to Elias, it is more apt to describe the African land ownership and protection system as corporate rather than communal.[43] Elias points out that the significance of this distinction is that the rights of individual members of the community co-exist with the rights of the community, rather than being subsumed in the African customary land ownership system, and therefore is more corporate than communal in nature.[44] However, notwithstanding having defined rights over land that co-exist with the rights of the community, individual member(s) cannot ordinarily alienate or deal with land to prejudice the vested interest of other members of the community, as outlined above.[45] The African customary law of land ownership and protection thus appear to be more inclusive and distributive in nature.

The distributive bent and character of African customary property ownership and protection regime is highlighted in the work of Kaunda.[46] According to him, African tribal societies were not individual but mutual societies, where human need was the supreme criterion of right behaviour and societies were structured in a way that satisfies the basic needs of all members. As Kaunda explained:

41 T.O. Elias, *The Nature of African Customary Law*, (Manchester: Manchester University Press, 1956), p. 162.

42 *Ibid.*, pp. 162–175.

43 *Ibid.*, pp. 163–164.

44 *Ibid.*, pp. 163–166.

45 *Ibid.*

46 K. Kaunda, *A Humanist in Africa*, ([add city or town of publishing house]: Longmans, Green and Co, 1966).

> Human need was the supreme criterion of behaviour. The hungry stranger, could, without penalty, enter the garden of a village and take, say, a bunch of bananas or a mealie cob to satisfy his hunger. His action only became theft if he took more than was necessary to satisfy his needs. For then he was depriving others.[47]

Under the inherited colonial laws, the scenario described by Kaunda above amounts to theft. Members of pre-colonial African communities were therefore not allowed to acquire or hoard goods or resources beyond their basic needs while other members of society were lacking. In fact, there was a standard below which no one in African societies was allowed to live without bring opprobrium or shame to the family or immediate community.[48] Given this contrast, I suggest that the African customary system of law and property protection is redistributive and not appropriative, and less class inclined to the individual protection of property under the inherited system of law in British colonial Africa.

A look at the way some property offences are framed and the exception or legally permissible excuses associated with them also reveals class bias. Take the provision relating to the theft of money under Section 383 (2) (f) of the Nigerian Criminal Code Act, for instance. The general rule is that the *actus reus* of taking property of another and the *mens rea* of intention to permanently deprive the owner thereof must concur and coincide for the offence of stealing to be determined. What this means is that if A takes the property of B without the latter's consent, but with the intention of later returning the property, the offence of stealing is not committed. With regard to money, however, Section 383 (2) (f) of the Criminal Code Act provides that a person who takes money not belonging to him or her and has the intention of using the money, is guilty of the crime of stealing, even if the perpetrator has the intention of later returning the amount taken to the owner. The question is, why is this exception made with for money and not for other types of property? While there may be other plausible explanations, I think the exception is actually targeted against eighteenth-century clerks and labourers who handled money for their merchants or other employers, in order to prevent the former from *borrowing* money entrusted to their care by propertied merchants and entrepreneurs. I suggest that the main aim of such an exception is to protect the money of the merchant and employer class from their needy clerks and labourers.

47 *Ibid.*, p. 25.

48 J. Nyerere, *Ujamaa: Essays on socialism* (Dar es Salaam: Oxford University Press, 1964), p. 107.

The third feature exhibited by the Nigerian criminal justice administration system that is similar to the criminal justice administration regime of eighteenth-century England is the supposed objectivity and neutral application of the criminal law. In fact, the notion of the neutral application of the law is the very foundation of all liberal societies. As rightly noted by Tushnet, "[t]he acquiescence of individuals to the liberal rule of law depends upon their continued unshakable faith in its objectivity. Thus the conflict between objectivity and subjectivity cannot readily be confronted within the legal sphere without undermining liberal society itself".[49]

As can be discerned from the analysis in Section 2 of this essay above, the supposition that the criminal law of eighteenth-century England objectively applied to the rich and poor alike was a core feature of that regime. The same is also the case in the Nigerian criminal justice administration system. This cannot in fact be otherwise without undermining the liberal legal nature of Nigerian society, as rightly noted by Tushnet above. Rather than applying equally and objectively to the rich and poor, however, the Nigerian criminal law regime is frequently applied against the poor and rarely against the monied members of the society. There are at least two reasons for this.

Firstly, the poor are most likely to run afoul of many of the offences in the Nigerian criminal law regime; and secondly, in the very few and rare instances when the rich run afoul of the law, they have the wherewithal and resources to escape the due application of the criminal law. Each of these claims is explained in turn below.

While the causal link between poverty per se and crime is still the subject of debate, theorists have traced unequal economic conditions to the prevalence and proliferation of crimes.[50] According to theorists, the unequal and unjust distribution of wealth in societies where great stock is placed on wealth provokes feelings of relative deprivation and resentment in the minds of those deprived and results in the proliferation of all manner of crimes in a bid by some to improve their lot, often at the expense of those that are not better off or who are only marginally better off than them.[51] The effect of this seems to be that

49 M. Tushnet, "Legal Scholarship: Its causes and cure", *Yale Law Journal*, 90 (1980/81), p. 1207.

50 W. Bonger, "Criminality and Economic Conditions", in J. Muncie *et al.* (eds.), *Criminological Perspectives: A reader* (London: Sage Publications, 1996), p. 40; J. Lea & J. Young, "Relative Deprivation", in J. Muncie *et al.* (eds.), *Criminological Perspectives: A reader* (London: Sage Publications,1996); W. Adebamwi & E. Obadare, "When Corruption Fights Back: Democracy and elite interest in Nigeria's Anti-Corruption war", p. 187.

51 K.S. Williams, *Textbook on Criminology* (6th ed.),(Oxford: Oxford University Press 2008), pp. 357–361; W. Bonger, "Criminality and Economic conditions"; J. Lea & J. Young, "Relative deprivation".

most of those who run afoul of the criminal law are poor, just as most offences committed are committed against the poor.[52] Nigeria is a capitalist state where unequal and unjust distribution of wealth is a feature of the political economy; the poor of Nigeria are therefore also the most susceptible to the violation of the criminal laws. The so-called equal or objective application of criminal laws to different social classes is thus a sham.

In addition to the above, however, Nigeria's criminal law regime also directly and indirectly targets the poor in many of its provisions. The provisions of Sections 249 and 250 of the Criminal Code Act are cases in point. Under Section 249, every common prostitute behaving indecently or in a disorderly manner and soliciting persons for prostitution in a public place; every person wandering or begging for alms or procuring any child or children to do so in a public place; every person gambling in any public place and every person who conducts himself or herself in a manner likely to cause a breach of the peace in any public place are deemed idle and disorderly persons and liable to imprisonment for one month.

Section 50 effectively states that every person previously convicted as an idle and disorderly person; every person who uses deformity or wounds to beg for alms; every person who gathers alms in public through false or fraudulent pretence; every suspected person or known thief with no visible means of subsistence or who cannot give a good account of himself; those generally referred to as pimps; and every person found wandering in or near any premises or upon any road or highway and is suspected to be there for illegal or disorderly purpose(s) are deemed to be rogues and vagabonds and liable on summary conviction to three months imprisonment for a first offence and one year's imprisonment for subsequent offences. A cursory glance at the acts and conducts prohibited in the provisions examined above show that they are primarily actions undertaken by society's lower strata.

A more invasive example in this regard, however, is the Street Trading and Illegal Markets Prohibition Law of Lagos State (the Street Trading Prohibition Law). The Law prohibits with penal consequences economic activities peculiar to most residents of Lagos State. The Law in Section 1 prohibits the selling or hawking of any goods or services in any street specified in the First Schedule of that Law or within the vicinity of any public building in the State. According to the First Schedule of the Law, streets referred to in Section 1 are all streets in Local Government Areas of the State other than those exempted by the

52 K.S. Williams, *Textbook on Criminology*, p. 327; J. Lea & J. Young, "Relative deprivation", pp. 136, 138–140.

relevant Commissioner. In effect, this means all streets in the State are out of bounds to street traders or hawkers.

Section 2 of the Law prohibits the setting up of markets by individuals other than the State, local governments, or statutory corporations. Section 3 prohibits extension of shops on walkways by occupants of shops in any part of the State. Section 4 prohibits the use of pedestrian bridges in the State as markets to sell goods or services. Goods of violators of the Law are liable to be seized and forfeited to the State (Sections 8 and 9 of the Law). First offenders against the Law are liable to a fine of ₦90,000 or to imprisonment for six months (Section 10 (1) (a) of the Law); second offenders are liable to a penalty of ₦135,000 and nine months in prison (Section 10 (1) (b) of the Law); while third offenders are liable to a fine of ₦180,000 and one year in prison (Section 10 (1) (c) of the Law). Any person who patronises or buys any goods or services in the prohibited areas is also guilty of an offence and is liable to a fine of ₦90,000 or imprisonment for six months, or both. The effect of the Street Trading Prohibition Law is to close virtually all public spaces where trading thrives and is profitable to the poor, thus foreclosing any possibility of economic well-being.

As stated above, even when the rich run afoul of the law they are unlikely to be brought to book to the same extent that the poor are. The reason for this is simple: Apart from the fact that a propertied liberal legal regime tilts the system in favour of the rich, the rich also have the requisite wherewithal to exploit the gaps and deficiencies in the system to escape due sanction. They have the money to hire the best legal representation when required; they are able to bribe judges where necessary; above all, they are generally able to tamper with a class-based system that is susceptible to the allure of money and influence.

Finally, the fourth feature of the Nigerian criminal justice administration system that mirrors that of eighteenth-century England is the pre-eminence and exclusive power of the courts in the determination of the guilt or innocence of persons accused of criminal offences. Like in eighteenth-century England, nobody is guilty of a crime unless pronounced so by a court of competent jurisdiction. This requirement for the application of the criminal law is constitutionally entrenched in Nigeria. The combined reading of Sections 6 and 36 (4) of the Nigerian Constitution, which vests judicial powers in the courts established under the Constitution and requires fair hearing in public and within a reasonable time before courts or tribunals vested with judicial power for any person charged with a criminal offence, respectively, confirms the exclusive power and competence of the courts to convict for crimes and impose requisite sanctions. As rightly noted by Nwabueze, "[…] conviction for a criminal offence and the imposition of sentence […] pertain exclusively to judicial power [...] so that only a court qualified under Section 6 of the Constitution to exercise judicial power can convict and sentence for a criminal offence".[53]

In addition, the illusion of mercy and pardoning of convicts upon which much of the charity of the English sovereign and the legitimacy of eighteenth-century criminal law regime rested was also largely a function of justices in Nigeria, as was the case in eighteenth century England. Although now mainly an executive act under Sections 175 and 212 of the Nigerian Constitution, state chief justices still participate in the pardon process through routine granting of reprieve to accused persons and awaiting trial inmates, especially during festive periods.[54]

Thus, almost six decades after independence, Nigeria's criminal justice administration system still closely resembles and exhibits the class nature and character of the eighteenth-century criminal justice system of England upon which it was based. As pointed out above, however, this is not peculiar to the Nigerian state; it is a phenomenon that is common to the criminal justice systems of former British dependencies. Although there have been some reform initiatives of the Nigerian criminal justice system at the federal and some states' levels, notably, the Administration of Criminal Justice Act, 2015 at the federal level and the Administration of Criminal Justice Law, 2011 and the Criminal Code Law, 2011, in Lagos State, the laws and other reform initiatives only tinkered at the fringes and failed to provide the necessary amendments that would transform Nigeria's criminal justice into a more equitable and inclusive system. The reform initiatives did not engage with or in any way affect the class domination tenets of the criminal justice system in Nigeria.

4 The Symbiotic Relationship of Nigeria's Class-Based Criminal Justice System, Illicit Interests, and a Corrupt Judiciary

Criminal justice has been referred to as "[...] the study of the various social institutions and practices concerned with identifying and responding to actual

53 B.O. Nwabueze, *The Presidential Constitution of Nigeria* (London: C. Hurst & Co, 1982), p. 431.

54 *Daily Post*, "Rivers Government Grants Pardon to 49 Prison Inmates", 9 May 2017 Retrieved from http://dailypost.ng/2017/05/09/rivers-government-grants-pardon-49-prison-inmates/ (accessed 6 June 2017); *Vanguard*, "CJ Pardons 28 Awaiting Trial Inmates", 8 February 2017. Retrieved from http://www.vanguardngr.com/2017/02/cj-pardons-28-awaiting-trial-inmates/ (accessed on 6 June 2017); Newsbreak, "Lagos Chief Judge Pardons 66 Inmates", 10 May 2017. Retrieved from https://www.newsbreak.ng/2017/05/lagos-chief-judge-pardons-66-inmates/ (accessed on 6 June 2017).

or suspected breaches of criminal law".[55] Criminal justice administration is therefore an expansive process that encompasses all the criminal law enforcement stages from investigation, arrest, and prosecution, to the conviction and punishment of offenders. The criminal justice system therefore revolves around four key state institutions: the police, the prosecutors, the courts, and prisons.[56]

Two different models of criminal justice administration have been identified by scholars: the crime control and the due process models.[57] The crime control model is synonymous with illiberal and authoritarian states and characterised by unrestrained power, extensive regulation, and coercion. The due process model, on the other hand, is synonymous with liberal democratic states and characterised by civil liberties, accountability, openness, and citizens' participation. Of the four state institutions involved in criminal justice administration, as pointed out above, the judiciary is probably the most significant. This is because it is the crucial institution for transforming the criminal justice system from a crime control model into a due process model more compatible with democratic norms.[58]

In addition, the judiciary also performs important checking functions on the other institutions in the criminal justice process that, incidentally, are agencies of the executive. The judiciary works to keep these within the bounds of the law and thus ensures the dispensation of criminal justice according to law, rather than according to the whims and caprices of state officials. Consequently, the judiciary represents the face of justice and is rightly regarded as the proverbial last hope of the common man.

It goes without saying, however, that a judiciary that creditably performs the critical functions in the criminal justice process highlighted above must be above board, impartial, and just in order to justify the confidence vested in it in and the high regard and esteem with which the institution is held by the general public. Recent reports that some members of the Nigerian judiciary, instead of upholding their judicial offices, have fallen for the allure of money and turned justice into a cash-and-carry affair with their corruption, are therefore disheartening. A brief recapitulation of what transpired will suffice in setting the requisite tone for the discussion that follows hereafter.

---

55 N. Lacey, "Introduction: Making sense of criminal justice", in N. Lacey (ed.), *A Reader on Criminal Justice* (New York: Oxford University Press, 1994), p. 3.

56 H.E. Sung, "Democracy and Criminal Justice in Cross-National Perspective: From crime control to due process", *The Annals of the American Academy of Political and Social Science*, 605 (2006), p. 313.

57 *Ibid.*, pp. 313–317.

58 *Ibid.*, pp. 311–337.

In the weekend of 8 and 9 October 2016, news broke that the Department of Security Services (DSS) and the Nigerian state secret police, in a two-day sting operation, besieged and arrested seven members of the Nigerian judiciary for bribery and corruption. Of the seven, two were serving Supreme Court Justices, one was a presiding justice of the Nigerian Court of Appeal, and the remaining four were High Court Justices.[59] Huge sums of money in both local and foreign currencies, far above the legitimate earnings of the judges, and documents evidencing ownership of landed property across Nigeria were allegedly discovered in the residences of some of the justices.[60] One was also alleged to have demanded a bribe of ₦200 million from a litigant to sway justice the litigant's way.[61] Others were alleged to have, among other malfeasances, collected bribes to compromise cases before them. Since the raid by the DSS, other justices and legal practitioners working in concert with them have been arrested for bribery and other corrupt practices and the trial of those indicted is ongoing.[62] It is unlikely, however, that anything concrete will emerge from the arrests and trials given the nature of Nigeria's criminal justice system and the symbiotic relationship between it, the illicit interests of elites, and corruption in the judiciary, which is the focus of this section of the essay.

Recent developments following the arrests of the judges confirm fears that nothing concrete is likely to come out of the furore. One of the judges indicted has been discharged and acquitted by the court trying him and six justices of those earlier indicted and suspended by the National Judicial Council (NJC), the institution responsible for the nomination and discipline of the judges, have been since been recalled by the NJC.[63] This recall attracted sharp criticism from some quarters, who alleged that the NJC was trying to shield the

59 Nigerian Monitor, "List Of Judges That Have Been Arrested By DSS Over Allegations Of Corruption", 16 October 2016. Retrieved from http://www.nigerianmonitor.com/list-of-judges-arrested-by-dss-over-allegations-of-corruption/ (accessed 22 March 2017).

60 *Business Today*, "Judges Arrest: DSS Gives Reasons for Arresting Judges", 9 October 2016. Retrieved from http://www.businesstodayng.com/judges-arrest-dss-gives-reasons-for-arresting-judges/ (accessed on 20 April 2017).

61 *The Nigeria Lawyer*, "Judges' Arrest: NJC Describes DSS Action as an Attempt to Ridicule, Harass and Intimidate Judiciary", 13 October 2016. Retrieved from http://thenigerialawyer.com/judges-arrest-njc-describing-dss-actions-as-an-attempt-to-ridicule-harass-and-intimidate-judges/ (accessed 17 March 2017).

62 *The Nigeria Lawyer*, "EFCC Witness Names 4 Judges Allegedly Involved in Nwobike's Bribe Scandal", 16 March 2017. Retrieved from http://thenigerialawyer.com/efcc-witness-names-bribe-taking-judges/ (accessed on 18 March 2017).

63 *Vanguard*, "NJC Recalls Justice Ademola, Five Other Judges Accused of Corruption", 3 June 2017. Retrieved from http://www.vanguardngr.com/2017/06/njc-recalls-justice-ademola-five-judges-accused-corruption/ (accessed on 10 June 2017).

indicted judges from prosecution.[64] This, in my view, is to be expected given the symbiotic relationship between the three musketeers of the Nigerian criminal justice system explained below.

The class-based criminal law regime, the elites' illicit interests, and a corrupt Nigerian judiciary legitimate and further each other in at least four ways. The first is that because the class-based regime is structured in such a way to protect and further the interests of the well-resourced, it is unable to perform the equitable distribution of wealth that political theorists have identified as central to a functioning government. To paraphrase Mill, the tendency of every man in the face of limited resources is to subject others, whenever he is able, to his will and power in order to appropriate the available materials and resources to maximise his own pleasure and happiness to the detriment of the interests and happiness of weaker men. Mill therefore sees the equitable distribution of society's scarce resources and the restraining of the avarice of those who will dispossess others as the primary duty of government.[65] Instead of restraining the avarice and illicit interests of the wealthy class, however, a class based regime is structured to do the exact opposite. It is a system that is arranged to help the rich dispossess the poor as relevant studies have revealed.[66] By working this way, the class-based regime facilitates the illicit interests and dispossession of the poor by rich elites.

Second, there is mutual legitimation and furthering of interests between a class-based legal regime and the judiciary in bourgeois legal orders. This is the kind of relationship Baxi referred to as the dialectics of the face and the mask.[67] According to Baxi, the judiciary in bourgeois legal orders is an organ of state power set up by those holding state power to dispense justice as defined by them.[68] The judiciary in such societies therefore represents the mask that covers the oppressive and dominating face of class power. By being given the appearance of autonomy and impartial interpreters of class laws, the judiciary in class societies legitimate class legal orders in the eyes of the oppressed, while the class-based system enhances and legitimates the judiciary by making it the

64 *Vanguard*, "Recall of Judges: NJC Trying to Shield Suspects from Trial – Presidency", 6 June 2017. Retrieved from http://www.vanguardngr.com/2017/06/recall-judges-njc-trying-shield-suspects-trial-presidency/ (accessed on 11 June 2017).

65 J.Mill, *Essays on Government*.1825.P.4 (Indianapolis: Liberty Fund Inc). Available at http://lf-oll.s3.amazonaws.com/titles/1761/Mill_0887_EBk_v6.opdf, retrieved 9 December 2018.

66 E.P. Thompson, *Whigs and Hunters: The origin of the Black Act*; D. Hay, "Poaching and the Game Laws on Cannock Chase", pp. 17–23.

67 U. Baxi, "Judicial Discourse: Dialectics of the face and the mask", *Journal of the Indian Law Institute*, 35 (1993), pp. 1–12.

68 *Ibid.*, pp. 1–7.

sole arbiter of class laws, as pointed out earlier. In such a regime, however, the judiciary is nothing more than "a selective instrument of class justice".[69]

Third, a mutual relationship is also deducible between a class-based regime, the illicit interests of elites, and a corrupt judiciary from the fact that all three belong to the same elite class and serve the same interests. Thus, even though they may not have a common intention, they do have a common object of mutual protection and furthering of each other illicit interests, which frequently culminates in the continued dispossession, subjugation, and oppression of the less privileged and less resourced class. I think the fact that there is actually such a common object and common interests of members of the ruling and well-resourced class in Nigeria in opposition to the interests and objects of the other members of the society is made clear by the sheer number of times that the Nigerian presidency has served as foster parents for high-profile crimes by the well-resourced and well-connected members of the Nigerian society as analysed by Adesanmi above.[70] The recent rallying around and recall of some judges indicted for corrupt practices by their brother judges and the National Judicial Council, in what has been said to resemble "[…] some sort of esprit de corps or solidarity with their brethren", appear to also confirm the common object or interests thesis of this essay.[71]

Lastly, a class-based regime is invariably a system founded on mutual exchange of favours, influence peddling, bribery, and corruption among members of the elite class. This is the conclusion of Hay's analysis of eighteenth-century England's criminal law regime examined in detail in Section 2 of this essay.[72] Hay further illustrates this point in his study of the ways game and the laws that protected it were used to maintain class distinction in eighteenth-century England.[73] According to Hay, game was a special currency through which class relations were sealed at the time. "It could be spent lavishly at dinners in order to command esteem, or given to others to mark important relationships: to inferiors as an indulgence, to superiors as a mark of respect".[74] Hay reported that

69 D. Hay, "Poaching and the Game Laws on Cannock Chase", p. 48.

70 P. Adesanmi, "The Nigerian Presidency As A Foster Parent Of Crimes".. *Sahara Reporters.* Retrieved from http://saharareporters.com/2017/04/15/nigerian-presidency-foster-parent-crimes-pius-adesanmi (accessed on 20-04-2017).

71 Itsey Sagay "Members of Judiciary Are Drifting In Wrong Direction – Sagay". 6 June 2017 Discussion Segment Retrieved from http://www.channelstv.com/2017/06/06/members-judiciary-drifting-wrong-direction-sagay/ (accessed 7 June 2017).

72 D. Hay, "Poaching and the Game Laws on Cannock Chase", pp. 189–253; *Idem*, "Property, Authority and the Criminal Law", in D Hay *et al.* (eds.), *Albion's Fatal Tree: Crime and society in eighteenth-century England* (London: Pantheon, 1975), pp. 17–63.

73 *Idem*, "Poaching and the Game Laws on Cannock Chase", p. 245.

74 *Ibid.*, p. 246.

game was given by the landed gentry as gifts to important personality to curry favour and seal class relations and it was also regularly used to bribe judges before or after important decisions in the giver's favour.[75]

With regard to Nigeria, there is an obvious link between bribery, corruption, the organised criminal state status of the state, and the elites in Nigeria as the literature examined in the introduction to this essay, among others, have shown. Adebanwi and Obadare have also pointed out that the most serious threat to the anti-corruption crusade in Nigeria is the illicit interests of the ruling elites and their cohorts, arising from their patrimonial domination of the system. According to these scholars, "anti-corruption campaigns by their very nature, pose a serious danger to the material basis of elites and the possibility of their continued reproduction".[76] The foregoing confirms the thesis in this essay that it is the elites that are benefiting from the ongoing rot, actively aided by a class-based criminal justice administration system. My point here is a simple one. We should not expect the situation to be other than it is, because where a class-based regime is combined with illicit interests and a corrupt judiciary, the three are bound to reinforce one another to the detriment of the rule of law, probity, and due process and can only result in gargantuan bribery, corruption, and the organised criminal state status that the Nigerian state currently enjoys. The mutual legitimation and reinforcement of these Three Musketeers have one end in sight, namely the primitive accumulation of wealth through the continued appropriation and dispossession of the Nigerian common wealth.

5 Conclusion

It is argued in this essay that the rot of bribery, corruption, and organised criminal state status of the Nigerian state cannot be divorced from the class character of its criminal justice system, which actively aids the class perpetrators of the rot. To buttress this argument, I examined the nature and character of eighteenth-century England's criminal justice system, from whence Nigeria inherited its criminal justice regime, and concluded that the inherited regime was clearly class-based and operates to further elites' illicit interests and appropriation of the property of the poor. The character and nature of present-day Nigeria's criminal justice administration system was also examined in Section 3 of the essay. It was found that despite having attained

75 *Ibid.*, pp. 246–247.
76 *Ibid.*

independence almost six decades ago, Nigeria's criminal justice regime still largely mirrors its eighteenth-century predecessor in class-based outlook and operation. Section 4 of the essay examined how Nigeria's class-based criminal justice system, elites' illicit interests, and a corrupt judiciary legitimate and re-inforce one another in the domination of the lower classes and continued appropriation of the Nigerian common patrimony. The conclusion, therefore, is that, given the ultimate aim of these three elements of the system, one should not expect anything other than the present rot in Nigeria's socio-political terrain. Indeed, the three elements can be compared to the Three Musketeers, whose motto is "All for one, and one for all". Consequently, if the Nigerian state is really concerned and honestly desirous to tackle the present rot, it should look to its bourgeois and class laws.

Bibliography

Adebamwi, W., and E. Obadare, "When Corruption FightsBack: Democracy and Elite Interest in Nigeria's Anti-Corruption War", *Journal of Modern African Studies*, 49: 2 (2011), pp. 1850–213.

Adesanmi, P., "The Nigerian Presidency As A Foster Parent Of Crimes", *Sahara Reporters,* 15 April 2017 Retrieved from http://saharareporters.com/2017/04/15/nigerian-presidency-foster-parent-crimes-pius-adesanmi (accessed on 17 April 2017).

Agbiboa, D.E., "Between Corruption and Development: The Political Economy of State Robbery in Nigeria", *Journal of Business Ethics*, 108: 3 (2012), pp. 325–345.

Akintayo, A.E., "Planning Law Versus the Right of the Poor to Adequate Housing: A Progressive Assessment of the Lagos State of Nigeria's Urban and Regional Planning and Development Law of 2010", *African Human Rights Law Journal*, 14: 2 (2014), pp. 553–579.

Baxi, U., "Judicial Discourse: Dialectics of the Face and the Mask", *Journal of the Indian Law Institute*, 35 (1993), pp. 1–12.

Beatie, J. "Looking Back at Property, Authority and the Criminal Law", *Legal History*, 10: 1–2, (2006), pp. 15–20.

Bonger, W., "Criminality and Economic Conditions", in J Muncie et al. (eds.), *Criminological Perspectives: A Reader*, London: Sage Publications, 1996.

Boone, C., "The Making of a Rentier Class: Wealth Accumulation and Political Control in Senegal", *The Journal of Development Studies*, 29: 3 (1990), pp. 425–449.

Business Today, "Judges Arrest: DSS Gives Reasons for Arresting Judges", 9 October 2016. Retrieved from http://www.businesstodayng.com/judges-arrest-dss-gives-reasons-for-arresting-judges/ (accessed on 20 April 2017).

Channels Television, "Members of Judiciary Are Drifting In Wrong Direction – Sagay". 6 June 2017 Retrieved from http://www.channelstv.com/2017/06/06/members-judiciary-drifting-wrong-direction-sagay/ (accessed 7 June 2017).

Chinedu, O.O., "Between Elite Interests and Pro-Poor Resistance: The Nigerian Courts and Labour-led Anti-Fuel Price Hike Struggles (1999–2007)", *Journal of African Law*, 54: 1 (2010), pp. 95–118.

Coldham, S., "Criminal Justice Policies in Commonwealth Africa: Trends and Prospects", *Journal of African Law*, 44: 2 (2000), pp. 218–238.

Daily Post, "Rivers Government Grants Pardon to 49 Prison Inmates", 9 May 2017 Retrieved from http://dailypost.ng/2017/05/09/rivers-government-grants-pardon-49-prison-inmates/ (accessed 6 June 2017).

Elias, T.O., *The Nature of African Customary Law*, Manchester: Manchester University Press, 1956.

Ellis, S., *This Present Darkness: A History of Nigerian Organised Crime*, London: C. Hurst & Co, 2016.

Hay, D., "Poaching and the Game Laws on Cannock Chase", in D. Hay et al.(eds.), *Albion's Fatal Tree: Crime and Society in Eighteenth-Century England*, London: Pantheon,1975, pp. 189–253.

Hay, D., "Property, Authority and the Criminal Law", in D. Hay et al.(eds.), *Albion's Fatal Tree: Crime and Society in Eighteenth-Century England*, London: Pantheon, 1975, pp. 17–63.

Joseph, R.A., *Democracy and Prebendal Politics in Nigeria*, Ibadan: Spectrum Books Ltd., 1991.

Karibi-Whyte, A.G.,*Groundwork of Nigerian Criminal Law*, Lagos: Nigerian Law Publications, 1986.

Kaunda, Kenneth, *A Humanist in Africa*,London: Longmans, Green and Co Ltd,1966.

Lacey, N., "Introduction: Making Sense of Criminal Justice", in N. Lacey (ed.),*A Reader on Criminal Justice*. New York: Oxford University Press, 1994.

Langbein, J.H., "Albion's Fatal Flaws, Past and Present", Faculty Scholarship Series; Paper 545, Harvard, (1983). Retrieved from http://www.law.harvard.edu/faculty/cdonahue/courses/lhsemelh/materials/Mats9F.pdf (accessed on 30 April 2017).

Lea, J. and, J. Young, "Relative Deprivation", in J. Muncie et al. (eds.), *Criminological Perspectives: A Reader*. London: Sage Publications, 1996.

Lewis, P., "From Prebendalism to Predation: The Political Economy of Decline in Nigeria", *The Journal of Modern African Studies*,34 (1996), pp. 79–103.

Mill, J., *Essays on Government*.1825. (Indianapolis: Liberty Fund Inc). Available at http://lf-oll.s3.amazonaws.com/titles/1761/Mill_0887_EBk_v6.0pdf, retrieved 9 December 2018.

Morris, H.F., "How Nigeria Got Its Criminal Code", *Journal of African Law*, 14: 3 (1970), pp. 137–154.

Morris, H.F., "A History of the Adoption of Codes of Criminal Law and Procedure in British Colonial Africa, 1876–1935", *Journal of African Law*, 18: 1 (1974), pp. 6–23.

Newsbreak, "Lagos Chief Judge Pardons 66 Inmates", 10 May 2017. Retrieved from https://www.newsbreak.ng/2017/05/lagos-chief-judge-pardons-66-inmates/ (accessed on 6 June 2017).

Nigerian Monitor, "List Of Judges That Have Been Arrested By DSS Over Allegations Of Corruption", 16 October 2016. Retrieved from http://www.nigerianmonitor.com/list-of-judges-arrested-by-dss-over-allegations-of-corruption/ (22 March 2017).

Nwabueze, B.O., *The Presidential Constitution of Nigeria*. London: C. Hurst &Co Ltd., 1982.

Nyerere, Julius, *Ujamaa: Essays on socialism*, Dar es Salaam: Oxford University Press, 1964.

Okonkwo, C.O., *Okonkwo and Naish: Criminal Law in Nigeria* (2nd.ed.), Ibadan: Spectrum Law Publishing, 1980.

Phillips, J., "Albion's Empire: Property, Authority and the Criminal Law in Eighteenth-Century Canada", *Legal History*, 10 (2006), pp. 21–27.

Seidman, R.B., "MensRea and the Reasonable African Man: The Pre-Scientific World-view and Mistake of Fact", *The International and Comparative Law Quarterly*, 15: 4(1966), pp. 1135–1164.

Sung, H.E., "Democracy and Criminal Justice in Cross-National Perspective: From Crime Control to Due Process", *The Annals of the American Academy of Political and Social Science*, 605 (2006), pp. 311–337.

The Nigeria Lawyer, "Judges' Arrest: NJC Describes DSS Action as an Attempt to Ridicule, Harass and Intimidate Judiciary", 13 October 2016. Retrieved from http://thenigerialawyer.com/judges-arrest-njc-describing-dss-actions-as-an-attempt-to-ridicule-harass-and-intimidate-judges/ (accessed on 17 March 2017).

The Nigeria Lawyer, "EFCC Witness Names 4 Judges Allegedly Involved in Nwobike's Bribe Scandal", 16 March 2017. Retrieved from http://thenigerialawyer.com/efcc-witness-names-bribe-taking-judges/ (accessed on 18 March 2017).

The Nigeria Lawyer, "Alleged N92m Bribe EFCC Secures Court Order to Detain Justice Rita Ofili-Ajumogobia", 12 November 2016. Retrieved from http://thenigerialawyer.com/alleged-n92m-bribe-efcc-secures-court-order-to-detain-justice-rita-ofili-ajumogobia-and-obla-san/ (19 March 2017).

Thompson, E.P., *Whigs and Hunters: The Origin of the Black Act,* London: Penguin Books, 1975.

Tushnet, M., "Legal Scholarship: Its Causes and Cure", *Yale Law Journal*, 90 (1980/81), pp. 1205–1223.

Vanguard, "CJ Pardons 28 Awaiting Trial Inmates", 8 February 2017. Retrieved from http://www.vanguardngr.com/2017/02/cj-pardons-28-awaiting-trial-inmates/ (accessed on 6 June 2017).

Vanguard, "NJC Recalls Justice Ademola, Five Other Judges Accused of Corruption", 3 June 2017. Retrieved from http://www.vanguardngr.com/2017/06/njc-recalls-justice-ademola-five-judges-accused-corruption/ (accessed on 10 June 2017).

Vanguard, "Recall of Judges: NJC Trying to Shield Suspects from Trial – Presidency", 6 June 2017. Retrieved from http://www.vanguardngr.com/2017/06/recall-judges-njc-trying-shield-suspects-trial-presidency/ (accessed on 11 June 2017).

Williams, K.S., *Textbook on Criminology* (6th ed.), Oxford: Oxford University Press, 2008.

Book Review

Stephen Ellis, (2016) *This Present Darkness: A History of Nigerian Organised Crime*. London: Hurst and Co.

Let me start by thanking Professors Ayodeji Olukoju and R.T. Akinyele and, of course, the entire Department of History and Strategic Studies, University of Lagos for inviting me to review this history book. In the context of today's multidisciplinary approach to scholarship, I consider this opportunity to be very significant. I am not very sure I thought the day would come when I, a legal scholar, would engage in an academic review of a book before an audience of academics and scholars in the field of history. When Prof. Akinyele invited me to do this review, I accepted because he said the book was about organised crime, a subject close to my heart. Indeed, I have taught the history of organised crime in two, separate postgraduate classes. As a criminology scholar who recognises the eclectic nature of criminology as a discipline, I could smell, from a distance, the potentialities of the book for expanding knowledge about organised crime in Nigeria. I was not disappointed. What actually distinguishes this history book is that it has emerged as a repertoire of evidence to validate various aetiological theories of crime as applied to Nigeria.

While appreciating this honour as a legal scholar, I wish to note that I had not completed reading the Introduction to the book, *This Present Darkness: A History of Nigerian Organised Crime*, when I concluded that agreeing to this review would, indeed, be one of the best services I could ever do myself. I say so for two reasons: First, as a Nigerian who loves her country so dearly and has tortuously tried to figure out how it became so embroiled in pervasive deviance and criminality; and second, as a criminologist with a keen interest in understanding criminality wherever, whenever, and howsoever it manifests.

The book has eleven chapters besides the Introduction. The captivating chapter titles: "Rules of Law" (note: not Rule of Law); "Wonder-Workers"; "Enter the Politicians"; "The National Cake"; "The Men in Uniform"; "Boom Time"; "Crime Goes Global"; "Godfathers"; "The Business of Crime"; "Cosmic Powers"; and "Nigerian Organised Crime" are very telling of how the book accounts for the trajectory of crime in Nigeria. Tracing the development of crime from the turn of the twentieth century, the book narrates how Nigeria and Nigerians have moved, in less than 100 years, from being relatively crime-free to being

 | DOI:10.1163/9789004396289_013

crime-infested. The Nigerian of old was apparently so indisposed to crime that the book reports that a British official writing in 1944 noted that the number of persistent and professional criminals was low and came to the conclusion that "Crime as a career has so far made little appeal to the young Nigerian".[1]

Noting that that is a world far removed from the Nigeria we know today, the author feels compelled to query what some others believe is the natural-ness of crime to the Nigerian, as exemplified in the view expressed by the former United States' Secretary of State Colin Powell, who suggested that crime is natural to Nigerians, because "it is in their natural culture".[2] The author, however, considers that it is important to query how such culture emerged and not just take it as a given. Thus, his guiding questions for the historical research into the development of crime in Nigeria are: "Can culture be an explanation for such behaviour? In any case, how does a specific culture come into being? Didn't the experience of colonial rule play some part?"[3] The author is unshaken in his belief that the political origins of organised crime in Nigeria are inextricably linked to the country's colonial experience. Giving direction to this historical study is the statement made early in the book that "[…] we need to study the colonial experience of Indirect Rule if we are to understand the origin of later practices of organised crime and corruption".[4]

Thus, Chapter 1 traces Nigeria's colonial history as characterised by Lugard's civilising mission, especially against the backdrop of indirect rule and the law. He points out how British law, imposed over colonised territory and its peoples, was radically different from the customary law that was indigenous to the people, in that the former had separated the idea of law from its divine attribute as God-directed or inspired and had evolved law into a body of man-made rules of a political community that governs itself (or is governed by a coercive foreign power). The natives, in that context, had trouble accepting the legitimacy of such laws, and even when they respected its precepts, *or pretended to*, it was less because of any perception of truth and more because it was imposed on them by an authority also able to impose punishment for disobedience. Hence, the mere introduction of English law with its commands did not turn colonised Nigerians completely away from adherence to a regime of law derived from religion.

At best, a dual religious heritage emerged that started to (re)shape Nigerians' idea about law and morality, all of which subsist today and contribute to

---

1 Stephen Ellis, *This Present Darkness: A History of Nigerian Organised Crime* (London: Hurst & Co., 2016), p. 4.

2 *Ibid.*, p. 3.

3 *Ibid.*

4 *Ibid.*, p. 4.

the significant role that religion and spirituality play in criminality in Nigeria, a reality the author returns to and devotes the whole of Chapter 10 to. How Nigerians negotiate the religious spheres is exemplified by the account the author presents of what Dr. Nnamdi Azikiwe (Zik) did when he was faced with the prospect of giving testimony to the Foster-Sutton tribunal established to investigate his insider dealings with the African Continental Bank. The author records that

> Zik was said to have sworn an oath at a traditional shrine with a key member of his cabinet, Eastern Region Financial Minister Mbonu Ojike, to protect one another. The fact that Zik lied under oath at the official enquiry indicates the greater importance he attached to an oath sworn at a shrine than one sworn on the Bible before a judicial hearing.[5]

Even today, most politicians continue to attach greater significance to oaths taken at traditional shrines and expect their colleagues to be (wo)men of honour who bind themselves to the oaths taken. The oath-taking between the duo of Uba and Ngige before the Okija shrine, an event the author returns to in Chapter 10, is evidence of such negotiations even today.

To the extent that the dual religious belief systems find an inseparable relationship between the spiritual and cosmic world, on the one hand, and the material world, on the other hand, they imbue adherents with the perception that material wealth and political power are evidence of blessings of God. This explains the persistent relationship between crime and religion – why many Nigerians seek and find help for success in criminal enterprise within the ambit of religion and spirituality. Without doubt, the book's exposé of how our traditional cultural norms, including our modern religious beliefs systems, fuel and sustain crime is incisive.

Although the author documents the view expressed by one writer as late as 1944 that Nigerians as a people were largely innocent when it came to modern forms of criminality, he however narrates the escapades of some of the early criminal careerists such as *The Professor of Wonders*, "Professor" Crentsil, arguably Nigeria's first known exponent of the modern "419" fraud,[6] a crime for which Nigerians have become globally notorious. In December 1921, Crentsil was convicted of fraud but received relatively light sentences for his offences; he was therefore able to boast that he got off on the strength of his "juju" powers. The various categories of 419-ers at this time included the "*wayo* trickster" (those who posed as agents of a foreign company and sold blank papers

5 *Ibid.*, p. 58.
6 This is a popular reference to Article 419 of Nigeria's criminal code.

with the promise that these could be turned into bank notes by application of a special chemical), "Ajasco Boys" (who were itinerant medicine sellers), and "Black Boys", who were money doublers and whose activities led to the criminalisation of the offence of money doubling under the colonial Criminal Code, an offence that is retained in the criminal statutes till today.

But the notoriety of a few offenders, such as Professor Crentsil, remained peculiar as it appears that Nigerians were more on the receiving end of "charlatanic correspondence"[7] at this time than they were perpetrators. So high was their vulnerability that a paternalistic colonial government even authorised the interception of postal materials to protect gullible Nigerians. It is doubtful, however, that the intervention helped much, as the Posts and Telegraphs Department (P&T as it was more popularly known) recorded an exponential growth of such offences from 2,855 in the years between 1935 and 1938 to 9,570 by 1947. One may therefore be forced to think that it is probably to avenge their forefathers' victimisation that today's Nigerian 419-ners have unleashed themselves on the descendants of those who once exploited their naivety.

What repeatedly stands out in Ellis's analysis is the uncanny similarity of criminal patterns of the past and the present. The author draws attention to the ease with which Nigerian criminals "self-fashion" (read: re-fashion themselves) and enter into politics with huge success simply by relying on the argument of persecution or victimisation. A good example is his story of one Prince Orizu, who was convicted on seven counts of fraud and theft of funds meant for scholarships for Nigerian students in the United States. It would appear he was the same person who transformed into Dr. Abyssinia Akweke Nwafor Orizu and who, as a stalwart of the National Council of Nigeria and the Cameroons (NCNC), became Nigeria's Senate President after independence. All that the apologists of history had to say of his earlier conviction was that "it was a miscarriage of justice".[8] One might feel the case is reminiscent of the case of former Governor Onanefe James Ibori, who was convicted of fraud in the United Kingdom but returned to a hero's welcome in his home state.

For those who struggle to figure out what appears to be the bizarre relationship between Nigerians and money/wealth and criminal risk-taking, Ellis's analysis shows that much of the trickery recorded in the colonial era was more commonly linked to Southern Nigeria, thus, in a sense demonstrating the relevance of Durkheim's and Merton's strands of anomie theory in explaining both historical and modern criminality in Nigeria. In the words of the author,

7 *Ibid.*, p. 26.
8 *Ibid.*, p. 28.

> people socialised in communities characterised by a relative lack of central authority and codified religion but, under colonial rule, [became] influenced by new structures of political authority...[offering] new possibilities for self-advancement [...]. New realms of risk, destiny and self-fashioning existed for people adventurous enough to explore them.[9]

And for anyone troubled trying to fathom how far some people are willing to go in the pursuit of wealth, Ellis devotes the section titled "*Wealth, risk, destiny*" to show how crime is inexorably linked to people's beliefs and attitudes.

Is there anything new under the sun?, is likely to be the constant refrain tugging at the reader's mind through the book, *This Present Darkness*. Many would think that the horrors of human trafficking as we know them today have never been known until they read of the report of an Assistant Commissioner of Police, Major J.W Garden, on professional slave-dealing and its modus operandi. I dare say that excerpts of the report quoted by the author would readily pass for findings relating to human trafficking involving Nigerians today. Garden noted that the children concerned were often escorted by women posing as mothers or sisters, "and armed men have been known to act as scouts".[10] Ellis records that so organised was the trafficking of girls and young women outside Nigeria that a 1939 investigation was initiated at the instance of a complaint by one Prince Eikineh, who suspected from the numbers of Nigerian girls and women who were coming to the Gold Coast to work in the sex business that the trade was systematically organised by older women. Subsequent police investigation not only confirmed this but found that

> the women concerned in this business were emigrating from Nigeria of their own free will, and that there was no kidnapping taking place [...] Further investigation [...] suggested that the women concerned considered their business to be no different from any other type of work. Some of them had even organised a trade union, with a recognised leadership.[11]

Indeed, the business was largely run by older women who had themselves worked as prostitutes before graduating to becoming organisers. Women with experience of the sex business in the Gold Coast returned to their home areas in Nigeria where they would

9 *Ibid.*, pp. 29–30.

10 *Ibid.*, p. 36.

11 *Ibid.*, p. 37.

> "obtain young girls on the pretext of marriage or in order to teach them trading and domestic work", but then requiring them to work in the sex trade for a couple of years. A girl wishing to enter this line of trade "first of all approaches one of the retired members from whom she obtains details as to route, transport costs to the [Gold] Coast and routine, also usually the name of the man from whom she can borrow the necessary funds".[12]

The preponderance of sex workers from the Cross River area involved in this trans-border sex trade led Ellis to allude to a "regional specialisation" of the trade "dominated by women who had experience of the trade and who passed on information on the business to others whom they knew, resulting in tight networks of patrons and clients that in some parts of the Cross River area involved almost every single family".[13] There is no doubt that historical trans-border sex trade is mimicked in many respects by the modern sex work in Europe involving Nigerian women from Benin. If nothing else, the accounts lend to the validity of criminological theories asserting that crime is learnt by differential association and that criminals learn not just the rationalisations for crime but also the skills and techniques, which learning is facilitated by the availability of criminal opportunities.[14]

In Chapter 3, the reader once again gets a sense of *déjà vu* as Ellis demonstrates that there is nothing new about the nature of Nigeria's money politics. As with today's politicians, early Nigerian professional politicians often found it hard to distinguish their personal financial ambitions from their political goals and in this, Ellis does not exclude notable politicians such as Dr. Nnamdi Azikiwe (Zik), Chief Obafemi Awolowo (Awo) and the Sardauna of Sokoto, Sir Ahmadu Bello.[15]

As colonialism opened up, new opportunities for acquiring wealth and consumer goods, corruption arrived in tow. Ellis records Otonti Nduka, a Nigerian university lecturer writing in 1964, as noting that "it was neither the science, philosophy nor even religion of the West which most impressed the natives: it was the material wealth, together with the power that was associated with it, which caught the imagination".[16] Culture conflict theory and anomie theory in Criminology immediately lunge forward again to provide explanations of how

12 *Ibid.*

13 *Ibid.*, p. 38.

14 Edwin Sutherland, "Differential Association: Theories of Criminal Behaviour", *Encyclopedia Britannica.* Retrieved from https://www.britannica.com/topic/differential-association (accessed 20 October 2017).

15 *Ibid.*, pp. 52–54.

16 *Ibid.*, p. 53.

the modern education that came with colonialism conduced to high levels of criminality. Explaining the higher preponderance of crime in the South, Ellis draws attention to the effects of school education which in Southern Nigeria produced a nationalist constituency in the form of "the Standard VI boys", for whom there was no equivalent in the North. They were joined by families and individuals moving from rural areas. There was an issue of vagrancy in all the main urban areas of Nigeria by the middle of the twentieth century.

> At the same time, the towns exerted a strong cultural attraction, since for young people especially, "anything seems better than the tight discipline of the family and the dreary monotony of village life in the bush". Traditional social life, suffused with "an elaborate and steady equilibration of rights, duties and loyalties, sanctified by usage and religion" was giving way to a new climate in the towns and cities especially. These were home to young men who were disposed to violence, not in the form of the gangsterism that was producing the very concept of organised crime in the United States, but in "a kind of diffuse, unregulated scramble stemming from the fluidity of the social structures and the absence of efficient organisation".[17]

As early as 1952, the ominous signs of the dangers of development-induced materialism were so glaring that Ellis reports that one Eyo A. Akak, a vocal anti-corruption crusader, together with like-minded individuals who believed that "bribery with its allied corruption is deeply planted in this country",[18] had formed themselves into the *Nigerian League of Bribe Scorners*. By this time, many people's eyes were already open to the prime responsibility of expatriates not only from Britain but elsewhere for the growth of bribery in the country. The corruptive influence of the private sector in Nigeria's public sector is no less dated, but what stands out is the extent to which it was predominantly a "foreign contribution" even as it is today, a fact acknowledged by even the first British High Commissioner to Nigeria. Ellis reports that as soon as Nigerian politicians began to acquire substantial power at the regional level in the 1950s foreign companies began to court them for contracts.[19] He cites the close relationship between the Leventis Group and Premier Akintola in Western Nigeria (with the latter's daughter employed as the former's public relations officer) and the widespread allegation that Mbonu Ojike received a kickback in 1955 for awarding the contract for a construction project to the Italian firm

17 *Ibid.*, p. 55.
18 *Ibid.*, p. 56.
19 *Ibid.*, p. 68.

Borini Prono. The persistent nemesis of the Nigerian economy, which is illegal expatriation of profits, is not differently dated. By 1962, it was already reported that foreign companies were systematically writing inflated invoices for goods that they imported in order to justify exporting excessive sums abroad, thus expatriating their profits. This was even different from when the foreign companies were cheating their Nigerian partners, by supplying sub-standard materials, which in one case provoked a court action in New York.

Ellis demonstrates that the entrance of political parties only heightened the tempo of corruption. The 1951 regional elections – much like those conducted in 1970, 1983, 1999, 2003, 2007, 2011, and 2015 – were reported to be "marked by great corruption".[20] The tenure of public office not only gave politicians influence over trade and production at that time, it also put politicians in a position where they could use government resources for their own private or party purpose. It was not thought to be stealing and defrauding the State; it was just taking one's legitimate share of "The National Cake".

Indeed, any scholar of Nigeria's current political structure and the role corrupt practices play in shaping it must take some time out to look at Chapter 3 of Ellis' book. By the 1960s, the Regional governments were already being accused of wasting money on "frivolities" such as new official residencies. Why, you might ask, does this read strangely familiar as if it were speaking of the 1990s and 2000s? By 1963, both the British High Commissioner and Prime Minister Tafawa Balewa were reported to have agreed that "party-funding was at the heart of the issue"[21] of corruption in government. If Sir Tafawa Balewa's effort then to negotiate some form of voluntary capping cost was said to have been unsuccessful because it was too feeble, sixty years on, not even the caps introduced by legislation were strong enough to disrupt the system.[22] Nigeria has remained true to the path of its hustling, one in which government at every level is a pump for redistributing money to the political barons who had spent their all to ensure electoral success.

Thanks to Stephen Ellis, we now know that the British-Polish sociologist Stanislav Andreski had invented the term "kleptocracy" to describe the system of government found in Nigeria in the early 1960s. On kleptocracy, Andreski notes that "[...] the functioning of the organs of authority is determined by the

20 *Ibid.*, p. 57.

21 *Ibid.*, p. 65.

22 "Section 91, Act no. 6, Electoral Act, 2010", Federal Government of Nigeria Official Gazette, 24 August 2010. Retrieved from http://www.parliament.am/library/norelectoral%20law/nigeria.pdf.

mechanisms of supply and demand rather than the laws and regulations".[23] Ellis further states:

> Regional governments were creating excessive numbers of local councils in order to satisfy local interests and opportunities for graft and to build a constituency for parliamentary candidates, who at election time could go to the local government councillors they had helped into office and call on their votes. Local councils gathered very little in the way of tax that made its way to the revenue authority. As a result, local government hardly functioned.[24]

With narratives such as this, it is hard not to ask: When will we learn from history?

Ellis clearly illustrates the meaning and historicity of the "kickback" syndrome in Nigeria with documented instances of kickbacks so bad that by 1966, the Swedish businessman A.A. Aklint described Nigeria as one of the most corrupt countries in Africa.[25] What was probably more unfortunate, however, was that corruption was not confined to government acts and activities, but had spread to daily life.[26]

Still more unfortunate is that sixty years later, little has changed in relation to Nigeria's ranking in the corruption league table(s). With these accounts in Ellis' book, it is difficult not to ask: "*What is history telling us for now?*" This question is critical especially when we are reflecting on what should be done to address Nigeria's problem of crime. Should we not listen carefully when we read that a senior judge had in 1964 stated: "[…] any hoped-for change in Nigerian politics will depend less on constitutional reform than upon reform in the minds of men".[27] It is this consideration that leads me to argue that a more critical investigation with hindsight would shed light on the trajectory of corruption and help us to understand how things managed to turn out this way. If we are confused at Nigerian citizens' ambivalent relationship with politics – one in which they are torn between their wish to benefit from the largesse distributed by politicians by joining their patronage systems and revulsion at the bribery involved and the consequent inefficiencies in providing public goods – the answer lies in the military intervention in Nigeria's politics.

23 *Ibid.*, p. 66.
24 *Ibid.*, p. 75.
25 *Ibid.*, p. 70.
26 *Ibid.*, pp. 74–77.
27 *Ibid.*, p. 75.

According to Ellis, just when things could get no worse, the *Men in Uniform* arrive with the promise to deliver the nation from rapid descent into the abyss of crime and they were initially lauded by citizens. But once it became clear the human losses to the coup were not evenly distributed across the ethnicities, the historical mutual suspicion of the various ethnic groups was escalated, but much more, a new criminality emerged with it.[28]

Ellis cites Wole Soyinka's summation of the scenario as one in which the success of the federal army resulted in "a consolidation of crime, an acceptance of the scale of values that created the conflict".[29] With the war over, and the military government in effective control, corruption permeated the security apparatus with even more dire consequences; armed with guns, police officers and military personnel simply took bribes openly at roadblocks, individual military strongmen, such as military governors, ran each federating state or parastatal he headed as a fiefdom.

Government corruption came to be seen as something close to patriotism, a feature of the national system which the military putsch had threatened but had been overcome. Could it be that the coup masterminds had clearly underestimated the scale, complexity and embeddedness of the corruption they desired to root out?

Ellis argues that there were at least three unanticipated consequences. First, it led to a situation where the military, having now taken control of the state, remained in that position for much of the twentieth century and became deeply politicised in the process. The depth of such politicisation reflects in the fact that since the country's return to democracy in 1999 ex-generals have continued to prosper by turning themselves into politicians. Second, a premodern form of state organisation became entrenched in modern form in a distinctive type of prebendalism. Third, the first set of coup-makers instituted a discourse of anti-corruption that came to be used by every group of coup plotters that followed.[30]

However, this went no further than a few years such that by 1967 the acceptance of tribes by government officials had become blatant and virtually universal. Ellis reports that a criminologist who was based in Ibadan during those years reported that his survey found that one in eight people in his sample had been victims of burglary. He concluded that in these circumstances the concepts of "crime" and "criminal" were ceasing to have much meaning.[31] By

28 *Ibid.*, pp. 89–93.

29 *Ibid.*, p. 89.

30 *Ibid.*, pp. 90–91.

31 *Ibid.*, p. 90.

this time, a population judged generally law-abiding just twenty years earlier had acquired a reputation for fraud.

The contours of a distinctive Nigerian pattern of criminality had been clearly established by the time of the two coups of 1966, although Ellis does admit that "[t]here does not seem to have been much organised crime in the modern meaning of the term".[32] While there is evidence that by 1952 Nigeria was being used as a staging post for heroin smuggling, thereby leading the military to take on the issues of drugs smuggling with the enactment of the decree of 1966 that provided a jail term of ten years for trafficking in hard drugs, it is also clear that foreigners of various nationalities were at the time already involved in currency frauds especially currency trafficking.[33] Ellis gives an account of the business dealings of one Mr. Colin Gold whose service was to assist his customers, including Nigerians and nationals of other countries around official foreign exchange controls.[34] Other than minor traces of organised crime like this, what existed on a large scale was a voracious and pervasive system of state corruption that was led by politicians.

By the end of the war, fortune had smiled on Nigeria and caused it to enter into "Boom Time". The country did not have to struggle to fund its post-war rebuilding. The victory of the Nigerian state in the war fired a wave of patriotism which the then US envoy to Nigeria, Ambassador John E. Reinhardt, labelled "Nigerianism" – a near-ideology that posited Nigerians had a manifest destiny comparable to that of Americans. The existence of oil in God-given abundance not only raised the country's status to that of an African superpower but resulted in a culture of conspicuous consumption characterised by the widespread feeling "that anything indigenous is inferior to its foreign counterpart".[35] Nigeria had shifted from the economic slow lane to the fast lane in the ten years from 1967; federal government revenue increased by a massive 2000 percent under a military government that was not accountable to anyone. In addition, professional smugglers developed business models that were adapted to their particular form of illegality. Indeed, by the late 1970s, the smuggling rings that operated between Dahomey (now Republic of Benin) and Nigeria were already being recognised as organised crime syndicates considering the efficiency and the amount of banned goods being brazenly displayed in the country. One writer had in fact compared the country's smuggling activities to those of the mafia organisation in the US. As many wondered at the source of their compatriot's "new wealth", they readily linked this to the invisible world. Many people

32 *Ibid.*, p. 91.
33 *Ibid.*, p. 92.
34 *Ibid.*
35 *Ibid.*, p. 95.

assumed that somewhere behind the most outrageous displays of wealth lay hidden networks and cults. Soon there was a rise in ritual killings. Rumours circulated that penis thieves were on the prowl and were thought to collect male organs for obscure ritual purposes. The military governments opted to deflect blame towards certain categories of criminals, especially armed robbers, a criminal phenomenon which though had been in existence for a long time but had assumed a more serious dimension in Kano.

At around the same time, Nigerianism was associated with accelerated development that caused the government to embark on prestige projects. It was in this context that a regime of senior civil servants known as "superpermsecs"[36] emerged. The boom turned many Nigerians into overnight businessmen – essentially middlemen rather than managers. All manner of irregular payments and trade-offs occurred as a result of these activities and by the late 1970s, a complex practice of influence-peddling had emerged, especially the offering of non-existent oil for sale.[37]

The book's narrative of the growth of Nigeria's criminal enterprise and the role of the State in its festering, both historically and even now, provides many lessons. Reading through the current "fight against corruption" one has many lessons to learn. There is a constant sense of *déjà vu* not only in terms of the manifestations of crime but also in terms of making sense of the official and unofficial understanding and approaches to crime, as well as the theories of anomie – both the Durkheimian and Mertonian strands – and the various theories of social disorganisation and gangs.

The chapter on globalisation of Nigerian criminality actually demonstrates how globalisation starting from colonisation provided opportunities for Nigerian criminality as victimisation. The book attempts to demonstrate the inextricable link between the different and seemingly disconnected types of crime and State failure as well as State criminality.

Little, one dares to say, appears to have changed 60 years later. Little wonder they say history is not was but is.

Does the Book Have Any Shortcoming?

While I thoroughly enjoyed every minute of reading the book for its content and style, I could not ignore two things that I thought took away from its perfection. It certainly bothered me by the time I got midway into it that the

36 *Ibid.*, pp. 96 and 107.

37 *Ibid.*, p. 97.

author had not attempted to clarify his conception of organised crime, nor had he identified any of the many types of criminal manifestations he documented as organised and fitting the sense in which the idea of "organised crime" is used in many intellectual discourses today. However, in the last chapter, the author explains that this was deliberate, as he thought that the nature, patterns and dimensions of the various types of organised crimes in Nigeria today cannot be divorced from the nation's historical pathways to modern criminality.

I also could not help wondering whether the title, "This Present Darkness: A *Political* History of Nigerian Organised Crime" would not have been more appropriate to foretell the direction of the analysis done in the work. However, I conceded that maybe the author left that keyword out of the title in order not to reveal everything upfront.

Finally, I note that whereas the book's coverage of Nigerian organised crime is broad and the author addresses different types of organised crime, the cover picture of a young lady simply dressed in a white tank top revealing the large tattoo on her chest may leave the reader initially thinking that the book is narrowly about the history of one of the many types of Nigerian organised crime – in this case human trafficking for *sexploitation*. I certainly thought so.

Conclusion

However, these shortcomings are not enough to take away from the fact that *This Present Darkness – A History of Nigerian Organised Crime* is a well written analysis of how organised crime in Nigeria has its own distinct history, which is closely linked with the country's political evolution and establishes that it does not merely ape forms of organised crime in other parts of the world. As a piece of scholarly work, the book presents records from unassailable sources to validate its content, and the references themselves are a rich field of knowledge. In terms of style, the writing is simple and easy to read and the book could pass for a novel, without this taking away from its quality as a reflective academic piece that is relevant to scholars across disciplines.

In conclusion, I unreservedly commend the book to anyone who is keen to understand how Nigeria has landed where she is.

Ayodele Atsenuwa

Short CV Stephen Ellis

2008–2015
Desmond Tutu professor, Faculty of Social Sciences, VU University Amsterdam.

2003–2004
Director Africa Programme International Crisis Group.

1994–2015
Senior researcher, African Studies Centre, University of Leiden.

1991–1994
Director, African Studies Centre, Leiden.

1986–1991
Editor, *Africa Confidential*, London.

1982–86
Researcher, Amnesty International, International Secretariat, Africa Department, London.

1979–1980
Lecturer, University of Madagascar.

1971–1972
Teacher, Collège Libermann, Douala, Cameroon.

Books

The Rising of the Red Shawls: A Revolt in Madagascar 1895–1899. Cambridge: Cambridge University Press, 1985.

French edition : *L'insurrection des menalamba: Une révolte à Madagascar (1895–1899)*. Paris : Éditions Karthala, 1998.

Un complot colonial à Madagascar : L'affaire Rainandriamampandry. Paris : Éditions Karthala, and Antananarivo: Éditions Ambozontany, 1990.

(with Tsepo Sechaba), *Comrades Against Apartheid: The South African Communist Party and the ANC in Exile.* London: James Currey, and Bloomington: Indiana University Press, 1992.

(with Yves Fauré, eds.), *Entreprises et entrepreneurs africains*. Paris: Éditions Karthala, and Orstom, 1995.

(ed.), *Africa Now: People, Policies and Institutions.* London: James Currey, 1995.

French edition: *L'Afrique maintenant.* Paris: Karthala, 1995.

Dutch edition: *Afrika Nu : Mensen, Beleid en Instellingen*. Den Haag: Ministerie van Buitenlandse Zaken, 1995.

(with Jean-François Bayart & Béatrice Hibou), *La criminalisation de l'Etat en Afrique.* Bruxelles: Editions Complexe, 1997.

English edition: *The Criminalization of the State in Africa*. Oxford: James Currey, and Bloomington: Indiana University Press, 1999.

The Mask of Anarchy: the Destruction of Liberia and the Religious Dimension of an African Civil War. London: Hurst & Co., and New York University Press, 1999.

Second edition, revised and updated with a new preface. London: Hurst & Co., and New York: New York University Press, 2007.

(with Gerrie ter Haar), *Worlds of Power: Religion and Politics in Africa.* London: Hurst & Co., and New York: University of Oxford Press, 2004. [Special edition: Johannesburg: Wits University Press, 2004].

Spanish edition: *Mundos de Poder: Pensiamento religioso y práctica política en África*. Barcelona: Edicions Bellaterra, 2005.

(with Solofo Randrianja), *Madagascar: A Short History.* London: Hurst & Co., and Chicago: Chicago University Press, 2009.

(with Ineke van Kessel, eds.), *Movers and Shakers: Social Movements in Africa.* Leiden: Brill, 2009.

South Africa and the Decolonization of the Mind. Inaugural Lecture, Desmond Tutu Chair in the Faculty of Social Sciences, VU University Amsterdam. Amsterdam: VUA, 2009.

Season of Rains: Africa in the World. London: Hurst & Co., and Johannesburg: Jacana, 2011; Chicago: University of Chicago Press, 2012.

Dutch edition: *Het Regenseizoen: Afrika in de Wereld.* Amsterdam: Prometheus/ Bert Bakker, Amsterdam, 2011.

External Mission: The ANC in Exile, 1960–1990. Johannesburg: Jonathan Ball, and Hurst & Co., London, 2012; New York: Oxford University Press, 2013.

This Present Darkness: A History of Nigerian Organised Crime. London: Hurst & Co., and New York: Oxford University Press, 2016. [South African edition: Pretoria: Jacana, 2016].

For an extensive list of publications: see Jos Damen, *Stephen Ellis Bibliography*. Second revised and enlarged edition, African Studies Centre, Leiden University, November 2018 (ASCL Occasional Publication 35).

Index

www.ingramcontent.com/pod-product-compliance
Lightning Source LLC
Chambersburg PA
CBHW071431230926
51846CB00001B/180

* 9 7 8 9 0 0 4 3 9 6 2 4 1 *